D0795059

20 YEARS OF BRITISH RECORD CHARTS 1955-1975

with commentary by
peter jones & tony jasper

*edited by
tony jasper*

QUEEN ANNE PRESS, LONDON

© Top Twenty charts Billboard Ltd./BMRB 1975.
© Supporting text Tony Jasper 1975.

All rights reserved. No part of this publication may be reproduced, stored in a retrieval system, transmitted in any form by any means electrical, mechanical or photocopied, recorded or otherwise without the prior permission of the publisher.

ISBN 0362 00263 0

House editor Kate Ritchie
Cover design Paul Chevannes

First published in 1976 by
Queen Anne Press Limited,
12 Vandy Street, London, EC2A 2EN

Printed in England by
Hazell Watson & Viney Ltd,
Aylesbury, Bucks

FOREWORD AND ACKNOWLEDGEMENTS

This volume publishes the Top Twenty singles charts as listed weekly in *Record Mirror* from early January 1955 to the end of September 1975. Chart information was made available to us by Billboard Limited and the tables and facts presented have appeared in the pages of *Record Mirror*. At one time the paper was published by Billboard but this ceased in 1974 when the paper was taken over by Spotlight Publications. However, the new company continues to glean its facts from the original chart source and credits Music Week and the British Market Research Bureau every week.

The British Market Research Bureau provided the first independently-prepared chart compilation in 1969, since prior to this singles charts had been compiled by various music trade papers and music newspapers. The chart published in *Music Week* and in the American *Billboard*, now printed with permission by *Record Mirror* and *Sounds*, is also used by the British Broadcasting Corporation. Prior to this, the BBC had compiled its own charts from all the charts published weekly by the musical press.

Each individual week's positions have been printed in the following way. The Top Twenty at the beginning of every month is given, with the records' positions for the ensuing weeks of the months in columns on the right-hand side of the page. Records which were not in the Top Twenty during the first week of the month are listed below the charts, with their Top Twenty positions for later weeks published in the right-hand columns.

Our reason for printing the chart list according to the date of the record paper's issue was quite simple. Though *Record Mirror* always printed a date seven days previous to the paper's publication at the top of its charts for many years, the chart provided was always taken as the 'best selling' list for the immediate period. Also, the paper is always available in mid-week.

We did find errors in other publications giving chart information and we suggest right lies on our side, though naturally this does not preclude us from making mistakes! Where the original charts contained mistakes, we noted them in this volume at the end of the appropriate month's charts. We did for instance find one memorable occasion when 21 records made up the chart, without two discs at Number Twenty!

We have printed the positions we found in the actual volumes instead of using the 'Five Years Ago' charts as given in the magazines. We found that such a process has been employed by music papers and publications concerned with the charts, and often with dire results!

The author would like to thank Rob and Tina Murdoch, David Armstrong, Deborah L. Dean and Merle Kessler for their help and interest, and also Martin Fraser for his opinions on chart matters and general assistance. He also acknowledges help and co-operation from the British Market Research Bureau and Mort L. Nasatir, the Managing Director of *Music Week* (U.K.), who is also a Vice-President of Billboard Publications Inc.

This volume is dedicated to all *Record Mirror* staff who worked on the paper at the time when the author was Charts Editor, with particular thanks to Peter Jones, the paper's former editor who is now associate editor of *Music Week*, and to Mike Hennessey, the former editorial director of *Record Mirror*.

JANUARY 1955

	22	29
1 Mambo Italiano *Rosemary Clooney* (Philips)		1
2 Finger of Suspicion *Dickie Valentine* (Decca)		2
3 Mr Sandman *The Chordettes* (Columbia)		–
4 Shake Rattle And Roll *Bill Haley* (Brunswick)		6
5 Naughty Lady Of Shady Lane *Dean Martin* (Capitol)		3
6 Happy Days And Lonely Nights *Suzi Miller* (Decca)		–
7 No One But You *Billy Eckstine* (MGM)		–
8 Softly Softly *Ruby Murray* (Columbia)		5
9 Don't Go To Strangers *Ronnie Harris* (Columbia)		8
10 Let Me Go *Teresa Brewer* (Vogue/Coral)		10
– Mr Sandman *The Four Aces* (Brunswick)		4
– Give Me Your Hand *Tennessee Ernie Ford* (Capitol)		7
– Mobile *Ray Burns* (Columbia)		9

22 January 1955 saw the first published chart, which consisted of a Top Ten only until 8 October 1955.

FEBRUARY 1955

	5	12	19	26
1 Mambo Italiano *Rosemary Clooney* (Philips)		2	4	3
2 Finger Of Suspicion *Dickie Valentine* (Decca)		6	8	7
3 Softly Softly *Ruby Murray* (Columbia)		3	2	2
4 Shake Rattle And Roll *Bill Haley* (Brunswick)		5	6	5
5 Naughty Lady Of Shady Lane *Dean Martin* (Capitol)		1	3	4
6 Give Me Your Word *Tennessee Ernie Ford* (Capitol)		4	1	1
7 Let Me Go *Teresa Brewer* (Vogue/Coral)		7	7	6
8 Mobile *Ray Burns* (Columbia)		8	–	10
9 A Blossom Fell *Various Artists* (Decca)		10	–	–
10 Mr Sandman *The Chordettes* (London)		–	–	–
– Beyond The Stars *David Whitfield* (Decca)		9	5	8
– Serenade/Donkey Song *Mario Lanza* (HMV)		–	10	–
– Heartbeat *Ruby Murray* (Columbia)		–	–	9

In the Record Mirror *issue of 19 February Dickie Valentine was credited with A Blossom Fell at the Number Nine position. The record was not listed for 26 February 1955.*

MARCH 1955

	5	12	19	26
1 Give Me Your Hand *Tennessee Ernie Ford* (Capitol)		2	1	1
2 Softly Softly *Ruby Murray* (Columbia)		1	2	2
3 Let Me Go *Teresa Brewer* (Vogue/Coral)		3	3	6
4 Naughty Lady Of Shady Lane *Dean Martin* (Capitol)		8	6	7
5 Shake Rattle And Roll *Bill Haley* (Brunswick)		9	10	–
6 Mambo Italiano *Rosemary Clooney* (Philips)		6	–	–
7 Mobile *Ray Burns* (Columbia)		5	4	4
8 Heartbeat *Ruby Murray* (Columbia)		–	–	–
9 Finger Of Suspicion *Dickie Valentine* (Decca)		–	–	–
10 A Blossom Fell *Nat 'King' Cole* (Capitol)		4	5	5
– Tomorrow *Johnny Brandon* (Polygon)		7	7	–
– Cherry Pink Apple Blossom *Perez Prado* (Columbia)		–	8	3
– If You Believe *Johnny Ray* (Philips)		10	–	–
– Let Me Go *Ruby Murray* (Columbia)		–	9	9
– If Anyone Finds This I Love You *Ruby Murray* (Columbia)		–	–	8
– A Blossom Fell *Dickie Valentine* (Decca)		–	–	10

APRIL 1955

2	9	16	23	30
1 Give Me Your Hand *Tennessee Ernie Ford* (Capitol)			1	1
2 Softly Softly *Ruby Murray* (Columbia)			5	8
3 Cherry Pink Apple Blossom *Perez Prado* (Columbia)			2	2
4 A Blossom Fell *Nat 'King' Cole* (Capitol)			–	–
5 Prize Of Old Gold *Joan Regan* (Decca)			6	–
6 Mobile *Ray Burns* (Columbia)			–	–
7 If Anyone Finds This I Love You *Ruby Murray* (Columbia)			10	9
8 Tomorrow *Johnny Brandon* (Polygon)			–	–
9 Mambo Rock *Bill Haley* (Brunswick)			–	–
10 Let Me Go *Teresa Brewer* (Vogue/Coral)			–	–
– Stranger In Paradise *Tony Bennett* (Philips)			3	3
– Wedding Bells *Eddie Fisher* (HMV)			4	7
– Cherry Pink Apple Blossom *Eddie Calvert* (Columbia)			7	4
– Earth Angel *The Crew Cuts* (Mercury)			8	5
– Under The Bridges Of Paris *Eartha Kitt* (HMV)			9	–
– Stranger In Paradise *Tony Martin* (HMV)			–	6
– Ready Willing And Able *Doris Day* (Philips)			–	10

The chart for 2 April was an official listing owing to a small number of shop returns caused by the Easter holidays. The 2 April chart was described by Record Mirror as for 'laughs'. There was no chart for 9 April and that of the 16 April was printed both to cover that week and the previous one.

MAY 1955

7	14	21	28
1 Stranger In Paradise *Tony Bennett* (Philips)	1	1	1
2 Cherry Pink Apple Blossom *Perez Prado* (Columbia)	2	2	3
3 Earth Angel *The Crew Cuts* (Mercury)	5	3	5
4 Cherry Pink Apple Blossom *Eddie Calvert* (Columbia)	3	4	4
5 Give Me Your Hand *Tennessee Ernie Ford* (Capitol)	4	6	7
6 Stranger In Paradise *Tony Martin* (HMV)	7	9	10
7 Ready Willing And Able *Doris Day* (Philips)	10	–	–
8 Wedding Bells *Eddie Fisher* (HMV)	9	–	–
9 If You Believe *Johnny Ray* (Philips)	6	7	6
10 You, My Love *Frank Sinatra* (Capitol)	–	–	–
– Unchained Melody *Al Hibbler* (Brunswick)	8	5	2
– Stranger In Paradise *The Four Aces* (Brunswick)	–	8	9
– Unchained Melody *Les Baxter* (Capitol)	–	10	–
– Unchained Melody *Jimmy Young* (Decca)	–	–	8

JUNE 1955

4	11	18	25
1 Stranger In Paradise *Tony Bennett* (Philips)	6	7	8
2 Unchained Melody *Al Hibbler* (Brunswick)	1	1	1
3 Cherry Pink *Perez Prado* (HMV)	4	6	6
4 Cherry Pink *Eddie Calvert* (Columbia)	2	2	5
5 Earth Angel *The Crew Cuts* (Mercury)	3	3	2
6 If You Believe *Johnny Ray* (Philips)	5	–	9
7 Give Me Your Hand *Tennessee Ernie Ford* (Capitol)	–	10	–
8 Unchained Melody *Jimmy Young* (Decca)	7	4	4
9 Stranger In Paradise *The Four Aces* (Brunswick)	10	9	–
10 Stranger In Paradise *Tony Martin* (HMV)	8	8	7
– Dreamboat *Alma Cogan* (HMV)	9	5	3
– Cool Water *Frankie Laine* (Philips)	–	–	10

The chart for 4 June was a repeat of that for 28 May.

JULY 1955

2		9	16	23	30
1	Unchained Melody *Al Hibbler* (Brunswick)	2	3	4	6
2	Dreamboat *Alma Cogan* (HMV)	1	1	2	3
3	Unchained Melody *Jimmy Young* (Decca)	3	2	5	5
4	Earth Angel *The Crew Cuts* (Mercury)	5	7	9	10
5	Cherry Pink *Eddie Calvert* (Columbia)	6	9	8	–
6	Stranger In Paradise *Tony Bennett* (Philips)	–	–	–	–
7	I Wonder *Dickie Valentine* (Decca)	4	5	7	7
8	Cool Water *Frankie Laine* (Philips)	7	6	3	2
9	Cherry Pink *Perez Prado* (HMV)	10	–	–	–
10	Where Will The Dimple Be *Rosemary Clooney* (Philips)	9	9	–	–
–	Evermore *Ruby Murray* (Columbia)	8	8	6	4
–	Rose Marie *Slim Whitman* (London)	–	4	1	1
–	Mama *David Whitfield* (Decca)	–	–	10	–
–	Strange Lady In Town *Frankie Laine* (Philips)	–	–	–	8
–	Ev'ry Day Of My Life *Malcolm Vaughan* (HMV)	–	–	–	9

AUGUST 1955

13		20	27
1	Rose Marie *Slim Whitman* (London)	1	1
2	Cool Water *Frankie Laine* (Philips)	2	3
3	Unchained Melody *Jimmy Young* (Decca)	9	–
4	Strange Lady In Town *Frankie Laine* (Philips)	6	5
5	Ev'ry Day Of My Life *Malcolm Vaughan* (HMV)	7	9
6	Evermore *Ruby Murray* (Columbia)	5	7
7	Ev'rywhere *David Whitfield* (Decca)	4	4
8	Dreamboat *Alma Cogan* (HMV)	–	–
9	Learnin' The Blues *Frank Sinatra* (Capitol)	3	2
10	I Wonder *Dickie Valentine* (Decca)	–	–
–	Indian Love Call *Slim Whitman* (London)	8	8
–	Unchained Melody *Al Hibbler* (Brunswick)	10	10
–	The Breeze And I *Caterina Valente* (Polydor)	–	6

The chart for 6 August was the same as that for 30 July, due to the August Bank Holiday.

SEPTEMBER 1955

3		10	17	24
1	Rose Marie *Slim Whitman* (London)	1	1	1
2	Cool Water *Frankie Laine* (Philips)	2	2	2
3	Learnin' The Blues *Frank Sinatra* (Capitol)	3	3	3
4	Ev'rywhere *David Whitfield* (Decca)	4	4	4
5	The Breeze And I *Caterina Valente* (Polydor)	5	6	7
6	Indian Love Call *Slim Whitman* (London)	7	5	6
7	Strange Lady In Town *Frankie Laine* (Philips)	6	7	10
8	Ev'ry Day Of My Life *Malcolm Vaughan* (HMV)	8	–	–
9	Evermore *Ruby Murray* (Columbia)	9	8	9
10	John And Julie *Eddie Calvert* (Columbia)	–	10	–
–	Love Me Or Leave Me *Sammy Davis Jnr.* (Brunswick)	–	9	8
–	The Man From Laramie *Jimmy Young* (Decca)	10	–	5

OCTOBER 1955

1		8	15	22	29
1	Cool Water *Frankie Laine* (Philips)	2	2	6	9
2	Rose Marie *Slim Whitman* (London)	3	3	3	6
3	The Man From Laramie *Jimmy Young* (Decca)	1	1	1	1
4	Learnin' The Blues *Frank Sinatra* (Capitol)	5	8	15	14
5	Ev'rywhere *David Whitfield* (Decca)	4	6	10	10
6	Indian Love Call *Slim Whitman* (London)	7	13	13	15
7	The Breeze And I *Caterina Valente* (Polydor)	9	9	11	12
8	Blue Star *Cyril Stapleton* (Decca)	6	5	4	4
9	Strange Lady In Town *Frankie Laine* (Philips)	17	–	–	–
10	Ev'ry Day Of My Life *Malcolm Vaughan* (HMV)	10	15	–	–
–	Yellow Rose Of Texas *Mitch Miller* (Philips)	8	4	2	2
–	Close The Door *The Stargazers* (Decca)	11	18	19	–
–	Hey, There *Rosemary Clooney* (Philips)	12	7	8	8
–	Humming Bird *Frankie Laine* (Philips)	13	16	16	18
–	Hernando's Hideaway *The Johnston Brothers* (Decca)	14	10	7	5
–	Love Me Or Leave Me *Sammy Davis Jnr.* (Brunswick)	15	17	19	–
–	Hernando's Hideaway *Johnny Ray* (Philips)	16	10	9	11
–	Hey, There *Johnny Ray* (Philips)	18	14	12	7
–	John And Julie *Eddie Calvert* (Columbia)	19	–	–	–
–	The Dam Busters March *R.A.F. Band* (HMV)	20	–	–	–
–	Rock Around The Clock *Bill Haley* (Brunswick)	–	12	5	3
–	Hey, There *Sammy Davis Jnr.* (Brunswick)	–	19	17	20
–	Love Me Or Leave Me *Doris Day* (Philips)	–	20	–	–
–	Yellow Rose Of Texas *Ronnie Hilton* (HMV)	–	20	–	–
–	I'll Come When You Call *Ruby Murray* (Columbia)	–	–	14	13
–	Hey, There *The Johnston Brothers* (Decca)	–	–	18	16
–	Bring Your Smile Along *Frankie Laine* (Philips)	–	–	–	17
–	That Old Black Magic *Sammy Davis Jnr.* (Brunswick)	–	–	–	18

It was for the first time that Record Mirror *published a Top Twenty on 8 October 1955.*

NOVEMBER 1955

5		12	19	26
1	The Man From Laramie *Jimmy Young* (Decca)	2	4	6
2	Yellow Rose Of Texas *Mitch Miller* (Philips)	3	2	3
3	Blue Star *Cyril Stapleton* (Decca)	5	8	10
4	Rock Around The Clock *Bill Haley* (Brunswick)	1	1	1
5	Hernando's Hideaway *The Johnston Brothers* (Decca)	4	3	4
6	Hey, There *Rosemary Clooney* (Philips)	6	7	7
7	Rose Marie *Slim Whitman* (London)	9	13	17
8	Cool Water *Frankie Laine* (Philips)	–	–	–
9	Hey, There *Johnny Ray* (Philips)	8	9	12
10	The Breeze And I *Caterina Valente* (Polydor)	15	–	–
11	Hey, There *The Johnston Brothers* (Decca)	–	–	14
12	I'll Come When You Call *Ruby Murray* (Columbia)	11	11	–
13	Hernando's Hideaway *Johnny Ray* (Philips)	12	14	–
14	Everywhere *David Whitfield* (Decca)	17	–	15
15	Indian Love Call *Slim Whitman* (London)	–	–	–
16	Love Is A Many Splendored Thing *The Four Aces* (Brunswick)	13	6	2
17	Yellow Rose Of Texas *Gary Miller* (Nixa)	–	–	–
18	Let's Have A Ding-Dong *Winifred Atwell* (Decca)	7	5	9
19	Love Is A Many Splendored Thing *Nat 'King' Cole* (Capitol)	–	15	–
20	Dam Busters March *Billy Cotton* (Decca)	–	–	–
–	Bring Your Smile Along *Frankie Laine* (Philips)	10	–	–
–	Ain't That A Shame *Pat Boone* (London)	14	10	5
–	Meet Me On The Corner *Max Bygraves* (HMV)	16	12	13

	12	19	26
– Singing Dogs *The Singing Dogs* (Nixa)	–	15	–
– Join In And Sing Again *The Johnston Brothers* (Decca)	–	17	–
– Seventeen *The Fontaine Sisters* (London)	–	18	–
– Twenty Tiny Fingers *The Stargazers* (Decca)	–	19	8
– Blue Star *Eve Boswell* (Parlophone)	–	20	10
– When You Lose The One You Love *David Whitfield* (Decca)	–	–	11
– Christmas Alphabet *Dickie Valentine* (Decca)	–	–	18
– Hawk Eye *Frankie Laine* (Philips)	–	–	16
– Suddenly There's A Valley *Lee Lawrence* (Decca)	–	–	19

Only 17 records were listed in the chart published for the 12 November 1955 issue of Record Mirror.

DECEMBER 1955

3	10	17	24
1 Rock Around The Clock *Bill Haley* (Brunswick)	1	1	1
2 Love Is A Many Splendored Thing *The Four Aces* (Brunswick)	2	2	3
3 Let's Have A Ding-Dong *Winifred Atwell* (Decca)	5	4	4
4 Twenty Tiny Fingers *The Stargazers* (Decca)	4	5	6
5 Ain't That A Shame *Pat Boone* (London)	6	6	7
6 Christmas Alphabet *Dickie Valentine* (Decca)	3	3	2
7 Yellow Rose Of Texas *Mitch Miller* (Philips)	7	8	10
8 Hernando's Hideaway *The Johnston Brothers* (Decca)	15	–	–
9 Hey, There *Rosemary Clooney* (Philips)	11	–	–
10 The Man From Laramie *Jimmy Young* (Decca)	19	–	–
11 Blue Star *Cyril Stapleton* (Decca)	16	17	–
12 Meet Me On The Corner *Max Bygraves* (HMV)	8	7	5
13 Hawk Eye *Frankie Laine* (Philips)	9	9	11
14 Hey, There *The Johnston Brothers* (Decca)	13	19	–
15 Cloudburst *Don Lang* (HMV)	10	13	14
16 Hey, There *Johnny Ray* (Philips)	–	–	–
17 I'll Come When You Call *Ruby Murray* (Columbia)	–	–	–
18 Caribbean *Mitchell Torok* (London)	–	–	–
19 Suddenly There's A Valley *Petula Clark* (Nixa)	14	10	8
20 I'll Never Stop Loving You *Doris Day* (Philips)	–	–	–
– When You Lose The One You Love *David Whitfield* (Decca)	12	14	15
– Singing Dogs *The Singing Dogs* (Nixa)	17	20	–
– The Very First Christmas Of All *Ruby Murray* (Columbia)	17	11	9
– Seventies *The Fontaine Sisters* (London)	20	–	–
– Suddenly There's A Valley *Lee Lawrence* (Columbia)	20	–	19
– The Shifting Whispering Sands *Billy Vaughan* (London)	–	12	13
– Suddenly There's A Valley *Julius La Rosa* (London)	–	14	16
– Join In And Sing Again *The Johnston Brothers* (Decca)	–	16	12
– Bluebell Polka *Jimmy Shand* (Parlophone)	–	18	20
– Tina Marie *Perry Como* (HMV)	–	–	17
– Pickin' A Chicken *Eve Boswell* (Parlophone)	–	–	18

1955

Ballads were the order of the day in 1955, with a host of hits from singers such as Johnny Ray, Frankie Laine, Guy Mitchell, Tony Bennett, Rosemary Clooney and Doris Day.

Ray was in the charts by April 1955 singing 'If You Believe', and ended the year with 'Song Of The Dreamer'. This pencil-slim half-Red Indian wept real tears as he emotionally sang songs such as 'Cry' and 'Little White Cloud That Cried'. A childhood accident had left him 52 per cent deaf, so he wore a hearing aid. Unkind critics said that he switched it off when he was performing so that he couldn't hear himself sing.

However, the hysteria which Ray created was phenomenal. George Cooper, an ex-stage doorman at the London Palladium lived through all the crazes in music, and he has said that nobody, not even The Beatles, created the fan furore that Ray did at that particular theatre. One night after a show Ray serenaded a vast crowd in Argyll Street from the Palladium roof, for his fans had made it clear that they were not going to leave the theatre until he had provided an unaccompanied encore.

Rosemary Clooney sang more jovial, fun songs such as 'Mambo Italiano' and 'Where Will The Dimple Be'. Doris Day entered the Top Twenty in April 1955 with 'Ready, Willing And Able', and Tony Bennett found a Number One with 'Stranger In Paradise' and engaged in a chart battle with both The Four Aces and Tony Martin who also entered the Top Ten with the same song.

Frankie Laine had already achieved an 18-week Number One hit in 1951 (the *New Musical Express* had begun the first pop chart ever in that year) with 'I Believe', and he went on to record a string of classic hit discs. His first record of 1955 was 'Rain Rain Rain', and he followed this with five other hits that year. Laine made a visit to Britain during the same year and was highly insulted for being criticised by the show business critic of one mass circulation newspaper, not for his voice but for the cut of his suit! Laine stood on the stage of the London Palladium and retorted 'Knock my talent if you must, but not my tailor'. He was sporting the new line in Italian-cut suits, with a square-shouldered short jacket, known as a 'bum freezer', and shoes with pointed toes.

Laine invited the audience on his second night at the Palladium to approve his suit, which they did in the same way as they approved of his voice which had bellowed its way through hits such as 'Shine', 'Mule Train' and 'Cry Of The Wild Goose'. Suitably mollified, Laine finished his act, but he had learned something that was to become more and more marked as pop music developed – that music and clothes were already linked. Clothes maketh the man, but they also help to make the music.

Apart from these American balladeers, Britain had her own hit makers, one of whom was Ruby Murray, a totally unsophisticated Irish girl who achieved five singles in the Top Twenty in one week. Ballads also came from singers such as Jimmy Young, Dickie Valentine, David Whitfield and Malcolm Vaughan. Many of these balladeers came from the most unlikely backgrounds – for example, Vaughan's high tenor voice had previously been one half of a knockabout comedy act. David Whitfield had been mixing cement on building sites in Hull until he entered the charts, and Dave King had been a mime artist in vaudeville until he learned how to sing suspiciously like Perry Como and Dean Martin.

Jimmy Young, who is now a successful Radio 2 disc-jockey, had two Number One hits in 1955 – 'Unchained Melody' and 'Man From Laramie'. Al Hibbler also achieved a Number One with 'Unchained Melody'.

1955 was a memorable year for Pat Boone, not in terms of a huge number of hits, but for his first British chart entry, 'Ain't That A Shame'. He reached Number Seven with this hit, which is perhaps more associated with Fats Domino in most people's minds.

Pop music was on the way in 1955, but generally speaking it was in the form of predictable songs from predictable artists. A new trend was needed and it came with the emergence of Bill Haley and The Comets who arrived in the Top Twenty with 'Shake, Rattle And Roll', a song which had been recorded on 12 April 1954 in the same session as 'Rock Around The Clock', which was to become their next hit. 'Rock Around The Clock' made little chart impression when it was first released in January 1955, but on its re-

release and chart entry in October the record was in the charts for four months.

The new craze brought its own Teddy Boy fashion following. Drainpipe trousers, bootlace ties, patches of velvet on lapels and pockets of drape jackets, 'brothel creeper' shoes, and the liberal application of Brylcreem to plastered-back quiffs of hair all added up to the Teddy Boys' uniform. However, the 'Teds' and their music certainly injected some much-needed excitement into the music scene of 1955.

JANUARY 1956

	7	14	21	28
1 Rock Around The Clock *Bill Haley* (Brunswick)		2	4	8
2 Love Is A Many Splendored Thing *The Four Aces* (Brunswick)		4	3	6
3 Rock-A-Beatin' Boogie *Bill Haley* (Brunswick)		5	6	7
4 Christmas Alphabet *Dickie Valentine* (Decca)		–	–	–
5 Meet Me On The Corner *Max Bygraves* (HMV)		8	13	16
6 Let's Have A Ding-Dong *Winifred Atwell* (Decca)		–	–	–
7 Ain't That A Shame *Pat Boone* (London)		12	17	–
8 Rock Island Line *Lonnie Donegan* (Decca)		9	8	9
9 The Ballad Of Davy Crockett *Bill Hayes* (London)		3	2	2
10 Twenty Tiny Fingers *The Stargazers* (Decca)		17	–	–
11 Sixteen Tons *Tennessee Ernie Ford* (Capitol)		1	1	1
12 Pickin' A Chicken *Eve Boswell* (Parlophone)		10	12	13
13 Tina Marie *Perry Como* (HMV)		–	–	–
14 When You Lose The One You Love *David Whitfield* (Decca)		13	10	10
15 Yellow Rose Of Texas *Mitch Miller* (Philips)		–	–	–
16 The Shifting Whispering Sands *Billy Vaughan* (London)		14	9	13
17 Suddenly There's A Valley *Petula Clark* (Nixa)		16	15	–
18 Cloudburst *Don Lang* (HMV)		11	–	–
19 Arriverderci, Darling *Edna Savage* (Parlophone)		–	20	–
20 Never Do A Tango With An Eskimo *Alma Cogan* (HMV)		20	16	–
20 Sixteen Tons *Frankie Laine* (Philips)		15	–	18
– Ballad Of Davy Crockett *Tennessee Ernie Ford* (Capitol)		6	7	4
– Love And Marriage *Frank Sinatra* (Capitol)		7	5	3
– Groce Di Oro *Joan Regan* (Decca)		18	–	–
– Robin Hood *Gary Miller* (Nixa)		19	13	12
– Love Is A Tender Trap *Frank Sinatra* (Capitol)		–	11	5
– Ballad Of Davy Crocket *Gary Miller* (Nixa)		–	18	–
– Robin Hood *Dick James* (Parlophone)		–	18	–
– Only You *The Hilltoppers* (London)		–	–	11
– Yellow Rose Of Texas *Stan Freburg* (Capitol)		–	–	15
– Zambesi *Lou Busch* (Capitol)		–	–	17
– Dreams Can Tell A Lie *Nat 'King' Cole* (Capitol)		–	–	18
– The Shifting Whispering Sands *Eamonn Andrews* (Parlophone)		–	–	20

FEBRUARY 1956

	4	11	18	25
1 Sixteen Tons *Tennessee Ernie Ford* (Capitol)		1	3	5
2 Ballad Of Davy Crockett *Bill Hayes* (London)		4	8	10
3 Love Is A Tender Trap *Frank Sinatra* (Capitol)		2	5	4
4 Love And Marriage *Frank Sinatra* (Capitol)		10	11	17
5 Ballad Of Davy Crockett *Tennessee Ernie Ford* (Capitol)		6	7	13
6 Rock-A-Beatin' Boogie *Bill Haley* (Brunswick)		9	19	15
7 Rock Island Line *Lonnie Donegan* (Decca)		6	12	11
8 When You Lose The One You Love *David Whitfield* (Decca)		15	–	–
9 Love Is A Many Splendored Thing *The Four Aces* (Brunswick)		14	–	–
10 Rock Around The Clock *Bill Haley* (Brunswick)		–	18	19
11 Robin Hood *Gary Miller* (Nixa)		13	15	–
12 Dreams Can Tell A Lie *Nat 'King' Cole* (Capitol)		20	16	16
13 Zambesi *Lou Busch* (Capitol)		5	1	1
14 Pickin' A Chicken *Eve Boswell* (Parlophone)		16	20	–
15 Only You *The Hilltoppers* (London)		8	6	6
16 It's Almost Tomorrow *The Dream Weavers* (Brunswick)		11	4	3
17 The Shifting Whispering Sands *Eamonn Andrews* (Parlophone)		–	–	–
18 Ain't That A Shame *Fats Domino* (London)		–	–	–
19 Sixteen Tons *Frankie Laine* (Philips)		18	–	–

4	11	18	25
20 With Your Love *Malcolm Vaughan* (HMV)	17	–	–
– Memories Are Made Of This *Dean Martin* (Capitol)	3	2	2
– Young And Foolish *Ronnie Hilton* (HMV)	12	–	–
– Young And Foolish *Edmund Hockeridge* (Nixa)	19	14	12
– Rock And Roll Waltz *Kay Starr* (HMV)	–	9	8
– Band Of Gold *Don Cherry* (Philips)	–	10	7
– Memories Are Made Of This *Dave King* (Decca)	–	13	9
– Who's Sorry Now *Johnny Ray* (Philips)	–	17	–
– With Your Love *Robert Earl* (Philips)	–	–	13
– Ballad Of Davy Crockett *Gary Miller* (Nixa)	–	–	18
– Young And Foolish *Dean Martin* (Capitol)	–	–	20

MARCH 1956

3	10	17	24	31
1 Memories Are Made Of This *Dean Martin* (Capitol)	1	3	4	5
2 Zambesi *Lou Busch* (Capitol)	2	2	3	4
3 It's Almost Tomorrow *The Dream Weavers* (Brunswick	3	1	1	1
4 Only You *The Hilltoppers* (London)	4	6	7	6
5 Rock And Roll Waltz *Kay Starr* (HMV)	6	4	2	2
6 Band Of Gold *Don Cherry* (Philips)	7	9	9	10
7 Love Is A Tender Trap *Frank Sinatra* (Capitol)	9	12	–	–
8 Memories Are Made Of This *Dave King* (Decca)	5	5	6	7
9 Sixteen Tons *Tennessee Ernie Ford* (Capitol)	12	–	–	–
10 Rock Island Line *Lonnie Donegan* (Decca)	10	10	10	–
11 Young And Foolish *Edmund Hockeridge* (Nixa)	11	15	17	–
12 Ballad Of Davy Crockett *Bill Hayes* (London)	19	19	–	–
13 Jimmy Unknown *Lita Rosa* (Decca)	13	20	13	17
14 Rock-A-Beatin' Boogie *Bill Haley* (Brunswick)	–	–	–	–
14 Ballad Of Davy Crockett *Tennessee Ernie Ford* (Capitol)	–	–	–	–
16 Dreams Can Tell A Lie *Nat 'King' Cole* (Capitol)	14	–	–	–
16 Love And Marriage *Frank Sinatra* (Capitol)	–	–	–	–
18 With Your Love *Robert Earl* (Philips)	–	–	–	–
19 Rock Around The Clock *Bill Haley* (Brunswick)	–	–	–	–
20 Tumbling Tumbleweeds *Slim Whitman* (London)	16	15	20	–
– Chain Gang *Jimmy Young* (Decca)	17	11	11	9
– Poor People Of Paris *Winifred Atwell* (Decca)	17	7	5	3
– My September Love *David Whitfield* (Decca)	20	–	18	19
– Rudder And Rock *David Whitfield* (Decca)	–	19	–	–
– See You Later Alligator *Bill Haley* (Brunswick)	8	8	8	8
– Great Pretender *Jimmy Parkinson* (Columbia)	15	13	11	11
– My September Love *Robert Earl* (Philips)	–	14	19	–
– I Hear You Knocking *Gale Storm* (London)	–	17	–	–
– Theme From The Threepenny Opera *Dick Hyman* (MGM)	–	–	16	12
– Seven Days *Anne Shelton* (Philips)	–	–	14	16
– Zambesi *Eddie Calvert* (Columbia)	–	–	15	13
– Theme From The Threepenny Opera *Billy Vaughan* (London)	–	–	20	15
– I'm A Fool *Slim Whitman* (London)	–	–	–	14
– A Tear Fell *Teresa Brewer* (Vogue/Coral)	–	–	–	20
– Willie Can *Alma Cogan* (HMV)	–	–	–	17

APRIL 1956

	7	14	21	28
1 Poor People Of Paris *Winifred Atwell* (Decca)		1	1	1
2 It's Almost Tomorrow *The Dream Weavers* (Brunswick)		2	2	2
3 Rock And Roll Waltz *Kay Starr* (HMV)		3	3	5
4 Zambesi *Lou Busch* (Capitol)		4	5	10
5 Memories Are Made Of This *Dave King* (Decca)		5	7	7
6 Only You *The Hilltoppers* (London)		6	4	5
7 Memories Are Made Of This *Dean Martin* (Capitol)		7	7	9
8 See You Later Alligator *Bill Haley* (Brunswick)		7	4	5
9 Chain Gang *Jimmy Young* (Decca)		16	–	–
10 Great Pretender *Jimmy Parkinson* (Columbia)		11	–	–
11 I'm A Fool *Slim Whitman* (London)		17	16	18
12 Band Of Gold *Don Cherry* (Philips)		18	–	–
12 Theme From The Threepenny Opera *Dick Hyman* (HMV)		9	11	11
14 Zambesi *Eddie Calvert* (Columbia)		–	–	–
15 Willie Can *Alma Cogan* (HMV)		14	14	15
16 Theme From The Threepenny Opera *Billy Vaughan* (London)		–	–	–
17 My September Love *David Whitfield* (Decca)		12	9	8
17 A Tear Fell *Teresa Brewer* (Vogue/Coral)		10	13	6
19 Rock Island Line *Lonnie Donegan* (Decca)		15	20	–
20 Seven Days *Anne Shelton* (Philips)		19	18	–
– You Can't Be True To Two *Dave King* (Decca)		12	10	13
– In A Little Spanish Town *Bing Crosby* (Brunswick)		20	–	–
– Nothin' To Do *Michael Holliday* (Columbia)		20	16	–
– No Other Love *Ronnie Hilton* (HMV)		–	12	4
– Theme From The Threepenny Opera *Louis Armstrong* (Philips)		–	15	16
– I'll Be Home *Pat Boone* (London)		–	19	14
– Lost John *Lonnie Donegan* (Nixa)		–	–	17
– Ain't Misbehavin' *Johnny Ray* (Philips)		–	–	18
– Main Title *Billy May* (Capitol)		–	–	20

MAY 1956

	5	12	19	26
1 Poor People Of Paris *Winifred Atwell* (Decca)		2	2	5
2 No Other Love *Ronnie Hilton* (HMV)		1	1	1
3 It's Almost Tomorrow *The Dream Weavers* (Brunswick)		5	10	12
4 A Tear Fell *Teresa Brewer* (Vogue/Coral)		3	3	2
5 Rock And Roll Waltz *Kay Starr* (HMV)		6	6	7
6 Only You *The Hilltoppers* (London)		8	8	10
7 My September Love *David Whitfield* (Decca)		4	5	4
8 Main Title *Billy May* (Capitol)		9	7	9
9 Theme From The Threepenny Opera *Dick Hyman* (HMV)		19	14	–
10 I'll Be Home *Pat Boone* (London)		7	4	3
11 Lost John *Lonnie Donegan* (Nixa)		10	9	6
12 Memories Are Made Of This *Dave King* (Decca)		12	–	–
13 Theme From The Threepenny Opera *Louis Armstrong* (Philips)		11	11	13
14 Memories Are Made Of This *Dean Martin* (Capitol)		19	–	18
15 See You Later Alligator *Bill Haley* (Brunswick)		16	18	19
16 Zambesi *Lou Busch* (Capitol)		–	–	–
17 You Can't Be True To Two *Dave King* (Decca)		14	13	14
18 Willie Can *Alma Cogan* (HMV)		17	19	–
19 Ain't Misbehavin' *Johnny Ray* (Philips)		–	–	–
20 Rock Island Line *Lonnie Donegan* (Decca)		13	–	16
– Mountain Greenery *Mel Torme* (Victor/Coral)		15	–	–
– No Other Love *Edmund Hockeridge* (Nixa)		18	16	–
– Port Au Prince *Winifred Atwell* (Decca)		–	20	–

5	12	19	26
– Heartbreak Hotel *Elvis Presley* (HMV)	–	17	11
– Too Young To Go Steady *Nat 'King' Cole* (Capitol)	–	15	17
– The Happy Whistler *Don Robertson* (Capitol)	–	12	8
– Blue Suede Shoes *Carl Perkins* (London)	–	–	15
– Hot Diggity *Perry Como* (HMV)	–	–	19

JUNE 1956

2	9	16	23	30
1 No Other Love *Ronnie Hilton* (HMV)	3	3	5	6
2 A Tear Fell *Teresa Brewer* (Vogue/Coral)	4	4	7	7
3 I'll Be Home *Pat Boone* (London)	1	1	1	1
4 Lost John *Lonnie Donegan* (Nixa)	2	2	2	2
5 My September Love *David Whitfield* (Decca)	7	8	8	9
6 Heartbreak Hotel *Elvis Presley* (HMV)	5	6	4	3
7 Poor People Of Paris *Winifred Atwell* (Decca)	9	14	–	–
8 The Happy Whistler *Don Robertson* (Capitol)	8	9	13	–
9 Main Title *Billy May* (Capitol)	10	11	16	–
10 Rock And Roll Waltz *Kay Starr* (HMV)	11	15	–	–
11 Saints Rock And Roll *Bill Haley* (Brunswick)	6	5	3	5
12 Only You *The Hilltoppers* (London)	20	–	–	–
13 Too Young To Go Steady *Nat 'King' Cole* (Capitol)	12	18	12	13
14 Theme From The Threepenny Opera *Louis Armstrong* (Philips)	20	–	–	–
15 Hot Diggity *Perry Como* (HMV)	13	7	6	4
16 You Can't Be True To Two *Dave King* (Decca)	–	–	–	–
17 Blue Suede Shoes *Carl Perkins* (London)	15	13	15	19
18 Blue Suede Shoes *Elvis Presley* (HMV)	14	9	10	12
19 Rock Island Line *Lonnie Donegan* (Decca)	–	–	–	–
19 It's Almost Tomorrow *The Dream Weavers* (Brunswick)	–	–	–	–
– Take It Satch (E.P.) *Louis Armstrong* (Philips)	20	–	–	–
– Out Of Town *Max Bygraves* (HMV)	18	–	–	–
– Hot Diggity *The Stargazers* (Decca)	17	–	–	–
– Moonglow And Theme From The Picnic *Morris Stoloff* (Brunswick)	16	12	9	11
– Hot Diggity *Michael Holliday* (Columbia)	–	16	11	15
– Gal In The Yaller Shoes *Michael Holliday* (Columbia)	–	20	17	10
– Mountain Greenery *Mel Torme* (Victor/Coral)	19	18	19	–
– Carousel (L.P.) *Soundtrack* (Capitol)	–	–	19	–
– Experiments In Mice *Johnny Dankworth* (Parlophone)	–	–	17	–
– Songs For Swingin' Lovers (L.P.) *Frank Sinatra* (Capitol)	–	–	13	13
– Why Do Fools Fall In Love *Frankie Lymon and The Teenagers* (Columbia)	–	–	–	15
– All Star Hit Parade *Various Artists* (Decca)	–	–	–	8
– Wayward Wind *Gogi Grant* (London)	–	–	–	17
– Portuguese Washer Woman *Joe 'Fingers' Carr* (Capitol)	–	–	–	19
– Wayward Wind *Tex Ritter* (Capitol)	–	–	–	18

No Number Seventeen was listed for 16 June 1956.

JULY 1956

7	14	21	28
1 I'll Be Home *Pat Boone* (London)	1	3	3
2 Lost John *Lonnie Donegan* (Nixa)	7	7	14
3 All Star Hit Parade *Various Artists* (Decca)	2	2	2
4 Heartbreak Hotel *Elvis Presley* (HMV)	6	6	5
5 Hot Diggity *Perry Como* (HMV)	9	9	12
6 Saints Rock And Roll *Bill Haley* (Brunswick)	8	11	9

7	14	21	28
7 Bluebottle Blues *The Goons* (Decca)	3	4	4
8 Experiments In Mice *Johnny Dankworth* (Parlophone)	5	5	8
9 Wayward Wind *Gogi Grant* (London)	10	8	10
10 No Other Love *Ronnie Hilton* (HMV)	16	–	–
11 My September Love *David Whitfield* (Decca)	15	–	–
12 Wayward Wind *Tex Ritter* (Capitol)	13	9	11
13 Why Do Fools Fall In Love *Frankie Lymon and The Teenagers* (Columbia)	4	1	1
14 Blue Suede Shoes *Elvis Presley* (HMV)	14	–	–
15 A Tear Fell *Teresa Brewer* (Vogue/Coral)	–	18	20
16 Songs For Swingin' Lovers (L.P.) *Frank Sinatra* (Capitol)	11	13	–
17 Moonglow And Theme From The Picnic *Morris Stoloff* (Brunswick)	12	16	18
18 I'm Walking Backwards *The Goons* (Decca)	–	–	–
20 Carousel (L.P.) *Various Artists* (Capitol)	–	–	–
20 Skiffle Session (E.P.) *Lonnie Donegan* (Nixa)	–	–	–
– Who Are We *Ronnie Hilton* (HMV)	17	15	13
– Whatever Will Be Will Be *Doris Day* (Philips)	18	14	9
– Badpenny Blues *Humphrey Lyttleton* (Parlophone)	19	17	18
– Portuguese Washer Woman *Joe 'Fingers' Carr* (Capitol)	20	–	–
– Walk Hand In Hand *Tony Martin* (HMV)	–	12	6
– A Sweet Old Fashioned Girl *Teresa Brewer* (Vogue/Coral)	–	19	15
– Hot Diggity *Michael Holliday* (Columbia)	–	20	–
– Mountain Greenery *Mel Torme* (Columbia)	–	–	16
– Be Bop A Lula *Gene Vincent* (Capitol)	–	–	17
– Serenade *Slim Whitman* (London)	–	–	20

AUGUST 1956

4	11	18	25
1 Why Do Fools Fall In Love *Frankie Lymon and The Teenagers* (Columbia)	2	2	5
2 Whatever Will Be Will Be *Doris Day* (Philips)	1	1	1
3 A Sweet Old Fashioned Girl *Teresa Brewer* (Vogue/Coral)	3	3	3
4 I'll Be Home *Pat Boone* (London)	6	6	8
5 Walk Hand In Hand *Tony Martin* (HMV)	4	5	4
6 Bluebottle Blues *The Goons* (Decca)	16	–	17
7 Mountain Greenery *Mel Torme* (Columbia)	5	4	5
8 All Star Hit Parade *Various Artists* (Decca)	7	9	12
9 Wayward Wind *Tex Ritter* (Capitol)	8	8	9
10 Wayward Wind *Gogi Grant* (Capitol)	11	11	16
11 Saints Rock And Roll *Bill Haley* (Brunswick)	10	9	13
12 Heartbreak Hotel *Elvis Presley* (HMV)	9	13	7
13 Who Are We *Ronnie Hilton* (HMV)	12	16	–
14 Experiments In Mice *Johnny Dankworth* (Columbia)	20	15	–
15 Serenade *Slim Whitman* (London)	14	14	11
16 Lost John *Lonnie Donegan* (Nixa)	17	–	–
17 The Faithful Hussar *Ted Heath* (Decca)	15	–	–
18 Walk Hand In Hand *Ronnie Carroll* (Philips)	13	12	10
19 Walk Hand In Hand *Jimmy Parkinson* (Columbia)	–	18	–
20 Hot Diggity *Perry Como* (HMV)	17	–	–
– Blue Suede Shoes *Elvis Presley* (HMV)	19	–	–
– Why Do Fools Fall In Love *Alma Cogan* (HMV)	20	19	–
– I Want You, I Need You, I Love You *Elvis Presley* (HMV)	–	20	15
– Rockin' Through The Rye *Bill Haley* (Brunswick)	–	7	6
– Be Bop A Lula *Gene Vincent* (Capitol)	–	17	20
– My Son John *David Whitfield* (Decca)	–	–	18
– You Are My First Love *Ruby Murray* (Columbia)	–	–	19
– I Almost Lost My Mind *Pat Boone* (London)	–	–	13
– Long Tall Sally *Little Richard* (London)	–	–	20

SEPTEMBER 1956

1	8	15	22	29
1 Whatever Will Be Will Be *Doris Day* (Philips)	1	1	2	2
2 Why Do Fools Fall In Love *Frankie Lymon and The Teenagers* (Columbia)	2	3	5	17
3 A Sweet Old Fashioned Girl *Teresa Brewer* (Vogue/ Coral)	5	5	8	11
4 Rockin' Through The Rye *Bill Haley* (Brunswick)	4	4	3	3
5 Walk Hand In Hand *Tony Martin* (HMV)	6	6	7	14
6 Mountain Greenery *Mel Torme* (Columbia)	7	7	13	15
7 I Almost Lost My Mind *Pat Boone* (London)	8	18	18	–
8 Wayward Wind *Tex Ritter* (Capitol)	15	19	–	–
9 Heartbreak Hotel *Elvis Presley* (HMV)	10	19	–	–
9 Serenade *Slim Whitman* (London)	13	12	17	20
11 I'll Be Home *Pat Boone* (London)	11	–	19	–
12 Born To Be With You *The Chordettes* (London)	13	14	15	16
13 My Son John *David Whitfield* (Decca)	–	–	–	–
14 I'm In Love Again *Fats Domino* (London)	9	17	–	19
15 Lay Down Your Arms *Anne Shelton* (Philips)	3	2	1	1
16 Saints Rock And Roll *Bill Haley* (Brunswick)	12	10	12	12
17 Walk Hand In Hand *Ronnie Carroll* (Philips)	16	–	–	–
18 Who Are We *Ronnie Hilton* (HMV)	–	–	–	–
19 Long Tall Sally *Little Richard* (London)	–	–	–	–
20 I Want You, I Need You, I Love You *Elvis Presley* (HMV)	19	19	–	–
– The Great Pretender *The Platters* (Mercury)	16	9	6	6
– Only You *The Platters* (Mercury)	18	11	11	10
– A Woman In Love *Frankie Laine* (Philips)	–	15	10	7
– Bring A Little Water Sylvia *Lonnie Donegan* (Nixa)	–	16	9	8
– Dead Or Alive *Lonnie Donegan* (Nixa)	–	13	14	9
– Ying Tong Song *The Goons* (Decca)	–	8	4	4
– Rock Around The Clock *Bill Haley* (Brunswick)	–	–	19	13
– Hound Dog *Elvis Presley* (HMV)	–	–	16	5
– When Mexico Gave Up The Rhumba *Mitchell Torok* (Brunswick)	–	–	–	18
– Moonglow And Theme From The Picnic *Morris Stoloff* (Brunswick)	19	–	–	–

OCTOBER 1956

6	13	20	27
1 Lay Down Your Arms *Anne Shelton* (Philips)	1	2	3
2 Woman In Love *Frankie Laine* (Philips)	2	1	1
3 Whatever Will Be Will Be *Doris Day* (Philips)	3	5	8
4 Hound Dog *Elvis Presley* (HMV)	5	3	2
5 Giddy Up A Ding Dong *Freddy Bell and The Bell Boys* (Mercury)	4	4	4
6 Rockin' Through The Rye *Bill Haley* (Brunswick)	6	6	6
7 Ying Tong Song *The Goons* (Decca)	8	7	10
8 The Great Pretender *The Platters* (Mercury)	11	12	–
9 Only You *The Platters* (Mercury)	7	8	15
10 Rock Around The Clock *Bill Haley* (Brunswick)	10	9	7
11 Bring A Little Water Sylvia *Lonnie Donegan* (Nixa)	9	10	11
12 Saints Rock And Roll *Bill Haley* (Brunswick)	15	19	19
13 Dead Or Alive *Lonnie Donegan* (Nixa)	13	15	17
14 See You Later Alligator *Bill Haley* (Brunswick)	17	13	16
15 When Mexico Gave Up The Rhumba *Mitchell Torok* (Brunswick)	14	11	9
16 Born To Be With You *The Chordettes* (London)	12	18	–
17 Walk Hand In Hand *Tony Martin* (HMV)	–	–	–
18 Razzle Dazzle *Bill Haley* (Brunswick)	16	16	20

6	13	20	27
19 Why Do Fools Fall In Love *Frankie Lymon and The Teenagers* (Columbia)	20	–	–
20 Woman In Love *Ronnie Hilton* (HMV)	–	–	–
– More *Perry Como* (HMV)	18	17	12
– Guys And Dolls (E.P.) *Marlon Brando and Jean Simmons* (Brunswick)	19	–	–
– Just Walking In The Rain *Johnny Ray* (Philips)	–	14	5
– Woman In Love *The Four Aces* (Brunswick)	–	20	–
– More *Jimmy Young* (Decca)	–	–	13
– Bluejean Bop *Gene Vincent* (Capitol)	–	–	14
– Rock With The Caveman *Tommy Steele* (Decca)	–	–	17

NOVEMBER 1956

3	10	17	24
1 Woman In Love *Frankie Laine* (Philips)	2	2	2
2 Hound Dog *Elvis Presley* (HMV)	3	3	4
3 Just Walking In The Rain *Johnny Ray* (Philips)	1	1	1
4 Lay Down Your Arms *Anne Shelton* (Philips)	7	11	18
5 Rockin' Through The Rye *Bill Haley* (Brunswick)	5	9	11
6 My Prayer *The Platters* (Mercury)	6	4	3
7 Giddy Up A Ding Dong *Freddie Bell and The Bell Boys* (Mercury)	8	13	–
8 More *Jimmy Young* (Decca)	4	5	6
9 When Mexico Gave Up The Rhumba *Mitchell Torok* (Brunswick)	10	7	8
10 Rock Around The Clock *Bill Haley* (Brunswick)	9	18	15
11 Rock With The Caveman *Tommy Steele* (Decca)	13	20	–
12 More *Perry Como* (HMV)	11	17	–
13 Whatever Will Be Will Be *Doris Day* (Philips)	20	–	–
14 Bluejean Bop *Gene Vincent* (Capitol)	12	–	–
15 Ying Tong Song *The Goons* (Decca)	–	–	–
16 Love Me As Though There Were No Tomorrow *Nat 'King' Cole* (Capitol)	–	16	20
17 See You Later Alligator *Bill Haley* (Brunswick)	–	–	–
18 Only You *The Platters* (Mercury)	17	18	17
18 Bring A Little Water Sylvia *Lonnie Donegan* (Nixa)	–	–	–
18 Make It A Party *Winifred Atwell* (Decca)	18	15	12
18 Autumn Concerto *George Melachrino* (HMV)	–	–	–
– Don't Be Cruel *Elvis Presley* (HMV)	19	–	–
– Green Door *Jim Lowe* (London)	13	10	12
– Green Door *Frankie Vaughan* (Philips)	15	6	5
– Rip It Up *Little Richard* (London)	16	8	7
– Blue Moon (E.P.) *Elvis Presley* (HMV)	–	12	10
– St Theresa Of The Roses *Malcolm Vaughan* (HMV)	–	14	9
– True Love *Bing Crosby and Grace Kelly* (Capitol)	–	–	16
– Rudy's Rock *Bill Haley* (Brunswick)	–	–	18
– Cindy, Oh Cindy *Eddie Fisher* (HMV)	–	–	14

DECEMBER 1956

1	8	15	22
1 Just Walking In The Rain *Johnny Ray* (Philips)	1	1	1
2 Woman In Love *Frankie Laine* (Philips)	6	9	10
3 Green Door *Frankie Vaughan* (Philips)	3	2	3
4 My Prayer *The Platters* (Mercury)	4	6	7
5 Rip It Up *Little Richard* (London)	2	4	5
6 St Theresa Of The Roses *Malcolm Vaughan* (HMV)	5	3	4
7 More *Perry Como* (HMV)	10	12	13

1	8	15	22
8 Hound Dog *Elvis Presley* (HMV)	7	8	8
9 Blue Moon (E.P.) *Elvis Presley* (HMV)	8	11	14
10 When Mexico Gave Up The Rhumba *Mitchell Torok* (Brunswick)	11	16	19
11 True Love *Bing Crosby and Grace Kelly* (Capitol)	12	10	9
12 Cindy, Oh Cindy *Eddie Fisher* (HMV)	9	7	6
13 Make It A Party *Winifred Atwell* (Decca)	15	13	11
14 Green Door *Jim Lowe* (London)	16	14	15
15 Rockin' Through The Rye *Bill Haley* (Brunswick)	14	16	18
16 Only You *The Platters* (Mercury)	17	20	–
17 Two Different Worlds *Ronnie Hilton* (HMV)	–	19	–
18 Giddy Up A Ding Dong *Freddie Bell and The Bell Boys* (Mercury)	–	–	–
19 Sing With Shand *Jimmy Shand* (Parlophone)	–	–	–
20 Don't Be Cruel *Elvis Presley* (HMV)	17	–	–
– Singing The Blues *Guy Mitchell* (Philips)	13	5	2
– Love Me Tender *Elvis Presley* (HMV)	20	15	12
– Singing The Blues *Tommy Steele* (Decca)	–	18	17
– Christmas Island *Dickie Valentine* (Decca)	–	–	20
– Rock Around The Clock *Bill Haley* (Brunswick)	19	–	16

No chart was published in Record Mirror *for 29 December 1956.*

1956

1956 saw the emergence of Elvis Presley, which was an event which dwarfed even the debut of Bill Haley during the previous year. The first year for Elvis meant no less than six hits in the Top Twenty, the first being the memorable 'Heartbreak Hotel', which was followed by 'Blue Suede Shoes'. Such was his popularity, particularly in his home country, that by the summer of that year Elvis was making a film, *Love Me Tender*. According to Derek Johnson in his book *Beat Music* (Wilhelm Hansen, 1969), Presley had sold ten million records by the end of 1956.

1956 began with Rock 'n' Roll and beat music, for the year opened with Bill Haley at Number One with 'Rock Around The Clock'. Haley achieved other hits during the year, including 'See You Later Alligator', 'Rockin' Through The Rye' and 'Saints Rock And Roll'. 'Rock Around The Clock' made a re-entry in October 1956, which was its third appearance in the charts.

The new Rock sounds resulted in some ballad singers having a thin time. Ruby Murray only managed one hit in 1956 in contrast to her seven hits of 1955, but Nat 'King' Cole continued some successful forays on the Top Twenty with three entries.

Another American singer, Perry Como, appeared on the British scene and was fairly successful with 'Hot Diggity', 'More' and 'Glendora' but, in comparison to Como's many chart appearances which were to occur in 1958, these three Top Twenty entries were just the beginning. Alma Cogan retained her popularity, while Pat Boone's first quiet one-hit quest for fame in 1955 blossomed into four hits in 1956, including the Forces' favourite, 'I'll Be Home'.

The arrival of Presley might possibly overshadow one other major event of 1956 – the arrival of Lonnie Donegan and skiffle music. Even if most of his records were derived from American music, Donegan was British and with his arrival, skiffle became the newest trend across the country. This one-time traditional jazzman had a staggering eight-year run of hits, beginning with 'Rock Island Line' and, even though Ken Colyer has more claim to fame as the gentleman responsible for bringing skiffle to the British public, it was Donegan who received media coverage.

Even though the sartorial style of skiffle was undistinguished, it did set off a trend for 'do-it-yourself' music, and thousands of skiffle groups throughout the British Isles made their own instruments such as tea-chest basses and home-made drum kits. One such skiffle group included a certain Richard Starkey, who was later to become the percussionist with a group called The Beatles. His first gig earned him 15 shillings, but the club secretary concerned was allegedly drunk and forgot to pay him!

Britain looked for her own rival to Presley and produced Gene Vincent, who became famous for 'Be Bop A Lula', but apart from this hit, Vincent was not a success in terms of the charts. 'Be Bop A Lula' stayed only two weeks in the Top Twenty and his follow-up hit, 'Bluejean Bop', had a one-week residence only.

Another British answer to Presley was an ex-Merchant Navy sailor known as Tommy Steele, whose image was carefully moulded by John Kennedy, a smart-talking publicist and ex-Fleet Street photographer. Kennedy stated 'Tommy is a natural to be the British Presley. But ... Presley's sullen approach, and all that hip-swivelling which gets him criticised so much isn't right. Nor is the fact that most people think Rock is a lower-class form of music, appealing only to the poor-paid yobboes. We must make Tommy into an upper-class hero'. So Steele was launched at a debutante party and for three weeks his 'Rock With The Caveman' remained in the Top Twenty.

Steele, in the same way as many other British singers of this era, then cast an eye to the American charts. In the American charts Steele covered two successive American hits of Guy Mitchell, reaching Number One with 'Singing The Blues' and Number Fifteen with 'Knee Deep In The Blues'. In February Guy Mitchell also reached Number One with 'Singing The Blues', and he won easily with his version of the latter song and reached Number Three.

After Steele came umpteen other British rockers blessed with surnames such as Goode, Power, Eager, Wilde and Fury, and by that time it was acceptable for rockers on stage to wear Italian-cut suits without being criticised as Frankie Laine had been.

Oddly enough, 1956 produced few one-hit wonders, but the ones who do belong in this category include Mitchell

Torok with 'When Mexico Gave Up The Rhumba', Don Cherry and 'Band Of Gold' and Joe 'Fingers' Carr with his 'Portuguese Washer Woman'. There were also several good instrumentals from one-hit orchestras such as those of Frank Chacksfield with 'In Old Lisbon' and the splendid 'Autumn Concerto' by The Melchrino Orchestra. But despite every ballad, orchestral piece or comedy record, 1956 was really concerned with solo singer Rock 'n' Roll, with Presley as the undisputed king.

5	12	19	26
1 Singing The Blues *Guy Mitchell* (Philips)	1	2	1
2 Just Walking In The Rain *Johnny Ray* (Philips)	3	8	12
3 Green Door *Frankie Vaughan* (Philips)	4	5	7
4 Singing The Blues *Tommy Steele* (Decca)	2	1	2
4 St Theresa Of The Roses *Malcolm Vaughan* (HMV)	5	7	6
6 Rip It Up *Little Richard* (London)	10	14	20
7 True Love *Bing Crosby and Grace Kelly* (Capitol)	6	4	4
7 Cindy, Oh Cindy *Eddie Fisher* (HMV)	7	9	11
9 Hound Dog *Elvis Presley* (HMV)	9	10	13
10 My Prayer *The Platters* (Mercury)	–	–	–
11 A Woman In Love *Frankie Laine* (Philips)	20	–	–
12 Love Me Tender *Elvis Presley* (HMV)	15	15	14
13 Blue Moon *Elvis Presley* (HMV)	19	17	–
14 Rock Around The Clock *Bill Haley* (Brunswick)	16	–	–
14 Rockin' Through The Rye *Bill Haley* (Brunswick)	–	–	–
16 Sing With Shand *Jimmy Shand* (Parlophone)	–	–	–
17 Make It A Party *Winifred Atwell* (Decca)	–	–	–
18 Blueberry Hill *Fats Domino* (London)	11	11	10
19 Friendly Persuasion *Pat Boone* (London)	8	6	5
20 A House With Love In It *Vera Lynn* (Decca)	–	–	–
– Moonlight Gambler *Frankie Laine* (Philips)	12	13	9
– Garden Of Eden *Gary Miller* (Nixa)	12	16	17
– Garden Of Eden *Frankie Vaughan* (Philips)	14	3	3
– More *Jimmy Young* (Decca)	16	–	–
– When Mexico Gave Up The Rhumba *Mitchell Torok* (Brunswick)	16	–	–
– Don't Be Cruel *Elvis Presley* (HMV)	20	–	–
– Don't You Rock Me Daddy-O *Lonnie Donegan* (Nixa)	–	12	8
– Garden Of Eden *Dick James* (Parlophone)	–	18	–
– Garden Of Eden *Joe Valino* (HMV)	–	19	17
– Two Different Worlds *Ronnie Hilton* (HMV)	–	20	–
– You Don't Owe Me A Thing *Johnny Ray* (Philips)	–	–	19
– Don't You Rock Me Daddy-O *The Vipers* (Columbia)	–	–	15
– Adoration Waltz *David Whitfield* (Decca)	–	–	16

2	9	16	23
1 Garden of Eden *Frankie Vaughan* (Philips)	1	1	2
2 Singing The Blues *Guy Mitchell* (Philips)	2	3	3
3 Singing The Blues *Tommy Steele* (Decca)	6	12	13
4 Friendly Persuasion *Pat Boone* (London)	3	6	8
5 True Love *Bing Crosby and Grace Kelly* (Capitol)	4	5	7
6 St Theresa Of The Roses *Malcolm Vaughan* (HMV)	9	9	12
7 Blueberry Hill *Fats Domino* (London)	7	7	11
8 Don't You Rock Me Daddy-O *Lonnie Donegan* (Nixa)	5	4	5
9 Moonlight Gambler *Frankie Laine* (Philips)	13	–	–
10 Hound Dog *Elvis Presley* (HMV)	12	20	–
11 Cindy, Oh Cindy *Eddie Fisher* (HMV)	16	17	–
12 Green Door *Frankie Vaughan* (Philips)	–	–	–
13 Don't You Rock Me Daddy-O *The Vipers* (Columbia)	8	13	15
14 Garden Of Eden *Gary Miller* (Nixa)	–	19	–
15 You Don't Owe Me A Thing *Johnny Ray* (Philips)	19	15	14
15 Adoration Waltz *David Whitfield* (Decca)	16	20	17
17 Just Walking In The Rain *Johnny Ray* (Philips)	18	–	–
18 Love Me Tender *Elvis Presley* (HMV)	–	–	–
19 Rock The Joint *Bill Haley* (Brunswick)	15	18	20

	9	16	23
20 Ain't That A Shame *Fats Domino* (London)	–	–	–
– Don't Forbid Me *Pat Boone* (London)	14	8	4
– Young Love *Tab Hunter* (London)	10	2	1
– Don't Knock The Rock *Bill Haley* (Brunswick)	11	10	10
– Rip It Up *Little Richard* (London)	20	–	–
– Young Love *Sonny James* (Capitol)	–	11	9
– Long Tall Sally *Little Richard* (London)	–	15	19
– Rock A Bye Your Baby *Jerry Lewis* (Brunswick)	–	14	16
– Knee Deep In The Blues *Tommy Steele* (Decca)	–	–	18
– Knee Deep In The Blues *Guy Mitchell* (Philips)	–	–	6
– You, Me And Us *Alma Cogan* (HMV)	–	–	20

MARCH 1957

2	9	16	23	30
1 Young Love *Tab Hunter* (London)	1	1	1	1
2 Don't Forbid Me *Pat Boone* (London)	2	2	2	2
3 Knee Deep In The Blues *Guy Mitchell* (Philips)	3	3	3	4
4 Garden Of Eden *Frankie Vaughan* (Philips)	5	9	10	–
5 Singing The Blues *Guy Mitchell* (Philips)	6	7	8	11
6 Don't You Rock Me Daddy-O *Lonnie Donegan* (Nixa)	4	4	5	6
7 True Love *Bing Crosby and Grace Kelly* (Capitol)	8	8	9	7
8 Long Tall Sally *Little Richard* (London)	7	5	4	3
9 Friendly Persuasion *Pat Boone* (London)	10	10	12	20
10 Young Love *Sonny James* (Capitol)	11	13	17	–
11 Adoration Waltz *David Whitfield* (Decca)	12	14	16	–
12 Blueberry Hill *Fats Domino* (London)	16	–	–	–
13 Banana Boat Song *Harry Belafonte* (HMV)	9	6	6	5
14 You Don't Owe Me A Thing *Johnny Ray* (Philips)	19	15	13	16
15 Don't Knock The Rock *Bill Haley* (Brunswick)	13	16	–	–
16 Knee Deep In The Blues *Tommy Steele* (Decca)	17	–	–	–
16 Banana Boat Song *The Tarriers* (Columbia)	14	12	11	15
17 Rip It Up *Bill Haley* (Brunswick)	18	19	–	–
18 St Theresa Of The Roses *Malcolm Vaughan* (HMV)	–	–	–	–
20 Rock A Bye Your Baby *Jerry Lewis* (Capitol)	19	18	–	19
– Banana Boat Song *Shirley Bassey* (Philips)	15	11	7	8
– Wisdom Of A Fool *Norman Wisdom* (Columbia)	–	20	20	–
– Look Homeward Angel *Johnny Ray* (Philips)	–	17	18	12
– She's Got It *Little Richard* (London)	–	–	14	13
– Only You *The Platters* (Mercury)	–	–	14	10
– The Girl Can't Help It *Little Richard* (London)	–	–	18	14
– The Great Pretender *The Platters* (Mercury)	–	–	20	17
– Cumberland Gap *The Vipers* (Columbia)	–	–	–	9
– Freight Train *Chas McDevitt and Nancy Whiskey* (Oriole)	–	–	–	18

APRIL 1957

6	13	20	27
1 Young Love *Tab Hunter* (London)	2	2	2
2 Don't Forbid Me *Pat Boone* (London)	3	5	6
3 Long Tall Sally *Little Richard* (London)	4	4	4
4 Knee Deep In The Blues *Guy Mitchell* (Philips)	6	8	20
5 Banana Boat Song *Harry Belafonte* (HMV)	5	3	3
6 Cumberland Gap *Lonnie Donegan* (Nixa)	1	1	1
7 Don't You Rock Me Daddy-O *Lonnie Donegan* (Nixa)	9	15	–
8 Look Homeward Angel *Johnny Ray* (Philips)	7	10	8
9 Cumberland Gap *The Vipers* (Columbia)	12	–	–
10 Only You *The Platters* (Mercury)	17	–	–
11 The Girl Can't Help It *Little Richard* (London)	10	12	11

	13	20	27
12 Banana Boat Song *Shirley Bassey* (Philips)	18	–	–
13 She's Got It *Little Richard* (London)	8	13	17
14 True Love *Bing Crosby and Grace Kelly* (Capitol)	14	20	20
15 Singing The Blues *Guy Mitchell* (Philips)	–	–	–
16 Friendly Persuasion *Pat Boone* (London)	–	–	–
17 The Great Pretender *The Platters* (Mercury)	–	–	–
18 Tutti Frutti *Little Richard* (London)	–	–	–
18 Heart *Max Bygraves* (Decca)	19	17	14
20 Banana Boat Song *The Tarriers* (Columbia)	–	–	–
– Freight Train *Chas McDevitt and Nancy Whiskey* (Oriole)	11	8	9
– I'm Not A Teenage Delinquent *Frankie Lymon and The Teenagers* (Columbia)	13	7	12
– Ninety-Nine Ways *Tab Hunter* (London)	15	11	13
– Singing The Blues *Tommy Steele* (Decca)	19	19	–
– Baby Baby *Frankie Lymon and The Teenagers* (Columbia)	16	6	5
– I'll Take You Home Again Kathleen *Slim Whitman* (London)	–	13	7
– Wear A Golden Ring *Frankie Laine* (Philips)	–	16	–
– Butterfly *Andy Williams* (London)	–	18	16
– I'm Walkin' *Fats Domino* (London)	–	20	15
– Maggie May *The Vipers* (Columbia)	–	20	–
– When I Fall In Love *Nat 'King' Cole* (Capitol)	–	–	10
– Butterfly *Charlie Gracie* (London)	–	–	17
– Butterfingers *Tommy Steele* (Decca)	–	–	19

MAY 1957

4	11	18	25
1 Cumberland Gap *Lonnie Donegan* (Nixa)	2	5	8
2 Baby Baby *Frankie Lymon and The Teenagers* (Columbia)	4	6	6
3 Banana Boat Song *Harry Belafonte* (HMV)	6	11	13
4 Long Tall Sally *Little Richard* (London)	10	13	16
5 Rock-A-Billy *Guy Mitchell* (Philips)	3	2	2
6 Young Love *Tab Hunter* (London)	11	15	–
7 When I Fall In Love *Nat 'King' Cole* (Capitol)	7	3	4
8 Butterfly *Andy Williams* (London)	1	1	1
9 Look Homeward Angel *Johnny Ray* (Philips)	13	12	18
10 Ninety-Nine Ways *Tab Hunter* (London)	5	8	10
11 I'll Take You Home Again Kathleen *Slim Whitman* (London)	9	9	5
12 Don't Forbid Me *Pat Boone* (London)	17	–	–
13 The Girl Can't Help It *Little Richard* (London)	4	14	20
14 Freight Train *Chas McDevitt and Nancy Whiskey* (Oriole)	8	10	9
15 I'm Not A Teenage Delinquent *Frankie Lymon and The Teenagers* (Columbia)	19	18	–
16 I'm Walkin' *Fats Domino* (London)	16	20	15
17 Wear A Golden Ring *Frankie Laine* (Philips)	–	–	–
18 Butterfingers *Tommy Steele* (Decca)	–	–	11
19 Butterfly *Charlie Gracie* (Parlophone)	–	19	14
20 She's Got It *Little Richard* (London)	20	–	–
– Yes Tonight Josephine *Johnny Ray* (Philips)	12	4	3
– Too Much *Elvis Presley* (HMV)	15	7	7
– Chapel Of The Roses *Malcolm Vaughan* (HMV)	18	16	19
– Why Baby Why *Pat Boone* (London)	–	17	–
– Party Doll *Buddy Knox* (Columbia)	–	–	17
– Mr Wonderful *Peggy Lee* (Capitol)	–	–	12

JUNE 1957

	8	15	22	29
1				
1 Butterfly *Andy Williams* (London)	2	3	5	9
2 Yes Tonight Josephine *Johnny Ray* (Philips)	1	1	1	1
3 Rock-A-Billy *Guy Mitchell* (Philips)	4	4	7	12
4 When I Fall In Love *Nat 'King' Cole* (Capitol)	3	2	3	3
5 I'll Take You Home Again Kathleen *Slim Whitman* (London)	6	14	17	–
6 Freight Train *Chas McDevitt and Nancy Whiskey* (Oriole)	5	11	12	18
7 Baby Baby *Frankie Lymon and The Teenagers* (Columbia)	14	19	18	–
8 Cumberland Gap *The Vipers* (Columbia)	11	13	15	19
9 Cumberland Gap *Lonnie Donegan* (Nixa)	–	–	–	–
10 Mr Wonderful *Peggy Lee* (Capitol)	9	9	8	11
11 Ninety-Nine Ways *Tab Hunter* (London)	17	20	–	–
12 Around The World *Bing Crosby* (Capitol)	8	7	4	7
13 Butterfingers *Tommy Steele* (Decca)	12	16	14	16
14 Around The World *Gracie Fields* (Columbia)	10	10	10	13
15 Around The World *Ronnie Hilton* (HMV)	7	6	6	5
16 Long Tall Sally *Little Richard* (London)	–	–	–	–
17 Look Homeward Angel *Johnny Ray* (Philips)	–	–	–	–
18 I'm Sorry *The Platters* (Mercury)	–	–	20	–
19 Chapel Of The Roses *Malcolm Vaughan* (HMV)	18	18	–	–
20 The Girl Can't Help It *Little Richard* (London)	–	–	–	–
– A White Sports Coat *Terry Dene* (Decca)	19	–	16	17
– Puttin' On The Style *Lonnie Donegan* (Nixa)	–	15	–	–
– A White Sports Coat *The King Brothers* (Parlophone)	19	17	11	10
– We Will Make Love *Russ Hamilton* (Oriole)	16	12	13	8
– Gambling Man *Lonnie Donegan* (Nixa)	15	8	2	2
– Little Darlin' *The Diamonds* (Mercury)	13	5	9	4
– Island In The Sun *Harry Belafonte* (RCA)	–	–	19	15
– All Shook Up *Elvis Presley* (HMV)	–	–	–	6
– Another School Day *Chuck Berry* (London)	–	–	–	20
– Fabulous *Charlie Gracie* (Parlophone)	–	–	–	14

JULY 1957

	13	20	27
6			
1 Gambling Man *Lonnie Donegan* (Nixa)	2	2	2
2 All Shook Up *Elvis Presley* (RCA)	1	1	1
3 Yes Tonight Josephine *Johnny Ray* (Philips)	4	7	7
4 Little Darlin' *The Diamonds* (Mercury)	6	5	5
5 Around The World *Ronnie Hilton* (HMV)	5	6	8
6 We Will Make Love *Russ Hamilton* (Oriole)	3	3	4
7 When I Fall In Love *Nat 'King' Cole* (Capitol)	7	13	11
8 Around The World *Bing Crosby* (Capitol)	9	10	13
9 A White Sports Coat *The King Brothers* (Parlophone)	8	11	12
10 Mr Wonderful *Peggy Lee* (Capitol)	13	17	18
11 Butterfingers *Tommy Steele* (Decca)	10	9	9
12 Butterfly *Andy Williams* (London)	–	–	–
13 Fabulous *Charlie Gracie* (Parlophone)	16	15	20
14 Freight Train *Chas McDevitt and Nancy Whiskey* (Oriole)	17	19	–
15 Around The World *Gracie Fields* (Columbia)	19	–	–
16 Rock-A-Billy *Guy Mitchell* (Philips)	–	–	–
17 Island In The Sun *Harry Belafonte* (RCA)	12	16	15
18 Lucille *Little Richard* (London)	15	12	10
19 I'm Sorry *The Platters* (Mercury)	–	–	–
20 I Like Your Kind Of Love *Andy Williams* (London)	18	18	19
– Last Train To San Fernando *Johnny Duncan* (Columbia)	–	–	17
– Teddy Bear *Elvis Presley* (RCA)	14	4	3

6		13	20	27
– Love Letters In The Sand *Pat Boone* (London)		11	8	6
– A White Sports Coat *Terry Dene* (Decca)		20	–	–
– Start Movin' *Sal Mineo* (Philips)		–	20	–
– Bye Bye Love *The Everly Brothers* (London)		–	14	14
– All Star Hit Parade Vol. 2 *Various Artists* (Decca)		–	–	16

AUGUST 1957

3	10	17	24	31
1 All Shook Up *Elvis Presley* (HMV)	1	1	1	3
2 Teddy Bear *Elvis Presley* (RCA)	3	2	4	5
3 Gambling Man/Puttin' On The Style *Lonnie Donegan* (Nixa)	2	5	8	12
4 We Will Make Love *Russ Hamilton* (Oriole)	4	6	10	10
5 Little Darlin' *The Diamonds* (Mercury)	6	9	9	16
6 Love Letters In The Sand *Pat Boone* (London)	5	3	3	2
7 Lucille *Little Richard* (London)	9	16	–	–
8 Around The World *Ronnie Hilton* (HMV)	12	18	18	–
9 Island In The Sun *Harry Belafonte* (RCA)	7	4	2	4
10 Yes Tonight Josephine *Johnny Ray* (Philips)	14	20	19	–
11 Butterfingers *Tommy Steele* (Decca)	11	15	15	17
12 Bye Bye Love *The Everly Brothers* (London)	8	7	6	7
13 Around The World *Bing Crosby* (Brunswick)	19	19	–	–
14 Start Movin' *Terry Dene* (Decca)	16	14	17	20
15 When I Fall In Love *Nat 'King' Cole* (Capitol)	15	17	–	–
16 Last Train To San Fernando *Johnny Duncan* (Columbia)	10	8	7	6
17 All Star Hit Parade Vol. 2 *Various Artists* (Decca)	13	10	11	19
18 A White Sports Coat *The King Brothers* (Parlophone)	–	–	–	–
19 Start Movin' *Sal Mineo* (Philips)	18	11	13	15
20 With All My Heart *Petula Clark* (Nixa)	17	12	14	9
– Fabulous *Charlie Gracie* (Parlophone)	20	–	16	13
– Diana *Paul Anka* (Columbia)	–	13	5	1
– Water Water/Handful Of Songs *Tommy Steele* (Decca)	–	–	12	8
– I'm Gonna Sit Right Down And Write Myself A Letter *Billy Williams* (Columbia)	–	–	20	–
– Wanderin' Eyes *Charlie Gracie* (London)	–	–	–	11
– Shiralee *Tommy Steele* (Decca)	–	–	–	14
– Paralysed *Elvis Presley* (HMV)	–	–	–	18

SEPTEMBER 1957

7	14	21	28
1 Diana *Paul Anka* (Columbia)	1	1	1
2 Love Letters In The Sand *Pat Boone* (London)	2	2	2
3 Last Train To San Fernando *Johnny Duncan* (Columbia)	3	3	3
4 All Shook Up *Elvis Presley* (HMV)	5	7	7
5 Island In The Sun *Harry Belafonte* (RCA)	4	4	4
6 Water Water/Handful Of Songs *Tommy Steele* (Decca)	6	5	5
7 Teddy Bear *Elvis Presley* (RCA)	10	12	14
8 Bye Bye Love *The Everly Brothers* (London)	11	11	13
9 With All My Heart *Petula Clark* (Nixa)	7	8	6
10 Paralysed *Elvis Presley* (HMV)	9	9	10
11 Wanderin' Eyes *Charlie Gracie* (London)	8	6	8
12 Fabulous *Charlie Gracie* (Parlophone)	13	16	–
13 We Will Make Love *Russ Hamilton* (Oriole)	17	–	16
14 Little Darlin' *The Diamonds* (Mercury)	18	19	–
15 Gambling Man/Puttin' On The Style *Lonnie Donegan* (Nixa)	14	14	–
16 Shiralee *Tommy Steele* (Decca)	16	15	17
17 Tammy *Debbie Reynolds* (Vogue/Coral)	12	10	9

7		14	21	28
18 Butterfingers *Tommy Steele* (Decca)		–	–	–
19 All Star Hit Parade Vol. 2 *Various Artists* (Decca)		–	–	–
20 Start Movin' *Sal Mineo* (Philips)		–	–	–
– Jenny Jenny *Little Richard* (London)		15	13	11
– Build Your Love *Johnny Ray* (Philips)		19	17	18
– Man On Fire *Frankie Vaughan* (Philips)		20	–	–
– Stardust *Billy Ward* (London)		–	20	20
– Whole Lotta Shakin' Goin' On *Jerry Lee Lewis* (London)		–	–	19
– That'll Be The Day *The Crickets* (Vogue/Coral)		–	–	12
– Short Fat Fannie *Larry Williams* (London)		–	18	15

OCTOBER 1957

5		12	19	26
1 Diana *Paul Anka* (Columbia)		1	1	2
2 Love Letters In The Sand *Pat Boone* (London)		2	5	6
3 Last Train To San Fernando *Johnny Duncan* (Columbia)		4	6	15
4 Wanderin' Eyes *Charlie Gracie* (London)		6	7	7
5 Island In The Sun *Harry Belafonte* (RCA)		9	8	12
6 Tammy *Debbie Reynolds* (Vogue/Coral)		3	3	4
7 Water Water/Handful Of Songs *Tommy Steele* (Decca)		8	9	9
8 With All My Heart *Petula Clark* (Nixa)		11	12	10
9 All Shook Up *Elvis Presley* (HMV)		10	13	16
10 That'll Be The Day *The Crickets* (London)		5	2	1
11 Paralysed *Elvis Presley* (HMV)		13	17	18
12 Jenny Jenny *Little Richard* (London)		20	–	–
13 Teddy Bear *Elvis Presley* (RCA)		14	15	8
14 Remember You're Mine *Pat Boone* (London)		16	10	5
15 Whole Lotta Shakin' Goin' On *Jerry Lee Lewis* (London)		12	14	11
16 Bye Bye Love *The Everly Brothers* (London)		17	–	–
17 Stardust *Billy Ward* (London)		–	–	–
18 Let's Have A Party *Elvis Presley* (RCA)		7	4	3
19 Short Fat Fannie *Larry Williams* (London)		–	–	–
20 In The Middle Of An Island *The King Brothers* (Parlophone)		–	–	–
– My Dixie Darlin' *Lonnie Donegan* (Nixa)		15	11	14
– Wedding Ring *Russ Hamilton* (Oriole)		18	19	20
– Man On Fire/Wanderin' Eyes *Frankie Vaughan* (Philips)*		19	16	13
– Call Rosie On The Phone *Guy Mitchell* (Philips)		–	18	17
– Be My Girl *Jim Dale* (Parlophone)		–	20	19

* Record Mirror *first listed this record as a one-selling side, namely 'Man On Fire', as seen in the September listings.*

NOVEMBER 1957

2	9	16	23	30
1 That'll Be The Day *The Crickets* (Vogue/Coral)	1	1	3	6
2 Let's Have A Party *Elvis Presley* (RCA)	2	2	2	3
3 Tammy *Debbie Reynolds* (Vogue/Coral)	3	3	9	12
4 Diana *Paul Anka* (Columbia)	4	9	11	16
5 Remember You're Mine *Pat Boone* (London)	5	8	8	7
6 Man On Fire/Wanderin' Eyes *Frankie Vaughan* (Philips)	7	10	12	15
7 Be My Girl *Jim Dale* (Parlophone)	6	6	5	2
8 Whole Lotta Shakin' Goin' On *Jerry Lee Lewis* (London)	9	14	20	–
9 Love Letters In The Sand *Pat Boone* (London)	13	17	–	–
10 Wanderin' Eyes *Charlie Gracie* (London)	16	–	–	–
11 Teddy Bear *Elvis Presley* (RCA)	14	19	–	–
12 Water Water/Handful Of Songs *Tommy Steele* (Decca)	15	–	–	–

2

	9	**16**	**23**	**30**
13 Island In The Sun *Harry Belafonte* (RCA)	18	–	–	–
14 With All My Heart *Petula Clark* (Nixa)	17	15	–	–
15 My Dixie Darlin' *Lonnie Donegan* (Nixa)	10	13	16	19
16 Last Train To San Fernando *Johnny Duncan* (Columbia)	20	–	–	–
17 Gotta Have Something In The Bank Frank *Frankie Vaughan and The Kaye Sisters* (Philips)	8	7	7	8
18 Lawdy Miss Clawdy/Tryin' To Get You *Elvis Presley* (HMV)	11	12	13	20
19 He's Got The Whole Wide World In His Hands *Laurie London* (Parlophone)	–	20	–	13
20 Honeycombe *Jimmy Rodgers* (Columbia)	–	–	–	–
– I Love You Baby *Paul Anka* (Columbia)	12	5	4	4
– Santa Bring Back My Baby to Me *Elvis Presley* (RCA)	–	16	10	9
– Mary's Boy Child *Harry Belafonte* (RCA)	–	4	1	1
– Wake Up Little Susie *The Everly Brothers* (London)	19	11	6	5
– Reet Petite *Jackie Wilson* (Coral)	–	18	17	18
– Alone *Petula Clark* (Pye/Nixa)	–	–	14	10
– Alone *The Shepherd Sisters* (HMV)	–	–	15	14
– Ma He's Making Eyes At Me *Johnny Otis Show* (Capitol)	–	–	18	11
– Alone *The Southlanders* (Decca)	–	–	19	17
– Keep A Knocking *Little Richard* (London)	–	–	–	20

DECEMBER 1957

	7	**14**	**21**
1 Mary's Boy Child *Harry Belafonte* (RCA)		1	1
2 Wake Up Little Susie *The Everly Brothers* (London)		2	3
3 I Love You Baby *Paul Anka* (Columbia)		3	3
4 Be My Girl *Jim Dale* (Parlophone)		4	6
5 Let's Have A Party *Elvis Presley* (RCA)		9	8
6 Ma He's Making Eyes At Me *Johnny Otis Show* (Capitol)		6	2
7 Remember You're Mine *Pat Boone* (London)		11	8
8 Santa Bring Back My Baby To Me *Elvis Presley* (RCA)		7	11
9 Alone *Petula Clark* (Pye/Nixa)		8	13
10 That'll Be The Day *The Crickets* (Vogue/Coral)		17	15
11 My Special Angel *Malcolm Vaughan* (HMV)		5	5
12 He's Got The Whole Wide World In His Hands *Laurie London* (Parlophone)		13	12
13 Gotta Have Something In The Bank Frank *Frankie Vaughan and The Kaye Sisters* (Philips)		–	–
14 Diana *Paul Anka* (Columbia)		15	17
15 Keep A Knocking *Little Richard* (London)		–	–
16 My Special Angel *Bobby Helms* (Brunswick)		18	20
17 Reet Petite *Jackie Wilson* (Coral)		12	14
17 Alone *The Southlanders* (Decca)		–	–
19 Tammy *Debbie Reynolds* (Vogue/Coral)		–	–
20 Alone *The Shepherd Sisters* (HMV)		–	–
– Wake Up Little Susie *The King Brothers* (Parlophone)		–	19
– Great Balls Of Fire *Jerry Lee Lewis* (London)		–	16
– Let's Have A Ball *Winifred Atwell* (Decca)		10	7
– All The Way *Frank Sinatra* (Capitol)		14	8
– April Love *Pat Boone* (London)		16	18

No chart was published for 28 December 1957.
We have found no record of the paper being published on 14 December and the listings for this date has been derived from the 'last week' figures of 21 December. However, such figures do not indicate the complete Top Twenty owing to records dropping out and being replaced in the charts.

1957

Bill Haley had arrived in the charts in January 1955 and, with 14 hits to his credit, he all but disappeared from the charts in 1957. Indeed, he was to return with 'Rock Around The Clock' in 1968 and 1974, but to all intents and purposes his chart impetus was never as strong once 'Rock The Joint' had left the Top Twenty.

However, there were several good newcomers on the music scene, including The Everly Brothers, Jerry Lee Lewis, Tab Hunter and Sonny James. Hunter and James both had a hit with 'Young Love', after which James did not appear in the charts again, and Hunter did not do much better, for he could only manage one more Top Ten hit, 'Ninety-Nine Ways' before he, too, faded into obscurity.

The Everley Brothers began their 19-hit trail in July 1957 with 'Bye Bye Love', and with their third record, 'All I Have To Do Is Dream' during the following year, they achieved their first Number One. Jerry Lee Lewis began with 'Whole Lotta Shakin' Goin' On', and in December 1957 he produced 'Great Balls Of Fire', a deserved Number One and one of pop's many classics.

For several newcomers of 1956, 1957 saw their fortunes continue to improve. Lonnie Donegan achieved five hits, of which two, 'Cumberland Gap' and 'Puttin' On The Style', reached the Number One position. The latter disc's B-side was the equally popular 'Gambling Man'.

Tommy Steele had four hits in 1957, as did Johnny Ray, but whereas Steele had a rosy future stretching ahead of him, Ray's chart career was drawing to an end, despite the fact that he achieved a Number One in 1957 with 'Yes Tonight Josephine'. However, his follow-up record, 'Build Your Love', only reached Number Seventeen and spent under a month in the Top Twenty.

Ray's recording company, Philips, had continued to have some measure of success with Frankie Laine, another of their artists, for he managed to achieve one hit with 'Love Is A Golden Ring', and the third of the famous Philips trio, Guy Mitchell, entered the Top Twenty three times throughout the year. One of his hits, 'Rock-A-Billy', reached the Number One position and he beat Tommy Steele in the chart listings with 'Knee Deep In The Blues'.

1957 also saw the first Number One record for the British singer, Frankie Vaughan, who covered 'Garden Of Eden', which had been an American hit. He was chased up the charts by Gary Miller but Miller's challenge proved weak, for he only reached the Number Fourteen position. Vaughan had three more hits including 'Gotta Have Something In The Bank Frank', for which he was joined by The Kaye Sisters.

Apart from the Top Twenty, 1957 also saw the birth of *6.5 Special*, the first British television pop series, which also tended to affect the charts themselves. Programme regulars such as Jim Dale, Terry Dene and Marty Wilde saw chart success following their television appearances. Dene promised much, but following two hits in 1957 and one in 1958, he disappeared from the charts.

Another major event was the advent of The Crickets and their lead singer, Buddy Holly in September 1957. Buddy Holly and The Crickets were living proof that for every trend in pop, there was a reaction countering it. For every menacing Gene Vincent, there was a melodic, clean-cut Buddy Holly. If the elder statesmen of pop became rather too old, there were always child stars of 13 or 14 years of age such as Laurie London, Jackie Dennis or Frankie Lymon ready to fill the gaps.

JANUARY 1958

4		11	18	25
1	Ma He's Making Eyes At Me *Johnny Otis Show* (Capitol)	1	2	3
2	Mary's Boy Child *Harry Belafonte* (RCA)	11	–	–
3	Wake Up Little Susie *The Everly Brothers* (London)	4	7	12
4	I Love You Baby *Paul Anka* (Columbia)	5	10	15
5	Great Balls Of Fire *Jerry Lee Lewis* (London)	2	1	2
6	My Special Angel *Malcolm Vaughan* (HMV)	3	5	7
7	Reet Petite *Jackie Wilson* (Coral)	7	3	9
8	All The Way *Frank Sinatra* (Capitol)	8	8	5
9	Kisses Sweeter Than Wine *Jimmy Rodgers* (Columbia)	6	9	8
10	Diana *Paul Anka* (Columbia)	14	–	–
11	Alone *Petula Clark* (Pye)	15	–	–
12	Party *Elvis Presley* (RCA)	16	13	–
13	Peggy Sue *Buddy Holly* (Coral)	10	4	6
14	Let's Have A Ball *Winifred Atwell* (Decca)	19	–	–
15	April Love *Pat Boone* (London)	12	12	16
16	Alone *The Southlanders* (Decca)	18	14	20
17	Oh! Boy *The Crickets* (Coral)	9	5	4
18	Jack O'Diamonds *Lonnie Donegan* (Pye)	17	16	–
19	Be My Girl *Jim Dale* (Parlophone)	–	–	–
20	Remember You're Mine *Pat Boone* (London)	–	20	–
–	Kisses Sweeter Than Wine *Frankie Vaughan* (Philips)	13	11	14
–	He's Got The Whole Wide World *Laurie London* (Parlophone)	20	17	–
–	Story Of My Life *Michael Holliday* (Columbia)	–	15	10
–	Wake Up Little Susie *The King Brothers* (Parlophone)	–	19	–
–	I'm Left, You're Right, She's Gone *Elvis Presley* (RCA)	–	18	17
–	The Story Of My Life *Gary Miller* (Nixa)	–	–	11
–	Bony Maronie *Larry Williams* (London)	–	–	13
–	Bye Bye Baby *Johnny Otis Show* (Capitol)	–	–	18
–	At The Hop *Danny and The Juniors* (HMV)	–	–	19
–	Jailhouse Rock *Elvis Presley* (RCA)	–	–	1

FEBRUARY 1958

1		8	15	22
1	Jailhouse Rock *Elvis Presley* (RCA)	1	2	3
2	The Story Of My Life *Michael Holliday* (Columbia)	2	1	1
3	Great Balls Of Fire *Jerry Lee Lewis* (London)	5	7	11
4	Oh! Boy *The Crickets* (Coral)	3	3	5
5	All The Way *Frank Sinatra* (Capitol)	6	6	7
6	Ma He's Making Eyes At Me *Johnny Otis Show* (Capitol)	11	14	17
7	Peggy Sue *Buddy Holly* (Coral)	8	11	10
8	Kisses Sweeter Than Wine *Jimmy Rodgers* (Columbia)	11	17	–
9	My Special Angel *Malcolm Vaughan* (HMV)	15	19	–
10	The Story Of My Life *Gary Miller* (Nixa)	10	13	14
11	April Love *Pat Boone* (London)	9	8	9
12	At The Hop *Danny and The Juniors* (HMV)	4	4	4
13	Bony Maronie *Larry Williams* (London)	14	12	12
14	Kisses Sweeter Than Wine *Frankie Vaughan* (Philips)	16	15	16
15	Reet Petite *Jackie Wilson* (Coral)	19	–	–
16	Love Me Forever *Marion Ryan* (Pye)	7	9	8
17	Bye Bye Baby *Johnny Otis Show* (Capitol)	18	18	–
18	Wake Up Little Susie *The Everly Brothers* (London)	–	–	–
19	I Love You Baby *Paul Anka* (Columbia)	–	–	–
20	I'm Left, You're Right, She's Gone *Elvis Presley* (RCA)	–	–	–
–	You Are My Destiny *Paul Anka* (Columbia)	13	10	6
–	Jailhouse Rock (E.P.) *Elvis Presley* (RCA)	16	16	15
–	Love Me Forever *Edyie Gormie* (CBS)	20	–	–

1	8	15	22
– Magic Moments *Perry Como* (RCA)	–	5	2
– Put A Light In The Window *The Southlanders* (HMV)	–	20	–
– Mandy *Eddie Calvert* (Columbia)	–	–	13
– Stood Up *Ricky Nelson* (London)	–	–	18
– At The Hop *Nick Todd* (London)	–	–	19
– Raunchy *Billy Vaughan* (London)	–	–	20

MARCH 1958

1	8	15	22	29
1 Magic Moments/Catch A Falling Star *Perry Como* (RCA)	1	1	1	1
2 The Story Of My Life *Michael Holliday* (Columbia)	2	2	3	4
3 Jailhouse Rock *Elvis Presley* (RCA)	3	4	5	6
4 At The Hop *Danny and The Juniors* (HMV)	4	5	6	9
5 Oh I Boy *The Crickets* (Coral)	7	7	11	13
6 You Are My Destiny *Paul Anka* (Columbia)	6	8	10	11
7 Love Me Forever *Marion Ryan* (Nixa)	8	12	13	–
8 All The Way/Chicago *Frank Sinatra* (Capitol)	10	13	15	12
9 April Love *Pat Boone* (London)	9	11	12	14
10 Peggy Sue *Buddy Holly* (Coral)	11	15	19	–
11 Don't/I Beg Of You *Elvis Presley* (RCA)	5	3	2	2
12 Great Balls Of Fire *Jerry Lee Lewis* (London)	–	–	–	–
13 Bony Moronie *Larry Williams* (London)	17	–	–	–
14 At The Hop *Nick Todd* (London)	–	–	–	–
15 Whole Lotta Woman *Marvin Rainwater* (MGM)	16	16	8	5
16 Mandy *Eddie Calvert* (Columbia)	19	18	18	15
17 Witchcraft *Frank Sinatra* (Capitol)	–	20	–	–
18 Raunchy *Billy Vaughan* (London)	–	–	–	–
19 Kisses Sweeter Than Wine *Frankie Vaughan* (Philips)	–	–	–	–
20 Sugartime *The McGuire Sisters* (London)	–	–	–	–
– Nairobi *Tommy Steele* (Decca)	12	6	4	3
– We Are Not Alone/Can't Get Along Without You *Frankie Vaughan* (Philips)	13	10	14	17
– Good Golly Miss Molly *Little Richard* (London)	14	9	7	8
– Baby Lover *Petula Clark* (Pye)	15	17	17	18
– Sugar Time/Don't Let Go *Jim Dale* (Parlophone)	17	–	–	–
– Jailhouse Rock (E.P.) *Elvis Presley* (RCA)	20	–	–	–
– Maybe Baby *The Crickets* (Coral)	–	14	9	7
– To Be Loved *Jackie Wilson* (Coral)	–	19	–	19
– Why Don't They Understand *George Hamilton IV* (Columbia)	–	20	16	20
– Swingin' Shepherd Blues *Mo Kauffman* (London)	–	–	20	–
– La Dee Dah *Jackie Dennis* (Decca)	–	–	–	10
– Big Beat *Fats Domino* (London)	–	–	–	16

APRIL 1958

5	12	19	26
1 Magic Moments/Catch A Falling Star *Perry Como* (RCA)	1	2	3
2 Don't/I Beg Of You *Elvis Presley* (RCA)	3	6	10
3 Whole Lotta Woman *Marvin Rainwater* (MGM)	2	1	1
4 Nairobi *Tommy Steele* (Decca)	5	5	9
5 Maybe Baby *The Crickets* (Coral)	4	4	5
6 La Dee Dah *Jackie Dennis* (Decca)	6	9	11
7 The Story Of My Life *Michael Holliday* (Columbia)	11	–	–
8 Good Golly Miss Molly *Little Richard* (London)	10	13	–
9 Swingin' Shepherd Blues *Ted Heath* (Decca)	7	8	4
10 Jailhouse Rock *Elvis Presley* (RCA)	12	–	–
11 At The Hop *Danny and The Juniors* (HMV)	–	–	–

5   **12 19 26**

	12	19	26
12 Too Soon To Know/A Wonderful Time Up There *Pat Boone* (London)	8	3	2
13 Tequila *The Champs* (London)	9	7	7
14 April Love *Pat Boone* (London)	15	14	15
15 Big Beat *Fats Domino* (London)	16	–	–
16 Mandy *Eddie Calvert* (Columbia)	14	19	–
17 Baby Lover *Petula Clark* (Pye)	18	–	–
18 Oh! I'm Falling In Love Again *Jimmy Rodgers* (Columbia)	–	15	–
19 To Be Loved *Jackie Wilson* (Coral)	17	17	17
20 You Are My Destiny *Paul Anka* (Columbia)	–	–	–
– Who's Sorry Now *Connie Francis* (MGM)	13	10	6
– To Be Loved *Malcolm Vaughan* (HMV)	17	20	16
– Breathless *Jerry Lee Lewis* (London)	20	11	8
– Happy Guitar/Princess *Tommy Steele* (Decca)	–	16	14
– Grand Coolie Dam/Nobody Loves Like An Irishman *Lonnie Donegan* (Pye)	–	12	12
– Sweet Little Sixteen *Chuck Berry* (London)	–	17	19
– Lollipop *The Chordettes* (London)	–	–	13
– Tom Hark *Elias and his Zig Zag Jive Flutes* (Columbia)	–	–	18
– The Clouds Will Soon Roll By *Tony Brent* (Columbia)	–	–	20

Record Mirror *in its issue of 12 April published a chart with two discs at Number Seventeen and then printed Number Eighteen and not a Nineteen and continued in numerical order.*

MAY 1958

3   **10 17 24 31**

	10	17	24	31
1 Whole Lotta Woman *Marvin Rainwater* (MGM)	1	4	7	7
2 It's Too Soon To Know/Wonderful Time Up There *Pat Boone* (London)	2	3	3	2
3 Who's Sorry Now *Connie Francis* (MGM)	3	1	1	1
4 Swingin' Shepherd Blues *Ted Heath* (Decca)	5	9	10	19
5 Magic Moments/Catch A Falling Star *Perry Como* (RCA)	10	10	–	–
6 Tequila *The Champs* (London)	11	13	20	–
6 Nobody Loves Like An Irishman/Grand Coolie Dam *Lonnie Donegan* (Nixa)	6	7	6	6
8 Lollipop *The Chordettes* (London	7	8	8	20
9 Breathless *Jerry Lee Lewis* (London)	13	14	19	–
10 Maybe Baby *The Crickets* (Coral)	12	20	–	–
11 Don't/I Beg Of You *Elvis Presley* (RCA)	17	–	–	–
12 Tom Hark *Elias and his Zig Zag Jive Flutes* (Columbia)	8	6	4	4
13 Sweet Little Sixteen *Chuck Berry* (London)	19	11	15	–
14 To Be Loved *Malcolm Vaughan* (HMV)	14	15	–	–
15 Lollipop *The Mudlarks* (Columbia)	9	5	5	5
16 Wear My Ring Around Your Neck *Elvis Presley* (RCA)	4	2	2	3
17 Princess/Happy Guitar *Tommy Steele* (Decca)	15	–	–	–
18 Nairobi *Tommy Steele* (Decca)	–	–	–	–
19 The Clouds Will Soon Roll By *Tony Brent* (Columbia)	16	–	–	–
20 April Love *Pat Boone* (London)	–	–	–	–
– La Dee Dah *Jackie Dennis* (Decca)	18	–	–	–
– I May Never Pass This Way Again *Robert Earl* (Philips)	20	–	–	–
– Stairway Of Love *Terry Dene* (Decca)	–	12	12	16
– Tulips From Amsterdam/Hands *Max Bygraves* (Decca)	–	16	13	13
– Kewpie Doll *Perry Como* (RCA)	–	17	11	11
– Stairway Of Love *Michael Holliday* (Columbia)	–	18	16	9
– On The Street Where You Live *David Whitfield* (Decca)	–	19	18	–
– Kewpie Doll *Frankie Vaughan* (Philips)	–	–	9	8
– Swingin' Shepherd Blues *Ella Fitzgerald* (HMV)	–	–	17	18
– Witch Doctor *Don Lang* (HMV)	–	–	–	10

3	10	17	24	31
– Witch Doctor *David Seville* (London)	–	–	–	15
– All I Have To Do Is Dream/Claudette *The Everly Brothers* (London)	–	–	–	12
– Twilight Time *The Platters* (Mercury)	–	–	–	17
– On The Street Where You Live *Vic Damone* (Philips)	–	–	14	14

JUNE 1958

7	14	21	28
1 Who's Sorry Now *Connie Francis* (MGM)	1	1	3
2 It's Too Soon To Know/Wonderful Time Up There *Pat Boone* (London)	3	5	11
3 Tom Hark *Elias and his Zig Zag Jive Flutes* (Columbia)	2	3	7
4 Wear My Ring Around Your Neck *Elvis Presley* (RCA)	8	12	15
5 Grand Coolie Dam/Nobody Loves Like An Irishman *Lonnie Donegan* (Nixa)	7	11	17
6 Lollipop *The Mudlarks* (Columbia)	11	18	–
7 Stairway Of Love *Michael Holliday* (Columbia)	6	8	6
8 Witch Doctor *Don Lang* (HMV)	4	6	8
9 All I Have To Do Is Dream/Claudette *The Everly Brothers* (London)	5	2	1
10 Tulips From Amsterdam/Hands *Max Bygraves* (HMV)	10	7	4
11 On The Street Where You Live *Vic Damone* (Philips)	9	4	2
12 Kewpie Doll *Frankie Vaughan* (Philips)	13	14	16
13 Whole Lotta Woman *Marvin Rainwater* (MGM)	19	–	–
14 Twilight Time *The Platters* (Mercury)	14	10	13
15 Witch Doctor *David Seville* (London)	17	16	19
16 Kewpie Doll *Perry Como* (RCA)	15	–	–
17 Johnny B Goode *Chuck Berry* (London)	–	–	–
18 Stairway Of Love *Terry Dene* (Decca)	–	–	–
19 The Army Game *TV Cast* (HMV)	12	9	5
20 Swingin' Shepherd Blues *Ella Fitzgerald* (HMV)	–	–	–
– Book Of Love *The Mudlarks* (Columbia)	16	13	10
– I Dig You Baby *Marvin Rainwater* (MGM)	18	20	14
– I May Never Pass This Way Again *Perry Como* (RCA)	20	–	20
– Big Man *The Four Preps* (Capitol)	–	15	9
– Purple People Eater *Sheb Wooley* (MGM)	–	17	12
– On The Street Where You Live *David Whitfield* (Decca)	–	18	–
– Rave On *Buddy Holly* (Coral)	–	–	18

JULY 1958

5	12	19	26
1 All I Have To Do Is Dream/Claudette *The Everly Brothers* (London)	1	1	1
2 On The Street Where You Live *Vic Damone* (Philips)	2	4	5
3 Tulips From Amsterdam/Hands *Max Bygraves* (HMV)	3	3	3
4 Big Man *The Four Preps* (Capitol)	4	2	2
5 Who's Sorry Now *Connie Francis* (MGM)	5	9	10
6 Book Of Love *The Mudlarks* (Columbia)	9	10	16
7 The Army Game *TV Cast* (HMV)	11	17	–
8 Witch Doctor *Don Lang* (HMV)	12	12	20
9 Stairway Of Love *Michael Holliday* (Columbia)	15	15	–
10 Tom Hark *Elias and his Zig Zag Jive Flutes* (Columbia)	14	16	–
11 Purple People Eater *Sheb Wooley* (MGM)	13	13	14
12 Twilight Time *The Platters* (Mercury)	6	8	8
13 Sugar Moon *Pat Boone* (London)	7	5	11
14 Rave On *Buddy Holly* (Coral)	8	6	4

5   **12 19 26**

	12	19	26
15 Wonderful Time Up There/It's Too Soon To Know *Pat Boone* (London)	20	–	–
16 Grand Coolie Dam/Nobody Loves Like An Irishman *Lonnie Donegan* (Nixa)	17	–	–
17 Kewpie Doll *Frankie Vaughan* (Philips)	–	–	–
18 On The Street Where You Live *David Whitfield* (Decca)	19	19	19
19 Lady Is A Tramp (E.P.) *Frank Sinatra* (Capitol)	–	–	–
20 Sally Don't You Grieve/Betty, Betty, Betty *Lonnie Donegan* (Pye)	10	7	7
– I'm Sorry I Made You Cry *Connie Francis* (MGM)	16	14	12
– I May Never Pass This Way Again *Perry Como* (RCA)	18	–	–
– The Only Man On The Island *Tommy Steele* (Decca)	20	18	15
– Endless Sleep *Marty Wilde* (Philips)	20	11	9
– A Very Precious Love *Doris Day* (Philips)	–	20	–
– Hard Headed Woman *Elvis Presley* (RCA)	–	–	6
– When *The Kalin Twins* (Brunswick)	–	–	13
– Return To Me *Dean Martin* (Capitol)	–	–	17
– Patricia *Perez Prado* (RCA)	–	–	18

AUGUST 1958

2	9	16	23	30
1 All I Have To Do Is Dream/Claudette *The Everly Brothers* (London)	1	1	1	2
2 Hard Headed Woman *Elvis Presley* (RCA)	2	2	3	5
3 Big Man *The Four Preps* (Capitol)	3	4	6	7
4 Rave On *Buddy Holly* (Coral)	4	6	8	8
5 When *The Kalin Twins* (Brunswick)	5	3	2	1
6 Tulips From Amsterdam/Hands *Max Bygraves* (HMV)	6	7	7	6
7 Endless Sleep *Marty Wilde* (Philips)	7	5	4	4
8 Twilight Time *The Platters* (Mercury)	8	9	9	14
9 On The Street Where You Live *Vic Damone* (Philips)	9	10	13	18
10 Return To Me *Dean Martin* (Capitol)	10	8	5	3
11 Sally Don't You Grieve/Betty, Betty, Betty *Lonnie Donegan* (Pye)	11	14	18	–
12 Sugar Moon *Pat Boone* (London)	12	12	10	13
13 I'm Sorry I Made You Cry *Connie Francis* (MGM)	13	15	19	20
14 Who's Sorry Now *Connie Francis* (MGM)	14	17	–	–
15 The Only Man On The Island *Tommy Steele* (Decca)	15	16	17	–
16 Think It Over *The Crickets* (Coral)	16	13	14	15
17 Patricia *Perez Prado* (RCA)	17	11	11	11
18 Yakety Yak *The Coasters* (London)	18	18	16	10
19 Stairway Of Love *Michael Holliday* (Columbia)	19	–	–	–
20 Purple People Eater *Sheb Wooley* (MGM)	20	20	–	–
– Splish Splash *Bobby Darin* (London)	–	19	15	16
– Splish Splash/Hello My Darlings *Charlie Drake* (Parlophone)	–	–	12	9
– Poor Little Fool *Ricky Nelson* (London)	–	–	20	12
– Fever *Peggy Lee* (Capitol)	–	–	–	17
– Early In The Morning *Buddy Holly* (Coral)	–	–	–	19

The 9 August chart was a repeat of that for 2 August.

SEPTEMBER 1958

6

		13	20	27
1	When *The Kalin Twins* (Brunswick)	1	1	1
2	All I Have To Do Is Dream *The Everly Brothers* (London)	4	5	6
3	Return To Me *Dean Martin* (Capitol)	2	4	4
4	Endless Sleep *Marty Wilde* (Philips)	5	9	11
5	Hard Headed Woman *Elvis Presley* (RCA)	13	11	–
6	Carolina Moon/Stupid Cupid *Connie Francis* (MGM)	3	2	2
7	Tulips From Amsterdam/Hands *Max Bygraves* (HMV)	12	10	16
8	Rave On *Buddy Holly* (Coral)	14	17	–
9	Patricia *Perez Prado* (RCA)	10	16	12
10	Yakety Yak *The Coasters* (London)	11	12	14
11	Poor Little Fool *Ricky Nelson* (London)	8	7	5
12	Fever *Peggy Lee* (Capitol)	6	8	9
13	Splish Splash/Hello My Darlings *Charlie Drake* (Parlophone)	9	6	7
14	Big Man *The Four Preps* (Capitol)	17	–	–
15	Splish Splash *Bobby Darin* (London)	18	20	–
16	Volare *Dean Martin* (Capitol)	7	3	3
17	Early In The Morning *Buddy Holly* (Coral)	15	–	–
18	Little Bernadette *Harry Belafonte* (RCA)	19	–	–
19	Sugar Moon *Pat Boone* (London)	–	–	–
20	Think It Over *The Crickets* (Coral)	20	–	–
–	Volare *Domenico Modugno* (Oriole)	16	15	13
–	Mad Passionate Love *Bernard Bresslaw* (HMV)	–	13	8
–	Bird Dog *The Everly Brothers* (London)	–	14	10
–	If Dreams Came True *Pat Boone* (London)	–	18	18
–	Rebel Rouser *Duane Eddy* (London)	–	19	17
–	Girl Of My Dreams *Tony Brent* (Columbia)	–	–	15
–	Moon Talk *Perry Como* (RCA)	–	–	19
–	Born Too Late *The Poni-Tails* (HMV)	–	–	20

OCTOBER 1958

4

		11	18	25
1	Stupid Cupid/Carolina Moon *Connie Francis* (MGM)	1	1	1
2	When *The Kalin Twins* (Brunswick)	3	3	7
3	Volare *Dean Martin* (Capitol)	2	2	3
4	Bird Dog *The Everly Brothers* (London)	4	6	5
5	Return To Me *Dean Martin* (Capitol)	8	12	20
6	Mad Passionate Love *Bernard Bresslaw* (HMV)	5	9	10
7	Poor Little Fool *Ricky Nelson* (London)	6	8	9
8	Splish Splash/Hello My Darlings *Charlie Drake* (Parlophone)	11	18	–
9	Endless Sleep *Marty Wilde* (Philips)	12	–	–
10	Fever *Peggy Lee* (Capitol)	13	15	–
11	All I Have To Do Is Dream/Claudette *The Everly Brothers* (London)	18	–	–
12	Born Too Late *The Poni-Tails* (HMV)	9	7	6
13	Rebel Rouser *Duane Eddy* (London)	–	19	20
14	If Dreams Came True *Pat Boone* (London)	16	–	18
15	Patricia *Perez Prado* (RCA)	19	20	16
16	Volare *Domenico Modugno* (Oriole)	17	14	14
17	Yakety Yak *The Coasters* (London)	–	–	–
18	Girl Of My Dreams *Tony Brent* (Columbia)	14	–	–
19	Move It *Cliff Richard* (Columbia)	10	5	4
20	Tulips From Amsterdam/Hands *Max Bygraves* (HMV)	–	–	–
–	King Creole *Elvis Presley* (RCA)	7	4	2
–	A Certain Smile *Johnny Mathis* (Fontana)	15	10	8
–	Little Star *The Elegants* (HMV)	20	–	–
–	Volare *Marino Marini* (Durium)	–	11	11

4

	11	18	25
– It's All In The Game *Tommy Edwards* (MGM)	–	13	12
– Western Movies *The Olympics* (HMV)	–	16	13
– Someday *Jodi Sands* (HMV)	–	17	17
– More Than Ever *Malcolm Vaughan* (HMV)	–	–	14

NOVEMBER 1958

1

	8	15	22	29
1 Stupid Cupid/Carolina Moon *Connie Francis* (MGM)	2	3	6	9
2 King Creole *Elvis Presley* (RCA)	5	8	9	12
3 Move It *Cliff Richard* (Columbia)	3	4	7	7
4 Bird Dog *The Everly Brothers* (London)	1	1	1	3
5 A Certain Smile *Johnny Mathis* (Fontana)	7	7	4	5
6 Come Prima *Marino Marini* (Durium)	4	5	5	8
7 Born Too Late *The Poni-Tails* (HMV)	8	9	12	–
8 Volare *Dean Martin* (Capitol)	11	15	–	–
9 It's All In The Game *Tommy Edwards* (MGM)	6	2	2	2
10 More Than Ever *Malcolm Vaughan* (HMV)	10	10	8	6
11 Mad Passionate Love *Bernard Bresslaw* (HMV)	17	20	–	–
12 When *The Kalin Twins* (Brunswick)	16	17	–	–
13 Western Movies *The Olympics* (HMV)	12	13	18	20
14 Poor Little Fool *Ricky Nelson* (London)	14	14	20	–
15 Hoots Mon *Lord Rockingham's XI* (Decca)	9	6	3	1
16 Volare *Domenico Modugno* (Oriole)	–	–	–	–
17 Someday *Jodi Sands* (HMV)	18	16	17	18
18 Tea For Two Cha-Cha *Tommy Dorsey Orchestra* (Brunswick)	15	12	14	16
19 Patricia *Perez Prado* (RCA)	–	–	–	–
20 Rebel Rouser *Duane Eddy* (London)	19	–	–	–
– My True Love *Jack Scott* (London)	13	11	10	10
– Moon Talk *Perry Como* (RCA)	20	19	–	–
– Love Makes The World Go Round *Perry Como* (RCA)	–	18	13	11
– It's Only Make Believe *Conway Twitty* (MGM)	–	–	11	4
– Come On Let's Go *Tommy Steele* (Decca)	–	–	15	14
– Someday *Ricky Nelson* (London)	–	–	16	13
– It's So Easy *The Crickets* (Coral)	–	–	19	–
– Tom Dooley *Lonnie Donegan* (Nixa)	–	–	–	15
– High Class Baby *Cliff Richard* (Columbia)	–	–	–	17
– I'll Get By/Fallin' *Connie Francis* (MGM)	–	–	–	19

DECEMBER 1958

5

	12	19	26
1 Hoots Mon *Lord Rockingham's XI* (Decca)	1	1	2
2 It's Only Make Believe *Conway Twitty* (MGM)	2	2	1
3 It's All In The Game *Tommy Edwards* (MGM)	4	5	8
4 Tom Dooley *Lonnie Donegan* (Nixa)	3	3	3
5 Bird Dog *The Everly Brothers* (London)	11	14	20
6 A Certain Smile *Johnny Mathis* (Fontana)	10	9	15
7 More Than Ever *Malcolm Vaughan* (HMV)	6	11	14
8 Come Prima/Volare *Marino Marini* (Durium)	9	12	12
9 Come On Let's Go *Tommy Steele* (Decca)	12	10	11
10 High Class Baby *Cliff Richard* (Columbia)	7	6	5
11 Love Makes The World Go Round *Perry Como* (RCA)	13	8	9
12 Somebody/I Got A Feeling *Ricky Nelson* (London)	14	13	13
13 Stupid Cupid/Carolina Moon *Connie Francis* (MGM)	15	20	–
14 Tea For Two Cha-Cha *Tommy Dorsey Orchestra* (Brunswick)	8	7	6
15 Move It *Cliff Richard* (Columbia)	16	16	17
16 My True Love *Jack Scott* (London)	–	–	–

39

	12	**19**	**26**
17 Tom Dooley *Kingston Trio* (Capitol)	5	4	4
18 Someday *Jodi Sands* (HMV)	19	17	19
19 King Creole *Elvis Presley* (RCA)	17	18	–
20 I'll Get by/Fallin' *Connie Francis* (MGM)	–	–	–
– The Day The Rains Came *Jane Morgan* (London)	18	15	7
– It's So Easy *The Crickets* (Brunswick)	20	–	–
– Mr Success *Frank Sinatra* (Capitol)	–	19	18
– Mary's Boy Child *Harry Belafonte* (RCA)	–	–	10
– More Party Pops *Russ Conway* (Columbia)	–	–	16

1958

1957 saw the arrival of Cliff Richard who, once he had been persuaded not to act like a direct copy of Elvis Presley, began a long and successful chart career. His first chart entry was in October 1958 with the classic song 'Move It', a number which was re-recorded in a different style in 1975 by Alvin Stardust.

1958 was also the year of Duane Eddy's first twanging guitar hit, and the emergence of Johnny Mathis, a singer who was still to be found enjoying increasing success as late as 17 years hence in 1975.

There was also the start of a somewhat brief but amazingly successful career in the charts for Connie Francis. She began with a Number One, 'Who's Sorry Now', and by the end of 1958 she had achieved another four hits.

The chart regulars managed fairly well, for Pat Boone had four hit records, Elvis achieved six and Lonnie Donegan mustered three. 'Tom Dooley', one of Donegan's hits, gave 1958 chart followers an exciting time as it battled in the charts with the original version by the American group, The Kingston Trio, a slightly folky group.

Even Ruby Murray reappeared after remaining dormant in the 1957 charts, and the year also saw seven hits from Perry Como. Como had indeed made chart impressions in 1956 with 'Hot Diggity', 'More' and 'Glendora', but had disappeared from the charts in 1957. However, few could have expected his startling comeback of 1958. though his television show of the time obviously brought him back into the public eye and aided his success a great deal.

The year also produced some pop classics including 'Twilight Time' from The Platters, 'Purple People Eater' from Sheb Wooley, Vic Damone's 'On The Street Where You Live', and 'Oh! Boy', 'Maybe Baby' and 'Think It Over' from The Crickets with Buddy Holly. Buddy Holly began his solo hit run with the mighty 'Peggy Sue', a record which was followed up 'Listen To Me', 'Rave On' and 'Early In The Morning'.

As always, big stars of the past failed to make the charts and therefore disappeared from the public eye. Winifred

Atwell's piano records failed to sell, although her Christmas hit of 1957 did mean that her name appeared in the 1958 listings. Eddie Calvert ended his trumpet successes with 'Mandy', and The Chordettes faded with the sickly strains of 'Lollipop'. The same song was also the swan-song of The Mudlarks.

However, another pianist appeared in the charts to fill the gaps left by both Joe Henderson and Winifred Atwell. This was Russ Conway, whose first hit was 'More Party Pops'.

Terry Dene appeared in the charts for the last time with 'Stairway Of Love', and Jackie Dennis had but a brief chart innings with 'La Dee Dah', not one of pop's most celebrated lyrics. The Four Preps came and went with the bouncy 'Big Man', a song best remembered for its piano chords. There was also a new but short-lived sound from Elias and his Zig Zag Jive Flutes with 'Tom Hark'.

Charlie Gracie was unsuccessful in 1958 despite four hits in 1957, including 'Fabulous' which had sounded very much like an early Presley record. Tab Hunter never found his way back into the charts, and the most important demise from the charts was that of Slim Whitman, who had achieved seven hits since 1955.

JANUARY 1959

3		**10**	**17**	**24**	**31**
1	It's Only Make Believe *Conway Twitty* (MGM)	1	1	3	7
2	Hoots Mon *Lord Rockingham's XI* (Decca)	2	2	8	14
3	Tom Dooley *Lonnie Donegan* (Nixa)	3	3	11	12
4	Tom Dooley *The Kingston Trio* (Capitol)	4	8	6	9
5	Love Makes The World Go Round *Perry Como* (RCA)	6	7	12	15
6	Tea For Two Cha-Cha *Tommy Dorsey Orchestra* (Brunswick)	5	9	9	11
7	It's All In The Game *Tommy Edwards* (MGM)	13	17	–	–
8	High Class Baby *Cliff Richard* (Columbia)	7	10	16	–
9	The Day The Rains Came *Jane Morgan* (London)	8	5	5	4
10	More Party Pops *Russ Conway* (Columbia)	15	–	–	–
11	Come On Let's Go *Tommy Steele* (Decca)	9	13	15	18
12	More Than Ever *Malcolm Vaughan* (HMV)	17	–	–	–
13	Someday *Ricky Nelson* (London)	16	19	–	–
14	Mary's Boy Child *Harry Belafonte* (RCA)	–	–	–	–
15	A Certain Smile *Johnny Mathis* (Fontana)	–	–	–	–
16	Come Prima *Marino Marini* (Durium)	–	–	–	–
17	Cannon Ball *Duane Eddy* (London)	14	14	20	–
18	Skiffle Party *Lonnie Donegan* (Nixa)	–	–	–	–
19	Son Of Mary *Harry Belafonte* (RCA)	–	–	–	–
20	Kiss Me Honey *Shirley Bassey* (Philips)	12	11	7	5
–	Baby Face *Little Richard* (London)	10	6	4	2
–	To Know Him Is To Love Him *The Teddy Bears* (London)	11	4	2	3
–	You Always Hurt The One You Love *Connie Francis* (MGM)	18	12	18	17
–	My Ukelele *Max Bygraves* (Decca)	19	16	–	–
–	King Creole *Elvis Presley* (RCA)	20	–	–	–
–	Smoke Gets In Your Eyes *The Platters* (Mercury)	–	15	10	8
–	Chantilly Lace *Big Bopper* (Mercury)	–	18	14	16
–	As I Love You *Shirley Bassey* (Philips)	–	20	13	10
–	High School Confidential *Jerry Lee Lewis* (London)	–	–	17	13
–	Problems *The Everly Brothers* (London)	–	–	19	6
–	All Of A Sudden My Heart Sings *Paul Anka* (Columbia)	–	–	–	19
–	I'll Remember Tonight *Pat Boone* (London)	–	–	–	20
–	I Got Stung/One Night *Elvis Presley* (RCA)	–	–	1	1

FEBRUARY 1959

7		**14**	**21**	**28**
1	I Got Stung/One Night *Elvis Presley* (RCA)	1	1	3
2	Baby Face *Little Richard* (London)	3	7	13
3	To Know Him Is To Love Him *The Teddy Bears* (London)	2	4	5
4	Kiss Me Honey *Shirley Bassey* (Philips)	4	6	8
5	Problems *The Everly Brothers* (London)	7	8	10
6	As I Love You *Shirley Bassey* (Philips)	6	2	2
7	Smoke Gets In Your Eyes *The Platters* (Mercury)	8	5	1
8	The Day The Rains Came *Jane Morgan* (London)	9	15	–
9	It's Only Make Believe *Conway Twitty* (MGM)	15	–	–
10	High School Confidential *Jerry Lee Lewis* (London)	13	13	–
11	Tea For Two Cha-Cha *Tommy Dorsey Orchestra* (Brunswick)	–	–	–
12	Does Your Chewing Gum Lose Its Flavour *Lonnie Donegan* (Nixa)	5	3	4
13	All Of A Sudden My Heart Sings *Paul Anka* (Columbia)	14	10	12
14	Tom Dooley *The Kingston Trio* (Capitol)	–	–	–
15	Hoots Mon *Lord Rockingham's XI* (Decca)	–	–	–
16	Wee Tom *Lord Rockingham's XI* (Decca)	11	12	16
17	I'll Be With You In Apple Blossom Time *Rosemary June* (Pye)	12	16	20

7	**14**	**21**	**28**
18 Chantilly Lace *Big Bopper* (Mercury)	20	20	–
19 Tom Dooley *Lonnie Donegan* (Nixa)	–	–	–
20 You Always Hurt The One You Love *Connie Francis* (MGM)	–	–	–
– Pub With No Beer *Slim Dusty* (Columbia)	10	9	6
– Petite Fleur *Chris Barber* (Nixa)	15	16	7
– I'll Remember Tonight *Pat Boone* (London)	17	–	–
– Stagger Lee *Lloyd Price* (HMV)	18	18	14
– Little Drummer Boy *The Beverley Sisters* (Mercury)	19	14	9
– My Happiness *Connie Francis* (MGM)	–	11	11
– Gigi *Billy Eckstine* (Mercury)	–	19	17
– Side Saddle *Russ Conway* (Columbia)	–	–	15
– Tomboy *Perry Como* (RCA)	–	–	18
– Wait For Me *Malcolm Vaughan* (HMV)	–	–	19

MARCH 1959

7	**14**	**21**	**28**
1 Smoke Gets In Your Eyes *The Platters* (Mercury)	1	1	1
2 As I Love You *Shirley Bassey* (Philips)	2	2	4
3 Does Your Chewing Gum Lose Its Flavour *Lonnie Donegan* (Nixa)	5	8	10
4 I Got Stung/One Night *Elvis Presley* (RCA)	8	12	17
5 Pub With No Beer *Slim Dusty* (Columbia)	3	5	7
6 Side Saddle *Russ Conway* (Columbia)	4	3	2
7 My Happiness *Connie Francis* (MGM)	7	4	3
8 Petite Fleur *Chris Barber* (Nixa)	6	6	5
9 Little Drummer Boy *The Beverley Sisters* (Mercury)	9	9	9
10 To Know Him Is To Love Him *The Teddy Bears* (London)	15	–	–
11 Kiss Me Honey *Shirley Bassey* (Philips)	12	14	18
12 Stagger Lee *Lloyd Price* (HMV)	10	7	6
13 Problems *The Everly Brothers* (London)	17	–	–
14 It Doesn't Matter Any More *Buddy Holly* (Coral)	11	10	8
15 All Of A Sudden My Heart Sings *Paul Anka* (Columbia)	13	16	14
16 Baby Face *Little Richard* (London)	16	19	–
17 Tomboy *Perry Como* (RCA)	14	15	12
18 Gigi *Billy Eckstine* (Mercury)	20	11	11
19 Manhattan Spiritual *Reg Owen* (Pye)	17	18	–
20 C'mon Everybody *Eddie Cochran* (London)	–	13	15
– I'll Remember Tonight *Pat Boone* (London)	19	–	–
– Sing Little Birdie *Pearl Carr and Teddy Johnson* (Columbia)	–	17	19
– Donna *Marty Wilde* (Philips)	–	20	16
– Charlie Brown *The Coasters* (London)	–	–	13
– Donna *Ritchie Valens* (London)	–	–	20

APRIL 1959

4	**11**	**18**	**25**
1 Side Saddle *Russ Conway* (Columbia)	1	1	2
2 Smoke Gets In Your Eyes *The Platters* (Mercury)	3	3	7
3 It Doesn't Matter Any More *Buddy Holly* (Coral)	2	1	1
4 My Happiness *Connie Francis* (MGM)	4	7	10
5 As I Love You *Shirley Bassey* (Philips)	5	9	13
6 Petite Fleur *Chris Barber* (Nixa)	5	6	4
7 Stagger Lee *Lloyd Price* (HMV)	7	10	11
8 Pub With No Beer *Slim Dusty* (Columbia)	10	13	14
9 Little Drummer Boy *The Beverley Sisters* (Mercury)	13	14	19
10 Gigi *Billy Eckstine* (Mercury)	11	11	16
11 Donna *Marty Wilde* (Philips)	8	4	6
12 Tomboy *Perry Como* (RCA)	14	15	15

4	11	18	25
13 Charlie Brown *The Coasters* (London)	9	5	5
14 C'mon Everybody *Eddie Cochran* (London)	12	8	8
15 Wait For Me *Malcolm Vaughan* (HMV)	16	19	—
16 Does Your Chewing Gum Lose Its Flavour *Lonnie Donegan* (Nixa)	19	—	—
17 By The Light Of The Silvery Moon *Little Richard* (London)	15	18	—
18 I Got Stung/One Night *Elvis Presley* (RCA)	—	19	—
19 Sing Little Birdie *Pearl Carr and Teddy Johnson* (Columbia)	17	12	—
20 Lonely One *Duane Eddy* (London)	—	—	—
– Maybe Tomorrow *Billy Fury* (Decca)	18	17	18
– Donna *Ritchie Valens* (London)	20	—	—
– It's Late/There'll Never Be Anyone But You *Ricky Nelson* (London)	—	16	9
– A Fool Such As I/I Need Your Love Tonight *Elvis Presley* (RCA)	—	—	3
– Come Softly To Me *The Fleetwoods* (London)	—	—	12
– Never Mind/Mean Streak *Cliff Richard* (Columbia)	—	—	17
– Come Softly To Me *Frankie Vaughan* (Philips)	—	—	20

MAY 1959

2	9	16	23	30
1 A Fool Such As I/I Need Your Love Tonight *Elvis Presley* (RCA)	1	1	1	1
2 It Doesn't Matter Any More *Buddy Holly* (Coral)	2	2	2	2
3 Side Saddle *Russ Conway* (Columbia)	5	4	5	9
4 Donna *Marty Wilde* (Philips)	4	7	7	6
5 Petite Fleur *Chris Barber* (Pye)	7	8	8	14
6 It's Late/There'll Never Be Anyone Else But You *Ricky Nelson* (London)	3	3	3	3
7 Charlie Brown *The Coasters* (London)	9	11	14	20
8 C'mon Everybody *Eddie Cochran* (London)	11	18	17	—
9 Smoke Gets In Your Eyes *The Platters* (Mercury)	15	16	18	—
10 Come Softly To Me *The Fleetwoods* (London)	6	6	6	10
11 Come Softly To Me *Frankie Vaughan and The Kaye Sisters* (Philips)	10	10	9	12
12 I Go Ape *Neil Sedaka* (RCA)	12	9	13	11
13 Idle On Parade (E.P.) *Anthony Newley* (Decca)	14	—	—	—
14 I've Waited So Long *Anthony Newley* (Decca)	8	5	4	4
15 My Happiness *Connie Francis* (MGM)	—	—	—	—
16 Mean Streak/Never Mind *Cliff Richard* (Columbia)	13	13	11	8
17 Stagger Lee *Lloyd Price* (HMV)	18	—	—	—
18 Tomboy *Perry Como* (RCA)	—	—	—	—
19 Wait For Me *Malcolm Vaughan* (HMV)	—	17	—	—
20 Lovin' Up A Storm *Jerry Lee Lewis* (London)	—	—	—	—
– Fort Worth Jail *Lonnie Donegan* (Nixa)	16	12	12	17
– Where Were You On Our Wedding Day *Lloyd Price* (HMV)	17	15	16	15
– Guitar Boogie Shuffle *Bert Weedon* (Top Rank)	19	14	10	7
– Maybe Tomorrow *Billy Fury* (Decca)	20	—	—	—
– Guitar Boogie Shuffle *The Virtues* (HMV)	—	19	19	19
– Hey Little Lucy *Conway Twitty* (MGM)	—	20	—	—
– Roulette *Russ Conway* (Columbia)	—	—	15	5
– Three Stars *Ruby Wright* (Parlophone)	—	—	20	18
– Poor Jenny/Take A Message To Mary *The Everly Brothers* (London)	—	—	—	13
– Margie *Fats Domino* (London)	—	—	—	16

6		13	20	27
1	A Fool Such As I/I Need Your Love Tonight *Elvis Presley* (RCA)	1	2	–
2	It Doesn't Matter Any More *Buddy Holly* (Coral)	4	7	–
3	Roulette *Russ Conway* (Columbia)	2	1	–
4	It's Late/There'll Never Be Anyone Else But You *Ricky Nelson* (London)	3	6	–
5	I've Waited So Long *Anthony Newley* (Decca)	6	5	–
6	Guitar Boogie Shuffle *Bert Weedon* (Top Rank)	7	8	–
7	Donna *Marty Wilde* (Philips)	15	20	–
8	Side Saddle *Russ Conway* (Columbia)	12	12	–
9	Mean Streak/Never Mind *Cliff Richard* (Columbia)	14	15	–
10	I Go Ape *Neil Sedaka* (RCA)	10	17	–
11	Take A Message To Mary/Poor Jenny *The Everly Brothers* (London)	11	13	–
12	Come Softly To Me *Frankie Vaughan and The Kaye Sisters* (Philips)	13	–	–
13	Dream Lover *Bobby Darin* (London)	5	3	–
14	Three Stars *Ruby Wright* (Parlophone)	8	9	–
15	Where Were You *Lloyd Price* (HMV)	–	–	–
16	May You Always *Joan Regan* (HMV)	20	16	–
17	Come Softly To Me *The Fleetwoods* (London)	18	–	–
18	Petite Fleur *Chris Barber* (Pye)	19	–	–
19	Margie *Fats Domino* (London)	–	–	–
20	A Teenager In Love *Marty Wilde* (Philips)	9	4	–
–	A Teenager In Love *Craig Douglas* (Top Rank)	16	14	–
–	Personality *Lloyd Price* (HMV)	17	11	–
–	Peter Gunn/Yep! *Duane Eddy* (London)	–	10	–
–	Personality *Anthony Newley* (Decca)	–	18	–
–	Goodbye Jimmy Goodbye *Ruby Murray* (Columbia)	–	19	–

There were no Top Twenty charts from 27 June until 8 August owing to a newspaper strike. During this time Record Mirror was not published.

8	15		22	29
1	1	Livin' Doll *Cliff Richard* (Columbia)	1	2
2	2	Dream Lover *Bobby Darin* (London)	5	6
3	3	Battle Of New Orleans *Lonnie Donegan* (Pye)	4	5
6	4	Lipstick On Your Collar *Connie Francis* (MGM)	6	4
4	5	Big Hunk Of Love *Elvis Presley* (RCA)	7	9
5	6	A Teenager In Love *Marty Wilde* (Philips)	8	11
18	7	Lonely Boy *Paul Anka* (Columbia)	3	3
7	8	Roulette *Russ Conway* (Columbia)	10	14
9	9	Heart Of A Man *Frankie Vaughan* (Philips)	9	7
–	10	Only Sixteen *Craig Douglas* (Top Rank)	2	1
8	11	Peter Gunn *Duane Eddy* (London)	–	–
12	12	It's Late/There'll Never Be Anyone Else But You *Ricky Nelson* (London)	–	–
10	13	Personality *Anthony Newley* (Decca)	16	19
11	14	Ragtime Cowboy Joe *The Chipmunks* (London)	13	–
13	15	Someone *Johnny Mathis* (Fontana)	12	10
14	16	I Know *Perry Como* (RCA)	11	–
–	17	Give, Give, Give *Tommy Steele* (Decca)	20	20
16	18	Twixt, Twelve And Twenty *Pat Boone* (London)	–	18
19	19	Personality *Lloyd Price* (HMV)	–	–
–	20	Mona Lisa *Conway Twitty* (MGM)	19	16

	8	15	22	29
– Only Sixteen *Sam Cooke* (HMV)	–	–	14	13
– China Tea *Russ Conway* (Columbia)	–	–	15	8
– Goodbye Jimmy Goodbye *Ruby Murray* (Columbia)	–	–	17	–
– Tallahassie Lassie *Freddie Cannon* (Top Rank)	–	–	18	15
– Here Comes Summer *Jerry Keller* (London)	–	–	–	12
– Only Sixteen *Al Saxon* (Fontana)	–	–	–	17

Owing to the newspaper strike, no chart was published in Record Mirror *for 8 August 1959, so those figures which appear under 8 August column were published as the 'last week' figures for 15 August 1959.*

SEPTEMBER 1959

	5	12	19	26
1 Only Sixteen *Craig Douglas* (Top Rank)		1	1	1
2 Livin' Doll *Cliff Richard* (Columbia)		2	2	2
3 Lonely Boy *Paul Anka* (Columbia)		3	4	4
4 Lipstick On Your Collar *Connie Francis* (MGM)		9	10	13
5 China Tea *Russ Conway* (Columbia)		4	5	5
6 Heart Of A Man *Frankie Vaughan* (Philips)		7	9	10
7 Battle Of New Orleans *Lonnie Donegan* (Pye)		6	11	15
8 Someone *Johnny Mathis* (Fontana)		11	12	12
9 Here Comes Summer *Jerry Keller* (London)		5	3	3
10 Dream Lover *Bobby Darin* (London)		13	19	–
11 Mona Lisa *Conway Twitty* (MGM)		10	6	6
12 Forty Miles Of Bad Road *Duane Eddy* (London)		8	7	7
13 Big Hunk Of Love *Elvis Presley* (RCA)		20	–	–
14 Just A Little Too Much *Ricky Nelson* (London)		12	8	9
15 Roulette *Russ Conway* (Columbia)		16	–	–
16 I Know *Perry Como* (RCA)		–	–	–
17 A Teenager In Love *Marty Wilde* (Philips)		–	–	–
18 Ragtime Cowboy Joe *The Chipmunks* (London)		–	–	–
19 Plenty Of Good Lovin' *Connie Francis* (MGM)		14	15	–
20 Only Sixteen *Sam Cooke* (HMV)		–	–	–
– 'Til I Kissed You *The Everly Brothers* (London)		15	13	8
– Three Bells *The Browns* (RCA)		17	18	11
– Peggy Sue Got Married *Buddy Holly* (Coral)		18	14	17
– Just Keep It Up *Dee Clarke* (London)		19	–	–
– Sal's Got A Sugar Lip *Lonnie Donegan* (Nixa)		–	16	18
– High Hopes *Frank Sinatra* (Capitol)		–	17	16
– I'm Gonna Get Married *Lloyd Price* (HMV)		–	20	20
– Sea Of Love *Marty Wilde* (Philips)		–	–	14
– Broken Hearted Melody *Sarah Vaughan* (Mercury)		–	–	19

OCTOBER 1959

	3	10	17	24	31
1 Only Sixteen *Craig Douglas* (Top Rank)		1	6	7	8
2 Here Comes Summer *Jerry Keller* (London)		2	4	6	7
3 Livin' Doll *Cliff Richard* (Columbia)		4	8	10	15
4 'Til I Kissed You *The Everly Brothers* (London)		3	2	3	3
5 China Tea *Russ Conway* (Columbia)		11	17	19	–
6 Forty Miles Of Bad Road *Duane Eddy* (London)		12	16	16	–
7 Mona Lisa *Conway Twitty* (MGM)		8	10	12	18
8 Lonely Boy *Paul Anka* (Columbia)		10	12	18	–
9 Just A Little Too Much *Ricky Nelson* (London)		13	13	14	–
10 Three Bells *The Browns* (RCA)		6	7	5	6
11 Mack The Knife *Bobby Darin* (London)		5	3	2	2
12 Someone *Johnny Mathis* (Fontana)		14	15	17	–

47

	3	10	17	24	31
13 Sea Of Love *Marty Wilde* (Philips)		9	5	4	4
14 Peggy Sue Got Married *Buddy Holly* (Coral)		16	18	15	16
15 Heart Of A Man *Frankie Vaughan* (Philips)		20	–	–	–
16 Broken Hearted Melody *Sarah Vaughan* (Mercury)		15	9	11	11
17 Lipstick On Your Collar *Connie Francis* (MGM)		–	–	–	–
18 High Hopes *Frank Sinatra* (Capitol)		18	20	13	10
19 Sal's Got A Sugar Lip *Lonnie Donegan* (Nixa)		–	–	–	–
20 Hold Back Tomorrow *Miki and Griff* (Pye)		–	–	–	–
– Travellin' Light *Cliff Richard* (Columbia)		7	1	1	1
– Red River Rock *Johnny and The Hurricanes* (London)		17	11	9	5
– Sleep Walk *Santo and Johnny* (Pye)		19	14	–	–
– Makin' Love *Floyd Robinson* (RCA)		–	19	8	9
– Mr Blue *Mike Preston* (Decca)		–	–	20	13
– What Do You Want To Make Those Eyes At Me For? *Emile Ford* (Pye)		–	–	–	12
– Put Your Head On My Shoulder *Paul Anka* (Columbia)		–	–	–	14
– Teen Beat *Sandy Nelson* (London)		–	–	–	17
– Mr Blue *David Macbeth* (Pye)		–	–	–	19
– One More Sunrise *Dickie Valentine* (Pye)		–	–	–	20

NOVEMBER 1959

	7	14	21	28
1 Travellin' Light *Cliff Richard* (Columbia)		1	1	1
2 Mack The Knife *Bobby Darin* (London)		2	4	5
3 Sea Of Love *Marty Wilde* (Philips)		4	5	9
4 Red River Rock *Johnny and The Hurricanes* (London)		3	2	3
5 'Til I Kissed You *The Everly Brothers* (London)		6	6	8
6 Three Bells *The Browns* (RCA)		11	12	–
7 Makin' Love *Floyd Robinson* (RCA)		8	14	17
8 Put Your Head On My Shoulder *Paul Anka* (Columbia)		7	7	7
9 What Do You Want To Make Those Eyes At Me For? *Emile Ford* (Pye)		5	3	2
10 Broken Hearted Melody *Sarah Vaughan* (Mercury)		10	12	14
11 Here Comes Summer *Jerry Keller* (London)		15	–	–
12 High Hopes *Frank Sinatra* (Capitol)		9	15	–
13 Mr Blue *Mike Preston* (Decca)		12	9	11
14 Mr Blue *David Macbeth* (Pye)		–	–	–
14 Teen Beat *Sandy Nelson* (Top Rank)		13	11	–
16 Only Sixteen *Craig Douglas* (Top Rank)		–	–	–
17 Mona Lisa *Conway Twitty* (MGM)		–	–	–
18 Livin' Doll *Cliff Richard* (Columbia)		–	–	–
19 I Want To Walk You Home *Fats Domino* (London)		19	–	–
20 One More Sunrise *Dickie Valentine* (Pye)		14	17	–
– Snow Coach *Russ Conway* (Columbia)		16	10	12
– Oh! Carol *Neil Sedaka* (RCA)		17	8	6
– Rawhide *Frankie Laine* (Philips)		18	19	–
– Always *Sammy Turner* (London)		20	–	–
– Seven Little Girls Sitting In The Back Seat *The Avons* (Columbia)		–	16	10
– What Do You Want *Adam Faith* (Parlophone)		–	18	4
– Poison Ivy *The Coasters* (London)		–	20	15
– More And More Party Pops *Russ Conway* (Columbia)		–	–	13
– Little White Bull *Tommy Steele* (Decca)		–	–	16
– The Best Of Everything *Johnny Mathis* (Fontana)		–	–	18
– Seven Little Girls Sitting In The Back Seat *P. Evans* (London)		–	–	18
– Heartaches By The Number *Guy Mitchell* (Philips)		–	–	20
– Little Donkey *The Beverley Sisters* (Decca)		–	–	20

5	12	19	26
1 What Do You Want *Adam Faith* (Parlophone)	1	1	1
2 What Do You Want To Make Those Eyes At Me For? *Emile Ford* (Pye)	2	2	2
3 Travellin' Light *Cliff Richard* (Columbia)	4	4	5
4 Oh! Carol *Neil Sedaka* (RCA)	3	3	3
5 Red River Rock *Johnny and The Hurricanes* (London)	6	6	12
6 Mack The Knife *Bobby Darin* (London)	8	16	–
7 Seven Little Girls Sitting In The Back Seat *The Avons* (Columbia)	5	5	4
8 Teen Beat *Sandy Nelson* (Top Rank)	7	8	14
8 Put Your Head On My Shoulder *Paul Anka* (Columbia)	9	18	–
10 'Til I Kissed You *The Everly Brothers* (London)	17	–	–
11 Snow Coach *Russ Conway* (Columbia)	10	9	6
12 Little White Bull *Tommy Steele* (Decca)	13	11	20
13 Sea Of Love *Marty Wilde* (Philips)	16	–	–
14 Rawhide *Frankie Laine* (Philips)	11	14	13
15 More And More Party Pops *Russ Conway* (Columbia)	15	11	9
16 Bad Boy *Marty Wilde* (Philips)	19	20	20
17 Heartaches By The Number *Guy Mitchell* (Philips)	–	–	–
18 Ivy Will Cling *Arnold Strang* (Fontana)	–	–	–
19 Piano Party *Winifred Atwell* (Decca)	20	15	18
20 Mr Blue *Mike Preston* (Decca)	–	–	–
– Among My Souvenirs *Connie Francis* (MGM)	12	10	8
– Some Kind-A-Earthquake *Duane Eddy* (London)	14	7	7
– Seven Little Girls In The Back Seat *Paul Evans* (London)	18	–	16
– Johnny Staccato Theme *Elmer Bernstein* (Capitol)	–	13	10
– Be My Guest *Fats Domino* (London)	–	17	19
– Deck Of Cards *Wink Martindale* (London)	–	19	–
– Jingle Bell Rock *Max Bygraves* (Decca)	–	–	11
– Reveille Rock *Johnny and The Hurricanes* (London)	–	–	15
– Little Donkey *The Beverley Sisters* (Decca)	–	–	16

1959

Most American Rock 'n' Roll heroes had hits during 1959 but Britain brought out some new pop heroes of her own for chart display. The American contingent included Pat Boone, Paul Anka, The Platters, Connie Francis, Buddy Holly, Ricky Nelson, Eddie Cochran and Fats Domino. On the British side, Tommy Steele continued in his flourishing career, and Billy Fury with 'Maybe To-morrow' and Adam Faith with 'What Do You Want' both entered the charts for the first time. One of Britain's home-grown black singers made the charts with the catchy 'What Do You Want To Make Those Eyes At Me For?'. His name was Emile Ford, and his chart life was short when compared to other singers of the time, although he did have four hits in 1960.

Frankie Vaughan, Russ Conway and Shirley Bassey all had hits in 1958. Bassey, after an absence from the charts in 1958, leapt to the fore with 'Kiss Me Honey Honey Kiss Me' and 'As I Love You'. Her success owed much to the Philips record company who took months in breaking the songs, such was their perseverance and faith in them, despite sceptical views from other record companies.

Chart fanatics observed some interesting battles in the record charts, for in the 1950s, unlike the 1970s, artists frequently competed for the top position with the same songs. Three versions of 'Come Softly To Me' made the Top Twenty. One of these was the original American version by The Fleetwoods, and the other two versions were by Craig Douglas and Frankie Vaughan, the latter being assisted by The Kaye Sisters, his high-stepping act and his Victor Mature type of beefcake appeal. The American version was the most popular, for it reached Number Six, while Frankie Vaughan and The Kaye Sisters lagged behind at Number Nine. However, both versions enjoyed two months in the charts. Craig Douglas' version only entered *Record Mirror*'s Top Ten British listing on several occasions, but with speed and alacrity he entered the charts for the first time with the disc's B-side, 'Teenager In Love'.

Douglas was a newcomer in 1959 and although 'Teenager In Love' was his first Top Twenty entry, he still lost to the more experienced opposition provided by Philips' recording artist, Marty Wilde, who took his version of the same song to the Number Two position.

Less exciting were the chart battles over the songs 'Only Sixteen' and 'Battle Of New Orleans'. Douglas featured again in the fight to take his version of the former song up the charts. This time he won and grabbed the Number One position. The classic version by the American singer, Sam Cooke, only reached Number Thirteen, and remained in the Top Twenty for only three weeks.

Lonnie Donegan spent 14 weeks in the Top Twenty, reaching Number Two with 'Battle Of New Orleans'. This was a case of a British artist, well-known in the popularity stakes, grabbing a song from an unknown American artist who had first made it a hit across the Atlantic. The 'unknown American' in this case was Johnny Horton, whose version of 'Battle Of New Orleans' stayed one solitary week in the British charts.

1959 saw a brief return of three heroes of the early 1950s, and at one time the charts almost contained all three at once. Frankie Laine galloped back with 'Rawhide', Guy Mitchell sang 'Heartaches By The Number', and Johnny Ray almost entered the Top Twenty with one of his best-ever, but unrecognised, discs called 'I'll Never Fall In Love Again'.

The early 1960s Trad Jazz boom in the charts was given its first breath of life in 1959 with 'Petite Fleur' by Chris Barber. The year's classics included 'To Know Him Is To Love Him' from The Teddy Bears, 'Dream Lover' by Bobby Darin, 'Here Comes Summer' from Jerry Keller, and Johnny and The Hurricanes' 'Red River Rock'. The most unexpected hit was 'A Pub With No Beer' from the Australian singer, Slim Dusty.

JANUARY 1960

9		16	23	30
1 What Do You Want To Make Those Eyes At Me For?				
Emile Ford (Pye)		1	3	5
2 What Do You Want Adam Faith (Parlophone)		2	4	7
3 Oh! Carol Neil Sedaka (RCA)	—	3	5	8
4 Seven Little Girls Sitting In The Back Seat The Avons				
(Columbia)		7	11	–
5 Johnny Staccato Theme Elmer Bernstein (Capitol)		5	6	12
6 Little White Bull Tommy Steele (Decca)		6	8	9
7 Bad Boy Marty Wilde (Philips)		8	14	19
8 Reveille Rock Johnny and The Hurricanes (London)		10	14	–
9 Travellin' Light Cliff Richard (Columbia)		14	–	–
10 Some Kind-A-Earthquake Duane Eddy (London)		13	17	–
11 Rawhide Frankie Laine (Philips)		15	12	17
12 Red River Rock Johnny and The Hurricanes (London)		20	–	–
13 Snow Coach Russ Conway (Columbia)		–	–	–
14 Starry-Eyed Michael Holliday (Columbia)		4	2	2
15 Teen Beat Sandy Nelson (Top Rank)		16	–	–
16 Be My Guest Fats Domino (London)		12	–	15
17 Among My Souvenirs Connie Francis (MGM)		17	–	–
18 More And More Party Pops Russ Conway (Columbia)		–	–	–
19 Too Good Little Tony (Decca)		19	13	13
20 Way Down Yonder Freddie Cannon (Top Rank)		9	7	4
– Why? Anthony Newley (Decca)		10	1	1
– In The Mood Ernie Fields (London)		18	–	–
– Heartaches By The Number Guy Mitchell (Philips)		–	9	6
– A Voice In The Wilderness Cliff Richard (Columbia)		–	10	3
– Expresso Bongo (E.P.) Cliff Richard (Columbia)		–	16	10
– Summer Set Acker Bilk (Columbia)		–	18	11
– Dance With Me The Drifters (London)		–	19	18
– Why? Frankie Avalon (HMV)		–	20	15
– Pretty Blue Eyes Craig Douglas (Top Rank)		–	–	14
– El Paso Marty Robbins (Fontana)		–	–	20

The chart for 2 January was a repeat of that for the last week in 1959.

FEBRUARY 1960

6	13	20	27
1 Why? Anthony Newley (Decca)	1	1	1
2 A Voice In The Wilderness Cliff Richard (Columbia)	2	2	3
3 Starry-Eyed Michael Holliday (Columbia)	3	7	11
4 Way Down Yonder Freddie Cannon (Top Rank)	4	4	4
5 Heartaches By The Number Guy Mitchell (Philips)	6	10	20
6 Poor Me Adam Faith (Parlophone)	5	3	2
7 What Do You Want To Make Those Eyes At Me For?			
Emile Ford (Pye)	9	11	18
8 Expresso Bongo (E.P.) Cliff Richard (Columbia)	16	–	–
9 Pretty Blue Eyes Craig Douglas (Top Rank)	7	5	6
10 Summer Set Acker Bilk (Columbia)	13	13	14
11 What Do You Want Adam Faith (Parlophone)	11	19	–
12 Oh! Carol Neil Sedaka (RCA)	19	–	–
13 Little White Bull Tommy Steele (Decca)	–	–	–
14 Beyond The Sea Bobby Darin (London)	10	9	8
15 Johnny Staccato Theme Elmer Bernstein (Columbia)	20	–	–
16 Misty Johnny Mathis (Fontana)	14	17	13
17 El Paso Marty Robbins (Fontana)	–	–	–

	13	20	27
18 Why? *Frankie Avalon* (HMV)	–	–	–
19 Be My Guest *Fats Domino* (London)	17	18	–
20 Harbour Lights *The Platters* (Mercury)	14	12	16
20 Slow Boat To China *Emile Ford* (Pye)	8	6	7
– Running Bear *Johnny Preston* (Mercury)	12	8	5
– You Got What It Takes *Marv Johnson* (London)	18	15	12
– Rawhide *Frankie Laine* (Philips)	20	–	–
– Be Mine *Lance Fortune* (Columbia)	–	14	10
– Bonnie Came Back *Duane Eddy* (London)	–	16	9
– Happy Anniversary *Joan Regan* (HMV)	–	20	–
– Royal Event *Russ Conway* (Columbia)	–	–	14
– Who Could Be Bluer *Jerry Lordan* (Parlophone)	–	–	17
– Delaware *Perry Como* (RCA)	–	–	19

MARCH 1960

5	12	19	26
1 Poor Me *Adam Faith* (Parlophone)	2	2	4
2 Running Bear *Johnny Preston* (Mercury)	1	1	2
3 Why? *Anthony Newley* (Decca)	6	7	8
4 A Voice In The Wilderness *Cliff Richard* (Columbia)	5	11	13
5 Slow Boat To China *Emile Ford* (Pye)	4	8	10
6 Way Down Yonder *Freddie Cannon* (Top Rank)	10	–	–
7 Delaware *Perry Como* (RCA),	3	3	3
8 Pretty Blue Eyes *Craig Douglas* (Top Rank)	8	9	18
9 Be Mine *Lance Fortune* (Pye)	7	5	11
10 Beyond The Sea *Bobby Darin* (London)	15	–	–
11 Summer Set *Acker Bilk* (Columbia)	11	13	–
12 Bonnie Came Back *Duane Eddy* (London)	19	–	–
13 Theme From A Summer Place *Percy Faith* (Philips)	12	5	5
14 You Got What It Takes *Marv Johnson* (London)	9	4	6
15 Royal Event *Russ Conway* (Columbia)	16	19	–
16 Who Could Be Bluer *Jerry Lordan* (Parlophone)	14	16	15
17 Harbour Lights *The Platters* (Mercury)	–	–	–
18 Starry-Eyed *Michael Holliday* (Columbia)	–	–	–
19 California Here I Come *Freddie Cannon* (Top Rank)	20	–	–
20 Hit And Miss *The John Barry Seven* (Columbia)	16	12	19
20 What In The World's Come Over You *Jack Scott* (Top Rank)	13	10	7
– Colette *Billy Fury* (London)	18	18	–
– Beatnik Fly *Johnny and The Hurricanes* (London)	–	14	12
– Fings Ain't What They Used To Be *Max Bygraves* (Decca)	–	15	14
– Handyman *Jimmy Jones* (MGM)	–	17	17
– Wild One *Bobby Rydell* (Columbia)	–	20	20
– My Old Man's A Dustman *Lonnie Donegan* (Pye)	–	–	1
– Fall In Love With You *Cliff Richard* (Columbia)	–	–	9
– Do You Mind? *Anthony Newley* (Decca)	–	–	16

APRIL 1960

2	9	16	23	30
1 My Old Man's A Dustman *Lonnie Donegan* (Pye)	1	1	1	7
2 Running Bear *Johnny Preston* (Mercury)	4	8	16	–
3 Fall In Love With You *Cliff Richard* (Columbia)	2	3	3	4
4 Theme From A Summer Place *Percy Faith* (Philips)	6	7	11	13
5 Delaware *Perry Como* (RCA)	10	11	–	–
6 What In The World's Come Over You *Jack Scott* (Top Rank)	11	18	–	18
7 Fings Ain't What They Used To Be *Max Bygraves* (Decca)	8	6	9	12
8 Poor Me *Adam Faith* (Parlophone)	15	–	–	–

	9	16	23	30
9 Handy man *Jimmy Jones* (MGM)	3	4	5	5
10 Do You Mind? *Anthony Newley* (Decca)	7	5	4	2
11 You Got What It Takes *Marv Johnson* (London)	14	15	–	–
12 Beatnik Fly *Johnny and The Hurricanes* (London)	9	9	12	14
13 Wild One *Bobby Rydell* (Columbia)	12	13	18	19
14 Hit And Miss *The John Barry Seven* (Columbia)	–	20	19	–
15 Who Could Be Bluer *Jerry Lordan* (Parlophone)	–	–	–	–
16 Slow Boat To China *Emile Ford* (Pye)	20	–	–	–
16 Why? *Anthony Newley* (Decca)	–	–	–	–
18 Willie And The Hand Jive *Cliff Richard* (Columbia)	–	–	–	–
19 Clementine *Bobby Darin* (London)	13	14	13	19
20 Summer Set *Acker Bilk* (Columbia)	19	–	–	–
– Stuck On You *Elvis Presley* (RCA)	5	2	2	6
– Looking High, High, High *Bryan Johnson* (Decca)	17	–	–	–
– Country Boy *Fats Domino* (London)	18	–	–	–
– Sweet Nuthin's *Brenda Lee* (Brunswick)	20	10	8	8
– Someone Else's Baby *Adam Faith* (Parlophone)	–	12	7	3
– Cathy's Clown *The Everly Brothers* (Warner Bros.)	–	16	6	1
– Footsteps *Steve Lawrence* (HMV)	–	17	10	11
– He'll Have To Go *Jim Reeves* (RCA)	–	19	15	16
– Standing On The Corner *The King Brothers* (Parlophone)	–	–	14	9
– Ooh! La La *Keith Kelly* (Parlophone)	–	–	17	17
– Heart Of A Teenage Girl *Craig Douglas* (Top Rank)	–	–	20	15
– Shazam *Duane Eddy* (London)	–	–	–	10

MAY 1960

	7	14	21	28
1 Cathy's Clown *The Everly Brothers* (Warner Bros.)		1	1	1
2 Do You Mind? *Anthony Newley* (Decca)		3	3	8
3 Someone Else's Baby *Adam Faith* (Parlophone)		2	2	3
4 Fall In Love With You *Cliff Richard* (Columbia)		6	7	11
5 Handyman *Jimmy Jones* (MGM)		5	6	7
6 Shazam *Duane Eddy* (London)		4	4	4
7 Sweet Nuthin's *Brenda Lee* (Brunswick)		7	8	5
8 Stuck On You *Elvis Presley* (RCA)		8	14	16
9 My Old Man's A Dustman *Lonnie Donegan* (Pye)		14	19	–
10 Standing On The Corner *The King Brothers* (Parlophone)		12	11	–
11 Footsteps *Steve Lawrence* (HMV)		13	10	9
12 Heart Of A Teenage Girl *Craig Douglas* (Top Rank)		10	12	14
13 Cradle Of Love *Johnny Preston* (Mercury)		9	5	2
14 Tease Me/Ooh! La La *Keith Kelly* (Parlophone)		17	13	17
15 Beatnik Fly *Johnny and The Hurricanes* (London)		15	16	–
16 Theme From A Summer Place *Percy Faith* (Philips)		16	18	–
17 He'll Have To Go *Jim Reeves* (RCA)		19	17	12
18 Fings Ain't What They Used To Be *Max Bygraves* (Decca)		–	–	–
19 Greenfields *The Brothers Four* (Philips)		–	–	–
20 Kookie-Kookie *Ed Byrnes* (Warner Bros.)		–	–	–
20 Mack The Knife *Ella Fitzgerald* (HMV)		–	–	–
– Three Steps To Heaven *Eddie Cochran* (London)		11	9	6
– Let The Little Girl Dance *Billy Bland* (London)		18	–	–
– Stairway To Heaven *Neil Sedaka* (RCA)		20	–	13
– Mama/Robot Man *Connie Francis* (MGM)		–	15	10
– Sixteen Reasons *Connie Stevens* (Warner Bros.)		–	20	–
– I Wanna Go Home *Lonnie Donegan* (Pye)		–	–	15
– The Urge *Freddie Cannon* (Top Rank)		–	–	18
– Lucky Five *Russ Conway* (Columbia)		–	–	19
– That's You *Nat 'King' Cole* (Capitol)		–	–	20

JUNE 1960

4		11	18	25
1	Cathy's Clown *The Everly Brothers* (Warner Bros.)	1	1	1
2	Cradle Of Love *Johnny Preston* (Mercury)	2	4	6
3	Shazam *Duane Eddy* (London)	7	7	13
4	Handyman *Jimmy Jones* (MGM)	5	6	7
5	Sweet Nuthin's *Brenda Lee* (Brunswick)	6	8	14
6	Three Steps To Heaven *Eddie Cochran* (London)	3	3	3
7	Mama/Robot Man *Connie Francis* (MGM)	3	2	2
8	Someone Else's Baby *Adam Faith* (Parlophone)	11	–	–
9	I Wanna Go Home *Lonnie Donegan* (Pye)	8	5	8
10	Footsteps *Steve Lawrence* (HMV)	10	–	–
11	Lucky Five *Russ Conway* (Columbia)	9	12	–
12	Heart Of A Teenage Girl *Craig Douglas* (Top Rank)	15	–	–
13	Stairway To Heaven *Neil Sedaka* (RCA)	16	14	17
14	Do You Mind? *Anthony Newley* (Decca)	–	–	–
15	He'll Have To Go *Jim Reeves* (RCA)	14	11	11
16	Fall In Love With You *Cliff Richard* (Columbia)	–	–	–
17	That's You *Nat 'King' Cole* (Capitol)	19	19	19
18	The Urge *Freddie Cannon* (Top Rank)	–	–	–
19	Sixteen Reasons *Connie Stevens* (Warner Bros.)	17	12	12
20	Let The Little Girl Dance *Billy Bland* (London)	–	–	–
–	Ain't Misbehavin' *Tommy Bruce* (Columbia)	12	9	4
–	Down Yonder *Johnny and The Hurricanes* (London)	12	10	9
–	You'll Never Know What You're Missing Till You Try *Emile Ford* (Pye)	18	18	–
–	That's Love *Billy Fury* (Decca)	20	–	–
–	Good Timin' *Jimmy Jones* (MGM)	–	15	5
–	River Stay Away From My Door *Frank Sinatra* (Capitol)	–	16	16
–	Angela Jones *Michael Cox* (Triumph)	–	17	10
–	Pistol Packing Mama *Gene Vincent* (Capitol)	–	20	15
–	Made You/When Johnny Comes Marching Home *Adam Faith* (Parlophone)	–	–	18
–	Talkin' Army Blues *Josh McCrae* (Top Rank)	–	–	20

JULY 1960

2		9	16	23	30
1	Good Timin' *Jimmy Jones* (MGM)	1	1	1	2
2	Mama/Robot Man *Connie Francis* (MGM)	6	7	8	9
3	Three Steps To Heaven *Eddie Cochran* (London)	8	9	15	19
4	Ain't Misbehavin' *Tommy Bruce* (Columbia)	4	5	6	8
5	Cathy's Clown *The Everly Brothers* (Warner Bros.)	10	12	20	–
6	What A Mouth *Tommy Steele* (Decca)	5	7	9	13
7	Please Don't Tease *Cliff Richard* (Columbia)	2	2	2	1
8	Made You/When Johnny Comes Marching Home *Adam Faith* (Parlophone)	3	4	4	7
9	Angela Jones *Michael Cox* (Triumph)	9	8	10	18
10	Shakin' All Over *Johnny Kidd* (HMV)	6	3	3	3
11	Handyman *Jimmy Jones* (MGM)	13	–	–	–
12	Cradle Of Love *Johnny Preston* (Mercury)	–	–	–	–
13	I Wanna Go Home *Lonnie Donegan* (Pye)	16	15	17	–
13	Down Yonder *Johnny and The Hurricanes* (London)	12	16	–	–
15	He'll Have To Go *Jim Reeves* (RCA)	15	17	–	17
16	Sixteen Reason *Connie Stevens* (Warner Bros.)	18	–	–	–
17	Pistol Packing Mama *Gene Vincent* (Capitol)	11	19	–	–
18	Shazam *Duane Eddy* (London)	–	–	–	–
19	Talkin' Army Blues *Josh McCrae* (Top Rank)	14	18	16	15
20	Sweet Nuthin's *Brenda Lee* (Brunswick)	20	–	–	–

2	9	16	23	30
– Look For A Star *Gary Mills* (Top Rank)	17	10	5	6
– I'm Sorry *Brenda Lee* (Brunswick)	19	11	14	15
– Yellow Polka Dot Bikini *Brian Hyland* (London)	–	13	12	14
– When Will I Be Loved *The Everly Brothers* (Warner Bros.)	–	14	7	5
– Elvis Is Back (L.P.) *Elvis Presley* (RCA)	–	20	–	–
– If She Should Come To You *Anthony Newley* (Decca)	–	–	11	12
– Because They're Young *Duane Eddy* (London)	–	–	13	11
– Love Is Like A Violin *Ken Dodd* (Columbia)	–	–	18	–
– Apache *The Shadows* (Columbia)	–	–	19	10
– The Girl Of My Best Friend *Elvis Presley* (RCA)	–	–	–	4
– Tie Me Kangaroo Down Sport *Rolf Harris* (Columbia)	–	–	–	20

AUGUST 1960

6	13	20	27
1 Please Don't Tease *Cliff Richard* (Columbia)	1	2	2
2 The Girl Of My Best Friend *Elvis Presley* (RCA)	3	3	3
3 Shakin' All Over *Johnny Kidd* (HMV)	4	6	6
4 Good Timin' *Jimmy Jones* (MGM)	7	11	–
5 Apache *The Shadows* (Columbia)	2	1	1
6 When Will I Be Loved *The Everly Brothers* (Warner Bros.)	5	4	5
7 Because They're Young *Duane Eddy* (London)	6	5	4
8 If She Should Come To You *Anthony Newley* (Decca)	9	7	8
9 Look For A Star *Gary Mills* (Top Rank)	11	17	20
10 Yellow Polka Dot Bikini *Brian Hyland* (London)	10	9	11
11 Made You/Johnny Comes Marching Home *Adam Faith* (Parlophone)	13	–	–
12 Tie Me Kangaroo Down Sport *Rolf Harris* (Columbia)	8	8	7
13 Talkin' Army Blues *Josh McCrae* (Top Rank)	12	14	13
14 I'm Sorry *Brenda Lee* (Brunswick)	18	10	10
15 Mama/Robot Man *Connie Francis* (MGM)	19	–	–
16 What A Mouth *Tommy Steele* (Decca)	14	–	–
17 Ain't Misbehavin' *Tommy Bruce* (Columbia)	15	–	–
18 Listen Little Girl *Keith Kelly* (Parlophone)	16	15	19
19 Love Is Like A Violin *Ken Dodd* (Decca)	19	20	15
20 Paper Roses *The Kaye Sisters* (Philips)	16	13	18
20 As Long As He Needs Me *Shirley Bassey* (Columbia)	–	20	–
– Everybody's Somebody's Fool *Connie Francis* (MGM)	–	12	9
– Please Help Me, I'm Falling *The Brook Brothers* (Top Rank)	–	16	–
– Only The Lonely *Roy Orbison* (London)	–	17	14
– Lorelei *Lonnie Donegan* (Pye)	–	–	12
– Tell Laura I Love Her *Ricky Valance* (Columbia)	–	–	15
– Image Of A Girl *Mark Wynter* (Decca)	–	–	17

SEPTEMBER 1960

3	10	17	24
1 Apache *The Shadows* (Columbia)	1	1	1
2 Because They're Young *Duane Eddy* (London)	3	3	5
3 The Girl Of My Best Friend *Elvis Presley* (RCA)	2	2	2
4 Please Don't Tease *Cliff Richard* (Columbia)	4	3	9
5 When Will I Be Loved *The Everly Brothers* (Warner Bros.)	6	7	14
6 Everybody's Somebody's Fool *Connie Francis* (MGM)	7	9	8
7 Shakin' All Over *Johnny Kidd* (HMV)	10	16	–
8 If She Should Come To You *Anthony Newley* (Decca)	11	19	–
9 Tie Me Kangaroo Down Sport *Rolf Harris* (Columbia)	14	20	–
10 Tell Laura I Love Her *Ricky Valance* (Columbia)	5	4	3
11 Lorelei *Lonnie Donegan* (Pye)	–	–	–

3

	10	**17**	**24**
12 Only The Lonely *Roy Orbison* (London)	8	6	4
13 Love Is Like A Violin *Ken Dodd* (Columbia)	12	15	–
14 I'm Sorry *Brenda Lee* (Brunswick)	–	–	–
15 Yellow Polka Dot Bikini *Brian Hyland* (London)	–	–	–
16 Talkin' Army Blues *Josh McCrae* (Top Rank)	–	17	–
17 As Long As He Needs Me *Shirley Bassey* (Columbia)	9	8	12
18 Caribbean Honeymoon *Frank Weir* (Oriole)	20	18	20
19 Paper Roses *The Kaye Sisters* (Philips)	15	10	15
20 Image Of A Girl *Mark Wynter* (Decca)	19	11	19
– How About That *Adam Faith* (Parlophone)	–	12	6
– Walk, Don't Run *The Ventures* (Top Rank)	–	14	10
– Nice 'n' Easy *Frank Sinatra* (Capitol)	–	20	–
– Nine Times Out Of Ten *Cliff Richard* (Columbia)	–	–	7
– So Sad/Lucille *The Everly Brothers* (Warner Bros.)	–	–	10
– Fish Man *Ian Menzies* (Pye)	–	–	16
– Walk, Don't Run *The John Barry Seven* (Columbia)	–	–	17
– I'll Be Your Hero/Jet Black Machine *Vince Taylor* (Palette)	–	–	18
– Please Help Me I'm Falling *Hank Locklin* (RCA)	13	13	13

For an unknown reason a chart was not published for 10 September 1960 in Record Mirror, so those figures which appear under 10 September column were published as the 'last week' figures for 17 September 1960.

OCTOBER 1960

1

	8	**15**	**22**	**29**
1 Tell Laura I Love Her *Ricky Valance* (Columbia)	1	2	3	5
2 Nine Times Out Of Ten *Cliff Richard* (Columbia)	3	4	6	7
3 Only The Lonely *Roy Orbison* (London)	2	1	1	1
4 How About That *Adam Faith* (Parlophone)	4	3	2	3
5 Apache *The Shadows* (Columbia)	7	10	13	16
6 The Girl Of My Best Friend/A Mess Of Blues *Elvis Presley* (RCA)	6	7	10	12
7 So Sad/Lucille *The Everly Brothers* (Warner Bros.)	5	5	5	4
8 Because They're Young *Duane Eddy* (London)	11	14	–	–
9 Walk, Don't Run *The Ventures* (Top Rank)	8	9	11	15
10 Please Help Me I'm Falling *Hank Locklin* (RCA)	10	12	14	17
11 Walk, Don't Run *The John Barry Seven* (Columbia)	9	8	7	10
12 Everybody's Somebody's Fool *Connie Francis* (MGM)	14	15	17	–
13 Image Of A Girl *Mark Wynter* (Decca)	18	–	–	–
14 As Long As He Needs Me *Shirley Bassey* (Columbia)	12	6	4	2
15 Fish Man *Ian Menzies* (Philips)	15	–	–	–
16 I'll Be Your Hero/Jet Black Machine *Vince Taylor* (Palette)	17	15	–	–
17 Please Don't Tease *Cliff Richard* (Columbia)	–	–	–	–
18 Let's Think About Living *Bob Luman* (Warner Bros.)	13	13	8	8
19 Chain Gang *Sam Cooke* (RCA)	16	11	9	11
20 When Will I Be Loved *The Everly Brothers* (Warner Bros.)	–	–	–	–
– Lonely/Sweetie Pie *Eddie Cochran* (London)	19	–	–	–
– Along Came Caroline *Michael Cox* (HMV)	20	20	–	–
– My Love For You *Johnny Mathis* (Fontana)	20	–	–	–
– McDonald's Cave *The Piltdown Men* (Capitol)	–	17	15	14
– Restless *Johnny Kidd* (HMV)	–	18	–	18
– Dreaming *Johnny Burnette* (London)	–	19	12	9
– Shortnin' Bread *The Viscounts* (Pye)	–	–	16	13
– Rocking Goose *Johnny and The Hurricanes* (London)	–	–	18	6
– Never On Sunday *Lyn Cornell* (Decca)	–	–	18	20
– Them There Eyes *Emile Ford* (Pye)	–	–	20	–
– Save The Last Dance For Me *The Drifters* (London)	–	–	–	18
– Top Teen Baby *Gary Mills* (Top Rank)	–	–	–	20

NOVEMBER 1960

5		12	19	26
1	It's Now Or Never *Elvis Presley* (RCA)	1	1	1
2	Only The Lonely *Roy Orbison* (London)	2	4	9
3	As Long As He Needs Me *Shirley Bassey* (Columbia)	3	5	6
4	Rocking Goose *Johnny and The Hurricanes* (London)	4	3	3
5	Nine Times Out Of Ten *Cliff Richard* (Columbia)	8	15	–
6	So Sad/Lucille *The Everly Brothers* (Warner Bros.)	11	–	–
7	Let's Think About Living *Bob Luman* (Warner Bros.)	9	11	16
8	Dreaming *Johnny Burnette* (London)	6	8	8
9	How About That *Adam Faith* (Parlophone)	15	20	–
10	Walk, Don't Run *The John Barry Seven* (Columbia)	17	18	–
11	Tell Laura I Love Her *Ricky Valance* (Columbia)	–	–	–
12	Chain Gang *Sam Cooke* (RCA)	14	–	–
13	My Heart Has A Mind Of Its Own *Connie Francis* (HMV)	5	2	5
14	My Love For You *Johnny Mathis* (Fontana)	–	16	–
15	McDonald's Cave *The Piltdown Men* (Capitol)	13	12	–
16	Please Help Me I'm Falling *Hank Locklin* (RCA)	18	–	–
16	Save The Last Dance For Me *The Drifters* (London)	7	6	4
18	Blue Angel/Today's Tear-Drops *Roy Orbison* (London)	16	13	15
19	Shortnin' Bread *The Viscounts* (Pye)	19	–	–
20	Mr Custer *Charlie Drake* (Parlophone)	20	14	17
20	The Girl Of My Best Friend/A Mess of Blues *Elvis Presley* (RCA)	–	–	–
–	Man Of Mystery *The Shadows* (Columbia)	10	7	2
–	Kommotion *Duane Eddy* (London)	12	10	12
–	Goodness Gracious Me *Peter Sellers and Sophia Loren* (Parlophone)	–	9	7
–	Milord *Edith Piaf* (Columbia)	–	17	19
–	Sorry Robbie *Bert Weedon* (Top Rank)	–	18	–
–	Lively *Lonnie Donegan* (Pye)	–	–	10
–	Strawberry Fair *Anthony Newley* (Decca)	–	–	11
–	Little Donkey *Nina and Frederik* (Columbia)	–	–	13
–	Ole McDonald *Frank Sinatra* (Capitol)	–	–	14
–	Wild Side Of Life *Josh McCrae* (Pye)	–	–	18
–	Poetry In Motion *Johnny Tilliston* (London)	–	–	20

DECEMBER 1960

3		10	17–24	31
1	It's Now Or Never *Elvis Presley* (RCA)	1	1	1
2	Save The Last Dance For Me *The Drifters* (London)	2	2	3
3	Man Of Mystery/The Stranger *The Shadows* (Columbia)	5	11	12
4	Strawberry Fair *Anthony Newley* (Decca)	3	4	5
5	Goodness Gracious Me *Peter Sellers and Sophia Loren* (Parlophone)	7	7	8
6	Rocking Goose *Johnny and The Hurricanes* (London)	8	8	11
7	My Heart Has A Mind Of Its Own *Connie Francis* (MGM)	11	13	–
8	I Love You *Cliff Richard* (Columbia)	4	3	2
9	As Long As He Needs Me *Shirley Bassey* (Columbia)	12	–	–
10	Little Donkey *Nina and Frederik* (Columbia)	6	5	6
11	Dreaming *Johnny Burnette* (London)	14	14	–
12	Poetry In Motion *Johnny Tilliston* (London)	9	6	4
13	Gurney Slade *Max Harris* (Fontana)	10	10	10
14	Ole McDonald *Frank Sinatra* (Capitol)	17	15	–
15	Lively *Lonnie Donegan* (Pye)	–	18	18
16	My Love For You *Johnny Mathis* (Fontana)	18	20	20
17	Wild Side Of Life *Josh McCrae* (Pye)	15	16	16
18	Blue Angel/Today's Tear-Drops *Roy Orbison* (London)	18	–	–

58

3

	10	17–24	31
19 Kicking Up The Leaves *Mark Wynter* (Decca)	–	–	–
20 Only The Lonely *Roy Orbison* (London)	–	–	–
– Lonely Pup *Adam Faith* (Parlophone)	13	9	7
– Perfidia *The Ventures* (London)	16	12	9
– Time Will Tell *Ian Gregory* (Pye)	20	17	19
– You Talk Too Much *Johnny Carson* (Fontana)	–	18	–
– Strawberry Blonde *Frank D'Rone* (Mercury)	–	–	13
– Ten Swinging Bottles *Pete Chester and The Chesternuts* (Pye)	–	–	14
– Pepe *Russ Conway* (Columbia)	–	–	15
– Portrait Of My Love *Matt Monro* (Parlophone)	–	–	17
– It's You That I Love *Marion Ryan* (Pye)	–	–	20

There was no Record Mirror for 24 December 1960.

59

1960

1960 was the year of the 'Itsy Bitsy Teeny Weeny Yellow Polka Dot Bikini', 'Beatnik Fly', 'Tie Me Kangaroo Down Sport', 'Even More Party Pops' and 'Ooh! La La'. Such a list is hardly likely to excite any pop connoisseur.

However, the year was a good one for such artists as The King Brothers, who finally made the charts once more with their cover version of The Four Lads' American hit 'Standing On The Corner'. The Kaye Sisters, noble assistants to several Frankie Vaughan hits, had their only Top Twenty hit in their own right with 'Paper Roses'. Johnny Kidd stirred females with his swashbuckling image and his first-ever Hit Parade successes with 'Shakin' All Over' and 'Restless'. The wait for further triumph for Kidd was long.

Gary Mills enjoyed brief fame with two hits, 'Look For A Star' and 'Top Teen Baby'. Johnny Mathis had his fifth and sixth hits, but then had to wait until 1975 for his next one. Ricky Valance had his one and only taste of fame in 1960 with 'Tell Laura I Love Her', and this record sparked off some predictions that there would be a spate of 'death' discs. However, four years were to pass until Twinkle's 'Terry' and 'Leader Of The Pack' from The Shangri-Las.

Freddie Cannon must have wondered what had happened to his chart career after his 1958 smash hit 'Tallahassie Lassie', particularly as he had ousted Tommy Steele's version of the same song from the top listings. However, 1960 saw a short but happy comeback for Cannon, as no less than three of his records made the Top Twenty throughout the year, starting with 'Way Down Yonder In New Orleans'.

Max Bygraves saw a nine-hit run end with 'Fings Ain't What They Used To Be', while Gene Vincent's chart career also came to an end with 'Pistol Packing Mama'. But if some stars disappeared, as always, newcomers saw a career of sorts begin. There was Mark Wynter embarking on his six-hit disc career with 'Image Of A Girl', and The Shadows began their careers in their own right without Cliff Richard. 'Apache' and 'Man Of Mystery' began their hit trail, and a year later they achieved four more hits. They had begun as The Drifters, and had to change this name to avoid confusion with the American band of the same name. They then changed it to The Shadows and learned that they now had the same name as Bobby Vee's American band, but they ignored *that* problem!

For some chart-established artists, life was good. Cliff Richard had no less than six hits; The Everly Brothers had four; and four hits were achieved by Duane Eddy. Adam Faith, with five hit records, almost equalled the amazing success of Cliff Richard, but Billy Fury remained comparatively quiet with only two hits.

Pat Boone did not appear in the 1960 charts, following his hit trail which had begun in 1955. However, he did have hits to come in 1961 and 1962.

For Frankie Laine it was goodbye with 'Rawhide', the fast-moving cowboy song of 1959, for after 1960 Laine did not appear in the charts again, in spite of continuing popularity into the 1970s.

In terms of success, then, 1960 belonged to Cliff Richard – with or without his Shadows.

JANUARY 1961

7		**14**	**21**	**28**
1	Poetry In Motion *Johnny Tilliston* (London)	1	1	2
2	Save The Last Dance For Me *The Drifters* (London)	3	5	12
3	I Love You *Cliff Richard* (Columbia)	2	3	4
4	It's Now Or Never *Elvis Presley* (RCA)	4	9	14
5	Lonely Pup *Adam Faith* (Parlophone)	10	–	–
6	Perifidia *The Ventures* (London)	5	8	15
7	Strawberry Fair *Anthony Newley* (Decca)	–	–	–
8	Man Of Mystery/The Stranger *The Shadows* (Columbia)	18	–	–
9	Counting Teardrops *Emile Ford* (Pye)	6	7	8
9	Goodness Gracious Me *Peter Sellers and Sophia Loren* (Parlophone)	11	16	–
11	Little Donkey *Nina and Frederik* (Columbia)	–	–	–
12	Portrait Of My Love *Matt Monro* (Parlophone)	7	6	5
13	Wild Side Of Life *Josh McCrae* (Pye)	–	–	–
14	Rocking Goose *Johnny and The Hurricanes* (London)	19	–	–
15	Strawberry Blonde *Frank D'Rone* (Mercury)	–	–	–
16	Ten Swinging Bottles *Pete Chester* (Pye)	–	–	–
17	Little Girl *Marty Wilde* (Philips)	20	20	20
18	Blue Angel *Roy Orbison* (London)	17	–	–
19	Stay *Maurice Williams* (Top Rank)	13	12	11
20	Buona Sera *Acker Bilk* (Columbia)	9	10	13
20	Like Strangers *The Everly Brothers* (London)	12	17	–
–	Pepe *Duane Eddy* (London)	8	4	3
–	Sway *Bobby Rydell* (Columbia)	14	18	–
–	Black Stockings *The John Barry Seven* (Columbia)	15	–	–
–	Piltdown Rides Again *The Piltdown Men* (London)	15	13	18
–	Are You Lonesome Tonight *Elvis Presley* (RCA)	–	2	1
–	You're Sixteen *Johnny Burnette* (London)	–	11	9
–	Pepe *Russ Conway* (Columbia)	–	14	–
–	North To Alaska *Johnny Horton* (Philips)	–	15	16
–	Chariot *Rhet Stoller* (Decca)	–	19	–
–	Rubber Ball *Bobby Vee* (London)	–	20	7
–	Sailor *Petula Clark* (Pye)	–	–	6
–	Rubber Ball *Marty Wilde* (Philips)	–	–	10
–	Many Years Ago *Connie Francis* (MGM)	–	–	17
–	Sailor *Anne Shelton* (Philips)	–	–	19
–	First Taste Of Love *Ben E. King* (London)	–	–	20

FEBRUARY 1961

4		**11**	**18**	**25**
1	Are You Lonesome Tonight *Elvis Presley* (RCA)	1	1	2
2	Sailor *Petula Clark* (Pye)	2	2	3
3	Pepe *Duane Eddy* (London)	4	9	12
4	Rubber Ball *Bobby Vee* (London)	3	5	7
5	Poetry In Motion *Johnny Tilliston* (London)	6	11	–
6	You're Sixteen *Johnny Burnette* (London)	5	6	11
7	Portrait Of My Love *Matt Monro* (Parlophone)	9	14	–
8	Sailor *Anne Shelton* (Philips)	7	10	15
9	Counting Teardrops *Emile Ford* (Pye)	13	–	–
10	Rubber Ball *Marty Wilde* (Philips)	10	–	16
11	I Love You *Cliff Richard* (Columbia)	17	18	–
12	Stay *Maurice Williams* (Top Rank)	–	–	–
13	Many Tears Ago *Connie Francis* (MGM)	–	–	–
14	Pepe *Russ Conway* (Columbia)	18	–	–
15	North To Alaska *Johnny Horton* (Philips)	19	–	–
16	Messing About On The River *Josh McCrae* (Pye)	16	15	–

4	11	18	25
17 First Taste Of Love *Ben E. King* (London)	–	16	–
18 Buona Sera *Acker Bilk* (Columbia)	11	12	14
19 It's Now Or Never *Elvis Presley* (RCA)	–	–	–
20 Calendar Girl *Neil Sedaka* (RCA)	20	13	10
– F.B.I. *The Shadows* (Columbia)	8	4	4
– Walk Right Back *The Everly Brothers* (Warner Bros.)	12	3	1
– Will You Love Me Tomorrow *The Shirelles* (Top Rank)	14	8	5
– Who Am I? /This Is It *Adam Faith* (Parlophone)	15	7	6
– Riders In The Sky *The Ramrods* (London)	–	17	8
– Pepy's Diary/Gather In The Mushrooms *Benny Hill* (Pye)	–	19	13
– Calcutta *Lawrence Welk* (London)	–	19	–
– Are You Sure? *The Allisons* (Fontana)	–	–	9
– Let's Jump The Broomstick *Brenda Lee* (Brunswick)	–	–	17
– Ja-Da *Johnny and The Hurricanes* (London)	–	–	17
– Wheels *The String-A-Longs* (London)	–	–	19
– New Orleans *The U.S. Bonds* (Top Rank)	–	–	20

MARCH 1961

4	11	18	25
1 Walk Right Back/Ebony Eyes *The Everly Brothers* (Warner Bros.)	1	1	2
2 Are You Sure? *The Allisons* (Fontana)	2	3	3
3 Sailor *Petula Clark* (Pye)	6	10	13
4 Will You Love Me Tomorrow *The Shirelles* (Top Rank)	3	5	5
5 Are You Lonesome Tonight *Elvis Presley* (RCA)	11	–	–
6 F.B.I. *The Shadows* (Columbia)	7	6	10
7 Theme For A Dream *Cliff Richard* (Columbia)	4	4	4
8 Riders In The Sky *The Ramrods* (London)	8	7	8
9 Who Am I?/This Is It *Adam Faith* (Parlophone)	9	11	20
10 Rubber Ball *Bobby Vee* (London)	–	–	–
11 Calendar Girl *Neil Sedaka* (RCA)	10	13	15
12 Wheels *The String-A-Longs* (London)	16	12	12
13 Samantha *Kenny Ball* (Pye)	12	14	13
14 Ja-Da *Johnny and The Hurricanes* (London)	18	–	–
15 Let's Jump The Broomstick *Brenda Lee* (Brunswick)	15	–	–
16 Baby Sittin' Boogie *Buzz Clifford* (Philips)	19	19	17
17 Pepe *Duane Eddy* (London)	–	–	–
18 Pepy's Diary/Gather In The Mushrooms *Benny Hill* (Parlophone)	20	–	–
18 Dream Girl *Mark Wynter* (Decca)	14	15	–
20 You're Sixteen *Johnny Burnette* (London)	–	–	–
– And The Heavens Cried *Anthony Newley* (Decca)	–	16	11
– Lazy River *Bobby Darin* (London)	–	17	9
– Goodnight Mrs Flintstone *The Piltdown Men* (Capitol)	–	18	19
– Warpaint *The Brook Brothers* (Pye)	–	20	17
– Wooden Heart *Elvis Presley* (RCA)	5	2	1
– My Kind Of Girl *Matt Monro* (Parlophone)	13	9	7
– Exodus *Ferrante and Teicher* (London)	17	8	6
– Marry Me *Mike Preston* (Decca)	–	–	16

APRIL 1961

1	8	15	22	29
1 Wooden Heart *Elvis Presley* (RCA)	1	2	2	1
2 Walk Right Back/Ebony Eyes *The Everly Brothers* (Warner Bros.)	3	3	5	13
3 Are You Sure? *The Allisons* (Fontana)	2	1	1	4
4 Theme For A Dream *Cliff Richard* (Columbia)	4	6	6	17

63

1	8	15	22	29
5 My Kind Of Girl *Matt Monro* (Parlophone)	6	12	16	18
6 Lazy River *Bobby Darin* (London)	5	4	7	5
7 Exodus *Ferranti and Teicher* (London)	9	10	14	14
8 And The Heavens Cried *Anthony Newley* (Decca)	8	8	9	19
8 Will You Love Me Tomorrow *The Shirelles* (Top Rank)	12	16	15	–
10 Riders In The Sky *The Ramrods* (London)	16	20	–	–
11 F.B.I. *The Shadows* (Columbia)	10	5	8	–
12 Warpaint *The Brook Brothers* (Pye)	13	11	11	7
13 Where The Boys Are *Connie Francis* (MGM)	7	9	10	16
13 Marry Me *Mike Preston* (Decca)	15	–	–	–
15 African Waltz *Johnny Dankworth* (Columbia)	–	13	17	12
16 Baby Sittin' Boogie *Buzz Clifford* (Fontana)	17	18	19	20
17 Calendar Girl *Neil Sedaka* (RCA)	–	–	–	–
17 Samantha *Kenny Ball* (Pye)	13	18	18	–
19 Goodnight Mrs Flintstone *The Piltdown Men* (Capitol)	–	–	–	–
20 Gee Whiz It's You *Cliff Richard* (Columbia)	–	15	12	8
– You're Driving Me Crazy *The Temperance Seven* (Parlophone)	11	7	4	1
– Blue Moon *The Marcels* (Pye)	18	14	3	3
– Pony Time *Chubby Checker* (Columbia)	19	–	–	–
– Exodus *Mantovani* (Decca)	20	–	–	–
– A Hundred Pounds Of Clay *Craig Douglas* (Top Rank)	–	17	13	11
– Theme From Dixie *Duane Eddy* (London)	–	–	20	6
– Little Boy Sad *Johnny Burnette* (London)	–	–	20	15
– Don't Treat Me Like A Child *Helen Shapiro* (Columbia)	–	–	–	9
– On The Rebound *Floyd Cramer* (RCA)	–	–	–	10

MAY 1961

6	13	20	27
1 You're Driving Me Crazy *The Temperance Seven* (Parlophone)	2	2	8
2 Blue Moon *The Marcels* (Pye)	1	1	3
3 Wooden Heart *Elvis Presley* (RCA)	3	7	12
4 Don't Treat Me Like A Child *Helen Shapiro* (Columbia)	4	8	7
5 On The Rebound *Floyd Cramer* (RCA)	5	5	5
6 Warpaint *The Brook Brothers* (Pye)	11	18	–
7 Theme From Dixie *Duane Eddy* (London)	8	16	15
8 A Hundred Pounds Of Clay *Craig Douglas* (Top Rank)	10	13	16
9 Gee Whiz It's You *Cliff Richard* (Columbia)	17	11	–
10 Lazy River *Bobby Darin* (London)	19	20	–
11 African Waltz *Johnny Dankworth* (Columbia)	12	15	20
12 Are You Sure *The Allisons* (Fontana)	15	–	–
13 Little Boy Sad *Johnny Burnette* (London)	16	19	17
14 Runaway *Del Shannon* (London)	7	3	1
15 More Than I Can Say *Bobby Vee* (London)	6	6	6
16 Easy Going Me *Adam Faith* (Parlophone)	14	9	18
17 Exodus *Ferranti and Teicher* (London)	20	–	–
18 Walk Right Back/Ebony Eyes *The Everly Brothers* (Warner Bros.)	–	–	–
19 Where The Boys Are *Connie Francis* (MGM)	–	–	–
20 Baby Sittin' Boogie *Buzz Clifford* (Fontana)	–	–	–
– The Frightened City *The Shadows* (Columbia)	9	4	4
– What'd I Say? *Jerry Lee Lewis* (London)	13	10	11
– Have A Drink On Me *Lonnie Donegan* (Pye)	18	17	14
– But I Do *Clarence Frogman Henry* (Pye)	–	12	10
– You'll Never Know *Shirley Bassey* (Columbia)	–	14	9
– Little Devil *Neil Sedaka* (RCA)	–	–	13
– Surrender *Elvis Presley* (RCA)	–	–	1
– Travellin' Man *Ricky Nelson* (London)	–	–	19

JUNE 1961

3		10	17	24
1 Surrender *Elvis Presley* (RCA)		1	1	1
2 Runaway *Del Shannon* (London)		2	2	2
3 More Than I Can Say *Bobby Vee* (London)		5	6	14
4 The Frightened City *The Shadows* (Columbia)		4	3	5
5 Blue Moon *The Marcels* (Pye)		9	–	–
6 On The Rebound *Floyd Cramer* (RCA)		13	18	–
7 You'll Never Know *Shirley Bassey* (Columbia)		3	8	7
8 What'd I Say? *Jerry Lee Lewis* (London)		10	13	17
9 But I Do *Clarence Frogman Henry* (Pye)		6	5	8
10 Don't Treat Me Like A Child *Helen Shapiro* (Columbia)		11	17	–
11 Have A Drink On Me *Lonnie Donegan* (Pye)		7	12	15
12 Little Devil *Neil Sedaka* (RCA)		14	19	18
13 You're Driving Me Crazy *The Temperance Seven* (Parlophone)		17	–	–
14 Hello Mary Lou/Travellin' Man *Ricky Nelson* (London)		12	4	6
15 Wooden Heart *Elvis Presley* (RCA)		15	20	–
16 Easy Going Me *Adam Faith* (Parlophone)		–	–	–
17 African Waltz *Johnny Dankworth* (Columbia)		–	–	–
18 I Still Love You All *Kenny Ball* (Pye)		19	–	–
19 Runnin' Scared *Roy Orbison* (London)		16	16	13
20 Halfway To Paradise *Billy Fury* (Decca)		8	10	10
– Well I Ask You *Eden Kane* (Decca)		20	14	16
– I Told Every Little Star *Linda Scott* (Columbia)		18	9	11
– Pop Goes The Weasel/Bee-Bom *Anthony Newley* (Decca)		–	15	9
– Temptation *The Everly Brothers* (Warner Bros.)		–	11	3
– Pasadena *The Temperance Seven* (Parlophone)		–	7	4
– A Girl Like You *Cliff Richard* (Columbia)		–	–	12
– Weekend *Eddie Cochran* (London)		–	–	19
– Ring Of Fire *Duane Eddy* (London)		–	–	20

JULY 1961

1		8	15	22	29
1 Runaway *Del Shannon* (London)		2	2	4	4
2 Surrender *Elvis Presley* (RCA)		6	8	9	14
3 Temptation *The Everly Brothers* (Warner Bros.)		1	1	1	1
4 Pasadena *The Temperance Seven* (Parlophone)		4	7	7	8
5 A Girl Like You *Cliff Richard* (Columbia)		5	3	3	6
6 Hello MaryLou/Travellin' Man *Ricky Nelson* (London)		3	4	5	3
7 Halfway To Paradise *Billy Fury* (Decca)		7	6	6	5
8 But I Do *Clarence Frogman Henry* (Pye)		8	13	19	16
9 The Frightened City *The Shadows* (Columbia)		12	19	–	–
10 You'll Never Know *Shirley Bassey* (Columbia)		19	–	–	–
11 Pop Goes The Weasel *Anthony Newley* (Decca)		10	11	15	–
12 Runnin' Scared *Roy Orbison* (London)		11	9	12	17
13 Well I Ask You *Eden Kane* (Decca)		9	5	2	2
14 I Told Every Little Star *Linda Scott* (Columbia)		17	–	–	–
15 Little Devil *Neil Sedaka* (RCA)		–	–	–	–
16 Have A Drink On Me *Lonnie Donegan* (Pye)		18	–	–	–
17 More Than I Can Say *Bobby Vee* (London)		–	–	–	20
18 Marcheta *Karl Denver* (Decca)		20	–	–	–
19 Ring Of Fire *Duane Eddy* (London)		13	15	20	–
20 Weekend *Eddie Cochran* (London)		15	18	18	15
– Breakin' In A Brand New Heart *Connie Francis* (MGM)		14	–	–	–
– Time *Craig Douglas* (Top Rank)		16	20	11	11
– You Don't Know *Helen Shapiro* (Columbia)		–	10	8	7
– Old Smokie/High Voltage *Johnny and The Hurricanes* (London)		–	12	14	19

1			**8**	**15**	**22**	**29**
– Romeo *Petula Clark* (Pye)			–	14	13	10
– Baby I Don't Care/Valley Of Tears *Buddy Holly* (Coral)			–	16	16	13
– Moody River *Pat Boone* (London)			–	17	16	–
– You Always Hurt The One You Love *Clarence Frogman Henry* (Pye)			–	–	10	9
– Don't You Know It *Adam Faith* (Parlophone)			–	–	–	12
– Quarter To Three *The U.S. Bonds* (Top Rank)			–	–	–	18
– That's My Home *Acker Bilk* (Columbia)			–	–	–	20

AUGUST 1961

5	**12**	**19**	**26**
1 Well I Ask You *Eden Kane* (Decca)	2	2	3
2 You Don't Know *Helen Shapiro* (Columbia)	1	1	2
3 Temptation *The Everly Brothers* (Warner Bros.)	5	12	11
4 Halfway To Paradise *Billy Fury* (Decca)	4	4	5
5 Pasadena *The Temperance Seven* (Parlophone)	12	9	15
6 A Girl Like You *Cliff Richard* (Columbia)	10	7	7
7 Runaway *Del Shannon* (London)	7	14	17
8 Hello Mary Lou/Travellin' Man *Ricky Nelson* (London)	8	10	9
9 Romeo *Petula Clark* (Pye)	6	5	6
10 Don't You Know It *Adam Faith* (Parlophone)	14	15	12
11 You Always Hurt The One You Love *Clarence Frogman Henry* (Pye)	11	12	10
12 Time *Craig Douglas* (Top Rank)	9	8	8
13 Johnny Remember Me *John Leyton* (Top Rank)	3	3	1
14 Baby I Don't Care/Valley Of Tears *Buddy Holly* (Coral)	13	–	14
15 Weekend *Eddie Cochran* (London)	–	–	19
16 Quarter To Three *The U.S. Bonds* (Top Rank)	15	13	13
17 Marcheta *Karl Denver* (Decca)	16	–	16
18 Reach For The Stars/Climb Every Mountain *Shirley Bassey* (Columbia)	–	6	4
19 Surrender *Elvis Presley* (RCA)	–	–	–
20 Runnin' Scared *Roy Orbison* (London)	–	–	–
– Cupid *Sam Cooke* (RCA)	17	17	18
– Moody River *Pat Boone* (London)	18	–	–
– But I Do *Clarence Frogman Henry* (Pye)	19	–	–
– Quite A Party *The Fireballs* (Pye)	20	–	–
– The Frightened City *The Shadows* (Columbia)	–	16	–
– The Writing On The Wall *Tommy Steele* (Decca)	–	18	–
– That's My Home *Acker Bilk* (Columbia)	–	19	–
– How Many Tears *Bobby Vee* (London)	–	20	–
– Ain't Gonna Wash For A Week *The Brook Brothers* (Pye)	–	–	20
– Too Many Beautiful Girls *Clinton Ford* (Oriole)	–	–	20

SEPTEMBER 1961

2	**9**	**16**	**23**	**30**
1 Johnny Remember Me *John Leyton* (Top Rank)	1	1	1	2
2 You Don't Know *Helen Shapiro* (Columbia)	2	3	4	5
3 Reach For The Stars/Climb Every Mountain *Shirley Bassey* (Columbia)	4	5	5	8
4 Romeo *Petula Clark* (Pye)	8	7	17	–
5 Well I Ask You *Eden Kane* (Decca)	5	8	14	–
6 Halfway To Paradise *Billy Fury* (Decca)	6	13	19	17
7 A Girl Like You *Cliff Richard* (Columbia)	–	–	–	–
8 Ain't Gonna Wash For A Week *The Brook Brothers* (Pye)	10	12	11	18
9 Cupid *Sam Cooke* (RCA)	12	9	9	14
10 Time *Craig Douglas* (Top Rank)	15	–	–	–

	9	16	23	30
11 Quarter To Three *The U.S. Bonds* (Top Rank)	13	20	–	–
12 That's My Home *Acker Bilk* (Columbia)	11	16	12	19
13 How Many Tears *Bobby Vee* (London)	17	17	18	–
14 Hello Mary Lou/Travellin' Man *Ricky Nelson* (London)	–	–	–	–
15 You Always Hurt The One You Love *Clarence Frogman Henry* (Pye)	20	–	–	–
16 Baby I Don't Care/Valley Of Tears *Buddy Holly* (Coral)	–	–	–	–
17 Marcheta *Karl Denver* (Decca)	–	–	–	–
18 Pasadena *The Temperance Seven* (Parlophone)	–	–	–	–
19 Pepito *Los Machucambos* (Decca)	19	–	–	–
20 Temptation *The Everly Brothers* (Warner Bros.)	–	–	–	–
– Kon-Tiki *The Shadows* (Columbia)	7	4	2	1
– Wild In The Country/I Feel So Bad *Elvis Presley* (RCA)	3	2	3	3
– Michael Row The Boat/Lumbered *Lonnie Donegan* (Pye)	9	6	7	12
– Sea Of Heartbreak *Don Gibson* (RCA)	14	18	20	15
– Hats Off To Larry *Del Shannon* (London)	16	14	15	9
– Drivin' Home *Duane Eddy* (London)	18	19	–	–
– Michael Row The Boat *The Highwaymen* (HMV)	–	10	6	4
– Together *Connie Francis* (MGM)	–	11	13	10
– Jealousy *Billy Fury* (Decca)	–	15	8	6
– Get Lost *Eden Kane* (Decca)	–	–	10	7
– You'll Answer To Me *Cleo Laine* (Fontana)	–	–	16	11
– Walkin' Back To Happiness *Helen Shapiro* (Columbia)	–	–	–	13
– Granada *Frank Sinatra* (Reprise)	–	–	–	16
– I'm Gonna Knock On Your Door *Eddie Hodges* (London)	–	–	–	20

OCTOBER 1961

7	14	21	28
1 Michael Row The Boat *The Highwaymen* (HMV)	3	3	4
2 Wild In The Country/I Feel So Bad *Elvis Presley* (RCA)	6	10	14
3 Walkin' Back To Happiness *Helen Shapiro* (Columbia)	1	1	1
4 Kon-Tiki *The Shadows* (Columbia)	7	8	15
5 Johnny Remember Me *John Leyton* (Top Rank)	9	15	–
6 Jealousy *Billy Fury* (Decca)	4	7	10
7 You'll Answer To Me *Cleo Laine* (Fontana)	5	4	6
8 Wild Wind *John Leyton* (Top Rank)	2	2	3
9 Sucu Sucu *Laurie Johnson* (Pye)	8	5	5
10 You Don't Know *Helen Shapiro* (Columbia)	12	–	–
11 Together *Connie Francis* (MGM)	10	12	–
12 Get Lost *Eden Kane* (Decca)	11	14	–
13 Hats Off To Larry *Del Shannon* (London)	14	9	11
14 Reach For The Stars/Climb Every Mountain *Shirley Bassey* (Columbia)	–	–	–
15 Granada *Frank Sinatra* (Reprise)	13	–	–
16 Muskrat *The Everly Brothers* (Warner Bros.)	–	–	–
17 Michael Row The Boat/Lumbered *Lonnie Donegan* (Pye)	16	17	–
18 Bless You *Tony Orlando* (Fontana)	19	11	7
19 Hard Hearted Hannah/Chilli Bom-Bom *The Temperance Seven* (Parlophone)	20	–	–
20 Sea Of Heartbreak *Don Gibson* (RCA)	–	20	20
– Who Put The Bomp *The Viscounts* (Nixa)	15	–	–
– Sucu Sucu *Nina and Frederik* (Columbia)	17	–	–
– My Boomerang Won't Come Back *Charlie Drake* (Parlophone)	18	16	13
– When The Girl In Your Arms Is The Girl In Your Heart *Cliff Richard* (Columbia)	–	6	2
– Mexicali Rose *Karl Denver* (Decca)	–	13	9
– You Must Have Been A Beautiful Baby *Bobby Darin* (London)	–	18	18
– Let's Get Together *Hayley Mills* (Decca)	–	19	12
– Hit The Road Jack *Ray Charles* (HMV)	–	–	8

7

		14	**21**	**28**
– Big Bad John *Jimmy Dean* (Philips)		–	–	16
– Take Five *Dave Brubeck* (Fontana)		–	–	17
– The Time Has Come *Adam Faith* (Parlophone)		–	–	19

NOVEMBER 1961

4

	11	**18**	**25**
1 Walkin' Back To Happiness *Helen Shapiro* (Columbia)	2	2	7
2 His Latest Flame *Elvis Presley* (RCA)	1	1	1
3 When The Girl In Your Arms Is The Girl In Your Heart *Cliff Richard* (Columbia)	3	5	11
4 Big Bad John *Jimmy Dean* (Philips)	5	4	2
5 Hit The Road Jack *Ray Charles* (HMV)	7	8	13
6 Wild Wind *John Leyton* (Top Rank)	9	13	–
7 Mexicali Rose *Karl Denver* (Decca)	11	16	14
8 Sucu Sucu *Laurie Johnson* (Pye)	12	18	16
9 Take Five *Dave Brubeck* (Fontana)	6	7	8
10 Michael Row The Boat *The Highwaymen* (HMV)	16	–	–
11 You'll Answer To Me *Cleo Laine* (Fontana)	14	17	–
12 Let's Get Together *Hayley Mills* (Decca)	13	11	–
13 Bless You *Tony Orlando* (Fontana)	10	15	19
14 Take Good Care Of My Baby *Bobby Vee* (London)	4	8	3
15 The Time Has Come *Adam Faith* (Parlophone)	8	6	5
16 You Don't Know What You've Got *Ral Donner* (Mercury)	18	–	–
17 Sucu Sucu *Nina and Frederik* (Columbia)	–	–	–
18 Tribute To Buddy Holly *Mike Berry* (HMV)	–	–	–
19 Kon-Tiki *The Shadows* (Columbia)	–	–	–
20 My Boomerang Won't Come Back *Charlie Drake* (Parlophone)	15	–	–
– Creole Jazz *Acker Bilk* (Columbia)	17	–	–
– Moon River *Danny Williams* (HMV)	19	9	6
– Runaround Sue *Dion* (Top Rank)	20	20	12
– Tower Of Strength *Frankie Vaughan* (Philips)	–	10	4
– The Savage *The Shadows* (Columbia)	–	12	9
– Midnight In Moscow *Kenny Ball* (Pye)	–	14	10
– Married *The Brook Brothers* (Pye)	–	19	17
– I'll Get By *Shirley Bassey* (Columbia)	–	–	15
– Fool No. 1 *Brenda Lee* (Brunswick)	–	–	18
– My Friend The Sea *Petula Clark* (Pye)	–	–	20

DECEMBER 1961

2

	9	**16**	**23**	**30**
1 Take Good Care Of My Baby *Bobby Vee* (London)	2	3	5	20
2 His Latest Flame/Little Sister *Elvis Presley* (RCA)	3	4	15	–
3 Big Bad John *Jimmy Dean* (Philips)	6	8	14	–
4 Tower Of Strength *Frankie Vaughan* (Philips)	1	1	1	1
5 Moon River *Danny Williams* (HMV)	4	2	3	3
6 The Time Has Come *Adam Faith* (Parlophone)	5	16	16	–
7 Walkin' Back To Happiness *Helen Shapiro* (Columbia)	8	6	9	14
8 Take Five *Dave Brubeck* (Fontana)	7	15	12	8
9 The Savage *The Shadows* (Columbia)	11	9	–	–
10 I'll Get By *Shirley Bassey* (Columbia)	9	12	10	–
11 When The Girl In Your Arms Is The Girl In Your Heart *Cliff Richard* (Columbia)	16	–	13	–
12 Midnight In Moscow *Kenny Ball* (Pye)	10	5	4	7
13 Runaround Sue *Dion* (Top Rank)	–	–	–	–
14 This Time *Troy Shondell* (London)	–	–	–	–
15 Hit The Road Jack *Ray Charles* (HMV)	18	–	–	–

2

	9	16	23	30
16 Mexicali Rose *Karl Denver* (Decca)	–	–	–	–
17 September In The Rain *Dinah Washington* (Mercury)	–	–	–	–
18 Stranger On The Shore *Acker Bilk* (Columbia)	13	7	2	–
19 Married *The Brook Brothers* (Pye)	–	–	–	–
20 Fool No. 1 *Brenda Lee* (Brunswick)	–	–	–	–
– You're The Only Good Thing That's Happened To Me *Jim Reeves* (RCA)	12	–	–	–
– The Charleston *The Temperance Seven* (Parlophone)	14	20	–	–
– Johnny Will *Pat Boone* (London)	15	14	6	4
– Toy Balloons *Russ Conway* (Columbia)	17	20	7	9
– Let True Love Begin *Nat 'King' Cole* (Capitol)	19	–	–	–
– Ever Lovin' *Ricky Nelson* (London)	20	–	–	–
– So Long Baby *Del Shannon* (London)	–	10	19	11
– Let There Be Drums *Sandy Nelson* (London)	–	11	8	5
– My Friend The Sea *Petula Clark* (Pye)	–	13	11	12
– Baby's First Christmas *Connie Francis* (MGM)	–	17	–	–
– I'd Never Find Another You *Billy Fury* (Decca)	–	18	–	10
– Son, This Is She *John Leyton* (HMV)	–	19	–	–
– I Know How You Love Me *Jimmy Crawford* (Columbia)	–	–	17	–
– Happy Birthday Sweet Sixteen *Neil Sedaka* (RCA)	–	–	18	18
– I Understand *The G-Clefs* (London)	–	–	20	–

A chart described as a 'skeleton' compilation was published in Record Mirror on 30 December 1961, and in the issue of 6 January 1962, a complete 'last week' column was published. We have not published the 30 December 'skeleton' chart as it was said at the time to be incorrect, and does not agree with the 'last week' placings of 6 January.

1961

1961 chart statistics provided very little evidence for those people who suggested that the British Top Twenty merely reflected the hits which had been in the American Hit Parade some weeks previously. During the year, of some 42 records which had made the American Top Three, only seven reached the same positions in the British Top Twenty. Six of these were Number One hits on both sides of the Atlantic and a further 17 made the British Top Twenty, but 24 hits which had been in the American Top Three failed to enter the British charts at all.

The six chart toppers on both sides of the Atlantic were 'Are You Lonesome Tonight' and 'Surrender' by Elvis Presley; 'Blue Moon' from The Marcels; 'Runaway' by Del Shannon; The Highwaymen's version of 'Michael Row The Boat'; and 'Take Good Care Of My Baby' from Bobby Vee.

Among the American discs failing to enter the British Top Twenty were 'Goodbye, Cruel World' by James Darren; 'A Hundred Pounds Of Clay' by Gene McDaniels; 'Let's Twist Again' from Chubby Checker; 'Dedicated To The One I Love' from The Shirelles; 'Stand By Me' from Ben E. King; and 'Please Mr Postman' from The Marvelettes.

One American artist, however, was busily chalking up hits on both sides of the Atlantic. This was Elvis Presley, who had five chart hits, all of which reached the Number One position except for 'Wild In The Country/Feel So Fine'.

A newcomer to the British charts from America was Del Shannon. Shannon's hit 'Runaway' started his hit trail which ended in a total of eight hits by 1965. Neil Sedaka, another American, had his most successful year with three Top Twenty hits, though only 'Happy Birthday Sweet Sixteen' reached the Top Five.

Anyway, there were plenty of British hit-makers. Cliff Richard had 'Theme For A Dream' in the February listings, and ended the year with 'When The Girl In Your Arms Is The Girl In Your Heart', his fourth hit of 1961. His back-

70

ing group, The Shadows, had one hit less than he, but they achieved something which Cliff failed to do in 1961 – they reached the Number One position with 'Kon-Tiki'.

The popularity of Trad Jazz continued, and Acker Bilk's run of hits continued after his 1960 success. He had three hits in 1961, one of which, 'Stranger On The Shore', was both a Number One and a record which sold a phenomenal number of copies. Kenny Ball entered the charts in February 1961 with 'Samantha' which he followed up with two more hits that year. 1962 was to yield a further three hits for Ball. Dave Brubeck, with a different Jazz sound, also made the charts with 'Take Five' a catchy, off-beat tune.

Adam Faith and Marty Wilde were also in the Hit Parade of 1961, but the latter was gradually running out of steam; he managed only one hit while Faith achieved four. The Allisons became one-hit wonders with the very successful Eurovision song 'Are You Sure?', but they then faded quickly from the scene. Tongue-in-cheek nostalgia came from The Temperance Seven, who had no less than four hits, though their popularity was waning by the time 'Pasadena', their second hit, reached its chart zenith of Number Four.

It was almost the last 1960s triumph for the twanging guitar of Duane Eddy, who achieved five hits in 1961. Three more lay in store for him in 1962, and then he disappeared into obscurity until he made a comeback in 1975 with 'Play Me Like You Play Your Guitar'.

Pop had began to see the wane of the rockers, with the leather clothes, the motorbikes and conversations filled with ton-up chat and argumentative clashes with authority. Certainly the onset of the Twist, spearheaded by Chubby Checker, changed dancehall tactics. Jiving turned to twisting, and the casualty wards of hospitals were full of ageing twisters whose enthusiasm got the better of their discretion. The Twist was only acceptable to the young until the old, too, cashed in on its popularity, by which time youth had dismissed such a dance and continued with its search for something or someone new.

6		13	20	27
1 Stranger On The Shore *Acker Bilk* (Columbia)		1	3	2
2 Moon River *Danny Williams* (HMV)		6	7	11
3 Let There Be Drums *Sandy Nelson* (London)		2	2	6
4 Johnny Will *Pat Boone* (London)		5	8	8
5 Tower Of Strength *Frankie Vaughan* (Philips)		9	17	–
6 Midnight In Moscow *Kenny Ball* (Pye)		4	9	15
7 So Long Baby *Del Shannon* (London)		11	11	19
8 Toy Balloons *Russ Conway* (Columbia)		13	20	–
9 I'd Never Find Another You *Billy Fury* (Decca)		8	4	4
10 My Friend The Sea *Petula Clark* (Pye)		–	–	–
11 Multiplication *Bobby Darin* (London)		10	5	3
12 Take Five *Dave Brubeck* (Fontana)		–	–	–
13 Happy Birthday Sweet Sixteen *Neil Sedaka* (RCA)		7	6	5
14 Don't Bring Lulu *Dorothy Provine* (Warner Bros.)		19	–	–
15 Banbino *The Springfields* (Philips)		–	–	–
16 September In The Rain *Dinah Washington* (Mercury)		–	–	–
17 Goodbye Cruel World *Jimmy Darren* (Pye)		15	15	–
18 Walkin' Back To Happiness *Helen Shapiro* (Columbia)		–	–	–
19 Run To Him *Bobby Vee* (London)		20	10	10
20 Take Good Care Of My Baby *Bobby Vee* (London)		–	–	–
– The Young Ones *Cliff Richard* (Columbia)		3	1	1
– Son, This Is She *John Leyton* (HMV)		12	–	20
– The Twist *Chubby Checker* (Columbia)		14	12	12
– Walk On By *Leroy Vandyke* (Mercury)		16	14	9
– The Lion Sleeps Tonight *The Tokens* (London)		18	19	–
– Peppermint Twist *Joey Dee and The Starlights* (Columbia)		17	16	13
– Let's Twist Again *Chubby Checker* (Columbia)		–	18	7
– The Language Of Love *John D. Loudermilk* (RCA)		–	13	14
– Forget Me Not *Eden Kane* (Decca)		–	–	16
– Crying In The Rain *The Everly Brothers* (Warner Bros.)		–	–	17
– The Comancheros *Lonnie Donegan* (Pye)		–	–	20

3		10	17	24
1 The Young Ones *Cliff Richard* (Columbia)		1	1	2
2 Rock-A-Hula Baby/Can't Help Falling In Love *Elvis Presley* (RCA)		2	2	1
3 Multiplication *Bobby Darin* (London)		8	11	20
4 Happy Birthday Sweet Sixteen *Neil Sedaka* (RCA)		7	6	11
5 Stranger On The Shore *Acker Bilk* (Columbia)		5	9	9
6 Let's Twist Again *Chubby Checker* (Columbia)		3	3	3
7 Forget Me Not *Eden Kane* (Decca)		4	4	4
8 I'd Never Find Another You *Billy Fury* (Decca)		9	7	10
9 Walk On By *Leroy Vandyke* (Mercury)		6	5	5
10 Let There Be Drums *Sandy Nelson* (London)		16	17	–
11 Crying In The Rain *The Everly Brothers* (Warner Bros.)		10	8	8
12 The Twist *Chubby Checker* (Columbia)		–	18	–
13 Run To Him *Bobby Vee* (London)		11	10	15
14 Lonesome *Adam Faith* (Parlophone)		12	16	–
15 Peppermint Twist *Joey Dee and The Starlights* (Columbia)		17	19	–
16 The Lion Sleeps Tonight *The Tokens* (RCA)		–	–	–
17 The Comancheros *Lonnie Donegan* (Pye)		–	20	–
18 Wimoweh *Karl Denver* (Decca)		–	12	6
19 Midnight In Moscow *Kenny Ball* (Pye)		15	–	–
20 The Language of Love *John D. Loudermilk* (RCA)		–	–	–
– Little Bitty Tear *Burl Ives* (Brunswick)		13	13	12

3	10	17	24
– Jeannie *Danny Williams* (HMV)	14	15	18
– Moon River *Danny Williams* (HMV)	18	–	–
– Johnny Will *Pat Boone* (London)	19	–	–
– Don't Stop, Twist *Frankie Vaughan* (Philips)	20	14	19
– March Of The Siamese Children *Kenny Ball* (Pye)	–	–	7
– Hole In The Ground *Bernard Cribbins* (Parlophone)	–	–	13
– Lesson No. 1 *Russ Conway* (Columbia)	–	–	14
– Tell Me What He Said *Helen Shapiro* (Columbia)	–	–	16
– The Wanderer *Dion* (HMV)	–	–	17

MARCH 1962

3	10	17	24	31
1 Rock-A-Hula Baby/Can't Help Falling In Love *Elvis Presley* (RCA)	1	1	3	3
2 Let's Twist Again *Chubby Checker* (Columbia)	4	6	5	5
3 March Of The Siamese Children *Kenny Ball* (Pye)	5	4	4	8
4 The Young Ones *Cliff Richard* (Columbia)	3	7	7	11
5 Tell Me What He Said *Helen Shapiro* (Columbia)	6	3	2	2
6 Walk On By *Leroy Vandyke* (Mercury)	12	11	15	17
7 Forget Me Not *Eden Kane* (Decca)	8	13	14	20
8 Wimoweh *Karl Denver* (Decca)	7	5	6	6
9 Wonderful Land *The Shadows* (Columbia)	2	2	1	1
10 Crying In The Rain *The Everly Brothers* (Warner Bros.)	9	8	13	16
11 Hole In The Ground *Bernard Cribbins* (Parlophone)	15	10	12	9
12 Little Bitty Tear *Burl Ives* (Brunswick)	14	18	16	–
13 The Wanderer *Dion* (HMV)	10	14	10	13
14 Softly As I Leave You *Matt Monro* (Parlophone)	13	12	11	10
15 Run To Him *Bobby Vee* (London)	–	–	–	–
16 Stranger On The Shore *Acker Bilk* (Columbia)	11	9	8	7
17 Happy Birthday Sweet Sixteen *Neil Sedaka* (RCA)	–	–	–	–
18 Don't Stop, Twist *Frankie Vaughan* (Philips)	17	–	–	–
19 I'd Never Find Another You *Billy Fury* (Decca)	–	–	–	–
20 Lesson No. 1 *Russ Conway* (Columbia)	16	–	–	–
– Theme From Z Cars *Johnny Keating* (Piccadilly)	18	15	17	14
– I'll See You In My Dreams *Pat Boone* (London)	19	19	–	–
– Frankie And Johnny *Acker Bilk* (Columbia)	20	–	–	–
– Dream Baby *Roy Orbison* (London)	–	16	9	4
– Twistin' The Night Away *Sam Cooke* (RCA)	–	17	18	15
– Letter Full Of Tears *Billy Fury* (Decca)	–	20	–	–
– Little Bitty Tear *Miki and Griff* (Pye)	–	–	19	–
– Jeannie *Danny Williams* (HMV)	–	–	20	–
– Hey! Baby *Bruce Channel* (Mercury)	–	–	25	12
– Hey Little Girl *Del Shannon* (London)	–	–	24	18
– Dr Kildare Theme *Johnny Spence* (Parlophone)	–	–	23	19

On 24 March 1962 Record Mirror began to list a Top Fifty. Its 'last week' figures at this date were those of its new chart source and did not correspond with its own former chart listing.

APRIL 1962

7	14	21	28
1 Wonderful Land *The Shadows* (Columbia)	1	1	1
2 Tell Me What He Said *Helen Shapiro* (Columbia)	3	5	5
3 Dream Baby *Roy Orbison* (London)	2	2	3
4 Can't Help Falling In Love/Rock-A-Hula Baby *Elvis Presley* (RCA)	4	6	6
5 Wimoweh *Karl Denver* (Decca)	8	11	20

7	**14**	**21**	**28**
6 Stranger On The Shore *Acker Bilk* (Columbia)	7	13	12
7 Twistin' The Night Away *Sam Cooke* (RCA)	6	7	7
8 Hey Little Girl *Del Shannon* (London)	5	3	4
9 Hole In The Ground *Bernard Cribbins* (Parlophone)	10	14	15
10 Softly As I Leave You *Matt Monro* (Parlophone)	14	16	–
11 Theme From Z Cars *Johnny Keating* (Piccadilly)	11	8	11
12 Hey! Baby *Bruce Channel* (Mercury)	5	4	2
13 Let's Twist Again *Chubby Checker* (Columbia)	13	15	19
14 March Of The Siamese Children *Kenny Ball* (Pye)	20	–	–
15 The Wanderer *Dion* (HMV)	18	–	–
16 The Young Ones *Cliff Richard* (Columbia)	17	19	–
17 Dr Kildare Theme *Johnny Spence* (Parlophone)	15	18	18
18 Never Goodbye *Karl Denver* (Decca)	12	9	10
19 Love Me Warm And Tender *Paul Anka* (RCA)	19	–	–
20 When My Little Girl Is Smiling *Craig Douglas* (Top Rank)	16	10	9
24 When My Little Girl Is Smiling *Jimmy Justice* (Pye)	22	12	13
47 Speak To Me Pretty *Brenda Lee* (Brunswick)	29	17	8
21 The Maigret Theme *Joe Loss* (HMV)	21	20	–
– Nut Rocker *B. Bumble* (Top Rank)	–	31	14
– Wonderful World Of The Young *Danny Williams* (HMV)	37	22	16
46 The Party's Over *Lonnie Donegan* (Pye)	25	21	**17**

MAY 1962

5	**12**	**19**	**26**
1 Wonderful Land *The Shadows* (Columbia)	1	3	6
2 Hey Little Girl *Del Shannon* (London)	5	8	8
3 Hey! Baby *Bruce Channel* (Mercury)	4	10	14
4 Nut Rocker *B. Bumble* (Top Rank)	2	1	2
5 Dream Baby *Roy Orbison* (London)	7	14	–
6 Tell Me What He Said *Helen Shapiro* (Columbia)	17	–	–
7 Speak To Me Pretty *Brenda Lee* (Brunswick)	3	5	7
8 Can't Help Falling In Love/Rock-A-Hula Baby *Elvis Presley* (RCA)	14	16	16
9 Never Goodbye *Karl Denver* (Decca)	10	11	15
10 Stranger On The Shore *Acker Bilk* (Columbia)	15	13	12
11 Wonderful World Of The Young *Danny Williams* (HMV)	8	12	13
12 Twistin' The Night Away *Sam Cooke* (RCA)	11	18	–
13 Theme From Z Cars *Johnny Keating* (Piccadilly)	18	–	–
14 When My Little Girl Is Smiling *Craig Douglas* (Top Rank)	13	20	–
15 When My Little Girl Is Smiling *Jimmy Justice* (Pye)	12	9	9
16 The Party's Over *Lonnie Donegan* (Pye)	9	17	19
17 Love Letters *Ketty Lester* (London)	6	6	4
18 Let's Twist Again *Chubby Checker* (Columbia)	–	–	–
19 Young World *Ricky Nelson* (London)	20	–	–
20 Dr Kildare Theme *Johnny Spence* (Parlophone)	–	–	–
– Good Luck Charm *Elvis Presley* (RCA)	16	2	1
– Do You Want To Dance *Cliff Richard* (Columbia)	20	4	3
42 As You Like It *Adam Faith* (Parlophone)	23	7	5
36 Last Night Was Made For Love *Billy Fury* (Decca)	26	15	11
– Ginny Come Lately *Brian Hyland* (HMV)	36	19	10
– Come Outside *Mike Sarne* (Parlophone)	46	29	17
– I Don't Know Why *Eden Kane* (Decca)	50	28	18
48 Lonely City *John Leyton* (HMV)	35	25	20

JUNE 1962

2		9	16	23	30
1	Good Luck Charm *Elvis Presley* (RCA)	1	1	1	3
2	I'm Looking Out The Window/Do You Want To Dance *Cliff Richard* (Columbia)	2	2	3	4
3	Nut Rocker *B. Bumble* (Top Rank)	3	5	9	10
4	Last Night Was Made For Love *Billy Fury* (Decca)	6	8	6	6
5	As You Like It *Adam Faith* (Parlophone)	5	6	8	14
6	Come Outside *Mike Sarne* (Parlophone)	4	3	2	1
7	Love Letters *Ketty Lester* (London)	11	13	–	–
8	I Don't Know Why *Eden Kane* (Decca)	9	7	7	11
9	Wonderful Land *The Shadows* (Columbia)	8	15	–	–
10	Ginny Come Lately *Brian Hyland* (HMV)	7	9	5	5
11	Stranger On The Shore *Acker Bilk* (Columbia)	12	11	11	9
12	When My Little Girl Is Smiling *Jimmy Justice* (Pye)	–	–	–	–
13	Wonderful World Of The Young *Danny Williams* (HMV)	19	–	–	–
14	Speak To Me Pretty *Brenda Lee* (Brunswick)	15	–	–	–
15	Hey Little Girl *Del Shannon* (London)	17	–	–	–
16	The Party's Over *Lonnie Donegan* (Pye)	20	–	–	–
17	Green Leaves Of Summer *Kenny Ball and his Jazzmen* (Pye)	13	10	10	12
18	A Picture Of You *Joe Brown* (Piccadilly)	10	4	4	2
19	How Can I Meet Her *The Everly Brothers* (Warner Bros.)	14	12	13	16
20	Lonely City *John Leyton* (HMV)	16	14	15	–
24	Unsquare Dance *Dave Brubeck* (CBS)	18	17	14	18
22	Lover Please *Maureen and The Vernon Girls* (Decca)	21	16	17	–
–	Sharing You *Bobby Vee* (Liberty)	41	18	–	17
30	Jezebel *Marty Wilde* (Philips)	23	19	20	–
–	A Little Love A Little Kiss *Karl Denver* (Decca)	32	20	–	19
–	Ain't That Funny *Jimmy Justice* (Pye)	–	30	18	15
–	I Can't Stop Loving You *Ray Charles* (HMV)	–	43	16	8
29	Deep In The Heart Of Texas *Duane Eddy* (RCA)	29	24	19	–
–	English Country Garden *Jimmy Rodgers* (Columbia)	–	34	21	7
–	Theme From Dr Kildare *Richard Chamberlain* (MGM)	40	24	13	12
–	Yes My Darling Daughter *Eydie Gorme* (CBS)	–	–	34	20

JULY 1962

7		14	21	28
1	Come Outside *Mike Sarne* (Parlophone)	2	4	7
2	A Picture Of You *Joe Brown* (Piccadilly)	3	3	3
3	Good Luck Charm *Elvis Presley* (RCA)	4	6	6
4	I Can't Stop Loving You *Ray Charles* (HMV)	1	1	2
5	Ginny Come Lately *Brian Hyland* (HMV)	5	8	11
6	I'm Looking Out The Window/Do You Want To Dance *Cliff Richard* (Columbia)	6	10	19
7	Green Leaves Of Summer *Kenny Ball and his Jazzmen* (Pye)	15	18	–
8	Ain't That Funny *Jimmy Justice* (Pye)	9	15	12
9	Stranger On The Shore *Acker Bilk* (Columbia)	17	19	18
10	Sharing You *Bobby Vee* (Liberty)	13	16	16
11	Last Night Was Made For Love *Billy Fury* (Decca)	12	14	20
12	English Country Garden *Jimmy Rodgers* (Columbia)	8	5	9
13	As You Like It *Adam Faith* (Parlophone)	19	–	–
14	Here Comes That Feeling *Brenda Lee* (Brunswick)	7	7	5
15	I Don't Know Why *Eden Kane* (Decca)	18	–	–
16	Yes My Darling Daughter *Eydie Gorme* (CBS)	10	11	17
17	Theme From Dr Kildare *Richard Chamberlain* (MGM)	–	–	–
18	Don't Ever Change *The Crickets* (Liberty)	14	12	8
19	Nut Rocker *B. Bumble* (Top Rank)	–	–	–

7		14	21	28
20	A Little Love A Little Kiss *Karl Denver* (Decca)	–	–	–
21	Our Favourite Melodies *Craig Douglas* (Columbia)	16	9	10
36	I Remember You *Frank Ifield* (Columbia)	11	2	1
25	Palisades Park *Freddy Cannon* (Stateside)	20	–	–
–	Speedy Gonzales *Pat Boone* (London)	40	13	4
46	Right, Said Fred *Bernard Cribbins* (Parlophone)	21	17	15
32	Ya Ya Twist *Petula Clark* (Pye)	23	20	14
–	Little Miss Lonely *Helen Shapiro* (Columbia)	48	23	13

AUGUST 1962

4		11	18	25
1	I Remember You *Frank Ifield* (Columbia)	1	1	1
2	I Can't Stop Loving You *Ray Charles* (HMV)	3	3	6
3	Speedy Gonzales *Pat Boone* (London)	2	2	2
4	A Picture Of You *Joe Brown* (Piccadilly)	4	6	13
5	Don't Ever Change *The Crickets* (Liberty)	5	9	10
6	Come Outside *Mike Sarne* (Parlophone)	9	17	18
7	Here Comes That Feeling *Brenda Lee* (Brunswick)	6	12	17
8	Little Miss Lonely *Helen Shapiro* (Columbia)	10	10	11
9	English Country Garden *Jimmy Rodgers* (Columbia)	14	19	19
10	Right, Said Fred *Bernard Cribbins* (Parlophone)	13	–	–
11	Let There Be Love *Nat 'King' Cole and George Shearing* (Capitol)	2	11	12
12	Our Favourite Melodies *Craig Douglas* (Columbia)	18	–	–
13	Good Luck Charm *Elvis Presley* (RCA)	–	–	–
14	Ya Ya Twist *Petula Clark* (Pye)	15	–	–
15	Sharing You *Bobby Vee* (Liberty)	20	–	–
16	Things *Bobby Darin* (London)	8	5	3
17	Ain't That Funny *Jimmy Justice* (Pye)	–	–	–
18	Ginny Come Lately *Brian Hyland* (HMV)	–	–	–
19	Cindy's Birthday *Shane Fenton* (Parlophone)	–	–	–
20	Stranger On The Shore *Acker Bilk* (Columbia)	19	18	–
23	Once Upon A Dream *Billy Fury* (Decca)	11	7	7
22	I'm Just A Baby *Louise Cordet* (Decca)	16	15	16
25	Breaking Up Is Hard To Do *Neil Sedaka* (RCA)	17	13	9
28	Guitar Tango *The Shadows* (Columbia)	7	4	4
43	Roses Are Red *Ronnie Carroll* (Philips)	23	8	5
40	Vacation *Connie Francis* (MGM)	24	14	14
50	Sealed With A Kiss *Brian Hyland* (HMV)	32	16	8
42	Roses Are Red *Bobby Vinton* (Columbia)	25	20	15
–	Dancin' Party *Chubby Checker* (Columbia)	42	26	20

SEPTEMBER 1962

1		8	15	22	29
1	I Remember You *Frank Ifield* (Columbia)	1	2	2	4
2	Speedy Gonzales *Pat Boone* (London)	5	6	8	15
3	Things *Bobby Darin* (London)	2	4	5	6
4	Guitar Tango *The Shadows* (Columbia)	6	9	10	11
5	Sealed With A Kiss *Brian Hyland* (HMV)	3	5	6	7
6	Roses Are Red *Ronnie Carroll* (Philips)	4	3	4	5
7	Once Upon A Dream *Billy Fury* (Decca)	9	11	16	20
8	Breaking Up Is Hard To Do *Neil Sedaka* (RCA)	7	8	7	9
9	I Can't Stop Loving You *Ray Charles* (HMV)	10	16	–	–
10	Vacation *Connie Francis* (MGM)	15	–	–	–
11	Little Miss Lonely *Helen Shapiro* (Columbia)	18	–	–	–
12	Let There Be Love *Nat 'King' Cole and George Shearing* (Capitol)	13	19	–	–

1	**8**	**15**	**22**	**29**
13 I'm Just A Baby *Louise Cordet* (Decca)	20	–		
14 So Do I *Kenny Ball* (Pye)	16	15	19	–
15 Pick A Bale Of Cotton *Lonnie Donegan* (Pye)	11	14	14	18
16 A Picture Of You *Joe Brown* (Piccadilly)	–	–	–	–
17 Ballad of Paladin *Duane Eddy* (RCA)	12	10	13	17
18 Don't Ever Change *The Crickets* (Liberty)	–	–	–	–
19 Dancing Party *Chubby Checker* (Columbia)	–	–	–	–
20 Main Theme From The Man With The Golden Arm *Jet Harris* (Decca)	14	12	15	16
34 She's Not For You *Elvis Presley* (RCA	8	1	1	1
41 Don't That Beat All *Adam Faith* (Parlophone)	19	13	9	8
– It'll Be Me *Cliff Richard* (Columbia)	17	7	3	2
50 Telstar *The Tornados* (Decca)	36	17	11	3
36 Will I What? *Mike Sarne* (Parlophone)	23	18	20	19
31 Spanish Harlem *Jimmy Justice* (Pye)	21	20	–	–
– Sheila *Tommy Roe* (HMV)	43	24	12	10
– Loco-Motion *Little Eva* (London)	42	25	17	13
38 What Now My Love *Shirley Bassey* (Columbia)	29	23	18	14
– You Don't Know Me *Ray Charles* (HMV)	–	47	23	12

OCTOBER 1962

6	**13**	**20**	**27**
1 Telstar *The Tornados* (Decca)	1	1	1
2 She's Not For You *Elvis Presley* (RCA)	5	6	9
3 It'll Be Me *Cliff Richard* (Columbia)	6	9	11
4 Sheila *Tommy Roe* (HMV)	3	4	3
5 Loco-Motion *Little Eva* (London)	2	2	2
6 It Might As Well Rain Until September *Carole King* (London)	4	3	2
7 Sealed With A Kiss *Brian Hyland* (HMV)	14	20	–
8 I Remember You *Frank Ifield* (Columbia)	8	8	14
9 You Don't Know Me *Ray Charles* (HMV)	9	10	12
10 Don't That Beat All *Adam Faith* (Parlophone)	10	12	20
11 Roses Are Red *Ronnie Carroll* (Philips)	12	16	19
12 Things *Bobby Darin* (London)	13	18	–
13 What Now My Love *Shirley Bassey* (Columbia)	7	5	8
14 Breaking Up Is Hard To Do *Neil Sedaka* (RCA)	16	–	–
15 Guitar Tango *The Shadows* (Columbia)	–	–	–
16 It Started All Over Again *Brenda Lee* (Brunswick)	15	17	18
17 Speedy Gonzales *Pat Boone* (London)	19	–	–
18 Reminiscing *Buddy Holly* (Coral)	17	–	–
19 Ramblin' Rose *Nat 'King' Cole* (Capitol)	11	7	5
20 Main Theme From The Man With The Golden Arm *Jet Harris* (Decca)	18	–	–
27 Lonely *Acker Bilk* (Columbia)	20	14	17
41 Venus In Blue Jeans *Mark Wynter* (Pye)	22	11	6
46 Let's Dance *Chris Montez* (London)	21	13	7
42 Sherry *The Four Seasons* (Stateside)	25	15	15
– Swiss Maid *Del Shannon* (London)	42	19	10
40 Devil Woman *Marty Robbins* (CBS)	26	21	13
– Lovesick Blues *Frank Ifield* (Columbia)	–	–	16

NOVEMBER 1962

3		10	17	24
1 Telstar *The Tornados* (Decca)		3	4	4
2 Let's Dance *Chris Montez* (London)		2	2	2
3 Loco-Motion *Little Eva* (London)		5	7	7
4 Venus In Blue Jeans *Mark Wynter* (Pye)		6	5	6
5 Lovesick Blues *Frank Ifield* (Columbia)		1	1	1
6 It Might As Well Rain Until September *Carole King* (London)		7	11	12
7 Ramblin' Rose *Nat 'King' Cole* (Capitol)		8	8	11
8 Swiss Maid *Del Shannon* (London)		4	3	3
9 Sheila *Tommy Roe* (HMV)		10	10	14
10 She's Not For You *Elvis Presley* (RCA)		17	–	–
11 Sherry *The Four Seasons* (Stateside)		9	9	8
12 Devil Woman *Marty Robbins* (CBS)		11	12	9
13 What Now My Love *Shirley Bassey* (Columbia)		12	16	20
14 You Don't Know Me *Ray Charles* (HMV)		15	17	–
15 It'll Be Me *Cliff Richard* (Columbia)		–	–	–
16 Lonely *Acker Bilk* (Columbia)		–	–	–
17 Bobby's Girl *Susan Maughan* (Philips)		13	6	5
18 I Remember You *Frank Ifield* (Columbia)		16	15	17
19 It Started All Over Again *Brenda Lee* (Brunswick)		–	–	–
20 No One Can Make My Sunshine Smile *The Everly Brothers* (Warner Bros.)		14	14	13
25 Because Of Love *Billy Fury* (Decca)		18	–	–
24 Oh Lonesome Me *Craig Douglas* (Decca)		19	19	16
33 Sun Arise *Rolf Harris* (Columbia)		20	13	15
– Dance With The Guitar Man *Duane Eddy* (RCA)		39	18	10
39 Must Be Madison *Joe Loss and his Orchestra* (HMV)		26	20	–
46 Love Me Tender *Richard Chamberlain* (MGM)		27	23	18
47 James Bond Theme *John Barry and his Orchestra* (Columbia)		24	21	19

DECEMBER 1962

1		8	15	22	29
1 Lovesick Blues *Frank Ifield* (Columbia)		1	2	3	5
2 Swiss Maid *Del Shannon* (London)		3	6	8	12
3 Bobby's Girl *Susan Maughan* (Philips)		4	4	5	9
4 Let's Dance *Chris Montez* (London)		5	7	12	10
5 Devil Woman *Marty Robbins* (CBS)		8	10	10	14
6 Dance With The Guitar Man *Duane Eddy* (RCA)		6	9	6	4
7 Venus In Blue Jeans *Mark Wynter* (Pye)		14	15	–	–
8 Sun Arise *Rolf Harris* (Columbia)		7	3	4	7
9 Telstar *The Tornados* (Decca)		9	8	9	8
10 Loco-Motion *Little Eva* (London)		17	–	–	–
11 No One Can Make My Sunshine Smile *The Everly Brothers* (Warner Bros.)		12	20	–	–
12 Ramblin' Rose *Nat 'King' Cole* (Capitol)		–	–	–	–
13 Sherry *The Four Seasons* (Stateside)		10	18	17	–
14 The Main Attraction *Pat Boone* (London)		15	12	14	16
15 Oh Lonesome Me *Craig Douglas* (Decca)		–	–	–	–
16 James Bond Theme *John Barry and his Orchestra* (Columbia)		13	–	16	–
17 Love Me Tender *Richard Chamberlain* (MGM)		19	16	15	–
18 It Might As Well Rain Until September *Carole King* (London)		–	–	–	–
19 I Remember You *Frank Ifield* (Columbia)		–	–	–	–
20 It Only Took A Minute *Joe Brown* (Piccadilly)		16	14	13	15
– Next Time *Cliff Richard* (Columbia)		18	5	2	2
24 Must Be Madison *Joe Loss and his Orchestra* (HMV)		20	–	–	–

1	8	15	22	29
30 Rockin' Around The Christmas Tree *Brenda Lee* (Brunswick)	11	11	7	6
– Return To Sender *Elvis Presley* (RCA)	2	1	1	1
27 Desafinado *Stan Getz and Charlie Byrd* (HMV)	21	13	18	11
25 A Forever Kind Of Love *Bobby Vee* (Liberty)	22	17	19	19
21 Love Me Do *The Beatles* (Parlophone)	26	19	–	17
– Dance On! *The Shadows* (Columbia)	–	24	11	3
50 Like I Do *Maureen Evans* (Oriole)	31	27	20	–
– Your Cheating Heart *Ray Charles* (HMV)	–	50	25	13
34 We're Gonna Go Fishin' *Hank Locklin* (RCA)	35	34	27	18
– Me And My Shadow *Frank Sinatra* (Capitol)	–	43	32	20

The chart for 29 December is the official chart published in New Record Mirror *on 12 January 1963. The chart given in* Record Mirror *for 29 December 1962 was a temporary listing and corrected on 12 January 1963.*

1962

The early 1960s heroes continued their successes, with three hits each for Adam Faith and The Everly Brothers, Billy Fury achieved four hits, as did Elvis Presley, but 1962 also saw the end of Lonnie Donegan's 26-hit chart career which had included three Number One records, and six others in the Top Five. The end of Donegan's career was slightly unexpected, even though his last Top Five disc had been in 1960.

Very similar to Donegan was the case of Pat Boone. His famous song 'Speedy Gonzales' reached the Number Two position in July, and 'The Main Attraction' took the Number Twelve position in December, after which Boone also departed from the charts. Apart from 'Speedy Gonzales' and 'Johnny Will', Pat Boone had made a series of discs beginning with 'If Dreams Came True' in 1958, and he had continued with six discs which reached no higher position in the charts than Number Sixteen.

Connie Francis had but one Top Twenty song, 'Vacation', in 1962. She lacked good material, as did Pat Boone.

It was also the end for Craig Douglas, whose 'Oh Lonesome Me' was as good a title as any with which to say goodbye! Douglas had scored a total of nine hits, including 'A Hundred Pounds Of Clay', a cover version which effectively prevented the American version from repeating its Stateside chart positioning.

Marty Wilde achieved his eighth hit during 1962 with 'Jezebel', but this version of the Frankie Laine song remained in the charts for only two weeks. But if the demise of Wilde was drawing near, the pace was beginning to quicken for American 'Little Miss Dynamite', Brenda Lee, for she achieved four hits records in 1962, as opposed to her two-hit track performance of the previous year.

Other new names appeared, though few of these made very much chart impression. The Four Seasons entered the Top Ten with 'Sherry', a song which made a comeback in 1975, sung by Adrian Baker. It was The Four Seasons' only 1962 hit. The Tornados promised much with their arrival on the scene, and their 'Telstar' stayed almost five months in the Top Twenty.

However, 1962 also marked the demise of the memorable Nat 'King' Cole and the pianist Russ Conway. Cole had achieved 10 hits since 1955, and there had been 12 hits for Russ Conway.

1962 was a historic year for a Liverpool foursome called The Beatles – the most significant new group of the year. The date of their first chart entry with 'Love Me Do' was 15 December 1962, the highest position they reached in the charts was Number Seventeen, and they remained in the Top Twenty for just two weeks. John, George, Paul and Ringo created a whole new trend of haircuts, neat suits and an explosion of music from the Merseyside areas.

Apart from the birth of the Mersey Sound in the charts, 1962 was also a year for television themes finding their way into the Top Twenty, including two versions of the 'Theme From Z Cars', two versions of the 'Dr Kildare Theme', and two instrumentals – the 'Theme From The Man With The Golden Arm' and 'Cutty Sark'.

Possibly the most surprising hit of the year was 'September In The Rain' from Dinah Washington and, according to some, the funniest discs of the year were 'Hole In The Ground' and 'Right, Said Fred' from Bernard Cribbins.

JANUARY 1963

5	12	19	26
1 Next Time *Cliff Richard* (Columbia)	1	1	2
2 Return To Sender *Elvis Presley* (RCA)	2	3	6
3 Lovesick Blues *Frank Ifield* (Columbia)	5	4	11
4 Sun Arise *Rolf Harris* (Columbia)	7	8	15
5 Dance With The Guitar Man *Duane Eddy* (RCA)	4	7	9
6 Bobby's Girl *Susan Maughan* (Philips)	9	14	19
7 Dance On! *The Shadows* (Columbia)	3	2	1
8 It Only Took A Minute *Joe Brown* (Piccadilly)	6	11	–
9 Telstar *The Tornados* (Decca)	11	10	20
10 Let's Dance *Chris Montez* (London)	13	16	–
11 Swiss Maid *Del Shannon* (London)	14	20	–
12 Rockin' Around The Christmas Tree *Brenda Lee* (Brunswick)	–	–	–
13 A Forever Kind Of Love *Bobby Vee* (Liberty)	18	–	–
14 Up On The Roof *Kenny Lynch* (HMV)	12	13	10
15 Your Cheating Heart *Ray Charles* (HMV)	16	17	–
16 Devil Woman *Marty Robbins* (CBS)	–	–	–
17 Go Away Little Girl *Mark Wynter* (Pye)	8.	6	7
18 Desafinado *Stan Getz and Charlie Byrd* (HMV)	15	–	–
19 Like I Do *Maureen Evans* (Oriole)	10	5	3
20 The Main Attraction *Pat Boone* (London)	20	–	–
30 He's A Rebel *The Crystals* (London)	19	–	–
24 Love Me Do *The Beatles* (Parlophone)	17	–	–
– Globe-Trotter *The Tornados* (Decca)	28	9	5
– Diamonds *Jet Harris and Tony Meehan* (Decca)	45	12	4
31 Don't You Think It's Time *Mike Berry and The Outlaws* (HMV)	21	15	8
44 Coming Home Baby *Mel Torme* (London)	24	18	13
26 Island Of Dreams *The Springfields* (Philips)	26	19	12
– Little Town Flirt *Del Shannon* (London)	–	41	14
– Some Kinda Fun *Chris Montez* (London)	–	42	16
– All Alone Am I *Brenda Lee* (Brunswick)	–	40	17
– Big Girls Don't Cry *The Four Seasons* (Stateside)	–	48	18

FEBRUARY 1963

2	9	16	23
1 Diamonds *Jet Harris and Tony Meehan* (Decca)	1	1	3
2 Next Time/Bachelor Boy *Cliff Richard* (Columbia)	2	5	9
3 Like I Do *Maureen Evans* (Oriole)	5	7	14
4 Dance On! *The Shadows* (Columbia)	9	11	–
5 Globe-Trotter *The Tornados* (Decca)	6	13	16
6 Don't You Think It's Time *Mike Berry and The Outlaws* (HMV)	8	8	13
7 Little Town Flirt *Del Shannon* (London)	7	4	5
8 Return To Sender *Elvis Presley* (RCA)	17	–	–
9 Wayward Wind *Frank Ifield* (Columbia)	4	2	1
10 Some Kinda Fun *Chris Montez* (London)	12	20	20
11 Go Away Little Girl *Mark Wynter* (Pye)	20	–	–
12 Up On The Roof *Kenny Lynch* (HMV)	18	–	–
13 Big Girls Don't Cry *The Four Seasons* (Stateside)	13	15	18
14 Island Of Dreams *The Springfields* (Philips)	10	12	8
15 All Alone Am I *Brenda Lee* (Brunswick)	11	9	7
16 Please Please Me *The Beatles* (Parlophone)	3	3	2
17 Dance With The Guitar Man *Duane Eddy* (RCA)	–	–	–
18 Coming Home Baby *Mel Torme* (London)	–	–	–
19 Suki Yaki *Kenny Ball* (Pye)	14	10	10
20 Lovesick Blues *Frank Ifield* (Columbia)	–	–	–
29 Loop-De-Loop *Frankie Vaughan* (Philips)	15	6	6
21 A Taste Of Honey *Acker Bilk* (Columbia)	16	16	17

2	9	16	23
23 My Little Girl *The Crickets* (Liberty)	19	17	17
– The Night Has A Thousand Eyes *Bobby Vee* (Liberty)	30	14	4
39 Walk Right In *The Rooftop Singers* (Fontana)	21	18	11
45 Hava Nagila *The Spotnicks* (Oriole)	26	19	15
– That's What Love Will Do *Joe Brown* (Piccadilly)	50	26	12

MARCH 1963

2	9	16	23	30
1 Wayward Wind *Frank Ifield* (Columbia)	1	7	10	17
2 Please Please Me *The Beatles* (Parlophone)	3	2	5	7
3 The Night Has A Thousand Eyes *Bobby Vee* (Liberty)	4	5	6	13
4 Diamonds *Jet Harris and Tony Meehan* (Decca)	7	14	18	–
5 Loop-De-Loop *Frankie Vaughan* (Philips)	8	13	15	–
6 That's What Love Will Do *Joe Brown* (Piccadilly)	5	3	3	8
7 Summer Holiday *Cliff Richard and The Shadows* (Columbia)	2	1	1	2
8 Little Town Flirt *Del Shannon* (London)	13	18	–	–
9 Island Of Dreams *The Springfields* (Philips)	9	6	7	5
10 Suki Yaki *Kenny Ball and his Jazzmen* (Pye)	17	20	–	–
11 Walk Right In *The Rooftop Singers* (Fontana)	10	15	17	–
12 All Alone Am I *Brenda Lee* (Brunswick)	15	19	–	–
13 Hava Nagila *The Spotnicks* (Oriole)	16	–	–	–
14 Like I've Never Been Gone *Billy Fury* (Decca)	6	4	4	3
15 Like I Do *Maureen Evans* (Oriole)	–	–	–	–
16 Next Time/Bachelor Boy *Cliff Richard* (Columbia)	19	–	–	–
17 Hey Paula *Paul and Paula* (Philips)	11	8	9	12
18 Charmaine *The Bachelors* (Decca)	12	11	8	6
19 Don't You Think It's Time *Mike Berry and The Outlaws* (HMV)	–	–	–	–
20 Globe-Trotter *The Tornados* (Decca)	–	–	–	–
21 Tell Him *Billie Davis* (Decca)	14	10	11	15
42 One Broken Heart For Sale *Elvis Presley* (RCA)	18	12	12	14
25 Hi Lili-Hi Lo *Richard Chamberlain* (MGM)	20	–	–	–
– Foot Tapper *The Shadows* (Columbia)	25	9	2	1
30 From A Jack To A King *Ned Miller* (London)	21	16	13	4
46 Rhythm Of The Rain *The Cascades* (Warner Bros.)	30	17	14	9
– Say Wonderful Things *Ronnie Carroll* (Philips)	37	21	16	11
– Brown Eyed Handsome Man *Buddy Holly* (Coral)	–	32	19	16
– How Do You Do It? *Gerry and The Pacemakers* (Columbia)	–	39	20	10
– Let's Turkey Trot *Little Eva* (London)	44	26	21	18
– The Folk Singer *Tommy Roe* (HMV)	–	–	31	19
– In Dreams *Roy Orbison* (London)	38	28	25	20

APRIL 1963

6	13	20	27
1 How Do You Do It? *Gerry and The Pacemakers* (Columbia)	1	1	1
2 From A Jack To A King *Ned Miller* (London)	2	2	2
3 Summer Holiday *Cliff Richard and The Shadows* (Columbia)	6	9	13
4 Foot Tapper *The Shadows* (Columbia)	3	6	9
5 Like I've Never Been Gone *Billy Fury* (Decca)	9	11	17
6 Say Wonderful Things *Ronnie Carroll* (Philips)	7	8	14
7 Rhythm Of The Rain *The Cascades* (Warner Bros.)	5	5	7
8 Charmaine *The Bachelors* (Decca)	8	12	15
9 Brown Eyed Handsome Man *Buddy Holly* (Coral)	4	3	10
10 That's What Love Will Do *Joe Brown* (Piccadilly)	14	–	–
11 Please Please Me *The Beatles* (Parlophone)	17	–	–

6		13	20	27
12 Hey Paula *Paul and Paula* (Philips)		18	–	–
13 The Folk Singer *Tommy Roe* (HMV)		10	4	4
14 Let's Turkey Trot *Little Eva* (London)		13	18	19
15 Island Of Dreams *The Springfields* (Philips)		15	16	20
16 Tell Him *Billie Davis* (Decca)		–	–	–
17 In Dreams *Roy Orbison* (London)		12	10	8
18 The Night Has A Thousand Eyes *Bobby Vee* (Liberty)		–	–	–
19 One Broken Heart For Sale *Elvis Presley* (RCA)		–	–	–
20 Wayward Wind *Frank Ifield* (Columbia)		–	–	–
22 Say I Won't Be There *The Springfields* (Philips)		11	7	5
23 Walk Like A Man *The Four Seasons* (Stateside)		16	13	12
24 Robot *The Tornados* (Philips)		19	17	–
21 End Of The World *Skeeter Davis* (RCA)		20	19	18
– Nobody's Darlin' But Mine *Frank Ifield* (Columbia)		30	14	6
28 Can't Get Used To Losing You *Andy Williams* (CBS)		21	15	11
35 Losing You *Brenda Lee* (Brunswick)		27	20	16
– From Me To You *The Beatles* (Parlophone)		–	23	3

MAY 1963

4		11	18	25
1 From Me To You *The Beatles* (Parlophone)		1	1	1
2 How Do You Do It? *Gerry and The Pacemakers* (Columbia)		2	4	8
3 From A Jack To A King *Ned Miller* (London)		3	7	12
4 Nobody's Darlin' But Mine *Frank Ifield* (Columbia)		4	8	11
5 Say I Won't Be There *The Springfields* (Philips)		8	12	14
6 Can't Get Used To Losing You *Andy Williams* (CBS)		5	2	5
7 In Dreams *Roy Orbison* (London)		6	6	7
8 Rhythm Of The Rain *The Cascades* (Warner Bros.)		12	15	17
9 Brown Eyed Handsome Man *Buddy Holly* (Coral)		11	13	18
10 Foot Tapper *The Shadows* (Columbia)		15	20	–
11 The Folk Singer *Tommy Roe* (HMV)		13	17	19
12 Walk Like A Man *The Four Seasons* (Stateside)		14	18	–
13 Losing You *Brenda Lee* (Brunswick)		10	11	10
14 Summer Holiday *Cliff Richard* (Columbia)		19	–	–
15 Scarlett O'Hara *Jet Harris and Tony Meehan* (Decca)		7	3	2
16 Say Wonderful Things *Ronnie Carroll* (Philips)		20	–	–
17 Two Kinds Of Teardrops *Del Shannon* (London)		9	5	6
18 He's So Fine *The Chiffons* (Stateside)		16	16	16
19 Like I've Never Been Gone *Billy Fury* (Decca)		–	–	–
20 End Of The World *Skeeter Davis* (RCA)		–	–	–
43 Do You Want To Know A Secret? *Billy J. Kramer and The Dakotas* (Parlophone)		17	10	3
24 Young Lovers *Paul and Paula* (Philips)		18	14	9
– Lucky Lips *Cliff Richard* (Columbia)		21	9	4
29 Deck Of Cards *Wink Martindale* (London)		22	19	13
– When Will You Say I Love You? *Billy Fury* (Decca)		–	28	15
37 Pipeline *The Chantays* (London)		32	22	20

JUNE 1963

1		8	15	22	29
1 From Me To You *The Beatles* (Parlophone)		1	1	2	4
2 Do You Want To Know A Secret? *Billy J. Kramer and The Dakotas* (Parlophone)		2	3	4	7
3 Scarlett O'Hara *Jet Harris and Tony Meehan* (Decca)		4	5	7	11
4 Lucky Lips *Cliff Richard* (Columbia)		8	6	10	12
5 Can't Get Used To Losing You *Andy Williams* (CBS)		10	14	14	19
6 Two Kinds Of Teardrops *Del Shannon* (London)		6	13	15	16

1	8	15	22	29
7 When Will You Say I Love You? *Billy Fury* (Decca)	3	4	5	10
8 In Dreams *Roy Orbison* (London)	11	10	11	13
9 Young Lovers *Paul and Paula* (Philips)	13	11	17	20
10 Deck Of Cards *Wink Martindale* (London)	9	9	8	8
11 Nobody's Darlin' But Mine *Frank Ifield* (Columbia)	14	15	18	–
12 Losing You *Brenda Lee* (Brunswick)	18	–	–	–
13 How Do You Do It? *Gerry and The Pacemakers* (Columbia)	15	20	19	–
14 Take These Chains From My Heart *Ray Charles* (HMV)	5	8	6	5
15 From A Jack To A King *Ned Miller* (London)	17	–	–	–
16 If You Gotta Make A Fool Of Somebody *Freddie and The Dreamers* (Columbia)	12	7	3	3
17 He's So Fine *The Chiffons* (Stateside)	20	–	–	–
18 Say I Won't Be There *The Springfields* (Philips)	–	–	–	–
19 Pipeline *The Chantays* (London)	16	19	–	–
20 Harvest Of Love *Benny Hill* (Pye)	–	–	20	–
22 I Like It *Gerry and The Pacemakers* (Columbia)	15	2	1	1
33 Falling *Roy Orbison* (London)	19	17	12	9
– Atlantis *The Shadows* (Columbia)	27	12	9	2
– Bo Diddley *Buddy Holly* (Coral)	35	16	13	6
29 Forget Him *Bobby Rydell* (Cameo-Parkway)	21	18	16	14
– Welcome To My World *Jim Reeves* (RCA)	–	41	26	15
– Da Doo Ron Ron *The Crystals* (London)	–	–	37	17
– The Ice Cream Man *The Tornados* (Decca)	34	25	22	18

JULY 1963

6	13	20	27
1 I Like It *Gerry and The Pacemakers* (Columbia)	1	2	7
2 Atlantis *The Shadows* (Columbia)	3	4	4
3 Confessin' *Frank Ifield* (Columbia)	2	1	1
4 If You Gotta Make A Fool Of Somebody *Freddie and The Dreamers* (Columbia)	8	14	16
5 Deck Of Cards *Wink Martindale* (London)	7	10	10
6 Take These Chains From My Heart *Ray Charles* (HMV)	5	6	6
7 Bo Diddley *Buddy Holly* (Coral)	4	8	13
8 From Me To You *The Beatles* (Parlophone)	13	16	15
9 Welcome To My World *Jim Reeves* (RCA)	6	12	11
10 Falling *Roy Orbison* (London)	11	13	14
11 Do You Want To Know A Secret? *Billy J. Kramer and The Dakotas* (Parlophone)	14	18	19
12 When Will You Say I Love You? *Billy Fury* (Decca)	16	19	–
13 Forget Him *Bobby Rydell* (Cameo-Parkway)	15	15	17
14 It's My Party *Lesley Gore* (Mercury)	9	9	9
15 In Dreams *Roy Orbison* (London)	20	–	–
16 Da Doo Ron Ron *The Crystals* (London)	12	5	6
17 Scarlett O'Hara *Jet Harris and Tony Meehan* (Decca)	–	–	–
18 The Ice Cream Man *The Tornados* (Decca)	–	–	–
19 Lucky Lips *Cliff Richard* (Columbia)	–	–	–
20 Two Kinds Of Teardrops *Del Shannon* (London)	–	–	–
27 Devil In Disguise *Elvis Presley* (RCA)	10	3	2
39 Sweets For My Sweet *The Searchers* (Pye)	17	7	3
22 You Can Never Stop Me Loving You *Kenny Lynch* (HMV)	18	20	18
48 Twist And Shout *Brian Poole and The Tremeloes* (Decca)	19	11	5
35 Suki Yaki *Kyu Sakamoto* (HMV)	25	17	12
– I Wonder *Brenda Lee* (Brunswick)	–	30	20

AUGUST 1963

3		10	17	24	31
1	Devil In Disguise *Elvis Presley* (RCA)	3	5	11	15
2	Confessin' *Frank Ifield* (Columbia)	2	2	4	9
3	Sweets For My Sweet *The Seachers* (Pye)	1	1	2	3
4	Twist And Shout *Brian Poole and The Tremeloes* (Decca)	4	4	7	13
5	Da Doo Ron Ron *The Crystals* (London)	5	8	8	14
6	I Like It *Gerry and The Pacemakers* (Columbia)	9	16	20	–
7	Atlantis *The Shadows* (Columbia)	7	11	16	–
8	Suki Yaki *Kyu Sakamoto* (HMV)	6	9	14	16
9	Welcome To My World *Jim Reeves* (RCA)	15	13	13	18
10	It's My Party *Lesley Gore* (Mercury)	12	19	–	–
11	Take These Chains From My Heart *Ray Charles* (HMV)	17	18	19	–
12	You Can Never Stop Me Loving You *Kenny Lynch* (HMV)	10	15	17	–
13	Deck Of Cards *Wink Martindale* (London)	–	–	–	–
14	I Wonder *Brenda Lee* (Brunswick)	18	17	15	–
15	Theme From The Legion's Last Patrol *Ken Thorne and his Orchestra* (HMV)	14	7	6	4
16	Bo Diddley *Buddy Holly* (Coral)	–	–	–	–
17	From Me To You *The Beatles* (Parlophone)	20	–	–	–
18	Falling *Roy Orbison* (London)	–	–	–	–
19	In Summer *Billy Fury* (Decca)	6	8	5	8
20	Wipeout *The Surfaris* (London)	13	10	10	5
34	Bad To Me *Billy J. Kramer and The Dakotas* (Parlophone)	11	3	1	1
21	I'll Never Get Over You *Johnny Kidd and The Pirates* (HMV)	16	12	9	6
22	The Cruel Sea *The Dakotas* (Parlophone)	19	22	21	20
–	I'm Telling You Now *Freddie and The Dreamers* (Columbia)	34	14	3	2
–	You Don't Have To Be A Baby To Cry *The Caravelles* (Decca)	36	20	12	7
–	Just Like Eddie *Heinz* (Decca)	38	26	18	11
–	It's All In The Game *Cliff Richard* (Columbia)	–	–	25	10
–	She Loves You *The Beatles* (Parlophone)	–	–	–	12
–	Dance On *Kathy Kirby* (Decca)	–	42	27	17
–	I Want To Stay Here *Steve Lawrence and Eydie Gorme* (CBS)	–	–	36	19

SEPTEMBER 1963

7		14	21	28
1	Bad To Me *Billy J. Kramer and The Dakotas* (Parlophone)	3	3	11
2	I'm Telling You Now *Freddie and The Dreamers* (Columbia)	5	6	14
3	She Loves You *The Beatles* (Parlophone)	1	1	1
4	It's All In The Game *Cliff Richard* (Columbia)	2	2	2
5	I'll Never Get Over You *Johnny Kidd and The Pirates* (HMV)	4	5	6
6	Sweets For My Sweet *The Searchers* (Pye)	12	17	–
7	You Don't Have To Be A Baby To Cry *The Caravelles* (Decca)	6	7	12
8	Wipeout *The Surfaris* (London)	8	10	13
9	Just Like Eddie *Heinz* (Decca)	9	8	5
10	I Want To Stay Here *Steve Lawrence and Eydie Gorme* (CBS)	7	4	3
11	Theme From The Legion's Last Patrol *Ken Thorne and his Orchestra* (HMV)	10	11	19
12	Confessin' *Frank Ifield* (Columbia)	15	20	–
13	In Summer *Billy Fury* (Decca)	14	19	–
14	Dance On *Kathy Kirby* (Decca)	11	14	16
15	Twist And Shout *Brian Poole and The Tremeloes* (Decca)	17	–	–
16	Da Doo Ron Ron *The Crystals* (London)	20	–	–
17	Still *Karl Denver* (Decca)	13	15	18

7	14	21	28
18 The Cruel Sea *The Dakotas* (Parlophone)	19	–	–
19 Suki Yaki *Kyu Sakamoto* (HMV)	–	–	–
20 Devil In Disguise *Elvis Presley* (RCA)	–	–	–
49 Applejack *Jet Harris and Tony Meehan* (Decca)	16	9	4
35 Wishing *Buddy Holly* (Coral)	18	13	10
– Do You Love Me? *Brian Poole and The Tremeloes* (Decca)	33	12	7
– If I Had A Hammer *Trini Lopez* (Reprise)	36	16	8
29 Whispering *The Bachelors* (Decca)	21	18	–
– Then He Kissed Me *The Crystals* (London)	–	22	9
– Shindig *The Shadows* (Columbia)	–	32	15
– Blue Bayou/Mean Woman Blues *Roy Orbison* (London)	–	41	17
38 Searchin' *The Hollies* (Parlophone)	32	26	20

OCTOBER 1963

5	12	19	26
1 She Loves You *The Beatles* (Parlophone)	3	3	3
2 Do You Love Me? *Brian Poole and The Tremeloes* (Decca)	1	1	1
3 Then He Kissed Me *The Crystals* (London)	2	2	4
4 It's All In The Game *Cliff Richard* (Columbia)	8	16	19
5 If I Had A Hammer *Trini Lopez* (Reprise)	4	6	7
6 I Want To Stay Here *Steve Lawrence and Eydie Gorme* (CBS)	11	14	–
7 Just Like Eddie *Heinz* (Decca)	15	17	20
8 Shindig *The Shadows* (Columbia)	6	8	12
9 Blue Bayou/Mean Woman Blues *Roy Orbison* (London)	5	4	5
10 I'll Never Get Over You *Johnny Kidd and The Pirates* (HMV)	20	–	–
11 Applejack *Jet Harris and Tony Meehan* (Decca)	9	12	15
12 Wishing *Buddy Holly* (Coral)	10	15	16
13 The First Time *Adam Faith* (Parlophone)	7	5	8
14 Still *Karl Denver* (Decca)	19	20	17
15 Bad To Me *Billy J. Kramer and The Dakotas* (Parlophone)	–	–	–
16 You Don't Have To Be A Baby To Cry *The Caravelles* (Decca)	–	–	–
17 Searchin' *The Hollies* (Parlophone)	12	13	13
18 Hello Little Girl *The Fourmost* (Parlophone)	14	11	9
19 I'm Telling You Now *Freddie and The Dreamers* (Columbia)	–	–	–
20 Hello Mudduh! Hello Fadduh! *Alan Sherman* (Warner Bros.)	17	18	14
27 I Who Have Nothing *Shirley Bassey* (Columbia)	13	10	6
25 Everybody *Tommy Roe* (HMV)	16	9	11
28 Somebody Else's Girl *Billy Fury* (Decca)	18	19	–
– You'll Never Walk Alone *Gerry and The Pacemakers* (Columbia)	22	7	2
– Let It Rock/Memphis Tennessee *Chuck Berry* (Pye)	25	21	10
– Be My Baby *The Ronettes* (London)	–	32	18

NOVEMBER 1963

2	9	16	23	30
1 You'll Never Walk Alone *Gerry and The Pacemakers* (Columbia)	1	1	1	2
2 She Loves You *The Beatles* (Parlophone)	2	3	2	1
3 Do You Love Me? *Brian Poole and The Tremeloes* (Decca)	5	8	12	16
4 Blue Bayou/Mean Woman Blues *Roy Orbison* (London)	3	4	7	9
5 Then He Kissed Me *The Crystals* (London)	9	10	14	17
6 If I Had A Hammer *Trini Lopez* (Reprise)	10	13	15	15
7 I Who Have Nothing *Shirley Bassey* (Columbia)	8	9	8	11
8 Sugar And Spice *The Searchers* (Pye)	4	2	3	6
9 Let It Rock/Memphis Tennessee *Chuck Berry* (Pye)	7	6	10	12
10 The First Time *Adam Faith* (Parlophone)	11	14	18	–
11 Be My Baby *The Ronettes* (London)	6	5	4	8

	9	16	23	30
12 Hello Little Girl *The Fourmost* (Parlophone)	13	20	–	–
13 Bossa Nova Baby *Elvis Presley* (RCA)	14	18	20	–
14 Hello Muddah! Hello Fadduh! *Alan Sherman* (Warner Bros.)	–	–	–	–
15 Everybody *Tommy Roe* (HMV)	17	–	–	–
16 Fools Rush In *Ricky Nelson* (Brunswick)	12	15	16	18
17 Miss You *Jimmy Young* (Columbia)	15	19	18	–
18 Shindig *The Shadows* (Columbia)	18	–	–	–
19 Searchin' *The Hollies* (Parlophone)	–	–	–	–
20 Still *Karl Denver* (Decca)	20	–	–	–
21 Blowin' In The Wind *Peter Paul and Mary* (Warner Bros.)	16	17	17	13
24 Memphis Tennessee *Dave Berry and The Cruisers* (Decca)	19	–	–	–
– Don't Talk To Him *Cliff Richard and The Shadows* (Columbia)	23	7	5	3
– I'll Keep You Satisfied *Billy J. Kramer and The Dakotas* (Parlophone)	–	11	9	4
– Secret Love *Kathy Kirby* (Decca)	–	12	6	5
44 Maria Elena *Los Indios Tabajaros* (RCA)	28	16	13	10
– You Were Made For Me *Freddie and The Dreamers* (Columbia)	39	23	11	7
– It's Almost Tomorrow *Mark Wynter* (Pye)	–	32	22	14
– Glad All Over *The Dave Clark Five* (Columbia)	–	–	38	19
– From Russia With Love *Matt Monro* (Parlophone)	–	43	27	20

DECEMBER 1963

	7	14	21
1 She Loves You *The Beatles* (Parlophone)		2	2
2 Don't Talk To Him *Cliff Richard* (Columbia)		6	10
3 You Were Made For Me *Freddie and The Dreamers* (Columbia)		3	3
4 You'll Never Walk Alone *Gerry and The Pacemakers* (Columbia)		8	12
5 Secret Love *Kathy Kirby* (Decca)		4	5
6 I'll Keep You Satisfied *Billy J. Kramer and The Dakotas* (Parlophone)		11	16
7 Maria Elena *Los Indios Tabajaros* (RCA)		5	7
8 Glad All Over *The Dave Clark Five* (Columbia)		9	4
9 I Only Want To Be With You *Dusty Springfield* (Philips)		7	6
10 I Want To Hold Your Hand *The Beatles* (Parlophone)		1	1
11 Be My Baby *The Ronettes* (London)		–	–
12 It's Almost Tomorrow *Mark Wynter* (Pye)		14	20
13 Sugar And Spice *The Searchers* (Pye)		–	–
14 Blue Bayou/Mean Woman Blues *Roy Orbison* (London)		16	–
15 I Who Have Nothing *Shirley Bassey* (Columbia)		12	–
16 I Wanna Be Your Man *The Rolling Stones* (Decca)		15	13
17 Deep Purple *April Stevens and Nino Tempo* (London)		18	–
18 Let It Rock/Memphis Tennessee *Chuck Berry* (Pye)		–	–
19 Blowin' In The Wind *Peter Paul and Mary* (Warner Bros.)		–	–
20 Hungry For Love *Johnny Kidd* (HMV)		–	–
24 Dominique *The Singing Nun* (Philips)		10	8
28 Geronimo *The Shadows* (Columbia)		13	11
27 Stay *The Hollies* (Parlophone)		17	19
23 Money *Bern Elliott and The Fenmen* (Decca)		19	14
33 24 Hours From Tulsa *Gene Pitney* (UA)		20	9
35 Swinging On A Star *Big Dee Irwin* (Colpix)		27	15
– Not Too Little Not Too Much *Chris Sandford* (Decca)		30	17
31 If I Ruled The World *Harry Secombe* (Philips)		22	18

There was no chart for 28 December 1963.

1963

1963 was definitely a year for British artists, for the charts produced names such as The Beatles, The Rolling Stones, Freddie and The Dreamers, Billy J. Kramer and The Dakotas, The Searchers, The Bachelors, Gerry and The Pacemakers, and Brian Poole and The Tremeloes.

The chart regulars also enjoyed various degrees of success. The Shadows had four hits which all entered the Top Ten, except for 'Geronimo'. Cliff also had four hits in 1963. One of these, 'Summer Holiday', was a Number One, 'It's All In The Game' and 'Don't Talk To Him' both reached the Number Two position, and 'Lucky Lips' settled at Number Four.

Billy Fury was another chart regular who achieved four chart successes in 1963, of which only one, 'Somebody Else's Girl', did not reach any of the Top Ten positions.

For the American contingent, Presley managed four hits, of which only 'Devil In Disguise' was a Number One. The other three hits did not make the Top Ten – a somewhat shattering change from 1962, when every Presley hit had been a Number One! However, what America did contribute to the British music scene of the time was a number of classic pop sounds, as opposed to successful artists. Some of these classics included 'He's So Fine' from The Chiffons; 'Rhythm Of The Rain' by The Cascades; 'Our Day Will Come' from Ruby and The Romantics; The Drifters' version of 'Up On The Roof'; 'Da Do Ron Ron', 'He's A Rebel' and 'Then He Kissed Me' all by The Crystals; The Surfaris with 'Wipeout'; and 'If I Had A Hammer' from Trini Lopez.

The Beatles had, of course, announced their arrival in December 1962 with 'Love Me Do', but this record had only achieved a brief Top Twenty innings. It was 'Please Please Me', their second release, which really set the ball rolling, though strangely this record failed to reach Number One. Their next 11 discs all reached the coveted Number One position, three of which were released in 1963 – 'From Me To You', 'She Loves You' and 'I Want To Hold Your Hand'.

Liverpool was the city with the sounds and Billy J. Kramer had a Number One with 'Bad To Me', though Kramer and his group, The Dakotas, are perhaps better remembered for their rendering of 'Do You Want To Know A Secret ?', a disc which reached the Number Two position. Gerry and The Pacemakers hit the Number One spot with their first record, 'How Do You Do It ?', which was followed by 'I Like It' and 'You'll Never Walk Alone', which both reached Number One, and so this Liverpudlian group ended 1963 with a hat-trick of hits.

Late in the year, Cilla Black, another Liverpudlian, entered the charts with 'Love Of The Loved' and Dusty Springfield made her first solo record, 'I Only Want To Be With You', which reached the Top Twenty in December. The Springfields, including Dusty, enjoyed several hits in 1963 including 'Island Of Dreams' and 'Say I Won't Be There'.

In America, The Beach Boys were becoming active and Bob Dylan arrived in Britain by means of one of his songs, 'Blowin' In The Wind', becoming a chart hit for Peter, Paul and Mary.

Amidst the Mersey Sound, The Beatles and other pop heroes such as 12-year-old Stevie Wonder came the march of the mods. The mod philosophy of life hinged onto French clothes, which were neat and casual, Italian scooters, and music drawn from the West Indies as well as from America and Britain. The mod life style was the complete antithesis of the rocker philosophy, and scooters and motorbikes clashed many times on pre-selected beaches or areas of waste ground. The two life styles, reflected in the music of the time, apparently could not exist side by side without essential ego-boosting and violent battles.

Television had done its best to fulfil the needs of the rockers, but with *Ready, Steady, Go* it set out to cater for the mods. Introduced by Cathy McGowan, the show poured forth the latest news for mods in terms of slang, clothes and music. Some of the mods later became involved in pop management, but in the end, as always, the movement burned itself out and pop continued in its usual habit of tottering between crazes, looking for something new to latch onto.

JANUARY 1964

4	11	18	25
1 I Want To Hold Your Hand *The Beatles* (Parlophone)	1	2	3
2 Glad All Over *The Dave Clark Five* (Columbia)	2	1	1
3 She Loves You *The Beatles* (Parlophone)	5	5	8
4 You Were Made For Me *Freddie and The Dreamers* (Columbia)	7	9	20
5 24 Hours From Tulsa *Gene Pitney* (UA)	6	6	5
6 I Only Want To Be With You *Dusty Springfield* (Philips)	4	4	4
7 Dominique *The Singing Nun* (Philips)	10	10	16
8 Maria Elena *Los Indios Tabajaros* (RCA)	13	11	19
9 Secret Love *Kathy Kirby* (Decca)	9	12	18
10 Don't Talk To Him *Cliff Richard* (Columbia)	14	–	–
11 Swinging On A Star *Big Dee Irwin* (Colpix)	8	7	7
12 Geronimo *The Shadows* (Columbia)	18	–	–
13 Hippy Hippy Shake *The Swinging Blue Jeans* (HMV)	3	3	2
14 Kiss Me Quick *Elvis Presley* (RCA)	15	15	14
15 I Wanna Be Your Man *The Rolling Stones* (Decca)	12	14	15
16 You'll Never Walk Alone *Gerry and The Pacemakers* (Parlophone)	17	20	–
17 Stay *The Hollies* (Parlophone)	11	8	12
18 Not Too Little Not Too Much *Chris Sandford* (Decca)	19	18	–
19 Money *Bern Elliott and The Fenmen* (Decca)	–	–	–
20 We Are In Love *Adam Faith* (Parlophone)	16	13	11
37 Do You Really Love Me Too? *Billy Fury* (Decca)	20	17	17
– Don't Blame Me *Frank Ifield* (Columbia)	38	19	13
– As Usual *Brenda Lee* (Brunswick)	29	16	9
– Needles And Pins *The Searchers* (Pye)	–	26	6
– I'm The One *Gerry and The Pacemakers* (Parlophone)	–	23	10

FEBRUARY 1964

1	8	15	22	29
1 Needles And Pins *The Searchers* (Pye)	1	1	3	3
2 Glad All Over *The Dave Clark Five* (Columbia)	4	6	10	14
3 Hippy Hippy Shake *The Swinging Blue Jeans* (HMV)	3	4	6	12
4 I'm The One *Gerry and The Pacemakers* (Columbia)	2	2	4	6
5 I Only Want To Be With You *Dusty Springfield* (Philips)	11	17	17	–
6 I Want To Hold Your Hand *The Beatles* (Parlophone)	7	15	15	17
7 24 Hours From Tulsa *Gene Pitney* (UA)	6	11	16	19
8 Stay *The Hollies* (Parlophone)	12	19	–	–
9 As Usual *Brenda Lee* (Brunswick)	5	7	7	9
10 Don't Blame Me *Frank Ifield* (Columbia)	10	8	12	15
11 We Are In Love *Adam Faith* (Parlophone)	18	–	–	–
12 Swinging On A Star *Big Dee Irwin* (Colpix)	16	20	–	–
13 Do You Really Love Me Too? *Billy Fury* (Decca)	14	–	8	10
14 5-4-3-2-1 *Manfred Mann* (HMV)	9	5	5	7
15 Kiss Me Quick *Elvis Presley* (RCA)	–	–	–	–
16 She Loves You *The Beatles* (Parlophone)	19	–	–	–
17 I Wanna Be Your Man *The Rolling Stones* (Decca)	–	–	–	–
18 Baby I Love You *The Ronettes* (London)	13	12	13	11
19 I Think Of You *The Merseybeats* (Fontana)	15	9	9	5
20 I'm In Love *The Fourmost* (Parlophone)	17	18	20	8
22 Diane *The Bachelors* (Decca)	8	3	1	1
26 Whispering *April Stevens and Nino Tempo* (London)	20	–	–	–
– Anyone Who Had A Heart *Cilla Black* (Parlophone)	28	10	2	2
42 Candy Man *Brian Poole and The Tremeloes* (Decca)	22	13	11	–
– I'm The Lonely One *Cliff Richard* (Columbia)	23	14	–	–
30 For You *Ricky Nelson* (Brunswick)	21	16	14	19

1	**8**	**15**	**22**	**29**
49 Boys Cry *Eden Kane* (Fontana)	33	24	18	13
– Bits And Pieces *The Dave Clark Five* (Columbia)	–	–	19	4
– Stay Awhile *Dusty Springfield* (Philips)	–	–	30	18
– Over You *Freddie and The Dreamers* (Columbia)	–	–	44	20

MARCH 1964

7	**14**	**21**	**28**
1 Anyone Who Had A Heart *Cilla Black* (Parlophone)	1	3	4
2 Bits And Pieces *The Dave Clark Five* (Columbia)	2	2	5
3 Diane *The Bachelors* (Decca)	4	6	11
4 Needles And Pins *The Searchers* (Pye)	7	10	–
5 I Think Of You *The Merseybeats* (Fontana)	8	7	13
6 Candy Man *Brian Poole and The Tremeloes* (Decca)	11	15	20
7 I'm The One *Gerry and The Pacemakers* (Columbia)	12	19	–
8 5-4-3-2-1 *Manfred Mann* (HMV)	20	–	–
9 Little Children *Billy J. Kramer and The Dakotas* (Parlophone)	3	1	1
10 As Usual *Brenda Lee* (Brunswick)	17	20	–
11 Not Fade Away *The Rolling Stones* (Decca)	5	4	3
12 Boys Cry *Eden Kane* (Fontana)	9	8	9
13 Over You *Freddie and The Dreamers* (Columbia)	18	16	18
14 I'm The Lonely One *Cliff Richard* (Columbia)	–	–	–
15 Baby I Love You *The Ronettes* (London)	19	–	–
16 Stay Awhile *Dusty Springfield* (Philips)	13	13	19
17 Borne On The Wind *Roy Orbison* (London)	15	17	–
18 Let Me Go Lover *Kathy Kirby* (Decca)	10	11	15
19 For You *Ricky Nelson* (Brunswick)	–	–	–
20 Just One Look *The Hollies* (Parlophone)	6	5	2
21 I Love You Because *Jim Reeves* (RCA)	14	9	6
28 That Girl Belongs To Yesterday *Gene Pitney* (UA)	16	12	8
36 Theme For Young Lovers *The Shadows* (Columbia)	22	14	14
47 Tell Me When *The Applejacks* (Decca)	29	18	12
– Can't Buy Me Love *The Beatles* (Parlophone)	–	–	7
– I Believe *The Bachelors* (Decca)	–	28	10
– World Without Love *Peter and Gordon* (Columbia)	39	36	16
– Viva Las Vegas *Elvis Presley* (RCA)	46	29	17

APRIL 1964

4	**11**	**18**	**25**
1 Can't Buy Me Love *The Beatles* (Parlophone)	1	1	2
2 Little Children *Billy J. Kramer and The Dakotas* (Parlophone)	2	4	9
3 Just One Look *The Hollies* (Parlophone)	5	6	10
4 Not Fade Away *The Rolling Stones* (Decca)	6	8	8
5 I Love You Because *Jim Reeves* (RCA)	7	5	6
6 I Believe *The Bachelors* (Decca)	3	3	3
7 Bits And Pieces *The Dave Clark Five* (Columbia)	10	14	–
8 Diane *The Bachelors* (Decca)	13	16	–
9 That Girl Belongs To Yesterday *Gene Pitney* (UA)	8	9	15
10 Anyone Who Had A Heart *Cilla Black* (Parlophone)	11	15	19
11 Tell Me When *The Applejacks* (Decca)	9	7	7
12 Boys Cry *Eden Kane* (Fontana)	–	–	–
13 World Without Love *Peter and Gordon* (Columbia)	4	2	1
14 Theme For Young Lovers *The Shadows* (Columbia)	12	19	20
15 I Think Of You *The Merseybeats* (Fontana)	20	–	–
16 Over You *Freddie and The Dreamers* (Columbia)	–	–	–
17 Let Me Go Lover *Kathy Kirby* (Decca)	19	–	–
18 Viva Las Vegas *Elvis Presley* (RCA)	17	18	–

4		11	18	25
19	Stay Awhile *Dusty Springfield* (Philips)	–	–	–
20	Good Golly Miss Molly *The Swinging Blue Jeans* (HMV)	14	11	14
–	Everything's All Right *The Mojos* (Decca)	18	13	12
–	Move Over Darling *Doris Day* (CBS)	15	12	11
–	My Boy Lollipop *Millie* (Fontana)	16	10	5
–	Mockingbird Hill *The Migil Five* (Pye)	30	17	13
–	Don't Throw Your Love Away *The Searchers* (Pye)	–	20	4
–	Hubble Bubble Toil And Trouble *Manfred Mann* (HMV)	–	29	16
–	Don't Let The Sun Catch You Crying *Gerry and The Pacemakers* (Columbia)	–	31	17
–	Juliet *The Four Pennies* (Philips)	36	32	18

MAY 1964

2		9	16	23	30
1	World Without Love *Peter and Gordon* (Columbia)	4	5	12	–
2	Don't Throw Your Love Away *The Searchers* (Pye)	1	1	3	8
3	I Believe *The Bachelors* (Decca)	2	4	6	9
4	Can't Buy Me Love *The Beatles* (Parlophone)	7	13	15	–
5	My Boy Lollipop *Millie* (Fontana)	3	3	2	3
6	I Love You Because *Jim Reeves* (RCA)	10	8	10	12
7	Don't Let The Sun Catch You Crying *Gerry and The Pacemakers* (Columbia)	6	9	7	15
8	Move Over Darling *Doris Day* (CBS)	8	15	17	19
9	Everything's All Right *The Mojos* (Decca)	17	18	–	–
10	Mockingbird Hill *The Migil Five* (Pye)	12	14	18	–
11	Hubble Bubble Toil And Trouble *Manfred Mann* (HMV)	15	19	–	–
12	Juliet *The Four Pennies* (Philips)	5	2	1	2
13	Not Fade Away *The Rolling Stones* (Decca)	19	–	–	–
14	Tell Me When *The Applejacks* (Decca)	19	–	–	–
15	Walk On By *Dionne Warwick* (Pye)	9	11	11	11
16	Little Children *Billy J. Kramer and The Dakotas* (Parlophone)	–	–	–	–
17	Don't Turn Around *The Merseybeats* (Fontana)	13	16	16	16
18	Just One Look *The Hollies* (Parlophone)	–	–	–	–
19	A Little Lovin' *The Fourmost* (Parlophone)	11	10	8	6
20	Good Golly Miss Molly *The Swinging Blue Jeans* (HMV)	–	–	–	–
31	It's Over *Roy Orbison* (London)	14	6	5	4
30	Constantly *Cliff Richard* (Columbia)	16	7	9	5
28	If I Loved You *Richard Anthony* (Columbia)	18	20	19	–
38	I Will *Billy Fury* (Decca)	20	17	14	14
–	You're My World *Cilla Black* (Parlophone)	30	12	4	1
–	The Rise And Fall Of Flingel Bunt *The Shadows* (Columbia)	37	21	13	7
–	No Particular Place To Go *Chuck Berry* (Pye)	42	26	20	10
–	Someone, Someone *Brian Poole* (Decca)	49	34	26	13
–	You're The One *Kathy Kirby* (Decca)	36	30	28	17
–	Here I Go Again *The Hollies* (Parlophone)	–	–	46	18
36	Non Ho L'Eta Per Amarti *Gigliola Cinquetti* (Decca)	28	24	22	20

JUNE 1964

6		13	20	27
1	You're My World *Cilla Black* (Parlophone)	1	1	3
2	It's Over *Roy Orbison* (London)	2	2	1
3	Juliet *The Four Pennies* (Philips)	5	13	15
4	Constantly *Cliff Richard* (Columbia)	6	9	16
5	The Rise And Fall Of Flingel Bunt *The Shadows* (Columbia)	7	8	13
6	No Particular Place To Go *Chuck Berry* (Pye)	3	6	11

	13	20	27
6			
7 My Boy Lollipop *Millie* (Fontana)	15	–	–
8 Someone, Someone *Brian Poole* (Decca)	4	3	2
9 A Little Lovin' *The Fourmost* (Parlophone)	14	19	–
10 Walk On By *Dionne Warwick* (Pye)	13	17	19
11 Here I Go Again *The Hollies* (Parlophone)	8	4	7
12 My Guy *Mary Wells* (Stateside)	9	5	5
13 I Love You Because *Jim Reeves* (RCA)	12	15	14
14 I Believe *The Bachelors* (Decca)	–	–	–
15 Don't Throw Your Love Away *The Searchers* (Pye)	–	–	–
16 I Will *Billy Fury* (Decca)	20	–	–
17 Shout *Lulu and The Luvvers* (Decca)	10	7	9
18 Non Ho L'Eta Per Amarti *Gigliola Cinquetti* (Decca)	17	18	–
19 You're The One *Kathy Kirby* (Decca)	–	–	–
20 I Love You Baby *Freddie and The Dreamers* (Columbia)	16	20	–
21 Can't You See She's Mine *The Dave Clark Five* (Columbia)	11	11	10
37 Hello Dolly *Louis Armstrong* (London)	18	10	4
29 Ramona *The Bachelors* (Decca)	19	12	6
39 Nobody I Know *Peter and Gordon* (Columbia)	23	14	12
34 You're No Good *The Swinging Blue Jeans* (HMV)	25	16	8
32 Hold Me *P. J. Proby* (Decca)	31	22	17
41 Hello Dolly *Frankie Vaughan* (Philips)	28	26	18
45 Bamalama Bamaloo *Little Richard* (London)	29	25	20

JULY 1964

	11	18	25
4			
1 It's Over *Roy Orbison* (London)	5	7	10
2 Someone, Someone *Brian Poole* (Decca)	4	10	15
3 You're No Good *The Swinging Blue Jeans* (HMV)	7	8	14
4 Ramona *The Bachelors* (Decca)	6	12	18
5 Hold Me *P. J. Proby* (Decca)	3	5	7
6 House Of The Rising Sun *The Animals* (Columbia)	1	2	5
7 You're My World *Cilla Black* (Parlophone)	15	20	–
8 Hello Dolly *Louis Armstrong* (London)	9	13	17
9 My Guy *Mary Wells* (Stateside)	12	16	19
10 Nobody I Know *Peter and Gordon* (Columbia)	11	14	–
11 Can't You See She's Mine *The Dave Clark Five* (Columbia)	14	15	–
12 I Won't Forget You *Jim Reeves* (RCA)	8	4	4
13 Shout *Lulu and The Luvvers* (Decca)	17	19	–
14 Here I Go Again *The Hollies* (Parlophone)	16	–	–
15 The Rise And Fall Of Flingel Bunt *The Shadows* (Columbia)	19	–	–
16 I Love You Because *Jim Reeves* (RCA)	–	–	–
17 Kissin' Cousins *Elvis Presley* (RCA)	10	11	11
18 Hello Dolly *Frankie Vaughan* (Philips)	20	–	–
19 No Particular Place To Go *Chuck Berry* (Pye)	–	–	–
20 Like Dreamers Do *The Applejacks* (Decca)	–	–	–
25 It's All Over Now *The Rolling Stones* (Decca)	2	1	2
31 On The Beach *Cliff Richard* (Columbia)	13	9	8
42 I Just Don't Know What To Do With Myself *Dusty Springfield* (Philips)	18	6	3
– A Hard Day's Night *The Beatles* (Parlophone)	–	3	1
– Call Up The Groups *The Barron-Knights* (Columbia)	38	17	6
– Wishin' And Hopin' *The Merseybeats* (Fontana)	30	18	16
– Do Wah Diddy Diddy *Manfred Mann* (HMV)	–	30	9
– Tobacco Road *The Nashville Teens* (Decca)	48	26	12
– Someday We're Gonna Love Again *The Searchers* (Pye)	–	22	13
– I Get Around *The Beach Boys* (Capitol)	46	32	20

		8	15	22	29
1					
1	A Hard Day's Night *The Beatles* (Parlophone)	1	2	2	5
2	It's All Over Now *The Rolling Stones* (Decca)	4	4	7	9
3	I Just Don't Know What To Do With Myself *Dusty Springfield* (Philips)	5	7	9	13
4	Call Up The Groups *The Barron-Knights* (Columbia)	3	3	5	10
5	Do Wah Diddy Diddy *Manfred Mann* (HMV)	2	1	1	2
6	Hold Me *P. J. Proby* (Decca)	13	18	–	–
7	House Of The Rising Sun *The Animals* (Columbia)	8	13	–	–
8	On The Beach *Cliff Richard* (Columbia)	7	9	11	15
9	I Won't Forget You *Jim Reeves* (RCA)	9	5	4	3
10	Tobacco Road *The Nashville Teens* (Decca)	6	6	6	6
11	I Get Around *The Beach Boys* (Capitol)	10	8	8	7
12	Someday We're Gonna Love Again *The Searchers* (Pye)	11	16	18	–
13	Wishin' And Hopin' *The Merseybeats* (Fontana)	14	15	17	–
14	It's Over *Roy Orbison* (London)	17	–	–	–
15	Kissin' Cousins *Elvis Presley* (RCA)	16	–	–	–
16	Someone, Someone *Brian Poole* (Decca)	20	–	–	–
17	You're No Good *The Swinging Blue Jeans* (HMV)	19	–	–	–
18	It's Only Make Believe *Billy Fury* (Decca)	12	10	12	17
19	Ramona *The Bachelors* (Decca)	–	–	–	–
20	Hello Dolly *Louis Armstrong* (London)	–	–	–	–
22	From A Window *Billy J. Kramer and The Dakotas* (Parlophone)	15	12	10	19
34	Have I The Right *The Honeycombs* (Pye)	18	11	3	1
25	I Found Out The Hard Way *The Four Pennies* (Philips)	23	14	14	18
–	It's For You *Cilla Black* (Parlophone)	28	17	13	8
23	I Love You Because *Jim Reeves* (RCA)	26	19	16	14
46	You'll Never Get To Heaven *Dionne Warwick* (Pye)	25	20	–	–
–	You Really Got Me *The Kinks* (Pye)	–	34	15	4
–	As Tears Go By *Marianne Faithfull* (Decca)	–	27	19	16
41	The Crying Game *Dave Berry* (Decca)	41	21	20	12
–	I Wouldn't Trade You For The World *The Bachelors* (Decca)	–	43	21	11
–	Such A Night *Elvis Presley* (RCA)	–	–	31	20

		11	18	25
4				
1	Have I The Right *The Honeycombs* (Pye)	2	2	3
2	You Really Got Me *The Kinks* (Pye)	1	1	5
3	I Won't Forget You *Jim Reeves* (RCA)	3	4	7
4	Do Wah Diddy Diddy *Manfred Mann* (HMV)	6	8	15
5	The Crying Game *Dave Berry* (Decca)	5	6	10
6	A Hard Day's Night *The Beatles* (Parlophone)	10	15	19
7	It's For You *Cilla Black* (Parlophone)	11	18	–
8	I Wouldn't Trade You For The World *The Bachelors* (Decca)	4	7	6
9	I Get Around *The Beach Boys* (Capitol)	15	–	–
10	It's All Over Now *The Rolling Stones* (Decca)	17	20	–
11	Call Up The Groups *The Barron-Knights* (Columbia)	19	–	–
12	I Love You Because *Jim Reeves* (RCA)	14	11	14
13	Such A Night *Elvis Presley* (RCA)	13	14	18
14	Tobacco Road *The Nashville Teens* (Decca)	20	–	–
15	As Tears Go By *Marianne Faithfull* (Decca)	9	10	9
16	She's Not There *The Zombies* (Decca)	12	12	16
17	Rag Doll *The Four Seasons* (Philips)	8	5	2
18	I'm Into Something Good *Herman's Hermits* (Columbia)	7	3	1
19	The Wedding *Julie Rogers* (Mercury)	16	13	11

4		**11**	**18**	**25**
20 I Just Don't Know What To Do With Myself *Dusty Springfield* (Philips)		–	–	–
32 Where Did Our Love Go *The Supremes* (Stateside)		18	9	4
29 Everybody Loves Somebody *Dean Martin* (Reprise)		21	16	12
– Oh Pretty Woman *Roy Orbison* (London)		36	17	8
39 Together *P. J. Proby* (Decca)		25	19	13
– Is It Time *Brenda Lee* (Brunswick)		30	23	17
– I'm Crying *The Animals* (Columbia)		–	40	20

OCTOBER 1964

3	**10**	**17**	**24**	**31**
1 I'm Into Something Good *Herman's Hermits* (Columbia)	2	2	5	10
2 Rag Doll *The Four Seasons* (Philips)	4	5	12	16
3 Where Did Our Love Go *The Supremes* (Stateside)	3	3	4	5
4 Oh Pretty Woman *Roy Orbison* (London)	1	1	2	2
5 I Wouldn't Trade You For The World *The Bachelors* (Decca)	6	6	11	15
6 I Won't Forget You *Jim Reeves* (RCA)	7	10	14	17
7 The Wedding *Julie Rogers* (Mercury)	5	4	6	3
8 Have I The Right *The Honeycombs* (Pye)	13	18	–	–
9 As Tears Go By *Marianne Faithfull* (Decca)	12	15	19	–
10 You Really Got Me *The Kinks* (Pye)	16	20	–	–
11 Together *P. J. Proby* (Decca)	8	14	16	–
12 Everybody Loves Somebody *Dean Martin* (Reprise)	11	13	17	19
13 The Crying Game *Dave Berry* (Decca)	–	–	–	–
14 She's Not There *The Zombies* (Decca)	20	–	–	–
15 I'm Crying *The Animals* (Columbia)	10	8	9	14
16 When You Walk In The Room *The Searchers* (Pye)	9	7	3	4
17 I Love You Because *Jim Reeves* (RCA)	19	–	–	–
18 Is It True *Brenda Lee* (Brunswick)	18	–	–	–
19 Bread And Butter *The Newbeats* (Hickory)	15	19	–	–
20 We're Through *The Hollies* (Parlophone)	14	9	8	7
22 Walk Away *Matt Monro* (Parlophone)	17	12	7	6
– (There's) Always Something There To Remind Me *Sandie Shaw* (Pye)	31	11	1	1
– Twelfth Of Never *Cliff Richard* (Columbia)	30	16	13	8
31 How Soon *Henry Mancini* (RCA)	23	17	10	12
42 One Way Love *Cliff Bennett* (Parlophone)	29	23	15	9
– Sha La La *Manfred Mann* (HMV)	–	43	18	11
– Maybe I Know *Lesley Gore* (Mercury)	–	21	20	–
– Baby Love *The Supremes* (Stateside)	–	–	24	13
– He's In Town *The Rockin' Berries* (Pye)	–	44	29	18
– Um, Um, Um, Um, Um, Um *Wayne Fontana* (Fontana)	34	29	22	20

NOVEMBER 1964

7	**14**	**21**	**28**
1 (There's) Always Something There To Remind Me *Sandie Shaw* (Pye)	2	7	16
2 Oh Pretty Woman *Roy Orbison* (London)	1	4	8
3 The Wedding *Julie Rogers* (Mercury)	9	12	18
4 Walk Away *Matt Monro* (Parlophone)	4	8	14
5 Sha La La *Manfred Mann* (HMV)	3	5	11
6 When You Walk In The Room *The Searchers* (Pye)	11	15	–
7 Baby Love *The Supremes* (Stateside)	5	1	1
8 Twelfth Of Never *Cliff Richard* (Columbia)	13	18	–
9 Where Did Our Love Go *The Supremes* (Stateside)	16	–	–
10 We're Through *The Hollies* (Parlophone)	20	–	–

7		14	21	28
11	How Soon *Henry Mancini* (RCA)	–	–	–
12	One Way Love *Cliff Bennett* (Parlophone)	14	–	–
13	Um, Um, Um, Um, Um, Um *Wayne Fontana* (Fontana)	8	6	5
14	He's In Town *The Rocking Berries* (Pye)	6	3	4
15	I'm Into Something Good *Herman's Hermits* (Columbia)	–	–	–
16	Google Eye *The Nashville Teens* (Decca)	10	13	–
17	Ain't That Lovin' You Baby *Elvis Presley* (RCA)	15	19	–
18	All Day And All Of The Night *The Kinks* (Pye)	7	2	2
19	I Won't Forget You *Jim Reeves* (RCA)	–	–	–
20	I Wouldn't Trade You For The World *The Bachelors* (Decca)	–	–	–
21	Tokyo Melody *Helmut Zacharias Orchestra* (Polydor)	12	9	12
29	Don't Bring Me Down *The Pretty Things* (Fontana)	17	10	13
26	Remember (Walkin' In The Sand) *The Shangri-Las* (Red Bird)	18	14	15
33	There's A Heartache Following Me *Jim Reeves* (RCA)	19	11	7
–	I'm Gonna Be Strong *Gene Pitney* (Stateside)	34	16	6
28	Losing You *Dusty Springfield* (Philips)	22	17	10
–	Downtown *Petula Clark* (Pye)	41	20	9
–	Little Red Rooster *The Rolling Stones* (Decca)	–	24	3
30	Walk Tall *Val Doonican* (Decca)	25	23	17
–	Pretty Paper *Roy Orbison* (London)	–	34	19
36	Black Girl *The Four Pennies* (Philips)	31	27	20

DECEMBER 1964

5		12	19	26
1	Little Red Rooster *The Rolling Stones* (Decca)	3	5	8
2	I'm Gonna Be Strong *Gene Pitney* (Stateside)	2	4	3
3	Baby Love *The Supremes* (Stateside)	8	10	15
4	Downtown *Petula Clark* (Pye)	4	2	2
5	All Day And All Of The Night *The Kinks* (Pye)	7	16	19
6	I Feel Fine *The Beatles* (Parlophone)	1	1	1
7	Um, Um, Um, Um, Um, Um *Wayne Fontana* (Fontana)	10	–	–
8	There's A Heartache Following Me *Jim Reeves* (RCA)	6	11	18
9	Losing You *Dusty Springfield* (Philips)	11	17	–
10	He's In Town *The Rocking Berries* (Pye)	13	–	–
11	Walk Tall *Val Doonican* (Decca)	5	3	4
12	Pretty Paper *Roy Orbison* (London)	9	6	6
13	Don't Bring Me Down *The Pretty Things* (Fontana)	17	–	–
14	Sha La La *Manfred Mann* (HMV)	–	–	–
15	Tokyo Melody *Helmut Zacharias Orchestra* (Polydor)	15	–	–
16	Oh Pretty Woman *Roy Orbison* (London)	–	–	–
17	I Understand *Freddie and The Dreamers* (Columbia)	12	7	5
18	Walk Away *Matt Monro* (Parlophone)	18	–	20
19	Show Me Girl *Herman's Hermits* (Columbia)	19	20	–
20	Black Girl *The Four Pennies* (Philips)	–	–	–
21	Message To Martha *Adam Faith* (Parlophone)	14	12	14
46	No Arms Could Ever Hold You *The Bachelors* (Decca)	16	8	7
–	I Could Easily Fall *Cliff Richard* (Columbia)	20	9	9
44	Blue Christmas *Elvis Presley* (RCA)	26	13	11
–	Somewhere *P. J. Proby* (Liberty)	30	14	10
30	Terry *Twinkle* (Decca)	24	15	12
–	Girl Don't Come *Sandie Shaw* (Pye)	38	18	13
49	What Have They Done To The Rain *The Searchers* (Pye)	27	19	16
–	Yeh, Yeh *Georgie Fame* (Columbia)	–	26	17

1964

The excitement of new stars and new sounds from 1963 continued into 1964, and the British dominance in the charts continued with The Beatles and The Rolling Stones both going from strength to strength following their first year of real success in 1963. The previous year's tentative attempts for success from Dusty Springfield and Cilla Black became much more certain as both girls launched into their long hit runs.

The new names of 1964 included The Animals, who arrived in the charts with the old folk song 'The House Of The Rising Sun'. Manfred Mann, with their lead singer, Paul Jones, began with '5-4-3-2-1', the first of many hits for the group. A record entitled 'Rosalyn' created much interest in The Pretty Things but though they received magazine coverage and were well-known on the pop scene, their ratings in terms of chart successes were never very high.

Liverpool produced yet another chart group in the form of The Merseybeats, but their eventual track performance was disappointing after initial promise. Their chart careers began and ended in 1964 with three hits, though they managed one more hit in 1966 under the name of The Merseys. The Zombies were another new group who promised much, but who were perhaps ahead of their time. Several years later ex-members of the group such as Rod Argent, Russ Ballard and Colin Blunstone enjoyed hits in their own right.

Liverpool was not the only centre of music, as Eric Burdon and The Animals from Newcastle proved. From the Midlands came The Hollies, who had been overshadowed in 1963 by the Mersey Sound. However, 'Just One Look' reached Number Two early in 1964 and their chart residency began, with the group appearing in the charts with the regularity of clockwork.

The Beach Boys arrived in 1964 with 'I Get Around', a record which remained in the charts for two months. The Beach Boys then disappeared from the Top Twenty until 1966, when they returned with a much bigger impact.

The two main pop heroes of 1963, The Beatles and The Rolling Stones, dominated the charts for most of the year.

The Beatles had three Number Ones and lent inspiration to Peter and Gordon, another new chart act, with 'World Without Love' which also reached the Number One position. The Rolling Stones had two Number Ones with 'It's All Over Now' and 'Little Red Rooster', while 'Not Fade Away' reached Number Three.

For a time it seemed that The Dave Clark Five were destined to chase The Beatles up and down the charts, for they had entered the charts for the first time in late November 1963 to topple The Beatles from their Number One position, and, until the end of July 1964, they were continually in the Top Twenty with hits such as 'Glad All Over', 'Bits And Pieces' and 'Can't You See That She's Mine'. Although all these records sold thousands of copies, The Dave Clark Five then had to wait almost a year before they achieved their next Top Twenty hit. Lulu, with her group, The Luvvers, began her long chart career and while The Kinks arrived in the charts with 'You Really Got Me', The Bachelors achieved even more hits than The Beatles, for they managed five songs in the charts, all of which were in the Top Ten.

Ballads were in vogue, so Julie Rogers had a hit with 'The Wedding Song', as did Frankie Vaughan with 'Hello Dolly', and The Four Pennies with 'Juliet'. Songs by The Four Seasons, Dionne Warwick, Doris Day and P. J. Proby also kept ballads to the fore.

1964 also yielded The Supremes, and the birth of the Tamla Motown sound.

JANUARY 1965

2	9	16	23	30
1 I Feel Fine *The Beatles* (Parlophone)	1	2	7	13
2 Downtown *Petula Clark* (Pye)	3	8	10	16
3 Walk Tall *Val Doonican* (Decca)	5	7	9	15
4 I'm Gonna Be Strong *Gene Pitney* (Stateside)	6	12	15	–
5 I Understand *Freddie and The Dreamers* (Columbia)	12	14	18	–
6 I Could Easily Fall *Cliff Richard* (Columbia)	9	11	13	18
7 Yeh, Yeh *Georgie Fame* (Columbia)	2	1	1	4
8 No Arms Could Ever Hold You *The Bachelors* (Decca)	11	13	16	–
9 Somewhere *P. J. Proby* (Liberty)	8	6	6	14
10 Terry *Twinkle* (Decca)	4	4	4	7
11 Girl Don't Come *Sandie Shaw* (Pye)	7	5	3	8
12 Message To Martha *Adam Faith* (Parlophone)	15	16	–	–
13 Pretty Paper *Roy Orbison* (London)	–	–	–	–
14 Little Red Rooster *The Rolling Stones* (Decca)	16	18	–	–
15 Blue Christmas *Elvis Presley* (RCA)	–	–	–	–
16 What Have They Done To The Rain *The Searchers* (Pye)	13	15	17	–
17 Cast Your Fate To The Winds *Sounds Orchestral* (Piccadilly)	17	10	5	10
18 Baby Love *The Supremes* (Stateside)	–	–	–	–
19 Go Now! *The Moody Blues* (Decca)	10	3	2	1
20 There's A Heartache Following Me *Jim Reeves* (RCA)	18	20	–	–
22 Ferry 'Cross The Mersey *Gerry and The Pacemakers* (Columbia)	14	9	8	9
24 Genie With The Light Brown Lamp *The Shadows* (Columbia)	20	17	–	–
– Baby Please Don't Go *Them* (Decca)	26	19	11	11
– You've Lost That Loving Feeling *Cilla Black* (Parlophone)	–	28	12	2
– Come Tomorrow *Manfred Mann* (HMV)	–	26	14	5
– Keep Searchin' *Del Shannon* (Stateside)	–	30	19	12
– You've Lost That Loving Feeling *The Righteous Brothers* (London)	–	35	20	3
– Tired Of Waiting For You *The Kinks* (Pye)	–	–	31	6
– Three Bells *Brian Poole and The Tremeloes* (Decca)	–	–	21	17
– I'll Never Find Another You *The Seekers* (Columbia)	48	33	32	19
– Leader Of The Pack *The Shangri-Las* (Red Bird)	–	42	27	20
– All Day And All Of The Night *The Kinks* (Pye)	19	–	–	–

FEBRUARY 1965

6	13	20	27
1 You've Lost That Loving Feeling *The Righteous Brothers* (London)	1	3	4
2 Tired Of Waiting For You *The Kinks* (Pye)	2	1	5
3 Go Now! *The Moody Blues* (Decca)	4	10	18
4 Come Tomorrow *Manfred Mann* (HMV)	6	8	16
5 You've Lost That Loving Feeling *Cilla Black* (Parlophone)	9	13	–
6 Keep Searchin' *Del Shannon* (Stateside)	3	4	6
7 Cast Your Fate To The Winds *Sounds Orchestral* (Piccadilly)	8	12	19
8 Yeh, Yeh *Georgie Fame* (Columbia)	15	–	–
9 Girl Don't Come *Sandie Shaw* (Pye)	18	–	–
10 Terry *Twinkle* (Decca)	17	–	–
11 Baby Please Don't Go *Them* (Decca)	10	16	–
12 Ferry 'Cross The Mersey *Gerry and The Pacemakers* (Columbia)	12	18	–
13 The Special Years *Val Doonican* (Decca)	7	7	7
14 I'll Never Find Another You *The Seekers* (Columbia)	5	2	1

6		**13**	**20**	**27**
15 Somewhere *P. J. Proby* (Liberty)		–	–	–
16 I'm Lost Without You *Billy Fury* (Decca)		16	20	–
17 Three Bells *Brian Poole and The Tremeloes* (Decca)		–	–	–
18 Leader Of The Pack *The Shangri-Las* (Red Bird)		11	14	–
19 I Feel Fine *The Beatles* (Parlophone)		–	–	–
20 Downtown *Petula Clark* (Pye)		–	–	–
33 Don't Let Me Be Misunderstood *The Animals* (Columbia)		13	6	3
27 Game Of Love *Wayne Fontana* (Fontana)		14	5	2
39 Funny How Love Can Be *The Ivy League* (Piccadilly)		19	9	9
41 It Hurts So Much *Jim Reeves* (RCA)		20	11	8
25 Yes I Will *The Hollies* (Parlophone)		22	15	12
– Goodnight *Roy Orbison* (London)		36	17	14
– It's Not Unusual *Tom Jones* (Decca)		39	19	10
– I Must Be Seeing Things *Gene Pitney* (Stateside)		–	24	11
– Silhouettes *Herman's Hermits* (Columbia)		–	41	13
– Come And Stay With Me *Marianne Faithfull* (Decca)		–	26	15
– I'll Stop At Nothing *Sandie Shaw* (Pye)		–	44	17
– Mary Anne *The Shadows* (Columbia)		35	25	20

MARCH 1965

6		**13**	**20**	**27**
1 I'll Never Find Another You *The Seekers* (Columbia)		2	4	6
2 It's Not Unusual *Tom Jones* (Decca)		1	2	2
3 Game Of Love *Wayne Fontana* (Fontana)		5	10	14
4 Silhouettes *Herman's Hermits* (Columbia)		3	3	3
5 Don't Let Me Be Misunderstood *The Animals* (Columbia)		8	12	19
6 I Must Be Seeing Things *Gene Pitney* (Stateside)		9	7	9
7 The Special Years *Val Doonican* (Decca)		12	15	16
8 Funny How Love Can Be *The Ivy League* (Piccadilly)		11	17	–
9 Come And Stay With Me *Marianne Faithfull* (Decca)		7	5	4
10 Tired Of Waiting For You *The Kinks* (Pye)		15	–	–
11 I'll Stop At Nothing *Sandie Shaw* (Pye)		4	8	7
12 It Hurts So Much *Jim Reeves* (RCA)		17	16	–
13 You've Lost That Loving Feeling *The Righteous Brothers* (London)		–	–	–
14 Yes I Will *The Hollies* (Parlophone)		10	9	11
15 Goodnight *Roy Orbison* (London)		14	14	–
16 Keep Searchin' *Del Shannon* (Stateside)		20	–	–
17 Mary Anne *The Shadows* (Columbia)		18	20	–
18 I Apologise *P. J. Proby* (Liberty)		16	11	12
19 Come Tomorrow *Manfred Mann* (HMV)		–	–	–
20 Cast Your Fate To The Winds *Sounds Orchestral* (Piccadilly)		–	–	–
31 The Last Time *The Rolling Stones* (Decca)		6	1	1
44 Goodbye My Love *The Searchers* (Pye)		13	6	5
21 Honey I Need *The Pretty Things* (Fontana)		19	13	18
35 Concrete And Clay *Unit 4 Plus 2* (Decca)		27	18	8
– Do The Clam *Elvis Presley* (RCA)		32	19	20
– The Minute You're Gone *Cliff Richard* (Columbia)		38	26	10
– For Your Love *The Yardbirds* (Columbia)		–	32	13
33 I Can't Explain *The Who* (Brunswick)		26	23	15
– I Know A Place *Petula Clark* (Pye)		30	21	17

APRIL 1965

3		10	17	24
1	The Last Time *The Rolling Stones* (Decca)	2	9	14
2	Concrete And Clay *Unit 4 Plus 2* (Decca)	1	3	13
3	It's Not Unusual *Tom Jones* (Decca)	7	18	–
4	Goodbye My Love *The Searchers* (Pye)	11	–	–
5	For Your Love *The Yardbirds* (Columbia)	3	2	4
6	The Minute You're Gone *Cliff Richard* (Columbia)	4	1	3
7	Catch The Wind *Donovan* (Pye)	5	4	5
8	Come And Stay With Me *Marianne Faithfull* (Decca)	8	–	–
9	Silhouettes *Herman's Hermits* (Columbia)	9	14	20
10	I'll Never Find Another You *The Seekers* (Columbia)	15	–	–
11	I'll Stop At Nothing *Sandie Shaw* (Pye)	20	–	–
12	I Can't Explain *The Who* (Brunswick)	10	8	10
13	I Must Be Seeing Things *Gene Pitney* (Stateside)	–	–	–
14	Here Comes The Night *Them* (Decca)	6	5	2
15	Times They Are A-Changin' *Bob Dylan* (CBS)	13	7	7
16	You're Breaking My Heart *Keeley Smith* (Reprise)	14	16	16
17	Yes I Will *The Hollies* (Parlophone)	–	–	–
18	I Know A Place *Petula Clark* (Pye)	–	–	–
19	I'll Be There *Gerry and The Pacemakers* (Columbia)	16	12	17
20	I Apologise *P. J. Proby* (Liberty)	–	–	–
23	Stop In The Name Of Love *The Supremes* (Tamla Motown)	12	6	6
26	Little Things *Dave Berry* (Decca)	17	11	8
29	Everybody's Gonna Be Happy *The Kinks* (Pye)	18	15	11
32	Pop Go The Workers *The Barron-Knights* (Columbia)	19	13	15
–	Ticket To Ride *The Beatles* (Parlophone)	–	10	1
–	Bring It On Home To Me *The Animals* (Columbia)	34	17	12
33	All Over The World *Francoise Hardy* (Pye)	28	19	19
35	King Of The Road *Roger Miller* (Philips)	26	20	9
–	True Love Ways *Peter and Gordon* (Columbia)	39	24	18

MAY 1965

1		8	15	22	29
1	Ticket To Ride *The Beatles* (Parlophone)	1	2	3	7
2	The Minute You're Gone *Cliff Richard* (Columbia)	7	9	17	–
3	Here Comes The Night *Them* (Decca)	3	6	19	–
4	King Of The Road *Roger Miller* (Philips)	2	1	4	5
5	Pop Go The Workers *The Barron-Knights* (Columbia)	6	8	10	15
6	Little Things *Dave Berry* (Decca)	10	15	–	–
7	Bring It On Home To Me *The Animals* (Columbia)	8	7	12	16
8	Concrete And Clay *Unit 4 Plus 2* (Decca)	13	19	–	–
9	Catch The Wind *Donovan* (Pye)	9	14	16	–
10	Stop In The Name Of Love *The Supremes* (Tamla Motown)	12	16	–	–
11	For Your Love *The Yardbirds* (Columbia)	18	–	–	–
12	The Last Time *The Rolling Stones* (Decca)	19	–	–	–
13	Times They Are A-Changin' *Bob Dylan* (CBS)	16	20	–	–
14	True Love Ways *Peter and Gordon* (Columbia)	5	4	2	3
15	World Of Our Own *The Seekers* (Columbia)	4	3	5	4
16	You're Breaking My Heart *Keeley Smith* (Reprise)	–	–	–	–
17	Oh No Not My Baby *Manfred Mann* (HMV)	11	12	11	13
18	I Can't Explain *The Who* (Brunswick)	–	–	–	–
19	Wonderful World *Herman's Hermits* (Columbia)	14	11	7	11
20	All Over The World *Francoise Hardy* (Pye)	20	–	18	17
25	Where Are You Now My Love *Jackie Trent* (Pye)	15	5	1	2
36	Subterranean Homesick Blues *Bob Dylan* (CBS)	17	10	9	9
–	This Little Bird *Marianne Faithfull* (Decca)	39	13	6	6
32	I've Been Wrong Before *Cilla Black* (Parlophone)	24	17	20	–

1		**8**	**15**	**22**	**29**
31	Not Until The Next Time *Jim Reeves* (RCA)	27	18	15	14
–	Long Live Love *Sandie Shaw* (Pye)	–	33	8	1
–	Poor Man's Son *The Rocking Berries* (Columbia)	–	28	13	8
–	The Clapping Song *Shirley Ellis* (London)	40	25	14	10
–	Trains And Boats And Planes *Burt Bacharach* (London)	–	–	27	12
–	Marie *The Bachelors* (Decca)	–	–	39	18
–	The Price Of Love *The Everly Brothers* (Warner Bros.)	–	–	29	19
–	Trains And Boats And Planes *Billy J. Kramer* (Parlophone)	–	–	35	20

JUNE 1965

5		**12**	**19**	**26**
1	Long Live Love *Sandie Shaw* (Pye)	1	3	7
2	Where Are You Now My Love *Jackie Trent* (Pye)	9	18	–
3	World Of Our Own *The Seekers* (Columbia)	3	8	12
4	True Love Ways *Peter and Gordon* (Columbia)	13	15	18
5	Poor Man's Son *The Rocking Berries* (Columbia)	5	6	8
6	This Little Bird *Marianne Faithfull* (Decca)	8	12	15
7	The Clapping Song *Shirley Ellis* (London)	7	7	6
8	Trains And Boats And Planes *Burt Bacharach* (London)	6	5	4
9	King Of The Road *Roger Miller* (Philips)	16	–	–
10	Ticket To Ride *The Beatles* (Parlophone)	14	–	–
11	The Price Of Love *The Everly Brothers* (Warner Bros.)	4	2	3
12	Subterranean Homesick Blues *Bob Dylan* (CBS)	20	–	–
13	Not Until The Next Time *Jim Reeves* (RCA)	18	–	–
14	Crying In The Chapel *Elvis Presley* (RCA)	2	1	2
15	Wonderful World *Herman's Hermits* (Columbia)	19	–	–
16	All Over The World *Francoise Hardy* (Pye)	–	–	–
17	Marie *The Bachelors* (Decca)	11	9	11
18	You've Never Been In Love Like This Before *Unit 4 Plus 2* (Decca)	15	16	14
19	Trains And Boats And Planes *Billy J. Kramer* (Parlophone)	12	14	–
20	Bring It On Home To Me *The Animals* (Columbia)	–	–	–
23	I'm Alive *The Hollies* (Parlophone)	10	4	1
22	Set Me Free *The Kinks* (Pye)	17	13	9
32	Colours *Donovan* (Pye)	21	10	5
26	Anyway, Anyhow, Anywhere *The Who* (Brunswick)	24	11	13
–	Looking Through The Eyes Of Love *Gene Pitney* (Stateside)	28	17	10
21	Come Home *The Dave Clark Five* (Columbia)	22	19	16
28	Love Her *The Walker Brothers* (Philips)	26	20	–
–	On My Word *Cliff Richard* (Columbia)	32	21	17
–	Stingray *The Shadows* (Columbia)	27	23	19
–	Heart Full Of Soul *The Yardbirds* (Columbia)	–	32	20

JULY 1965

3		**10**	**17**	**24**	**31**
1	Crying In The Chapel *Elvis Presley* (RCA)	2	5	6	14
2	I'm Alive *The Hollies* (Parlophone)	1	1	4	7
3	The Price Of Love *The Everly Brothers* (Warner Bros.)	6	9	15	20
4	Colours *Donovan* (Pye)	7	11	12	–
5	Looking Through The Eyes Of Love *Gene Pitney* (Stateside)	3	4	7	13
6	Trains And Boats And Planes *Burt Bacharach* (London)	12	–	–	–
7	Long Live Love *Sandie Shaw* (Pye)	15	17	–	–
8	The Clapping Song *Shirley Ellis* (London)	16	–	–	–
9	Set Me Free *The Kinks* (Pye)	14	20	–	–
10	Anyway, Anyhow, Anywhere *The Who* (Brunswick)	11	12	14	–
11	Heart Full Of Soul *The Yardbirds* (Columbia)	4	2	2	2

3	10	17	24	31
12 On My Word *Cliff Richard* (Columbia)	17	13	20	–
13 Leave A Little Love *Lulu* (Decca)	9	8	8	15
14 World Of Our Own *The Seekers* (Columbia)	18	–	–	–
15 To Know You Is To Love You *Peter and Gordon* (Columbia)	5	6	5	9
16 Marie *The Bachelors* (Decca)	–	–	–	–
17 Poor Man's Son *The Rocking Berries* (Piccadilly)	–	–	–	–
18 You've Never Been In Love Like This Before *Unit 4 Plus 2* (Decca)	–	–	–	–
19 Mr Tambourine Man *The Byrds* (CBS)	8	3	1	1
20 Come Home *The Dave Clark Five* (Columbia)	–	–	–	–
21 Tossing And Turning *The Ivy League* (Piccadilly)	10	7	3	4
23 In The Middle Of Nowhere *Dusty Springfield* (Philips)	13	10	9	8
25 She's About A Mover *Sir Douglas Quintet* (London)	19	15	16	–
28 Just A Little Bit Too Late *Wayne Fontana* (Fontana)	20	–	–	–
29 Wooly Bully *Sam The Sham and The Pharaohs* (MGM)	23	14	13	12
– There But For Fortune *Joan Baez* (Fontana)	32	16	11	10
– You've Got Your Troubles *The Fortunes* (Decca)	37	18	10	3
36 Goodbyee *Peter Cook and Dudley Moore* (Decca)	28	19	19	18
– We've Got To Get Out Of This Place *The Animals* (Columbia)	–	41	17	6
– He's Got No Love *The Searchers* (Pye)	48	31	18	16
– Catch Us If You Can *The Dave Clark Five* (Columbia)	–	38	23	11
– With These Hands *Tom Jones* (Decca)	49	33	21	17
– Let The Water Run Down *P. J. Proby* (Liberty)	33	24	22	19
– Help *The Beatles* (Parlophone)	–	–	–	5

AUGUST 1965

7	14	21	28
1 Help *The Beatles* (Parlophone)	1	1	2
2 Mr Tambourine Man *The Byrds* (CBS)	4	8	14
3 You've Got Your Troubles *The Fortunes* (Decca)	3	2	8
4 We've Got To Get Out Of This Place *The Animals* (Columbia)	2	3	6
5 Tossing And Turning *The Ivy League* (Piccadilly)	6	13	20
6 Heart Full Of Soul *The Yardbirds* (Columbia)	11	20	–
7 Catch Us If You Can *The Dave Clark Five* (Columbia)	5	7	9
8 There But For Fortune *Joan Baez* (Fontana)	8	12	17
9 In The Middle Of Nowhere *Dusty Springfield* (Philips)	16	–	–
10 I'm Alive *The Hollies* (Parlophone)	18	–	–
11 Wooly Bully *Sam The Sham and The Pharaohs* (MGM)	15	18	–
12 He's Got No Love *The Searchers* (Pye)	17	19	–
13 With These Hands *Tom Jones* (Decca)	13	15	–
14 Crying In The Chapel *Elvis Presley* (RCA)	19	–	–
15 Summer Nights *Marianne Faithfull* (Decca)	10	11	13
16 To Know You Is To Love You *Peter and Gordon* (Columbia)	–	–	–
17 Looking Through The Eyes Of Love *Gene Pitney* (Stateside)	–	–	–
18 Everyone's Gone To The Moon *Jonathan King* (Decca)	7	6	4
19 A Walk In The Black Forest *Horst Jankowski* (Mercury)	14	5	3
20 In Thoughts Of You *Billy Fury* (Decca)	9	10	11
22 Zorba's Dance *Marcello Minerbi* (Durium)	12	9	7
40 Don't Make My Baby Blue *The Shadows* (Columbia)	20	17	10
– I Got You Babe *Sonny and Cher* (Atlantic)	30	4	1
– All I Really Want To Do *The Byrds* (CBS)	26	14	5
39 See My Friend *The Kinks* (Pye)	24	16	12
– Satisfaction *The Rolling Stones* (Decca)	–	–	15
– What's New Pussycat *Tom Jones* (Decca)	47	21	16
– Make It Easy On Yourself *The Walker Brothers* (Philips)	–	31	18
– Like A Rolling Stone *Bob Dylan* (CBS)	–	42	19

SEPTEMBER 1965

4		11	18	25
1	I Got You Babe *Sonny and Cher* (Atlantic)	2	2	4
2	Help *The Beatles* (Parlophone)	5	8	13
3	Satisfaction *The Rolling Stones* (Decca)	1	1	2
4	All I Really Want To Do *The Byrds* (CBS)	9	12	–
5	A Walk In The Black Forest *Horst Jankowski* (Mercury)	4	6	7
6	Zorba's Dance *Marcello Minerbi* (Durium)	8	10	8
7	Everyone's Gone To The Moon *Jonathan King* (Decca)	15	19	–
8	Make It Easy On Yourself *The Walker Brothers* (Philips)	3	3	1
9	Like A Rolling Stone *Bob Dylan* (CBS)	6	4	6
10	See My Friend *The Kinks* (Pye)	18	–	–
11	What's New Pussycat *Tom Jones* (Decca)	12	14	20
12	We've Got To Get Out Of This Place *The Animals* (Columbia)	20	–	–
13	All I Really Want To Do *Cher* (Liberty)	9	11	17
14	You've Got Your Troubles *The Fortunes* (Decca)	19	–	–
15	Don't Make My Baby Blue *The Shadows* (Columbia)	17	–	–
16	In Thoughts Of You *Billy Fury* (Decca)	–	–	–
17	Catch Us If You Can *The Dave Clark Five* (Columbia)	–	–	–
18	That's The Way *The Honeycombs* (Pye)	13	13	12
19	Laugh At Me *Sonny* (Atlantic)	10	9	10
20	Summer Nights *Marianne Faithfull* (Decca)	–	–	–
32	Look Through Any Window *The Hollies* (Parlophone)	11	5	5
21	Unchained Melody *The Righteous Brothers* (London)	15	15	19
37	Tears *Ken Dodd* (Columbia)	16	7	3
30	Just A Little Bit Better *Herman's Hermits* (Columbia)	21	16	15
28	Il Silenzio *Nini Rosso* (Durium)	23	17	14
–	Eve Of Destruction *Barry McGuire* (RCA)	39	18	9
50	Hang On Sloopy *The McCoys* (Immediate)	29	20	16
–	If You Gotta Go, Go Now *Manfred Mann* (HMV)	–	37	11
–	Almost There *Andy Williams* (CBS)	–	27	18

OCTOBER 1965

2		9	16	23	30
1	Tears *Ken Dodd* (Columbia)	1	1	1	1
2	Make It Easy On Yourself *The Walker Brothers* (Philips)	3	6	7	15
3	Satisfaction *The Rolling Stones* (Decca)	8	10	15	20
4	Look Through Any Window *The Hollies* (Parlophone)	7	7	14	19
5	If You Gotta Go, Go Now *Manfred Mann* (HMV)	2	3	3	7
6	Eve Of Destruction *Barry McGuire* (RCA)	4	4	4	3
7	I Got You Babe *Sonny and Cher* (Atlantic)	14	15	20	–
8	Like A Rolling Stone *Bob Dylan* (CBS)	10	16	–	–
9	A Walk In The Black Forest *Horst Jankowski* (Mercury)	13	12	16	–
10	Il Silenzio *Nini Rosso* (Durium)	9	8	11	9
11	Hang On Sloopy *The McCoys* (Immediate)	6	5	5	8
12	Almost There *Andy Williams* (CBS)	5	2	2	2
13	That's The Way *The Honeycombs* (Pye)	16	18	–	–
14	Laugh At Me *Sonny* (Atlantic)	20	–	–	–
15	Just A Little Bit Better *Herman's Hermits* (Columbia)	17	19	–	–
16	Zorba's Dance *Marcello Minerbi* (Durium)	18	20	–	–
17	Baby Don't Go *Sonny and Cher* (Atlantic)	11	11	13	16
18	Help *The Beatles* (Parlophone)	–	–	–	–
19	Whatcha Gonna Do About It *The Small Faces* (Decca)	15	14	19	18
20	All I Really Want To Do *Cher* (Liberty)	–	–	–	–
23	Message Understood *Sandie Shaw* (Pye)	12	9	6	12
22	Some Of Your Lovin' *Dusty Springfield* (Philips)	19	13	8	11
31	In The Midnight Hour *Wilson Pickett* (Atlantic)	22	17	12	13
44	It's Good News Week *Hedgehoppers Anonymous* (Decca)	31	21	10	6

2	9	16	23	30
– Evil Hearted You/Still I'm Sad *The Yardbirds* (Columbia)	–	22	9	4
– Here It Comes Again *The Fortunes* (Decca)	45	29	17	9
– Yesterday Man *Chris Andrews* (Decca)	44	31	18	5
– Get Off Of My Cloud *The Rolling Stones* (Decca)	–	–	–	17
– Yesterday *Matt Monro* (Parlophone)	–	–	26	10

NOVEMBER 1965

6	13	20	27
1 Get Off Of My Cloud *The Rolling Stones* (Decca)	1	1	3
2 Tears *Ken Dodd* (Columbia)	2	4	5
3 Evil Hearted You/Still I'm Sad *The Yardbirds* (Columbia)	5	9	14
4 Yesterday Man *Chris Andrews* (Decca)	3	3	6
5 It's Good News Week *Hedgehoppers Anonymous* (Decca)	6	12	17
6 Here It Comes Again *The Fortunes* (Decca)	4	8	9
7 Almost There *Andy Williams* (CBS)	9	13	16
8 Yesterday *Matt Monro* (Parlophone)	8	11	13
9 Eve Of Destruction *Barry McGuire* (RCA)	13	17	–
10 It's My Life *The Animals* (Columbia)	7	7	7
11 Hang On Sloopy *The McCoys* (Immediate)	16	–	–
12 If You Gotta Go, Go Now *Manfred Mann* (HMV)	17	–	–
13 The Carnival Is Over *The Seekers* (Columbia)	10	2	1
14 Love Is Strange *The Everly Brothers* (Warner Bros.)	11	14	15
15 Positively 4th Street *Bob Dylan* (CBS)	12	10	10
16 Some Of Your Lovin' *Dusty Springfield* (Philips)	18	–	–
17 But You're Mine *Sonny and Cher* (Atlantic)	–	20	–
18 In The Midnight Hour *Wilson Pickett* (Atlantic)	–	–	–
19 Message Understood *Sandie Shaw* (Pye)	–	–	–
20 Until It's Time For You To Go *The Four Pennies* (Philips)	20	19	–
33 My Generation *The Who* (Brunswick)	14	5	2
31 1-2-3 *Len Barry* (Brunswick)	15	6	4
22 Baby I'm Yours *Peter and Gordon* (Columbia)	19	–	–
39 A Lover's Concerto *The Toys* (Stateside)	23	15	11
48 Wind Me Up *Cliff Richard* (Columbia)	29	16	8
46 Princess In Rags *Gene Pitney* (Stateside)	31	18	12
– Tell Me Why *Elvis Presley* (RCA)	40	22	18
– The River *Ken Dodd* (Columbia)	–	37	19
– Don't Bring Me Your Heartaches *Paul and Barry Ryan* (Decca)	38	26	20

DECEMBER 1965

4	11	18	25
1 The Carnival Is Over *The Seekers* (Columbia)	1	2	4
2 My Generation *The Who* (Brunswick)	3	5	7
3 1-2-3 *Len Barry* (Brunswick)	6	4	8
4 Get Off Of My Cloud *The Rolling Stones* (Decca)	9	16	–
5 A Lover's Concerto *The Toys* (Stateside)	5	9	9
6 Tears *Ken Dodd* (Columbia)	8	7	5
7 Wind Me Up *Cliff Richard* (Columbia)	4	3	2
8 Positively 4th Street *Bob Dylan* (CBS)	11	15	17
9 Princess In Rags *Gene Pitney* (Stateside)	10	12	16
10 Yesterday Man *Chris Andrews* (Decca)	19	17	20
11 The River *Ken Dodd* (Columbia)	7	6	3
12 It's My Life *The Animals* (Columbia)	14	–	–
13 Don't Bring Me Your Heartaches *Paul and Barry Ryan* (Decca)	15	18	–
14 Maria *P. J. Proby* (Liberty)	12	8	4
15 Tell Me Why *Elvis Presley* (RCA)	17	20	–
16 Yesterday *Matt Monro* (Parlophone)	20	–	–
17 Is It Really Over *Jim Reeves* (RCA)	(–)	19	–

4

1965

1965 produced some exciting chart entries in its own right, even though 1963 and 1964 had provided two outstanding vintage pop years. The year had some classic records and saw the emergence of some new and exciting pop figures.

Many of the regulars such as Cliff Richard, The Beatles, The Rolling Stones, Elvis Presley and The Kinks accumulated hits, particularly the latter who had their finest year ever with no less than five Top Ten hits.

Not all previous chart regulars stayed the pace. There were notable absences from the Top Twenty of such stars as Freddie and The Dreamers, Billy Fury and Adam Faith. Fury had accumulated 19 hits during his career, while Faith had managed 16. Frank Ifield disappeared, so too Brenda Lee. Brian Poole and The Tremeloes just managed to remain in the charts with one hit only, before the group split up. It was the same story for Billy J. Kramer and The Dakotas, whose swan-song was 'Trains And Boats And Planes'.

The new names in the Top Twenty included The Who, heralded as a pop art group, The Yardbirds, The Moody Blues, Bob Dylan, Donovan, The Righteous Brothers, The Seekers, The Walker Brothers and Them, with Van Morrison as their lead singer.

There were the usual one-hit wonders, some of whom recorded songs which have become classics in pop history. Such was the case of Barry McGuire with 'Eve of Destruction'; 'Gettin' Mighty Crowded' from Betty Everett; 'She's About A Mover' by The Sir Douglas Quintet; The Shangri-Las with 'Leader Of The Pack'; and Dobie Gray's 'In Crowd'.

Beatle records remained in the charts for 29 weeks altogether, while The Kinks came a close second with a 28-week chart residency, and The Rolling Stones' records remained in the charts for a total of 27 weeks. These three top groups were ousted from their Number One positions at various times by artists such as The Righteous Brothers whose song, 'You've Lost That Loving Feeling', had a chart battle with a cover version by Cilla Black. A hit was achieved by the ballad singer Ken Dodd, whose record 'Tears' proved to be the single which reached the highest rating in 1965, and it stayed a staggering 21 weeks in the Top Twenty – a week longer than the chart residency achieved by 'Telstar' from The Tornados in 1962.

More sweet pop sounds came from The Seekers, who took the Number One spot with 'I'll Never Find Another You'. The Shadows did well with five hits during the year, but then finished their chart run with 'War Lord', although they were still voted the top instrumental group in a pop poll. However, they re-emerged in 1974 as a chart force, with vocals added to their distinctive sound.

Bob Dylan entered the British charts in April with 'The Times They Are A-Changin'', which was quickly followed by 'Subterranean Homesick Blues', 'Like A Rolling Stone' and 'Positively Fourth Street'. Britain's answer to Dylan was in the form of Donovan, whose song 'Catch The Wind' made the charts. Donovan soon built his own fan following, but his music and lyrics seemed rather lightweight when compared to those of the mighty Mr Zimmerman.

Dylan's ex-girlfriend Joan Baez also made the 1965 charts with 'There But For Fortune' and she also entered the Top Fifty with the Dylan composition 'It's All Over Now Baby Blue'.

1965 saw the chart debut of a Cambridge University undergraduate, Jonathan King, with 'Everyone's Gone To The Moon'. He also wrote 'It's Good News Week' for Hedgehoppers Anonymous.

There was hope for the newcomers to the charts such as Bob Dylan, The Yardbirds, Donovan and The Walker Brothers, who all looked to 1966 with expectancy, but for several long-established chart artists, there was nothing but gloom awaiting them in 1966.

JANUARY 1966

1		8	15	22	29
1	Day Tripper/We Can Work It Out *The Beatles* (Parlophone)	1	1	2	4
2	Wind Me Up *Cliff Richard* (Columbia)	2	3	5	16
3	The River *Ken Dodd* (Columbia)	4	6	9	9
4	The Carnival Is Over *The Seekers* (Columbia)	3	4	7	14
5	Tears *Ken Dodd* (Columbia)	7	11	15	19
6	My Ship Is Coming In *The Walker Brothers* (Philips)	6	5	3	7
7	My Generation *The Who* (Brunswick)	12	16	–	–
8	1-2-3 *Len Barry* (Brunswick)	11	13	17	–
9	A Lover's Concerto *The Toys* (Stateside)	17	19	–	–
10	Let's Hang On *The Four Seasons* (Philips)	8	7	4	5
11	Rescue Me *Fontella Bass* (Chess)	13	14	18	–
12	Maria *P. J. Proby* (Liberty)	14	–	–	–
13	To Whom It Concerns *Chris Andrews* (Decca)	15	18	–	–
14	Till The End Of The Day *The Kinks* (Pye)	10	8	10	8
15	Keep On Runnin' *The Spencer Davis Group* (Fontana)	5	2	1	2
16	Princess In Rags *Gene Pitney* (Stateside)	18	1	–	–
17	Positively 4th Street *Bob Dylan* (CBS)	–	–	–	–
18	War Lord *The Shadows* (Columbia)	–	–	–	–
19	Merrie Gentle Pops *The Barron-Knights* (Columbia)	9	10	16	–
20	Yesterday Man *Chris Andrews* (Decca)	–	–	–	–
37	A Hard Day's Night *Peter Sellers* (Parlophone)	16	15	14	20
33	A Must To Avoid *Herman's Hermits* (Columbia)	19	9	8	6
22	My Girl *Otis Redding* (Atlantic)	20	17	12	11
30	Spanish Flea *Herb Alpert* (Pye)	21	12	6	3
–	Michelle *The Overlanders* (Pye)	–	36	11	1
–	Take Me To Your Heart Again *Vince Hill* (Columbia)	49	29	13	–
–	England Swings *Roger Miller* (Pye)	31	24	19	13
31	Take Me For What I'm Worth *The Searchers* (Pye)	27	22	20	–
–	You Were On My Mind *Crispian St. Peters* (Decca)	45	28	27	10
–	Michelle *David and Jonathan* (Columbia)	–	39	24	12
–	Love's Just A Broken Heart *Cilla Black* (Parlophone)	–	48	31	15
–	Can You Please Crawl Out Your Window *Bob Dylan* (CBS)	–	–	–	17
–	A Groovy Kind Of Love *The Mindbenders* (Fontana)	–	34	29	18
–	If I Needed Someone *The Hollies* (Parlophone)	–	20	–	–

FEBRUARY 1966

5		12	19	26
1	Michelle *The Overlanders* (Pye)	1	5	11
2	Keep On Runnin' *The Spencer Davis Group* (Fontana)	6	8	20
3	Spanish Flea *Herb Alpert* (Pye)	3	4	6
4	You Were On My Mind *Crispian St. Peters* (Decca)	2	3	4
5	Love's Just A Broken Heart *Cilla Black* (Parlophone)	5	7	10
6	A Must To Avoid *Herman's Hermits* (Columbia)	8	11	–
7	Day Tripper/We Can Work It Out *The Beatles* (Parlophone)	13	–	–
8	Let's Hang On *The Four Seasons* (Philips)	15	–	–
9	My Ship Is Coming In *The Walker Brothers* (Philips)	17	–	–
10	Till The End Of The Day *The Kinks* (Pye)	20	–	–
11	Michelle *David and Jonathan* (Columbia)	16	20	–
12	The River *Ken Dodd* (Columbia)	–	–	–
13	My Girl *Otis Redding* (Atlantic)	12	16	–
14	A Groovy Kind Of Love *The Mindbenders* (Fontana)	7	6	3
15	The Carnival Is Over *The Seekers* (Columbia)	–	–	–
16	Like A Baby *Len Barry* (Brunswick)	10	13	19
17	England Swings *Roger Miller* (Philips)	–	–	–
18	These Boots Are Made For Walkin' *Nancy Sinatra* (Reprise)	4	1	1
19	Girl *St. Louis Union* (Decca)	11	12	16

5		12	19	26
20	Wind Me Up *Cliff Richard* (Columbia)	–	–	–
–	Mirror, Mirror *Pinkerton's Assorted Colours* (Decca)	9	10	12
–	19th Nervous Breakdown *The Rolling Stones* (Decca)	14	2	2
37	Have Pity On The Boy *Paul and Barry Ryan* (Decca)	18	19	–
42	Tomorrow *Sandie Shaw* (Pye)	19	9	9
29	Second Hand Rose *Barbra Streisand* (CBS)	26	14	14
–	My Love *Petula Clark* (Pye)	35	15	5
31	Little By Little *Dusty Springfield* (Philips)	21	17	17
–	Sha La La La Lee *The Small Faces* (Decca)	30	18	7
–	Barbara Ann *The Beach Boys* (Capitol)	–	35	8
–	Inside Looking Out *The Animals* (Decca)	–	38	13
–	Backstage *Gene Pitney* (Stateside)	–	45	15
40	Uptight *Stevie Wonder* (Tamla Motown)	31	26	18

MARCH 1966

5		12	19	26
1	These Boots Are Made For Walkin' *Nancy Sinatra* (Reprise)	1	9	12
2	19th Nervous Breakdown *The Rolling Stones* (Decca)	8	12	17
3	A Groovy Kind Of Love *The Mindbenders* (Fontana)	2	4	7
4	My Love *Petula Clark* (Pye)	9	14	16
5	Sha La La La Lee *The Small Faces* (Decca)	6	3	4
6	Barbara Ann *The Beach Boys* (Capitol)	3	5	5
7	Backstage *Gene Pitney* (Stateside)	4	7	9
8	Spanish Flea *Herb Alpert* (Pye)	5	13	19
9	You Were On My Mind *Crispian St. Peters* (Decca)	13	20	–
10	Make The World Go Away *Eddie Arnold* (RCA)	16	10	10
11	Tomorrow *Sandie Shaw* (Pye)	11	–	–
12	Inside Looking Out *The Animals* (Decca)	12	17	–
13	Love's Just A Broken Heart *Cilla Black* (Parlophone)	–	–	–
14	Uptight *Stevie Wonder* (Tamla Motown)	18	–	–
15	Girl *St. Louis Union* (Decca)	–	–	–
16	Lightning Strikes *Lou Christie* (MGM)	14	11	11
17	Mirror, Mirror *Pinkerton's Assorted Colours* (Decca)	–	–	–
18	I Can't Let Go *The Hollies* (Parlophone)	7	2	2
19	Michelle *The Overlanders* (Pye)	–	–	–
20	Little By Little *Dusty Springfield* (Philips)	–	–	–
26	The Sun Ain't Gonna Shine Any More *The Walker Brothers* (Philips)	10	1	1
31	This Golden Ring *The Fortunes* (Decca)	15	16	–
28	Shapes Of Things *The Yardbirds* (Columbia)	17	6	3
22	What Now My Love *Sonny and Cher* (Atlantic)	19	15	13
34	Dedicated Follower Of Fashion *The Kinks* (Pye)	20	8	6
–	Substitute *The Who* (Reaction)	33	18	15
–	May Each Day *Andy Williams* (CBS)	36	19	–
–	Elusive Butterfly *Bob Lind* (Fontana)	48	21	8
44	Hold Tight *Dave Dee, Dozy, Beaky, Mick and Tich* (Fontana)	31	23	14
–	Elusive Butterfly *Val Doonican* (Decca)	–	35	18
–	Sound Of Silence *The Bachelors* (Decca)	–	39	20

APRIL 1966

2		9	16	23	30
1	The Sun Ain't Gonna Shine Any More *The Walker Brothers* (Philips)	1	2	7	14
2	I Can't Let Go *The Hollies* (Parlophone)	3	–	–	–
3	Shapes Of Things *The Yardbirds* (Columbia)	8	14	19	–
4	Dedicated Follower Of Fashion *The Kinks* (Pye)	4	9	13	20
5	Elusive Butterfly *Bob Lind* (Fontana)	5	7	11	–

	9	16	23	30
6 Elusive Butterfly *Val Doonican* (Decca)	7	6	5	16
7 Sha La La La Lee *The Small Faces* (Decca)	12	–	–	–
8 Make The World Go Away *Eddie Arnold* (RCA)	10	8	16	17
9 Barbara Ann *The Beach Boys* (Capitol)	14	19	–	–
10 Somebody Help Me *The Spencer Davis Group* (Fontana)	2	1	1	3
11 Hold Tight *Dave Dee, Dozy, Beaky, Mick and Tich* (Fontana)	6	4	4	5
12 Sound Of Silence *The Bachelors* (Decca)	9	3	3	7
13 What Now My Love *Sonny and Cher* (Atlantic)	17	–	–	–
14 Substitute *The Who* (Reaction)	11	5	8	11
15 A Groovy Kind Of Love *The Mindbenders* (Fontana)	–	–	–	–
16 Backstage *Gene Pitney* (Stateside)	–	–	–	–
17 These Boots Are Made For Walkin' *Nancy Sinatra* (Reprise)	20	–	–	–
18 Lightning Strikes *Lou Christie* (MGM)	–	–	–	–
19 Blue Turns To Grey *Cliff Richard* (Columbia)	15	16	18	18
20 Spanish Flea *Herb Alpert* (Pye)	–	–	–	–
34 Alfie *Cilla Black* (Parlophone)	13	18	12	20
41 You Don't Have To Say You Love Me *Dusty Springfield* (Philips)	16	10	2	1
39 Bang, Bang *Cher* (Liberty)	18	13	6	4
21 Someday One Day *The Seekers* (Columbia)	19	11	14	15
38 I Put A Spell On You *Alan Price* (Decca)	24	12	9	9
48 Pied Piper *Crispian St. Peters* (Decca)	26	15	10	8
29 Homeward Bound *Simon and Garfunkel* (CBS)	27	17	15	12
25 You Won't Be Leavin' *Herman's Hermits* (Columbia)	21	20	20	–
– Day Dream *The Lovin' Spoonful* (Pye)	–	23	17	6
– Pretty Flamingo *Manfred Mann* (HMV)	–	–	22	2
– Sloop John B. *The Beach Boys* (Capitol)	–	–	36	13
31 Super Girl *Graham Bonney* (Columbia)	32	27	24	19

MAY 1966

7		14	21	28
1 Pretty Flamingo *Manfred Mann* (HMV)		1	1	4
2 Day Dream *The Lovin' Spoonful* (Pye)		2	3	11
3 Bang, Bang *Cher* (Liberty)		4	11	16
4 You Don't Have To Say You Love Me *Dusty Springfield* (Philips)		6	7	14
5 Sloop John B. *The Beach Boys* (Capitol)		3	2	6
6 Pied Piper *Crispian St. Peters* (Decca)		5	8	13
7 Hold Tight *Dave Dee, Dozy, Beaky, Mick and Tich* (Fontana)		7	13	18
8 Sound Of Silence *The Bachelors* (Decca)		8	18	–
9 Alfie *Cilla Black* (Parlophone)		11	20	–
10 Homeward Bound *Simon and Garfunkel* (CBS)		9	16	17
11 Somebody Help Me *The Spencer Davis Group* (Fontana)		16	–	–
12 Substitute *The Who* (Reaction)		18	–	–
13 I Put A Spell On You *Alan Price* (Decca)		17	–	–
14 Someday One Day *The Seekers* (Columbia)		20	–	–
15 Elusive Butterfly *Val Doonican* (Decca)		–	–	–
16 That's Nice *Neil Christian* (Strike)		14	–	–
17 Make The World Go Away *Eddie Arnold* (RCA)		–	–	–
18 Blue Turns To Grey *Cliff Richard* (Columbia)		–	–	–
19 Soul And Inspiration *The Righteous Brothers* (Verve)		15	19	19
20 Shotgun Wedding *Roy C.* (Island)		10	6	7
28 Sorrow *The Merseys* (Fontana)		12	9	5
42 Wild Thing *The Troggs* (Fontana)		13	4	2
27 How Does That Grab You Darlin' *Nancy Sinatra* (Reprise)		19	–	–
– Paint It, Black *The Rolling Stones* (Decca)		–	5	1
– Rainy Day Women *Bob Dylan* (CBS)		32	10	9
– Strangers In The Night *Frank Sinatra* (Reprise)		40	12	3

7	**14**	**21**	**28**
– Promises *Ken Dodd* (Columbia)	26	14	12
– Hey Girl *The Small Faces* (Decca)	23	15	10
– Monday, Monday *The Mamas and Papas* (RCA)	31	17	8
– When A Man Loves A Woman *Percy Sledge* (Atlantic)	49	34	15
– I Love Her *Paul and Barry Ryan* (Decca)	44	30	20

JUNE 1966

4	**11**	**18**	**25**
1 Strangers In The Night *Frank Sinatra* (Reprise)	1	1	2
2 Paint It, Black *The Rolling Stones* (Decca)	2	6	12
3 Wild Thing *The Troggs* (Fontana)	3	9	15
4 Sorrow *The Merseys* (Fontana)	4	4	9
5 Monday, Monday *The Mamas and Papas* (RCA)	5	3	3
6 Sloop John B. *The Beach Boys* (Capitol)	9	13	16
7 Rainy Day Women *Bob Dylan* (CBS)	10	15	–
8 Promises *Ken Dodd* (Columbia)	6	8	13
9 When A Man Loves A Woman *Percy Sledge* (Atlantic)	7	5	4
10 Hey Girl *The Small Faces* (Decca)	11	17	–
11 Shotgun Wedding *Roy C.* (Island)	12	–	–
12 Pretty Flamingo *Manfred Mann* (HMV)	13	–	–
13 Don't Bring Me Down *The Animals* (Decca)	8	7	6
14 Nothing Comes Easy *Sandie Shaw* (Pye)	14	16	17
15 Day Dream *The Lovin' Spoonful* (Pye)	20	–	–
16 Pied Piper *Crispian St. Peters* (Decca)	–	–	–
17 You Don't Have To Say You Love Me *Dusty Springfield* (Philips)	19	–	–
18 Come On Home *Wayne Fontana* (Fontana)	16	20	–
19 I Love Her *Paul and Barry Ryan* (Decca)	17	–	–
20 Once There Was A Time/Not Responsible *Tom Jones* (Decca)	18	19	18
21 Under Over Sideways Down *The Yardbirds* (Columbia)	15	10	10
– Paperback Writer *The Beatles* (Parlophone)	–	2	1
– Don't Answer Me *Cilla Black* (Parlophone)	25	11	7
– River Deep, Mountain High *Ike and Tina Turner* (London)	33	12	8
– Sunny Afternoon *The Kinks* (Pye)	31	14	5
– Nobody Needs Your Love *Gene Pitney* (Stateside)	37	18	11
– Hideaway *Dave Dee, Dozy, Beaky, Mick and Tich* (Fontana)	38	21	14
– Bus Stop *The Hollies* (Parlophone)	–	–	19
45 Opus 17 *The Four Seasons* (Philips)	34	25	20

JULY 1966

2	**9**	**16**	**23**	**30**
1 Paperback Writer *The Beatles* (Parlophone)	2	7	14	19
2 Strangers In The Night *Frank Sinatra* (Reprise)	5	6	11	15
3 Sunny Afternoon *The Kinks* (Pye)	1	1	2	5
4 River Deep, Mountain High *Ike and Tina Turner* (London)	3	3	4	9
5 Nobody Needs Your Love *Gene Pitney* (Stateside)	4	2	5	11
6 Don't Answer Me *Cilla Black* (Parlophone)	8	12	17	–
7 When A Man Loves A Woman *Percy Sledge* (Atlantic)	9	13	19	–
8 Monday, Monday *The Mamas and Papas* (RCA)	11	15	20	–
9 Bus Stop *The Hollies* (Parlophone)	6	5	8	12
10 Hideaway *Dave Dee, Dozy, Beaky, Mick and Tich* (Fontana)	10	10	15	17
11 Don't Bring Me Down *The Animals* (Decca)	14	–	–	–
12 Get Away *Georgie Fame* (Columbia)	7	4	1	4
13 Over Under Sideways Down *The Yardbirds* (Columbia)	12	–	–	–
14 Promises *Ken Dodd* (Columbia)	16	–	–	–
15 Sorrow *The Merseys* (Fontana)	–	–	–	–

2	9	16	23	30
16 Paint It, Black *The Rolling Stones* (Decca)	–	–	–	–
17 I Am A Rock *Simon and Garfunkel* (CBS)	17	–	–	–
18 Wild Thing *The Troggs* (Fontana)	–	–	–	–
19 Sloop John B. *The Beach Boys* (Capitol)	19	–	–	–
20 Lana *Roy Orbison* (London)	15	16	16	20
21 It's A Man's Man's Man's World *James Brown* (Pye)	13	19	–	–
– Out Of Time *Chris Farlowe* (Immediate)	20	9	3	1
34 I Couldn't Live Without Your Love *Petula Clark* (Pye)	21	8	7	6
35 Black Is Black *Los Bravos* (Decca)	25	11	6	2
– Love Letters *Elvis Presley* (RCA)	37	14	9	8
– Goin' Back *Dusty Springfield* (Philips)	30	17	12	10
39 The More I See You *Chris Montez* (Pye)	26	18	13	7
23 This Door Swings Both Ways *Herman's Hermits* (Columbia)	18	20	–	–
– With A Girl Like You *The Troggs* (Fontana)	–	29	10	3
37 Mama *Dave Berry* (Decca)	34	25	18	14
– (Baby) You Don't Have To Tell Me *The Walker Brothers* (Philips)	–	27	21	13
– Summer In The City *The Lovin' Spoonful* (Kama Sutra)	–	43	28	16
– Visions *Cliff Richard* (Columbia)	–	–	29	18

AUGUST 1966

6	13	20	27
1 With A Girl Like You *The Troggs* (Fontana)	1	2	3
2 Out Of Time *Chris Farlowe* (Immediate)	2	9	15
3 Black Is Black *Los Bravos* (Decca)	4	4	6
4 The More I See You *Chris Montez* (Pye)	3	6	8
5 Get Away *Georgie Fame* (Columbia)	11	–	–
6 Love Letters *Elvis Presley* (RCA)	7	11	19
7 Mama *Dave Berry* (Decca)	6	5	5
8 I Couldn't Live Without Your Love *Petula Clark* (Pye)	10	13	20
9 Sunny Afternoon *The Kinks* (Pye)	13	–	–
10 Goin' Back *Dusty Springfield* (Philips)	14	19	–
11 River Deep, Mountain High *Ike and Tina Turner* (London)	18	–	–
12 Summer In The City *The Lovin' Spoonful* (Kama Sutra)	9	8	12
13 (Baby) You Don't Have To Tell Me *The Walker Brothers* (Philips)	–	–	–
14 Nobody Needs Your Love *Gene Pitney* (Stateside)	19	–	–
15 Visions *Cliff Richard* (Columbia)	12	7	7
16 God Only Knows *The Beach Boys* (Capitol)	5	3	2
17 Hi-Lili-Hi-Lo *The Alan Price Set* (Decca)	15	12	11
18 I Want You *Bob Dylan* (CBS)	16	17	18
19 Bus Stop *The Hollies* (Parlophone)	–	–	–
20 Strangers In The Night *Frank Sinatra* (Reprise)	20	–	–
– Yellow Submarine *The Beatles* (Parlophone)	8	1	1
24 I Saw Her Again *The Mamas and Papas* (RCA)	17	15	13
42 They're Coming To Take Me Away Ha-Haa! *Napoleon XIV* (Warner Bros.)	31	10	4
28 Lovers Of The World Unite *David and Jonathan* (Columbia)	24	14	10
34 More Than Love *Ken Dodd* (Columbia)	22	16	14
37 Just Like A Woman *Manfred Mann* (Fontana)	27	18	16
– All Or Nothing *The Small Faces* (Decca)	39	20	9
– Too Soon To Know *Roy Orbison* (London)	–	25	17

SEPTEMBER 1966

3		10	17	24
1	Yellow Submarine/Eleanor Rigby *The Beatles* (Parlophone)	1	3	5
2	God Only Knows *The Beach Boys* (Capitol)	3	5	8
3	All Or Nothing *The Small Faces* (Decca)	2	1	2
4	They're Coming To Take Me Away Ha-Haa! *Napoleon XIV* (Warner Bros.)	4	7	16
5	With A Girl Like You *The Troggs* (Fontana)	9	–	–
6	Mama *Dave Berry* (Decca)	8	11	15
7	Visions *Cliff Richard* (Columbia)	12	19	–
8	Too Soon To Know *Roy Orbison* (London)	5	4	3
9	Lovers Of The World Unite *David and Jonathan* (Columbia)	7	9	11
10	Summer In The City *The Lovin' Spoonful* (Kama Sutra)	17	–	–
11	I Saw Her Again *The Mamas and Papas* (RCA)	13	17	–
12	Hi-Lili-Hi-Lo *The Alan Price Set* (Decca)	14	20	–
13	Just Like A Woman *Manfred Mann* (Fontana)	11	10	20
14	The More I See You *Chris Montez* (Pye)	18	–	–
15	More Than Love *Ken Dodd* (Columbia)	16	18	–
16	Black Is Black *Los Bravos* (Decca)	19	–	–
17	Distant Drums *Jim Reeves* (RCA)	6	2	1
18	Got To Get You Into My Life *Cliff Bennett* (Parlophone)	15	6	9
19	Working In The Coal-Mine *Lee Dorsey* (Stateside)	10	8	10
20	I Want You *Bob Dylan* (CBS)	–	–	–
–	Little Man *Sonny and Cher* (Atlantic)	35	12	6
–	You Can't Hurry Love *The Supremes* (Tamla Motown)	38	13	7
–	I'm A Boy *The Who* (Reaction)	20	14	4
38	When I Come Home *The Spencer Davis Group* (Fontana)	23	15	12
29	Ashes To Ashes *The Mindbenders* (Fontana)	22	16	14
–	Bend It *Dave Dee, Dozy, Beaky, Mick and Tich* (Fontana)	–	38	13
–	Walk With Me *The Seekers* (Columbia)	31	23	17
–	Winchester Cathedral *New Vaudeville Band* (Fontana)	43	26	18
–	All I See Is You *Dusty Springfield* (Philips)	–	41	19

OCTOBER 1966

1		8	15	22	29
1	Distant Drums *Jim Reeves* (RCA)	1	1	1	3
2	I'm A Boy *The Who* (Reaction)	3	3	5	8
3	You Can't Hurry Love *The Supremes* (Tamla Motown)	4	6	9	12
4	Little Man *Sonny and Cher* (Atlantic)	5	8	13	–
5	Too Soon To Know *Roy Orbison* (London)	8	14	15	20
6	Bend It *Dave Dee, Dozy, Beaky, Mick and Tich* (Fontana)	2	2	3	6
7	Winchester Cathedral *New Vaudeville Band* (Fontana)	6	4	6	5
8	All Or Nothing *The Small Faces* (Decca)	13	–	–	–
9	Yellow Submarine/Eleanor Rigby *The Beatles* (Parlophone)	18	–	–	–
10	Walk With Me *The Seekers* (Columbia)	11	11	12	16
11	All I See Is You *Dusty Springfield* (Philips)	9	10	11	11
12	Lovers Of The World Unite *David and Jonathan* (Columbia)	–	–	–	–
13	Working In The Coal-Mine *Lee Dorsey* (Stateside)	19	–	–	–
14	Sunny *Bobby Hebb* (Philips)	12	15	–	–
15	Got To Get You Into My Life *Cliff Bennett* (Parlophone)	–	–	–	–
16	God Only Knows *The Beach Boys* (Capitol)	–	–	–	–
17	Have You Seen Your Mother Baby, Standing In The Shadow *The Rolling Stones* (Decca)	7	5	8	10
18	Guantanamera *The Sandpipers* (Pye)	10	7	7	7
19	When I Come Home *The Spencer Davis Group* (Fontana)	20	–	–	–
20	Ashes To Ashes *The Mindbenders* (Fontana)	–	–	–	–

	8	15	22	29
– Another Tear Falls *The Walker Brothers* (Philips)	14	12	18	–
– Sunny *Georgie Fame* (Columbia)	15	13	14	19
– I Don't Care *Los Bravos* (Decca)	16	17	19	–
– I Can't Control Myself *The Troggs* (Page One)	17	9	4	2
30 Lady Godiva *Peter and Gordon* (Columbia)	24	16	16	17
42 I've Got You Under My Skin *The Four Seasons* (Reprise)	29	18	20	14
– Reach Out I'll Be There *The Four Tops* (Tamla Motown)	–	19	2	1
– No Milk Today *Herman's Hermits* (Columbia)	35	20	17	9
– Stop Stop Stop *The Hollies* (Parlophone)	–	27	10	4
– Time Drags By *Cliff Richard* (Columbia)	–	34	21	13
– High Time *Paul Jones* (HMV)	49	39	28	15
– If I Were A Carpenter *Bobby Darin* (Atlantic)	–	44	29	18

NOVEMBER 1966

5	12	19	26
1 Reach Out I'll Be There *The Four Tops* (Tamla Motown)	1	3	4
2 Stop Stop Stop *The Hollies* (Parlophone)	2	7	8
3 I Can't Control Myself *The Troggs* (Page One)	6	8	11
4 Distant Drums *Jim Reeves* (RCA)	7	11	12
5 Winchester Cathedral *New Vaudeville Band* (Fontana)	10	14	–
6 High Time *Paul Jones* (HMV)	4	5	6
7 No Milk Today *Herman's Hermits* (Columbia)	9	12	18
8 Guantanamera *The Sandpipers* (Pye)	12	15	19
9 Bend It *Dave Dee, Dozy, Beaky, Mick and Tich* (Fontana)	15	19	–
10 Time Drags By *Cliff Richard* (Columbia)	11	18	–
11 Semi-Detached Suburban Mr James *Manfred Mann* (Fontana)	3	2	5
12 I've Got You Under My Skin *The Four Seasons* (Philips)	17	–	–
13 If I Were A Carpenter *Bobby Darin* (Atlantic)	13	9	10
14 A Fool Am I *Cilla Black* (Parlophone)	14	13	20
15 Good Vibrations *The Beach Boys* (Capitol)	5	1	1
16 I'm A Boy *The Who* (Reaction)	19	–	–
17 All I See Is You *Dusty Springfield* (Philips)	–	–	–
18 All That I Am *Elvis Presley* (RCA)	–	–	–
19 Have You Seen Your Mother Baby, Standing In The Shadow *The Rolling Stones* (Decca)	–	–	–
20 You Can't Hurry Love *The Supremes* (Tamla Motown)	–	–	–
26 Gimme Some Loving *The Spencer Davis Group* (Fontana)	8	4	2
25 Holy Cow *Lee Dorsey* (Stateside)	16	6	7
22 Beauty Is Only Skin Deep *The Temptations* (Tamla Motown)	18	–	–
27 Help Me Girl *Eric Burdon* (Decca)	20	17	14
– Green, Green Grass Of Home *Tom Jones* (Decca)	35	10	3
47 What Would I Be *Val Doonican* (Decca)	31	16	9
39 Friday On My Mind *The Easybeats* (UA)	33	20	17
– Just One Smile *Gene Pitney* (Stateside)	46	28	13
– My Mind's Eye *The Small Faces* (Decca)	–	29	15
32 A Love Like Yours *Ike and Tina Turner* (London)	26	21	16

DECEMBER 1966

3	10	17	24	31
1 Green, Green Grass Of Home *Tom Jones* (Decca)	1	1	1	1
2 Good Vibrations *The Beach Boys* (Capitol)	2	5	9	11
3 Gimme Some Loving *The Spencer Davis Group* (Fontana)	5	8	11	–
4 What Would I Be *Val Doonican* (Decca)	3	2	3	6
5 Semi-Detached Suburban Mr James *Manfred Mann* (Fontana)	7	12	15	–
6 Holy Cow *Lee Dorsey* (Stateside)	10	15	19	14
7 Reach Out I'll Be There *The Four Tops* (Tamla Motown)	13	18	–	–

1966

Seven of the top 10 names of 1965 lost their chart ascendancy during 1966. The departure which perhaps left the largest gap was that of The Seekers. However, a new group who appeared on the scene continued to have hit after hit. This was the Fontana recording team with the endless name, Dave Dee, Dozy, Beaky, Mick and Tich. The last week of March saw their first assault on the charts with 'Hold Tight'. They did indeed 'hold tight' as far as 1966's charts were concerned, for they chalked up a further three successes before the year was finished.

The year's success story lay with The Beach Boys, who had enjoyed their first chart entry in 1964 with 'I Get Around', though they had no Top Twenty entry in 1965. Among their 1966 hits was 'Good Vibrations', a classic song which deservedly reached the Number One position.

For Dusty Springfield, 1966 saw further improvements on her career as a solo singer, for she had a major hit with 'You Don't Have To Say You Love Me'. Elvis Presley was to take the same song to the Number One position in 1971.

The year produced its classic songs such as Ike and Tina Turner's 'River Deep Mountain High', a song produced by Phil Spector and strangely unacclaimed in the United States, the land of its birth. There was also 'These Boots Are Made For Walkin'' from Nancy Sinatra, and two Beatle classics, 'Yellow Submarine' and the superb 'Eleanor Rigby'. The Walker Brothers had a huge hit with 'The Sun Ain't Gonna Shine Any More', and altogether the year was something of a revival for the Philips record company, whose stable of artists included the Dave Dee group, Dusty Springfield, Spencer Davis, The Walker Brothers, Manfred Mann, The Mindbenders and The Merseys.

As with most years, 1966 was host to one-hit wonders. The Overlanders promised much with the Beatle classic 'Michelle' taking them to Number One, but unfortunately this was their only Top Twenty entry in the annals of pop history. In much the same way, fortune awarded only two hits each to David and Jonathan, Crispian St. Peters, and the legendary Lovin' Spoonful.

For some artists, 1966 was the year which saw their total decline after some measure of success in previous years. This was true of Marianne Faithfull who, during 1964 and 1965, had achieved four Top Twenty hits. It was also true of P. J. Proby, who disappeared after six successive hits. For some artists, 1966 was the beginning of a long spell with no hits; Sonny and Cher were just one duo who fall into this category. Since their first chart entry in 1965, they had achieved five hits, then 1966 saw a decline in their fortunes and chart appearances until 1972 when 'All I Ever Need Is You' brought them back into both the public eye and the charts.

Most artists disappear from the pop scene once their fortunes wane, and few make a comeback. However, at least one chart artist did make a reappearance on the pop scene as late as 1975. This was Chris Farlowe, who twice made The Rolling Stones' excellent song 'Out Of Time' a hit.

Apart from Dave Dee, Dozy, Beaky, Mick and Tich, 1966 also laid foundations for The Small Faces, another major chart force from whence other groups and singers eventually sprang. They entered the charts in September 1965 and 1966 saw four further hits, including 'All Or Nothing', their first Number One.

JANUARY 1967

	7	14	21	28
1 Green, Green Grass Of Home *Tom Jones* (Decca)	1	1	2	4
2 Morningtown Ride *The Seekers* (Columbia)	2	2	4	8
3 Sunshine Superman *Donovan* (Pye)	3	3	5	14
4 Save Me *Dave Dee, Dozy, Beaky, Mick and Tich* (Fontana)	5	5	8	16
5 Happy Jack *The Who* (Reaction)	6	6	3	5
6 Dead End Street *The Kinks* (Pye)	9	9	15	20
7 What Would I Be *Val Doonican* (Decca)	10	10	18	18
8 You Keep Me Hangin' On *The Supremes* (Tamla Motown)	11	11	17	—
9 In The Country *Cliff Richard* (Columbia)	7	7	6	10
10 My Mind's Eye *The Small Faces* (Decca)	20	20	—	—
11 Good Vibrations *The Beach Boys* (Capitol)	15	15	—	—
12 Friday On My Mind *The Easybeats* (UA)	14	14	—	—
13 Any Way That You Want Me *The Troggs* (Page One)	8	8	9	13
14 What Becomes Of The Broken Hearted *Jimmy Ruffin* (Tamla Motown)	16	16	—	—
15 Under New Management *The Barron-Knights* (Columbia)	18	18	—	—
16 Pamela, Pamela *Wayne Fontana* (Fontana)	12	12	14	15
17 Distant Drums *Jim Reeves* (RCA)	—	—	—	—
18 Just One Smile *Gene Pitney* (Stateside)	—	—	—	—
19 Sittin' In The Park *Georgie Fame* (Columbia)	13	13	12	12
20 Reach Out I'll Be There *The Four Tops* (Tamla Motown)				
42 I'm A Believer *The Monkees* (RCA)	4	4	1	1
32 Night Of Fear *The Move* (Deram)	17	17	7	2
23 (I Know) I'm Losing You *The Temptations* (Tamla Motown)	19	19	19	—
— Standing In The Shadows Of Love *The Four Tops* (Tamla Motown)		23	10	6
— Matthew And Son *Cat Stevens* (Deram)		33	11	3
25 I Feel Free *Cream* (Reaction)	21	21	13	11
41 Hey Joe *Jimi Hendrix* (Polydor)	32	32	16	9
48 A Place In The Sun *Stevie Wonder* (Tamla Motown)	46	46	20	—
— Let's Spend The Night Together/Ruby Tuesday *The Rolling Stones* (Decca)		—	26	7
— I've Been A Bad, Bad Boy *Paul Jones* (HMV)		—	38	17
43 Single Girl *Sandy Posey* (MGM)	36	36	27	19

FEBRUARY 1967

	4	11	18	25
1 I'm A Believer *The Monkees* (RCA)	1	1	2	3
2 Matthew And Son *Cat Stevens* (Deram)	2	2	5	9
3 Night Of Fear *The Move* (Deram)	4	4	7	17
4 Let's Spend The Night Together/Ruby Tuesday *The Rolling Stones* (Decca)	3	3	3	6
5 Green, Green Grass Of Home *Tom Jones* (Decca)	7	7	12	18
6 Hey Joe *Jimi Hendrix* (Polydor)	6	6	14	—
7 I've Been A Bad, Bad Boy *Paul Jones* (HMV)	5	5	6	11
8 Standing In The Shadows Of Love *The Four Tops* (Tamla Motown)	13	13	—	—
9 Happy Jack *The Who* (Reaction)	—	—	—	—
10 Morningtown Ride *The Seekers* (Columbia)	—	—	—	—
11 Pamela, Pamela *Wayne Fontana* (Fontana)	18	18	—	—
12 I Feel Free *Cream* (Reaction)	16	16	—	—
13 Sittin' In The Park *Georgie Fame* (Columbia)	20	20	—	—
14 Sugar Town *Nancy Sinatra* (Reprise)	10	10	8	14
15 Single Girl *Sandy Posey* (MGM)	19	19	19	20
16 In The Country *Cliff Richard* (Columbia)	—	—	—	—
17 Snoopy Vs The Red Baron *The Royal Guardsmen* (Stateside)	14	14	9	8

4	**11**	**18**	**25**
18 Let Me Cry On Your Shoulder *Ken Dodd* (Columbia)	11	15	–
19 I'm A Man *The Spencer Davis Group* (Fontana)	9	16	–
20 Any Way That You Want Me *The Troggs* (Page One)	–	–	–
43 This Is My Song *Petula Clark* (Pye)	8	1	1
23 Release Me *Engelbert Humperdinck* (Decca)	12	4	2
24 I Won't Come In While He's There *Jim Reeves* (RCA)	15	13	12
32 Peek-A-Boo *New Vaudeville Band* (Fontana)	17	11	7
34 Here Comes My Baby *The Tremeloes* (CBS)	24	10	4
– Mellow Yellow *Donovan* (Pye)	37	17	10
29 It Takes Two *Marvin Gaye and Kim Weston* (Tamla Motown)	22	18	16
– Edelweiss *Vince Hill* (Columbia)	40	20	13
– Penny Lane/Strawberry Fields Forever *The Beatles* (Parlophone)	–	–	5
– On A Carousel *The Hollies* (Parlophone)	–	34	15
– There's A Kind Of Hush *Herman's Hermits* (Columbia)	48	32	19

MARCH 1967

4	**11**	**18**	**25**
1 Release Me *Engelbert Humperdinck* (Decca)	1	1	1
2 Penny Lane/Strawberry Fields Forever *The Beatles* (Parlophone)	2	2	5
3 This Is My Song *Petula Clark* (Pye)	3	3	4
4 Here Comes My Baby *The Tremeloes* (CBS)	6	9	13
5 I'm A Believer *The Monkees* (RCA)	7	14	17
6 Edelweiss *Vince Hill* (Columbia)	4	5	2
7 On A Carousel *The Hollies* (Parlophone)	5	4	7
8 Mellow Yellow *Donovan* (Pye)	9	17	–
9 Peek-A-Boo *New Vaudeville Band* (Fontana)	13	15	20
10 Snoopy Vs The Red Baron *The Royal Guardsmen* (Stateside)	10	10	14
11 There's A Kind Of Hush *Herman's Hermits* (Columbia)	8	7	10
12 Let's Spend The Night Together/Ruby Tuesday *The Rolling Stones* (Decca)	18	–	–
13 Detroit City *Tom Jones* (Decca)	11	8	11
14 I Won't Come In While He's There *Jim Reeves* (RCA)	15	–	–
15 Matthew And Son *Cat Stevens* (Deram)	–	–	–
16 It Takes Two *Marvin Gaye and Kim Weston* (Tamla Motown)	16	19	–
17 Single Girl *Sandy Posey* MGM)	19	–	–
18 Georgy Girl *The Seekers* (Columbia)	12	6	3
19 Sugar Town *Nancy Sinatra* (Reprise)	–	–	–
20 I've Been A Bad, Bad Boy *Paul Jones* (HMV)	–	–	–
22 Give It To Me *The Troggs* (Page One)	14	12	15
31 This Is My Song *Harry Secombe* (Philips)	17	11	9
32 I'll Try Anything *Dusty Springfield* (Philips)	20	13	18
37 Memories Are Made Of This *Val Doonican* (Decca)	21	16	12
44 I Was Kaiser Bill's Batman *Whistling Jack Smith* (Deram)	29	18	8
– Simon Smith And His Amazing Dancing Bear *Alan Price* (Decca)	–	20	6
– Puppet On A String *Sandie Shaw* (Pye)	–	27	16
41 Love Is Here And Now You're Gone *The Supremes* (Tamla Motown)	24	22	19

APRIL 1967

1		8	15	22	29
1	Release Me *Engelbert Humperdinck* (Decca)	1	2	5	8
2	This Is My Song *Harry Secombe* (Philips)	3	5	7	14
3	Edelweiss *Vince Hill* (Columbia)	7	10	17	20
4	Simon Smith And His Amazing Dancing Bear *Alan Price* (Decca)	5	7	11	18
5	I Was Kaiser Bill's Batman *Whistling Jack Smith* (Deram)	6	8	13	17
6	Puppet On A String *Sandie Shaw* (Pye)	4	3	2	1
7	Georgy Girl *The Seekers* (Columbia)	10	14	–	–
8	This Is My Song *Petula Clark* (Pye)	9	18	–	–
9	Somethin' Stupid *Frank and Nancy Sinatra* (Reprise)	2	1	1	2
10	Penny Lane/Strawberry Fields Forever *The Beatles* (Parlophone)	8	12	–	–
11	Memories Are Made Of This *Val Doonican* (Decca)	12	17	–	–
12	On A Carousel *The Hollies* (Parlophone)	16	–	–	–
13	There's A Kind Of Hush *Herman's Hermits* (Columbia)	15	–	–	–
14	It's All Over *Cliff Richard* (Columbia)	11	9	9	18
15	Touch Me, Touch Me *Dave Dee, Dozy, Beaky, Mick and Tich* (Fontana)	13	16	–	–
16	Detroit City *Tom Jones* (Decca)	19	–	–	–
17	Love Is Here And Now You're Gone *The Supremes* (Tamla Motown)	20	–	–	–
18	Give It To Me *The Troggs* (Page One)	–	–	–	–
19	I'll Try Anything *Dusty Springfield* (Philips)	–	–	–	–
20	Al Capone *Prince Buster* (Blue Beat)	18	–	–	–
–	A Little Bit Me, A Little Bit You *The Monkees* (RCA)	14	4	3	3
46	Ha! Ha! Said The Clown *Manfred Mann* (Fontana)	17	6	4	4
39	Purple Haze *Jimi Hendrix* (Track)	22	11	6	5
33	Bernadette *The Four Tops* (Tamla Motown)	25	13	8	10
28	Because I Love You *Georgie Fame* (CBS)	23	15	15	–
36	Happy Together *The Turtles* (London)	27	19	12	12
23	Knock On Wood *Eddie Floyd* (Atlantic)	21	20	19	19
48	I'm Gonna Get Me A Gun *Cat Stevens* (Deram)	34	21	10	6
40	Seven Drunken Nights *The Dubliners* (Major Minor)	33	25	14	11
–	I Can Hear The Grass Grow *The Move* (Deram)	39	30	16	7
–	Dedicated To The One I Love *The Mamas and Papas* (RCA)	47	35	18	9
41	Arnold Layne *Pink Floyd* (Columbia)	31	26	20	–
–	Funny Familiar Forgotten Feeling *Tom Jones* (Decca)	–	39	24	13
–	The Boat That I Row *Lulu* (Columbia)	–	46	33	16

MAY 1967

6		13	20	27
1	Puppet On A String *Sandie Shaw* (Pye)	1	3	5
2	Somethin' Stupid *Frank and Nancy Sinatra* (Reprise)	2	5	10
3	Purple Haze *Jimi Hendrix* (Track)	7	10	16
4	A Little Bit Me, A Little Bit You *The Monkees* (RCA)	10	11	18
5	I Can Hear The Grass Grow *The Move* (Deram)	9	13	20
6	Dedicated To The One I Love *The Mamas and Papas* (RCA)	3	2	3
7	Ha! Ha! Said The Clown *Manfred Mann* (Fontana)	12	18	–
8	I'm Gonna Get Me A Gun *Cat Stevens* (Deram)	13	20	–
9	Funny Familiar Forgotten Feeling *Tom Jones* (Decca)	8	7	11
10	The Boat That I Row *Lulu* (Columbia)	6	6	8
11	Release Me *Engelbert Humperdinck* (Decca)	15	–	19
12	Bernadette *The Four Tops* (Tamla Motown)	18	–	–
13	Seven Drunken Nights *The Dubliners* (Major Minor)	11	8	7
14	Happy Together *The Turtles* (London)	16	19	–

6	**13**	**20**	**27**
15 Silence Is Golden *The Tremeloes* (CBS)	4	1	1
16 Pictures Of Lily *The Who* (Track)	5	4	6
17 Hi Ho Silver Lining *Jeff Beck* (Columbia)	14	14	14
18 It's All Over *Cliff Richard* (Columbia)	–	–	–
19 Knock On Wood *Eddie Floyd* (Atlantic)	20	–	–
20 This Is My Song *Harry Secombe* (Philips)			
37 New York Mining Disaster 1941 *The Bee Gees* (Polydor)	17	16	12
34 Then I Kissed Her *The Beach Boys* (Capitol)	19	12	4
– Waterloo Sunset *The Kinks* (Pye)	29	9	2
– The Wind Cries Mary *Jimi Hendrix* (Track)	27	15	9
– Sweet Soul Music *Arthur Conley* (Stax)	21	17	15
– The Happening *The Supremes* (Tamla Motown)	41	23	13
– Finchley Central *New Vaudeville Band* (Fontana)	46	25	17

JUNE 1967

3	**10**	**17**	**24**
1 Silence Is Golden *The Tremeloes* (CBS)	2	4	4
2 Waterloo Sunset *The Kinks* (Pye)	3	3	5
3 Dedicated To The One I Love *The Mamas and Papas* (RCA)	7	9	12
4 A Whiter Shade Of Pale *Procol Harum* (Deram)	1	1	1
5 Then I Kissed Her *The Beach Boys* (Capitol)	5	8	10
6 The Wind Cries Mary *Jimi Hendrix* (Track)	8	15	–
7 There Goes My Everything *Engelbert Humperdinck* (Decca)	4	2	2
8 The Happening *The Supremes* (Tamla Motown)	6	6	7
9 Pictures of Lily *The Who* (Track)	10	–	–
10 Seven Drunken Nights *The Dubliners* (Major Minor)	12	16	–
11 Puppet On A String *Sandie Shaw* (Pye)	13	20	–
12 Somethin' Stupid *Frank and Nancy Sinatra* (Reprise)	18	–	–
13 Sweet Soul Music *Arthur Conley* (Stax)	9	7	9
14 The Boat That I Row *Lulu* (Columbia)			
15 New York Mining Disaster 1941 *The Bee Gees* (Polydor)	15	–	–
16 Finchley Central *New Vaudeville Band* (Fontana)	11	11	13
17 Funny Familiar Forgotten Feeling *Tom Jones* (Decca)	20	–	–
18 Roses Of Picardy *Vince Hill* (Columbia)	16	13	18
19 Hi Ho Silver Lining *Jeff Beck* (Columbia)	–	–	–
20 Purple Haze *Jimi Hendrix* (Track)	–	–	–
24 Okay *Dave Dee, Dozy, Beaky, Mick and Tich* (Fontana)	14	10	6
41 Carrie Anne *The Hollies* (Parlophone)	17	5	3
22 The First Cut Is The Deepest *P. P. Arnold* (Immediate)	19	18	20
44 Paper Sun *Traffic* (Island)	26	12	8
36 Groovin' *The Young Rascals* (Atlantic)	23	14	11
25 If I Were A Rich Man *Topol* (CBS)	21	17	14
39 Night Of The Long Grass *The Troggs* (Page One)	25	19	17
48 Don't Sleep In The Subway *Petula Clark* (Pye)	34	22	15
– Here Comes The Nice *The Small Faces* (Immediate)	37	26	16
– She'd Rather Be With Me *The Turtles* (London)	–	40	19

JULY 1967

1	**8**	**15**	**22**	**29**
1 A Whiter Shade Of Pale *Procol Harum* (Deram)	1	1	4	7
2 There Goes My Everything *Engelbert Humperdinck* (Decca)	2	4	6	8
3 Carrie Anne *The Hollies* (Parlophone)	5	7	19	16
4 Okay *Dave Dee, Dozy, Beaky, Mick and Tich* (Fontana)	7	19	–	–
5 Paper Sun *Traffic* (Island)	8	15	–	–
6 She'd Rather Be With Me *The Turtles* (London)	4	5	7	5
7 Alternate Title *The Monkees* (RCA)	3	3	2	4

1		**8**	**15**	**22**	**29**
8	Groovin' *The Young Rascals* (Atlantic)	9	11	–	15
9	Silence Is Golden *The Tremeloes* (CBS)	20			
10	The Happening *The Supremes* (Tamla Motown)	14	16	–	–
11	If I Were A Rich Man *Topol* (CBS)	10	9	9	–
12	Don't Sleep In The Subway *Petula Clark* (Pye)	16	20	–	–
13	Sweet Soul Music *Arthur Conley* (Stax)	13	12	–	–
14	Here Comes The Nice *The Small Faces* (Immediate)	12	14	17	18
15	Waterloo Sunset *The Kinks* (Pye)	–	–	–	–
16	Then I Kissed Her *The Beach Boys* (Capitol)	–	–	–	–
17	Seven Rooms Of Gloom *The Four Tops* (Tamla Motown)	15	18	12	19
18	Finchley Central *New Vaudeville Band* (Fontana)	–	–	–	–
19	Strange Brew *Cream* (Reaction)	18	17	18	–
20	It Must Be Him *Vikki Carr* (Liberty)	6	6	3	2
25	Respect *Aretha Franklin* (Atlantic)	11	10	16	12
28	See Emily Play *Pink Floyd* (Columbia)	17	8	8	6
29	Give Me Time *Dusty Springfield* (Philips)	19	–	–	–
–	All You Need Is Love *The Beatles* (Parlophone)	–	2	1	1
–	San Francisco (Flowers In Your Hair) *Scott McKenzie* (CBS)	–	13	5	3
45	With A Little Help From My Friends *The Young Idea* (Columbia)	35	29	10	–
–	You Only Live Twice *Nancy Sinatra* (Reprise)	36	25	11	17
–	When You're Young And In Love *The Marvelettes* (Tamla Motown)	28	21	13	–
–	Somewhere My Love *The Michael Sammes Singers* (HMV)	–	31	14	–
30	Take Me In Your Arms And Love Me *Gladys Knight and The Pips* (Tamla Motown)	21	22	15	13
–	Marta *The Bachelors* (Decca)	40	35	20	–
–	Up, Up And Away *The Johnnie Mann Singers* (Liberty)	–	47	26	9
–	Death Of A Clown *Dave Davies* (Pye)	–	–	23	10
42	Let's Pretend *Lulu* (Columbia)	32	32	35	11
–	007 *Desmond Dekker* (Pyramid)	–	49	27	14
43	Just Loving You *Anita Harris* (CBS)	30	33	39	20

AUGUST 1967

5		**12**	**19**	**26**
1	All You Need Is Love *The Beatles* (Parlophone)	2	2	3
2	San Francisco (Flowers In Your Hair) *Scott McKenzie* (CBS)	1	1	1
3	Death Of A Clown *Dave Davies* (Pye)	3	4	7
4	It Must Be Him *Vikki Carr* (Liberty)	5	10	13
5	Alternate Title *The Monkees* (RCA)	9	14	–
6	I'll Never Fall In Love Again *Tom Jones* (Decca)	4	3	2
7	She'd Rather Be With Me *The Turtles* (London)	6	11	15
8	I Was Made To Love Her *Stevie Wonder* (Tamla Motown)	7	5	8
9	See Emily Play *Pink Floyd* (Columbia)	10	13	–
10	A Whiter Shade Of Pale *Procol Harum* (Deram)	17	–	–
11	Up, Up And Away *The Johnnie Mann Singers* (Liberty)	8	6	10
12	There Goes My Everything *Engelbert Humperdinck* (Decca)	13	–	16
13	Let's Pretend *Lulu* (Columbia)	14	17	–
14	Just Loving You *Anita Harris* (CBS)	11	7	6
15	Respect *Aretha Franklin* (Atlantic)	–	–	–
16	Groovin' *The Young Rascals* (Atlantic)	–	–	–
17	Creeque Alley *The Mamas and Papas* (RCA)	12	12	9
18	Take Me In Your Arms And Love Me *Gladys Knight and The Pips* (Tamla Motown)	–	–	–
19	007 *Desmond Dekker* (Pyramid)	19	19	–
20	You Only Live Twice *Nancy Sinatra* (Reprise)	16	15	–
38	Even The Bad Times Are Good *The Tremeloes* (CBS)	15	8	4
27	Gin House *Amen Corner* (Deram)	18	16	12

5		12	19	26
37	The House That Jack Built *The Alan Price Set* (Decca)	20	9	5
21	Tramp *Otis Redding and Carla Thomas* (Stax)	22	18	–
–	Itchycoo Park *The Small Faces* (Immediate)	43	20	14
–	Pleasant Valley Sunday *The Monkees* (RCA)	–	22	11
–	We Love You/Dandelion *The Rolling Stones* (Decca)	–	–	17
–	Excerpt From A Teenage Opera *Keith West* (Parlophone)	40	25	18
–	Last Waltz *Engelbert Humperdinck* (Decca)	–	–	19
49	A Bad Night *Cat Stevens* (Deram)	26	24	20

SEPTEMBER 1967

2		9	16	23	30
1	San Francisco (Flowers In Your Hair) *Scott McKenzie* (CBS)	3	3	6	9
2	I'll Never Fall In Love Again *Tom Jones* (Decca)	2	2	5	8
3	Last Waltz *Engelbert Humperdinck* (Decca)	1	1	1	1
4	The House That Jack Built *The Alan Price Set* (Decca)	5	12	17	–
5	Even The Bad Times Are Good *The Tremeloes* (CBS)	6	7	11	12
6	All You Need Is Love *The Beatles* (Parlophone)	13	15	–	–
7	Just Loving You *Anita Harris* (CBS)	7	9	14	16
8	I Was Made To Love Her *Stevie Wonder* (Tamla Motown)	9	11	16	19
9	Death Of A Clown *Dave Davies* (Pye)	16	–	–	–
10	We Love You/Dandelion *The Rolling Stones* (Decca)	8	10	9	15
11	Pleasant Valley Sunday *The Monkees* (RCA)	11	17	–	–
12	Excerpt From A Teenage Opera *Keith West* (Parlophone)	4	4	2	2
13	Heroes And Villains *The Beach Boys* (Capitol)	12	8	12	13
14	Up, Up And Away *The Johnnie Mann Singers* (Liberty)	20	–	–	–
15	Creeque Alley *The Mamas and Papas* (RCA)	19	–	–	–
16	Gin House *Amen Corner* (Deram)	17	–	–	–
17	It Must Be Him *Vikki Carr* (Liberty)	–	–	–	–
18	Itchycoo Park *The Small Faces* (Immediate)	10	6	3	4
19	Everything *Engelbert Humperdinck* (Decca)	–	–	–	–
20	You Only Live Twice *Nancy Sinatra* (Reprise)	–	–	–	–
23	The Day I Met Marie *Cliff Richard* (Columbia)	14	14	15	10
25	Let's Go To San Francisco *The Flowerpot Men* (Deram)	15	5	4	6
32	Burning Of The Midnight Lamp *Jimi Hendrix* (Track)	18	19	19	20
43	Reflections *Diana Ross and The Supremes* (Tamla Motown)	23	13	7	5
33	There Must Be A Way *Frankie Vaughan* (Columbia)	27	16	13	11
22	You Keep Me Hanging On *Vanilla Fudge* (Atlantic)	22	18	20	–
–	Flowers In The Rain *The Move* (Regal Zonophone)	40	20	8	3
–	Hole In My Shoe *Traffic* (Island)	44	23	10	7
41	Black Velvet Band *The Dubliners* (Major Minor)	28	22	18	18
–	The Letter *The Box Tops* (Stateside)	–	45	24	14
–	Massachusetts *The Bee Gees* (Polydor)	–	–	31	17

OCTOBER 1967

7		14	21	28
1	Last Waltz *Engelbert Humperdinck* (Decca)	3	3	2
2	Flowers In The Rain *The Move* (Regal Zonophone)	2	4	5
3	Hole In My Shoe *Traffic* (Island)	4	2	5
4	Excerpt From A Teenage Opera *Keith West* (Parlophone)	5	9	13
5	Reflections *Diana Ross and The Supremes* (Tamla Motown)	8	10	11
6	Massachusetts *The Bee Gees* (Polydor)	1	1	1
7	Itchycoo Park *The Small Faces* (Immediate)	10	12	16
8	Let's Go To San Francisco *The Flowerpot Men* (Deram)	12	17	–
9	The Letter *The Box Tops* (Stateside)	6	5	6
10	The Day I Met Marie *Cliff Richard* (Columbia)	14	15	18

7		**14**	**21**	**28**
11 There Must Be A Way *Frankie Vaughan* (Columbia)		7	7	10
12 Just Loving You *Anita Harris* (CBS)		17	–	17
13 I'll Never Fall In Love Again *Tom Jones* (Decca)		–	–	–
14 San Francisco *Scott McKenzie* (CBS)		20	–	–
15 Ode To Billy Joe *Bobby Gentry* (Capitol)		16	18	14
16 When Will The Good Apple Fall *The Seekers* (Columbia)		13	11	12
17 Even The Bad Times Are Good *The Tremeloes* (CBS)		–	–	–
18 From The Underworld *The Herd* (Fontana)		11	8	8
19 Black Velvet Band *The Dubliners* (Major Minor)		15	16	–
20 Good Times *Eric Burdon and The Animals* (MGM)		–	–	–
34 Homburg *Procol Harum* (Regal Zonophone)		9	6	9
22 King Midas In Reverse *The Hollies* (Parlophone)		18	20	19
23 Five Little Fingers *Frankie McBride* (Emerald)		19	–	–
48 Baby Now That I've Found You *The Foundations* (Pye)		21	13	4
– Zabadak *Dave Dee, Dozy, Beaky, Mick and Tich* (Fontana)		35	14	7
41 You've Not Changed *Sandie Shaw* (Pye)		23	19	20
– Autumn Almanac *The Kinks* (Pye)		–	42	15

NOVEMBER 1967

4		**11**	**18**	**25**
1 Massachusetts *The Bee Gees* (Polydor)		2	2	4
2 Baby Now That I've Found You *The Foundations* (Pye)		1	1	2
3 Zabadak *Dave Dee, Dozy, Beaky, Mick and Tich* (Fontana)		3	4	7
4 Last Waltz *Engelbert Humperdinck* (Decca)		4	5	8
5 Hole In My Shoe *Traffic* (Island)		11	16	20
6 From The Underworld *The Herd* (Fontana)		6	12	17
7 Homburg *Procol Harum* (Regal Zonophone)		9	14	19
8 Autumn Almanac *The Kinks* (Pye)		5	3	6
9 Flowers In The Rain *The Move* (Regal Zonophone)		12	18	–
10 The Letter *The Box Tops* (Stateside)		15	19	–
11 There Must Be A Way *Frankie Vaughan* (Columbia)		10	15	14
12 When Will The Good Apple Fall *The Seekers* (Columbia)		19	–	–
13 Ode To Billy Joe *Bobby Gentry* (Capitol)		20	–	–
14 Excerpt From A Teenage Opera *Keith West* (Parlophone)		–	–	–
15 San Franciscan Nights *Eric Burdon and The Animals* (MGM)		8	7	13
16 Love Is All Around *The Troggs* (Page One)		7	6	5
17 Reflections *Diana Ross and The Supremes* (Tamla Motown)		–	–	–
18 There Is A Mountain *Donovan* (Pye)		14	8	10
19 Just Loving You *Anita Harris* (CBS)		17	–	–
20 If The Whole World Stopped Loving *Val Doonican* (Pye)		16	11	9
21 I Can See For Miles *The Who* (Track)		13	10	12
22 You've Not Changed *Sandie Shaw* (Pye)		18	20	–
– Let The Heartaches Begin *Long John Baldry* (Pye)		31	9	1
49 Everybody Knows *The Dave Clark Five* (Columbia)		26	13	3
33 I Feel Love Coming On *Felice Taylor* (President)		25	17	11
42 Careless Hands *Des O'Connor* (Columbia)		28	27	15
– All My Love *Cliff Richard* (Columbia)		–	28	16
– Something's Gotten Hold Of My Heart *Gene Pitney* (Stateside)		–	36	18

DECEMBER 1967

2	9	16	23	30
1 Let The Heartaches Begin *Long John Baldry* (Pye)	2	3	6	8
2 Everybody Knows *The Dave Clark Five* (Columbia)	3	2	13	16
3 If The Whole World Stopped Loving *Val Doonican* (Pye)	4	4	4	4
4 Baby Now That I've Found You *The Foundations* (Pye)	8	17	–	–
5 Last Waltz *Engelbert Humperdinck* (Decca)	13	16	12	13
6 Love Is All Around *The Troggs* (Page One)	7	15	–	–
7 Something's Gotten Hold Of My Heart *Gene Pitney* (Stateside)	5	6	5	5
8 All My Love *Cliff Richard* (Columbia)	11	11	7	6
9 Hello, Goodbye *The Beatles* (Parlophone)	1	1	1	1
10 Careless Hands *Des O'Connor* (Columbia)	6	7	11	11
11 Zabadak *Dave Dee, Dozy, Beaky, Mick and Tich* (Fontana)	16	–	–	–
12 I Feel Love Coming On *Felice Taylor* (President)	12	14	19	–
13 I'm Coming Home *Tom Jones* (Decca)	10	5	2	3
14 There Is A Mountain *Donovan* (Pye)	–	–	–	–
15 World *The Bee Gees* (Polydor)	9	9	14	15
16 Massachusetts *The Bee Gees* (Polydor)	–	–	–	–
17 Autumn Almanac *The Kinks* (Pye)	20	–	–	–
18 I Can See For Miles *The Who* (Track)	–	–	–	–
19 Daydream Believer *The Monkees* (RCA)	15	13	8	7
20 San Franciscan Nights *Eric Burdon and The Animals* (MGM)	–	–	–	–
24 Thank U Very Much *The Scaffold* (Columbia)	14	10	9	9
21 Kites *Simon Dupree* (Columbia)	17	12	15	14
37 In And Out Of Love *The Supremes* (Tamla Motown)	18	18	17	17
42 Here We Go Round The Mulberry Bush *Traffic* (Island)	19	8	10	12
– There Must Be A Way *Frankie Vaughan* (Columbia)	22	19	20	20
– Magical Mystery Tour *The Beatles* (Parlophone)	–	20	3	2
– Walk Away Renee *The Four Tops* (Tamla Motown)	–	25	16	10
– Tin Soldier *The Small Faces* (Immediate)	49	29	18	19
– Ballad Of Bonnie And Clyde *Georgie Fame* (CBS)	–	33	22	18

1967

The charts of 1967 reflected Flower Power and its accompanying drug culture. The American West Coast world was given attention as a result of 'San Francisco' by Scott McKenzie, as well as the even more artificial 'Let's Go To San Francisco' from The Flowerpot Men.

The editor of a short-lived paper, *Flower Scene*, which was devoted to the movement wrote 'What the world needs now is love, just love, and let the people leading us to hatred and war go jump in a lake'. The magazine even ran a 'hippie of the month' campaign!

The underlying philosophy of Flower Power was a three-pronged edict stating that firstly people were to do their own thing, wherever and whenever they wanted; secondly, they were to drop out and leave conventional society; and thirdly hippies were to blow the mind of every 'straight' person with whom they came into contact and turn them on to beauty, love, honesty and fun.

Carnaby Street shop owners rubbed their hands in readiness for the wave of business in bells, beads, kaftans, frilly shirts and flower-patterned suits. Concert promoters staged shows featuring popular musicians and called them 'love ins'.

Flower Power and its consequent ethos also included The Move with two of their hits entitled 'I Can Hear The Grass Grow' and 'Flowers In The Rain'. The Rolling Stones sang 'We Love You', a double A-sided hit coupled with 'Dandelion', and produced the album 'Their Satanic Majesties Request'. The Beatles issued their famous 'Sergeant Pepper' album featuring tracks such as 'Lucy In The Sky With Diamonds' and 'A Day In The Life'.

One of 1967's greatest singles, 'A Whiter Shade Of Pale', came from Procol Harum in June. Even if the lyrics were beautifully incomprehensible, the record reached the Number One position and remained in the Top Twenty for three months all but a week. The disc was reissued in June 1972, but did not achieve anything like its previous success.

Jimi Hendrix arrived in 1967 and his songs, in the same way as the Procol Harum single, became vital material for alternative 'underground' groups. Hendrix had four hits – 'Hey Joe', 'Purple Haze', 'And The Wind Cries Mary' and 'Burning Of The Midnight Lamp'.

Another new group arrived, too, but they were a somewhat different kettle of fish. They were The Monkees, an American group who had been created originally for a television series about a group of comedy musicians. The Monkees became teen sensations as a result of this television show, and they achieved five hits in 1967, the first of which was 'I'm A Believer'.

Female hearts fluttered for Cat Stevens, another chart artist who emerged in 1967. His songs were among the first from British artists which reflected an individual's personal reflection on life as a young person. This song formula was particularly in evidence in 'Matthew And Son', his first hit.

Tongue-in-cheek nostaglia had been given a lift in 1961 with The Temperance Seven and in 1967, The New Vaudeville Band continued their success following their 1966 hit, 'Winchester Cathedral'. The year's most unlikely hits were The Dubliners with 'Seven Drunken Nights' and possibly from Prince Buster with 'Al Capone'. Pink Floyd, never in the future a singles chart force, arrived with a line-up including Syd Barrett and two singles, 'See Emily Play' and 'Arnold Layne'.

The Hollies, The Tremeloes, The Supremes, Stevie Wonder, Cliff Richard and Tom Jones all did very well in the charts of 1967, and there were three hits for the Small Faces, but the Spencer Davis group failed to maintain their 1966 momentum and could manage only one hit. The Beach Boys managed two chart entries and Elvis Presley had his only fruitless year since his arrival with a hit record in 1956!

JANUARY 1968

6		13	20	27
1 Hello, Goodbye *The Beatles* (Parlophone)		1	1	8
2 Magical Mystery Tour *The Beatles* (Parlophone)		2	4	5
3 I'm Coming Home *Tom Jones* (Decca)		7	7	16
4 Thank U Very Much *The Scaffold* (Columbia)		6	10	19
5 Walk Away Renee *The Four Tops* (Tamla Motown)		3	5	7
6 Daydream Believer *The Monkees* (RCA)		5	6	6
7 Something's Gotten Hold Of My Heart *Gene Pitney* (Stateside)	11	15	–
8 If The Whole World Stopped Loving *Val Doonican* (Pye)		8	9	18
9 Kites *Simon Dupree* (Columbia)		9	12	20
10 Ballad Of Bonnie And Clyde *Georgie Fame* (CBS)		4	2	1
11 Here We Go Round The Mulberry Bush *Traffic* (Island)		10	16	–
12 World *The Bee Gees* (Polydor)		12	11	12
13 In And Out Of Love *The Supremes* (Tamla Motown)		14	19	–
14 Careless Hands *Des O'Connor* (Columbia)		13	17	–
15 Let The Heartaches Begin *Long John Baldry* (Pye)		18	–	–
16 Last Waltz *Engelbert Humperdinck* (Decca)		19	–	–
17 Everybody Knows *The Dave Clark Five* (Columbia)		–	–	–
18 All My Love *Cliff Richard* (Columbia)		17	–	–
19 Tin Soldier *The Small Faces* (Immediate)		16	14	9
20 Jackie *Scott Walker* (Philips)		–	–	–
36 Everlasting Love *The Love Affair* (CBS)		15	3	2
22 The Other Man's Grass *Petula Clark* (Pye)		20	–	–
– Am I That Easy To Forget *Engelbert Humperdinck* (Decca)	33	8	3
48 Judy In Disguise *John Fred and his Playboy Band* (Pye)	23	13	4
39 She Wears My Ring *Solomon King* (Columbia)		25	18	13
23 Paradise Lost *The Herd* (Fontana)		21	20	15
– Everything I Am *Plastic Penny* (Page One)		27	22	10
– Bend Me Shape Me *Amen Corner* (Deram)		–	33	11
– Suddenly You Love Me *The Tremeloes* (CBS)		–	46	14
– I Can Take Or Leave Your Loving *Herman's Hermits* (Columbia)		–	34	17

FEBRUARY 1968

3		10	17	24
1 Everlasting Love *The Love Affair* (CBS)		1	2	4
2 Ballad Of Bonnie And Clyde *Georgie Fame* (CBS)		7	14	–
3 Am I That Easy To Forget *Engelbert Humperdinck* (Decca)		4	4	6
4 Judy In Disguise *John Fred and his Playboy Band* (Pye)		3	6	9
5 Bend Me Shape Me *Amen Corner* (Deram)		5	3	5
6 Everything I Am *Plastic Penny* (Page One)		10	15	20
7 The Mighty Quinn *Manfred Mann* (Fontana)		2	1	1
8 She Wears My Ring *Solomon King* (Columbia)		9	5	3
9 Suddenly You Love Me *The Tremeloes* (CBS)		6	7	11
10 Tin Soldier *The Small Faces* (Immediate)		17	–	–
11 Daydream Believer *The Monkees* (RCA)		16	17	–
12 Magical Mystery Tour *The Beatles* (Parlophone)		18	–	–
13 Walk Away Renee *The Four Tops* (Tamla Motown)		20	–	–
14 I Can Take Or Leave Your Loving *Herman's Hermits* (Columbia)		11	11	16
15 Gimme Little Sign *Brenton Wood* (Liberty)		8	8	10
16 Hello, Goodbye *The Beatles* (Parlophone)		–	–	–
17 Darlin' *The Beach Boys* (Capitol)		15	12	14
18 World *The Bee Gees* (Polydor)		–	–	–
19 Paradise Lost *The Herd* (Fontana)		–	–	–
20 I'm Coming Home *Tom Jones* (Decca)		19	20	–
30 Pictures Of Matchstick Men *Status Quo* (Pye)		12	9	7

3		10	17	24
37 Don't Stop The Carnival *Alan Price* (Decca)		13	16	15
41 Words *The Bees Gees* (Polydor)		14	13	12
– Fire Brigade *The Move* (Regal Zonophone)		22	10	8
38 Back On My Feet Again *The Foundations* (Pye)		23	18	18
26 Nights In White Satin *The Moody Blues* (Deram)		21	19	–
– Cinderella Rockafella *Esther and Abi Ofarim* (Philips)		–	32	2
– Legend Of Xanadu *Dave Dee, Dozy, Beaky, Mick and Tich* (Fontana)		–	35	13
– Green Tambourine *The Lemon Pipers* (Kama Sutra)		40	23	17
– Rosie *Don Partridge* (Columbia)		35	22	19

MARCH 1968

2		9	16	23	30
1 Cinderella Rockafella *Esther and Abi Ofarim* (Philips)		1	1	2	4
2 The Mighty Quinn *Manfred Mann* (Fontana)		3	8	15	–
3 Legend Of Xanadu *Dave Dee, Dozy, Beaky, Mick and Tich* (Fontana)		2	2	1	5
4 Bend Me Shape Me *Amen Corner* (Deram)		8	14	18	–
5 She Wears My Ring *Solomon King* (Columbia)		9	12	12	15
6 Fire Brigade *The Move* (Regal Zonophone)		4	3	7	13
7 Pictures Of Matchstick Men *Status Quo* (Pye)		7	13	19	–
8 Words *The Bee Gees* (Polydor)		11	15	16	–
9 Everlasting Love *The Love Affair* (CBS)		17	20	–	–
10 Suddenly You Love Me *The Tremeloes* (CBS)		16	16	–	–
11 Green Tambourine *The Lemon Pipers* (Kama Sutra)		10	7	8	16
12 Gimme Little Sign *Brenton Wood* (Liberty)		15	18	–	–
13 Am I That Easy To Forget *Engelbert Humperdinck* (Decca)		18	19	–	–
14 Rosie *Don Partridge* (Columbia)		5	4	4	7
15 Jennifer Juniper *Donovan* (Pye)		6	5	6	9
16 Darlin' *The Beach Boys* (Capitol)		13	11	14	17
17 Judy In Disguise *John Fred and his Playboy Band* (Pye)		–	–	–	–
18 Don't Stop The Carnival *Alan Price* (Decca)		–	–	–	–
19 Back On My Feet Again *The Foundations* (Pye)		19	–	–	–
20 I Can Take Or Leave Your Loving *Herman's Hermits* (Columbia)		–	–	–	–
36 Delilah *Tom Jones* (Decca)		12	6	3	2
21 Dock Of The Bay *Otis Redding* (Stax)		14	9	5	3
34 Me, The Peaceful Heart *Lulu* (Columbia)		20	10	9	11
26 Wonderful World *Louis Armstrong* (Stateside)		26	17	10	6
– Lady Madonna *The Beatles* (Parlophone)		–	–	11	1
– If I Were A Carpenter *The Four Tops* (Tamla Motown)		–	30	13	10
31 Love Is Blue *Paul Mauriat* (Philips)		24	21	17	14
24 Guitar Man *Elvis Presley* (RCA)		23	24	20	19
– Congratulations *Cliff Richard* (Columbia)		–	–	32	8
– Step Inside Love *Cilla Black* (Parlophone)		–	35	22	12
– If I Only Had Time *John Rowles* (MCA)		–	40	40	18
– Ain't Nothin' But A Houseparty *The Showstoppers* (Beacon)		–	38	29	20

APRIL 1968

6		13	20	27
1 Lady Madonna *The Beatles* (Parlophone)		4	6	18
2 Delilah *Tom Jones* (Decca)		2	4	5
3 Congratulations *Cliff Richard* (Columbia)		1	1	2
4 Dock Of The Bay *Otis Redding* (Stax)		6	8	9
5 Wonderful World *Louis Armstrong* (Stateside)		3	2	1

6	**13**	**20**	**27**
6 Cinderella Rockafella *Esther and Abi Ofarim* (Philips)	11	16	–
7 If I Were A Carpenter *The Four Tops* (Tamla Motown)	9	11	17
8 Legend of Xanadu *Dave Dee, Dozy, Beaky, Mick and Tich* (Fontana)	18	–	–
9 Step Inside Love *Cilla Black* (Parlophone)	8	9	14
10 Rosie *Don Partridge* (Columbia)	15	20	–
11 If I Only Had Time *John Rowles* (MCA)	5	3	4
12 Love Is Blue *Paul Mauriat* (Philips)	19	19	–
13 Jennifer Juniper *Donovan* (Pye)	–	–	–
14 Me, The Peaceful Heart *Lulu* (Columbia)	–	–	–
15 Captain Of Your Ship *Reparata and The Delrons* (Bell)	13	15	13
16 Ain't Nothin' But A Houseparty *The Showstoppers* (Beacon)	16	14	11
17 Fire Brigade *The Move* (Regal Zonophone)	–	–	–
18 Simon Says *The 1910 Fruitgum Co.* (Pye)	7	5	3
19 Valleri *The Monkees* (RCA)	12	12	16
20 Can't Keep My Eyes Off You *Andy Williams* (CBS)	17	10	6
23 Jennifer Eccles *The Hollies* (Parlophone)	10	7	7
27 I Can't Let Maggie Go *The Honey Bus* (Deram)	14	13	8
24 Cry Like A Baby *The Box Tops* (Bell)	23	17	15
31 Something Here In My Heart *The Paper Dolls* (Pye)	22	18	12
– Lazy Sunday *The Small Faces* (Immediate)	–	31	10
– White Horses *Jacky* (Philips)	42	22	19
– Hello How Are You *The Easybeats* (UA)	35	26	20
42 Rock Around The Clock *Bill Haley* (MCA)	20	–	–

MAY 1968

4	**11**	**18**	**25**
1 Wonderful World *Louis Armstrong* (Stateside)	1	1	5
2 Simon Says *The 1910 Fruitgum Co.* (Pye)	3	6	7
3 Lazy Sunday *The Small Faces* (Immediate)	2	4	4
4 If I Only Had Time *John Rowles* (MCA)	8	8	11
5 Can't Keep My Eyes Off You *Andy Williams* (CBS)	6	9	8
6 Congratulations *Cliff Richard* (Columbia)	11	12	17
7 Man Without Love *Engelbert Humperdinck* (Decca)	4	2	2
8 Jennifer Eccles *The Hollies* (Parlophone)	10	13	–
9 I Can't Let Maggie Go *The Honey Bus* (Deram)	14	18	–
10 Delilah *Tom Jones* (Decca)	15	20	–
11 Something Here In My Heart *The Paper Dolls* (Pye)	13	17	–
12 I Don't Want Our Loving To Die *The Herd* (Fontana)	5	7	6
13 Ain't Nothin' But A Houseparty *The Showstoppers* (Beacon)	16	16	16
14 White Horses *Jacky* (Philips)	12	10	10
15 Cry Like A Baby *The Box Tops* (Bell)	17	19	–
16 Young Girl *The Union Gap* (CBS)	7	3	1
17 Captain Of Your Ship *Reparata and The Delrons* (Bell)	–	–	–
18 Valleri *The Monkees* (RCA)	–	–	–
19 Somewhere In The Country *Gene Pitney* (Stateside)	20	–	–
20 Honey *Bobby Goldsboro* (UA)	9	5	3
24 Rainbow Valley *The Love Affair* (CBS)	18	11	9
22 Little Green Apples *Roger Miller* (Philips)	19	–	20
40 Sleepy Joe *Herman's Hermits* (Columbia)	22	14	12
38 Joanna *Scott Walker* (Philips)	23	15	13
– Helule Helule *The Tremeloes* (CBS)	41	25	14
– This Wheel's On Fire *Julie Driscoll, Brian Auger and The Trinity* (Marmalade)	26	23	15
– U.S. Male *Elvis Presley* (RCA)	–	40	18
– Do You Know The Way To San Jose *Dionne Warwick* (Pye)	–	32	19

JUNE 1968

1		8	15	22	29
1	Young Girl *The Union Gap* (CBS)	1	1	2	2
2	Honey *Bobby Goldsboro* (UA)	3	3	6	10
3	Man Without Love *Engelbert Humperdinck* (Decca)	2	4	10	14
4	Wonderful World *Louis Armstrong* (Stateside)	11	12	20	20
5	Lazy Sunday *The Small Faces* (Immediate)	9	–	–	–
6	I Don't Want Our Loving To Die *The Herd* (Fontana)	6	10	14	–
7	Rainbow Valley *The Love Affair* (CBS)	5	5	11	17
8	Joanna *Scott Walker* (Philips)	7	11	15	19
9	Do You Know The Way To San Jose *Dionne Warwick* (Pye)	8	9	8	13
10	This Wheel's On Fire *Julie Driscoll, Brian Auger and The Trinity* (Marmalade)	10	6	5	8
11	Simon Says *The 1910 Fruitgum Co.* (Pye)	13	16	17	–
12	Sleepy Joe *Herman's Hermits* (Columbia)	12	17	16	–
13	Can't Keep My Eyes Off You *Andy Williams* (CBS)	–	–	–	–
14	White Horses *Jacky* (Philips)	16	19	19	–
15	Helule Helule *The Tremeloes* (CBS)	14	15	18	–
16	U.S. Male *Elvis Presley* (RCA)	15	–	–	–
17	If I Only Had Time *John Rowles* (MCA)	18	–	–	–
18	Jumping Jack Flash *The Rolling Stones* (Decca)	4	2	1	1
19	Delilah *Tom Jones* (Decca)	–	–	–	–
20	Baby Come Back *The Equals* (President)	19	14	7	3
32	Blue Eyes *Don Partridge* (Columbia)	17	7	3	5
33	Hurdy Gurdy Man *Donovan* (Pye)	20	8	4	4
22	I Pretend *Des O'Connor* (Columbia)	22	13	9	6
43	Lovin' Things *The Marmalade* (CBS)	31	18	12	9
45	Son Of Hickory Hollers Tramp *O. C. Smith* (CBS)	30	20	13	7
–	My Name Is Jack *Manfred Mann* (Fontana)	–	50	21	11
–	Yummy Yummy *The Ohio Express* (Pye)	50	35	25	12
–	Boys *Lulu* (Columbia)	33	30	22	15
–	Yesterday Has Gone *Cupid's Inspiration* (NEMS)	–	–	37	16
–	Hush Not A Word To Mary *John Rowles* (MCA)	–	–	36	18

JULY 1968

6		13	20	27
1	Baby Come Back *The Equals* (President)	1	1	3
2	Son Of Hickory Hollers Tramp *O. C. Smith* (CBS)	2	2	6
3	Jumping Jack Flash *The Rolling Stones* (Decca)	5	9	19
4	Hurdy Gurdy Man *Donovan* (Pye)	6	20	–
5	I Pretend *Des O'Connor* (Columbia)	5	3	1
6	Lovin' Things *The Marmalade* (CBS)	7	14	–
7	Blue Eyes *Don Partridge* (Columbia)	10	11	16
8	Yesterday Has Gone *Cupid's Inspiration* (NEMS)	4	4	7
9	My Name Is Jack *Manfred Mann* (Fontana)	8	10	13
10	Young Girl *The Union Gap* (CBS)	13	15	–
11	Yummy Yummy *The Ohio Express* (Pye)	9	5	5
12	Hush Not A Word To Mary *John Rowles* (MCA)	14	12	14
13	This Wheel's On Fire *Julie Driscoll, Brian Auger and The Trinity* (Marmalade)	16	–	–
14	Mony Mony *Tommy James and The Shondells* (Ember)	11	6	2
15	One More Dance *Esther and Abi Ofarim* (Philips)	15	13	15
16	Honey *Bobby Goldsboro* (UA)	20	–	–
17	Do You Know The Way To San Jose *Dionne Warwick* (Pye)	19	–	–
18	Boys *Lulu* (Columbia)	–	–	–
19	Macarthur Park *Richard Harris* (RCA)	12	7	4
20	D. W. Washburn *The Monkees* (RCA)	17	–	–
30	Fire *The Crazy World of Arthur Brown* (Track)	18	8	8

6

	13	20	27
46 This Guy's In Love *Herb Alpert* (A & M)	28	16	9
– Mrs Robinson *Simon and Garfunkel* (CBS)	42	17	10
31 Gotta See Jane *R. Dean Taylor* (Tamla Motown)	23	18	20
33 Where Will You Be *Sue Nicholls* (Pye)	24	19	17
– I Close My Eyes And Count To Ten *Dusty Springfield* (Philips)	31	22	11
48 Last Night In Soho *Dave Dee* (Fontana)	30	24	12
– Universal *The Small Faces* (Immediate)	37	23	18

AUGUST 1968

3

	10	17	24	31
1 Mony Mony *Tommy James and The Shondells* (Major Minor)	1	2	1	4
2 I Pretend *Des O'Connor* (Columbia)	3	5	12	14
3 Fire *The Crazy World of Arthur Brown* (Track)	2	1	2	6
4 Macarthur Park *Richard Harris* (RCA)	8	15	–	–
5 Mrs Robinson *Simon and Garfunkel* (CBS)	4	6	11	17
6 Baby Come Back *The Equals* (President)	11	16	–	–
7 I Close My Eyes And Count To Ten *Dusty Springfield* (Philips)	6	4	6	13
8 Last Night In Soho *Dave Dee* (Fontana)	9	10	15	20
9 Son Of Hickory Hollers Tramp *O. C. Smith* (CBS)	16	–	–	–
10 Yummy Yummy *The Ohio Express* (Pye)	13	18	18	–
11 This Guy's In Love *Herb Alpert* (A & M)	5	3	3	3
12 Help Yourself *Tom Jones* (Decca)	7	9	5	5
13 Yesterday Has Gone *Cupid's Inspiration* (NEMS)	20	–	–	–
14 Dance To The Music *Sly and The Family Stone* (CBS)	12	7	10	10
15 Sunshine Girl *Herman's Hermits* (Columbia)	10	8	8	9
16 Universal *The Small Faces* (Immediate)	18	20	19	–
17 Gotta See Jane *R. Dean Taylor* (Tamla Motown)	–	–	–	–
18 Keep On *Bruce Channel* (Bell)	14	14	13	12
19 Days *The Kinks* (Pye)	15	12	14	15
20 Here Comes The Judge *Pigmeat Markham* (Chess)	19	19	–	–
26 Do It Again *The Beach Boys* (Capitol)	17	11	4	1
– I Gotta Get A Message To You *The Bee Gees* (Polydor)	27	13	7	2
44 High In The Sky *Amen Corner* (Deram)	23	17	9	7
37 On The Road Again *Canned Heat* (Liberty)	29	27	16	16
– Say A Little Prayer *Aretha Franklin* (Atlantic)	37	26	17	8
– Hold Me Tight *Johnny Nash* (Regal Zonophone)	42	38	20	11
– Dream A Little Dream Of Me *Mama Cass* (RCA)	–	46	28	18
46 Hard To Handle *Otis Redding* (Atlantic)	31	24	23	19

SEPTEMBER 1968

7

	14	21	28
1 I Gotta Get A Message To You *The Bee Gees* (Polydor)	2	3	4
2 This Guy's In Love *Herb Alpert* (A & M)	6	10	15
3 Help Yourself *Tom Jones* (Decca)	8	14	13
4 Do It Again *The Beach Boys* (Capitol)	3	5	7
5 Say A Little Prayer *Aretha Franklin* (Atlantic)	4	4	6
6 High In The Sky *Amen Corner* (Deram)	9	11	11
7 Hold Me Tight *Johnny Nash* (Regal Zonophone)	5	7	5
8 Dance To The Music *Sly and The Family Stone* (CBS)	20	–	–
9 Mony Mony *Tommy James and The Shondells* (Major Minor)	14	–	–
10 Fire *The Crazy World of Arthur Brown* (Track)	15	–	–
11 Keep On *Bruce Channel* (Bell)	–	–	–
12 Dream A Little Dream Of Me *Mama Cass* (RCA)	11	12	14
13 Sunshine Girl *Herman's Hermits* (Columbia)	16	20	–
14 I Pretend *Des O'Connor* (Columbia)	18	18	–

7	**14**	**21**	**28**
15 Lady Will Power *The Union Gap* (CBS)	13	9	10
16 Little Arrows *Leapy Lee* (MCA)	17	13	9
17 On The Road Again *Canned Heat* (Liberty)	10	8	8
18 Days *The Kinks* (Pye)	–	–	–
19 Hard To Handle *Otis Redding* (Atlantic)	19	15	16
20 Yesterday's Dream *The Four Tops* (Tamla Motown)	–	–	–
27 Hey Jude *The Beatles* (Apple)	1	1	2
– Those Were The Days *Mary Hopkin* (Apple)	7	2	1
26 Jezamine *The Casuals* (Decca)	12	6	3
29 Classical Gas *Mason Williams* (Warner Bros.)	25	16	12
33 Ice In The Sun *Status Quo* (Pye)	22	17	17
– Hello, I Love You *The Doors* (Elektra)	32	19	18
– Red Balloon *The Dave Clark Five* (Columbia)	–	39	19
31 I Live For The Sun *Vanity Fare* (Page One)	28	26	20

OCTOBER 1968

5	**12**	**19**	**26**
1 Those Were The Days *Mary Hopkin* (Apple)	1	1	1
2 Hey Jude *The Beatles* (Apple)	4	3	2
3 Jezamine *The Casuals* (Decca)	3	2	3
4 Little Arrows *Leapy Lee* (MCA)	2	4	4
5 Hold Me Tight *Johnny Nash* (Regal Zonophone)	10	15	16
6 I Gotta Get A Message To You *The Bee Gees* (Polydor)	13	16	20
7 Lady Will Power *The Union Gap* (CBS)	5	5	9
8 Say A Little Prayer *Aretha Franklin* (Atlantic)	12	–	–
9 Red Balloon *The Dave Clark Five* (Columbia)	7	8	14
10 High In The Sky *Amen Corner* (Deram)	18	–	–
11 Ice In The Sun *Status Quo* (Pye)	8	14	18
12 Do It Again *The Beach Boys* (Capitol)	20	–	–
13 Classical Gas *Mason Williams* (Warner Bros.)	9	11	15
14 On The Road Again *Canned Heat* (Liberty)	–	–	–
15 Dream A Little Dream Of Me *Mama Cass* (RCA)	16	–	–
16 Hello, I Love You *The Doors* (Elektra)	15	19	19
17 A Day Without Love *The Love Affair* (CBS)	11	9	6
18 My Little Lady *The Tremeloes* (CBS)	6	6	8
19 Help Yourself *Tom Jones* (Decca)	–	–	–
20 Hard To Handle *Otis Redding* (Atlantic)	–	–	–
32 Les Bicyclettes De Belsize *Engelbert Humperdinck* (Decca)	14	7	5
12 Light My Fire *Jose Feliciano* (RCA)	17	10	10
43 Wreck Of The Antoinette *Dave Dee, Dozy, Beaky, Mick and Tich* (Fontana)	19	18	17
27 The Good, The Bad And The Ugly *Hugo Montenegro* (Warner Bros.)	21	12	7
33 Listen To Me *The Hollies* (Parlophone)	23	13	11
34 Only One Woman *The Marbles* (Polydor)	26	17	12
42 With A Little Help From My Friends *Joe Cocker* (Regal Zonophone)	38	20	13

NOVEMBER 1968

2	**9**	**16**	**23**	**30**
1 Those Were The Days *Mary Hopkin* (Apple)	2	5	9	11
2 With A Little Help From My Friends *Joe Cocker* (Regal Zonophone)	1	2	5	10
3 The Good, The Bad And The Ugly *Hugo Montenegro* (RCA)	3	1	1	1
4 Little Arrows *Leapy Lee* (MCA)	8	14	13	20
5 Only One Woman *The Marbles* (Polydor)	6	8	8	12

2

	9	**16**	**23**	**30**
6 Light My Fire *Jose Feliciano* (RCA)	7	7	11	13
7 Hey Jude *The Beatles* (Apple)	10	11	—	—
8 Jezamine *The Casuals* (Decca)	11	10	16	—
9 Les Bicyclettes De Belsize *Engelbert Humperdinck* (Decca)	12	12	19	—
10 My Little Lady *The Tremeloes* (CBS)	13	17	—	—
11 A Day Without Love *The Love Affair* (CBS)	15	20	—	—
12 Listen To Me *The Hollies* (Parlophone)	14	15	18	—
13 Red Balloon *The Dave Clark Five* (Columbia)	—	—	—	—
14 Wreck Of The Antoinette *Dave Dee, Dozy, Beaky, Mick and Tich* (Fontana)	18	—	—	—
15 Lady Will Power *The Union Gap* (CBS)	19	—	—	—
16 Eloise *Barry Ryan* (MGM)	4	3	2	2
17 Classical Gas *Mason Williams* (Warner Bros.)	20	—	—	—
18 All Along The Watchtower *Jimi Hendrix* (Track)	9	6	.6	5
19 This Old Heart Of Mine *The Isley Brothers* (Tamla Motown)	5	4	3	3
20 Breaking Down The Walls Of Heartache *The Bandwagon* (Direction)	16	9	4	6
21 Mexico *Long John Baldry* (Pye)	17	16	15	19
41 Eleanore *The Turtles* (London)	23	13	7	8
35 Ain't Got No – I Got Life/Do What You Gotta Do *Nina Simone* (RCA)	28	18	10	7
23 You're All I Need To Get By *Marvin Gaye and Tammi Terrell* (Tamla Motown)	21	19	—	—
– Lily The Pink *The Scaffold* (Columbia)	41	23	12	4
34 If I Knew Then What I Know Now *Val Doonican* (Pye)	27	26	14	17
– I'm A Tiger *Lulu* (Columbia)	50	30	17	9
47 May I Have The Next Dream With You *Malcolm Roberts* (Major Minor)	31	24	20	14
27 Harper Valley P.T.A. *Jeannie C. Riley* (Polydor)	24	21	22	15
– One, Two, Three O'Leary *Des O'Connor* (Columbia)	—	—	31	16
– The Urban Spaceman *The Bonzo Dog Doo Dah Band* (Liberty)	44	34	25	18

DECEMBER 1968

7	**14**	**21**
1 The Good, The Bad And The Ugly *Hugo Montenegro* (RCA)	2	6
2 Lily The Pink *The Scaffold* (Columbia)	1	1
3 Eloise *Barry Ryan* (MGM)	8	18
4 This Old Heart Of Mine *The Isley Brothers* (Tamla Motown)	7	10
5 Breaking Down The Walls Of Heartache *The Bandwagon* (Direction)	10	11
6 One, Two, Three O'Leary *Des O'Connor* (Columbia)	4	4
7 Ain't Got No – I Got Life/Do What You Gotta Do *Nina Simone* (RCA)	3	2
8 May I Have The Next Dream With You *Malcolm Roberts* (Major Minor)	9	15
9 I'm A Tiger *Lulu* (Columbia)	12	12
10 Eleanore *The Turtles* (London)	14	—
11 All Along The Watchtower *Jimi Hendrix* (Track)	—	—
12 Harper Valley P.T.A. *Jeannie C. Riley* (Polydor)	15	17
13 The Urban Spaceman *The Bonzo Dog Doo Dah Band* (Liberty)	6	5
14 Build Me Up Buttercup *The Foundations* (Pye)	5	3
15 Race With The Devil *The Gun* (CBS)	13	8
16 Those Were The Days *Mary Hopkin* (Apple)	18	—
17 Only One Woman *The Marbles* (Polydor)	—	—
18 With A Little Help From My Friends *Joe Cocker* (Regal Zonophone)	—	—

7		14	21
19 Love Child *Diana Ross and The Supremes* (Tamla Motown)		17	19
20 If I Knew Then What I Know Now *Val Doonican* (Pye)		–	–
22 Sabre Dance *Love Sculpture* (Parlophone)		11	7
26 A Minute Of Your Time *Tom Jones* (Decca)		15	16
23 Private Number *Judy Clay and William Bell* (Stax)		19	14
30 Albatross *Fleetwood Mac* (Blue Horizon)		20	13
45 Ob-La-Di-Ob-La-Da *The Marmalade* (CBS)		22	9
44 Son Of A Preacher Man *Dusty Springfield* (Philips)		24	20

The chart for 28 December 1968 is a repeat of that for the previous week.

1968

Donovan continued his success of 1967 by providing songs which continued in the same vein as the previous year, seemingly preoccupied with flowers, beads, drugs, love, peace and happiness. He added three more hits in 1968 to his previous two of 1967, so obviously a market still existed for gentle, wafting lullabies which avoided the harshness of reality.

Music in 1968 lacked any real identity of its own, for there were few new stars, though the year did produce some fine songs. The outstanding records included two from The Beatles, 'Lady Madonna' and 'Hey Jude'. Early in January, The Beatles fought themselves for top chart placing as 'Hello, Goodbye' and 'Magical Mystery Tour' strove for the Number One position.

The Herd looked as though they would be labelled as the next 'teen' group and their key figure, Peter Frampton, received extensive teen magazine coverage. However, the group achieved only two hits in 1968, 'Paradise Lost' and 'I Don't Want Our Loving To Die', which followed their 1967 hit record, 'From The Underworld'. Peter Frampton, a good musician, was so horrified by the trimmings of teeny-bop fame that he made for the hills and The Herd were heard of no more. Later, Frampton was to emerge as an accepted and progressive musician.

There was also Julie Driscoll with Brian Auger and The Trinity, who excited the pop world and promised much, but 'This Wheel's On Fire' was their only Top Twenty hit. Blues-styled music continued from Chicken Shack and Christine Perfect but the group were to score only one hit in 1969 with 'I'd Rather Go Blind'.

The most unexpected hit was from a street busker called Don Partridge who sang 'Rosie', and many experienced pop commentators were thrown into confusion somewhat by the alarming speed with which 'Cinderella Rockafella' from Esther and Abi Ofarim travelled up the charts.

Amen Corner surfaced in style in 1968 under Andy Fairweather-Low after their first tentative chart entry with 'Gin House' during September 1967. Whereas 'Gin

House' had reached Number Twelve and no more, their three 1968 hits all made the Top Six. Likewise Dave Dee, Dozy, Beaky, Mick and Tich had three hits, but the last of these three in October entitled 'Wreck Of The Antoinette' was the group's final chart appearance. Altogether, the group had achieved 10 Top Twenty discs.

Some noteworthy hits which emerged from the otherwise dull charts included The Love Affair's cover version of the American Robert Knight's smash hit 'Everlasting Love'; Joe Cocker with the superb 'With A Little Help From My Friends'; The Union Gap with 'Young Girl' and 'Lady Will Power'; Nina Simone's 'Ain't Got No – I Got Life'; 'Dock Of The Bay' by Otis Redding and, late in 1968, 'Son Of A Preacher Man' from Dusty Springfield.

Altogether, the music scene of 1968 leaned towards 'heavy' and progressive music, and audiences listened to lengthy tuning up sessions which were followed by long solos which hardly merited an admission fee. Many businessmen and concert promoters would have preferred a return to Flower Power, when they could sell the accessories which accompanied the music, but with the new progressive music, none of the trappings of fashion or cults were necessary.

JANUARY 1969

4		11	18	25
1 Ob-La-Di-Ob-La-Da *The Marmalade* (CBS)		3	1	1
2 Lily The Pink *The Scaffold* (Columbia)		1	4	4
3 Build Me Up Buttercup *The Foundations* (Pye)		2	3	6
4 Albatross *Fleetwood Mac* (Blue Horizon)		4	2	2
5 The Urban Spaceman *The Bonzo Dog Doo Dah Band* (Liberty)		5	7	9
6 Sabre Dance *Love Sculpture* (Parlophone)		6	8	11
7 Ain't Go No – I Got Life/Do What You Gotta Do *Nina Simone* (RCA)		7	9	14
8 One, Two, Three O'Leary *Des O'Connor* (Columbia)		13	14	17
9 Son Of A Preacher Man *Dusty Springfield* (Philips)		9	11	13
10 Something's Happening *Herman's Hermits* (Columbia)		8	6	7
11 Race With The Devil *The Gun* (CBS)		14	19	–
12 For Once In My Life *Stevie Wonder* (Tamla Motown)		10	5	3
13 I'm A Tiger *Lulu* (Columbia)		11	18	20
14 Private Number *Judy Clay and William Bell* (Stax)		12	10	8
15 The Good, The Bad And The Ugly *Hugo Montenegro* (RCA)		16	15	19
16 May I Have The Next Dream With You *Malcolm Roberts* (Major Minor)		18	–	–
17 A Minute Of Your Time *Tom Jones* (Decca)		17	20	18
18 Love Child *Diana Ross and The Supremes* (Tamla Motown)		15	17	16
19 Breaking Down The Walls Of Heartache *The Bandwagon* (Direction)		19	–	–
20 Ob-La-Di-Ob-La-Da *The Bedrocks* (Columbia)		–	–	–
22 This Old Heart Of Mine *The Isley Brothers* (Tamla Motown)		20	–	–
32 Fox On The Run *Manfred Mann* (Fontana)		23	12	10
29 Blackberry Way *The Move* (Regal Zonophone)		29	13	5
31 S.O.S./Headline News *Edwin Starr* (Polydor)		22	16	12
– You Got Soul *Johnny Nash* (Major Minor)		37	23	15

FEBRUARY 1969

1		8	15	22
1 Albatross *Fleetwood Mac* (Blue Horizon)		2	2	6
2 Blackberry Way *The Move* (Regal Zonophone)		1	3	5
3 For Once In My Life *Stevie Wonder* (Tamla Motown)		3	4	10
4 Ob-La-Di-Ob-La-Da *The Marmalade* (CBS)		10	9	14
5 Fox On The Run *Manfred Mann* (Fontana)		11	13	16
6 Something's Happening *Herman's Hermits* (Columbia)		14	14	20
7 Lily The Pink *The Scaffold* (Columbia)		–	19	–
8 Private Number *Judy Clay and William Bell* (Stax)		13	–	–
9 You Got Soul *Johnny Nash* (Major Minor)		6	7	8
10 Build Me Up Buttercup *The Foundations* (Pye)		–	–	–
11 S.O.S./Headline News *Edwin Starr* (Polydor)		15	18	–
12 Dancing In The Street *Martha Reeves and The Vandellas* (Tamla Motown)		4	5	7
13 The Urban Spaceman *The Bonzo Dog Doo Dah Band* (Liberty)		–	–	–
14 To Love Somebody *Nina Simone* (RCA)		5	10	12
15 Sabre Dance *Love Sculpture* (Parlophone)		–	–	–
16 Please Don't Go *Donald Peers* (Columbia)		8	6	4
17 I Guess I'll Always Love You *The Isley Brothers* (Tamla Motown)		12	11	15
18 Love Child *Diana Ross and The Supremes* (Tamla Motown)		–	–	–
19 Quick Joey Small *Kasenatz Katz* (Buddah)		–	–	–
20 Ain't Got No – I Got Life/Do What You Gotta Do *Nina Simone* (RCA)		–	–	–
37 I'm Gonna Make You Love Me *The Supremes* (Tamla Motown)		7	8	3

1	8	15	22
27 Mrs Robinson (E.P.) *Simon and Garfunkel* (CBS)	9	–	–
24 People *The Tymes* (Direction)	16	–	18
28 I'll Pick A Rose *Marv Johnson* (Tamla Motown)	17	16	13
33 Half As Nice *Amen Corner* (Immediate)	19	1	1
42 Soul Sister Brown Sugar *Sam and Dave* (Stax)	20	–	17
– The Way It Used To Be *Engelbert Humperdinck* (Decca)	39	15	9
21 Hey Jude *Wilson Pickett* (Atlantic)	21	16	–
26 Going Up The Country *Canned Heat* (Liberty)	26	19	–
47 Wichita Lineman *Glen Campbell* (Ember)	24	26	11
– Surround Yourself With Sorrow *Cilla Black* (Parlophone)	–	41	19
– Where Do You Go To My Lovely *Peter Sarstedt* (UA)	18	12	2

MARCH 1969

1	8	15	22	29
1 Where Do You Go To My Lovely *Peter Sarstedt* (UA)	1	1	1	2
2 Half As Nice *Amen Corner* (Immediate)	2	11	15	–
3 I'm Gonna Make You Love Me *Diana Ross and The Supremes and The Temptations* (Tamla Motown)	6	9	19	–
4 Please Don't Go *Donald Peers* (Columbia)	3	10	4	20
5 The Way It Used To Be *Engelbert Humperdinck* (Decca)	9	3	3	13
6 Dancing In The Street *Martha Reeves and The Vandellas* (Tamla Motown)	14	17	–	–
7 Blackberry Way *The Move* (Regal Zonophone)	18	–	–	–
8 Albatross *Fleetwood Mac* (Blue Horizon)	19	–	–	–
9 Wichita Lineman *Glen Campbell* (Ember)	7	8	8	14
10 I'll Pick A Rose *Marv Johnson* (Tamla Motown)	12	16	–	–
11 Surround Yourself With Sorrow *Cilla Black* (Parlophone)	4	4	6	3
12 You Got Soul *Johnny Nash* (Major Minor)	–	–	–	–
13 For Once In My Life *Stevie Wonder* (Tamla Motown)	20	–	–	–
14 I Guess I'll Always Love You *The Isley Brothers* (Tamla Motown)	–	–	–	–
15 You've Lost That Loving Feeling *The Righteous Brothers* (London)	13	12	10	17
16 To Love Somebody *Nina Simone* (RCA)	–	–	–	–
17 Gentle On My Mind *Dean Martin* (Capitol)	10	5	4	5
18 Soul Sister Brown Sugar *Sam and Dave* (Stax)	15	–	–	–
19 I Heard It Through The Grapevine *Marvin Gaye* (Tamla Motown)	5	2	2	1
20 Monsieur Dupont *Sandie Shaw* (Pye)	8	7	7	8
26 First Of May *The Bee Gees* (Polydor)	11	6	9	7
36 Good Times *Cliff Richard* (Columbia)	16	15	13	12
– Sorry Suzanne *The Hollies* (Parlophone)	33	14	12	4
40 One Road *The Love Affair* (CBS)	21	18	16	19
36 Windmills Of Your Mind *Noel Harrison* (Reprise)	34	19	–	16
– Games People Play *Joe South* (Capitol)	30	20	14	6
– Get Ready *The Temptations* (Tamla Motown)	39	21	17	10
47 I Can Hear Music *The Beach Boys* (Capitol)	26	27	20	18
– Boom Bang-A-Bang *Lulu* (Columbia)	–	22	22	9
– If I Can Dream *Elvis Presley* (RCA)	17	13	11	11
– In The Bad Bad Old Days *The Foundations* (Pye)	–	–	18	15

5		12	19	26
1	I Heard It Through The Grapevine *Marvin Gaye* (Tamla Motown)	11	3	6
2	Gentle On My Mind *Dean Martin* (Capitol)	2	5	5
3	Sorry Suzanne *The Hollies* (Parlophone)	3	7	18
4	Boom Bang-A-Bang *Lulu* (Columbia)	4	4	7
5	The Israelites *Desmond Dekker and The Aces* (Pyramid)	5	1	2
6	Monsieur Dupont *Sandie Shaw* (Pye)	6	13	–
7	Where Do You Go To My Lovely *Peter Sarstedt* (UA)	7	–	–
8	Games People Play *Joe South* (Capitol)	8	9	15
9	In The Bad Bad Old Days *The Foundations* (Pye)	9	8	10
10	First Of May *The Bee Gees* (Polydor)	10	–	–
11	Surround Yourself With Sorrow *Cilla Black* (Parlophone)	11	17	–
12	Good Times *Cliff Richard* (Columbia)	12	19	–
13	Get Ready *The Temptations* (Tamla Motown)	13	20	–
14	Windmills Of Your Mind *Noel Harrison* (Reprise)	14	10	9
15	If I Can Dream *Elvis Presley* (RCA)	15	–	–
16	The Way It Used To Be *Engelbert Humperdinck* (Decca)	16	–	–
17	Pinball Wizard *The Who* (Track)	17	6	4
18	I Can Hear Music *The Beach Boys* (Capitol)	18	11	12
19	Wichita Lineman *Glen Campbell* (Ember)	18	–	–
20	You've Lost That Loving Feeling *The Righteous Brothers* (London)	20	–	–
–	Goodbye *Mary Hopkin* (Apple)	25	2	3
28	Cupid *Johnny Nash* (Major Minor)	28	12	13
22	Hello World *The Tremeloes* (CBS)	22	14	19
35	Come Back And Shake Me *Clodagh Rodgers* (RCA)	35	15	8
21	Harlem Shuffle *Bob and Earl* (Island)	21	16	11
26	I Don't Know Why *Stevie Wonder* (Tamla Motown)	26	18	14
–	Man Of The World *Fleetwood Mac* (Blue Horizon)	–	20	–
–	Get Back *The Beatles* (Apple)	–	–	1
–	Road Runner *Jnr. Walker and The All Stars* (Tamla Motown)	–	26	16
–	Passing Strangers *Sarah Vaughan and Billy Eckstine* (Mercury)	27	23	17
–	Badge *Cream* (Polydor)	–	36	20

3		10	17	24	31
1	Get Back *The Beatles* (Apple)	1	1	1	2
2	Goodbye *Mary Hopkin* (Apple)	2	5	8	20
3	The Israelites *Desmond Dekker and The Aces* (Pyramid)	6	8	17	–
4	Pinball Wizard *The Who* (Track)	4	10	11	–
5	Come Back And Shake Me *Clodagh Rodgers* (RCA)	3	4	7	10
6	Cupid *Johnny Nash* (Major Minor)	10	14	19	–
7	Harlem Shuffle *Bob and Earl* (Island)	11	13	16	–
8	Windmills Of Your Mind *Noel Harrison* (Reprise)	19	17	–	–
9	I Heard It Through The Grapevine *Marvin Gaye* (Tamla Motown)	–	–	–	–
10	Boom Bang-A-Bang *Lulu* (Columbia)	–	17	–	–
11	Man Of The World *Fleetwood Mac* (Blue Horizon)	7	3	3	2
12	Gentle On My Mind *Dean Martin* (Reprise)	13	16	–	–
13	Road Runner *Jnr. Walker and The All Stars* (Tamla Motown)	12	12	12	17
14	In The Bad Bad Old Days *The Foundations* (Pye)	–	–	–	–
15	My Sentimental Friend *Herman's Hermits* (Columbia)	5	2	2	4
16	My Way *Frank Sinatra* (Capitol)	9	6	6	5
17	I Don't Know Why *Stevie Wonder* (Tamla Motown)	16	–	–	–

3	10	17	24	31
18 I Can Hear Music *The Beach Boys* (Capitol)	–	–	–	–
19 Games People Play *Joe South* (Capitol)	–	–	–	–
20 Behind The Painted Smile *The Isley Brothers* (Tamla Motown)	8	7	5	6
29 Living In Shame *Diana Ross and The Supremes* (Tamla Motown)	14	–	15	16
25 The Boxer *Simon and Garfunkel* (CBS)	15	9	9	7
24 Dizzy *Tommy Roe* (Stateside)	17	11	4	3
28 Badge *Cream* (Polydor)	18	–	20	–
21 Passing Strangers *Sarah Vaughan and Billy Eckstine* (Mercury)	20	20	–	–
36 Ragamuffin Man *Manfred Mann* (Fontana)	23	15	10	8
– Love Me Tonight *Tom Jones* (Decca)	–	19	14	9
35 Aquarius/Let The Sunshine In *Fifth Dimension* (Bell)	25	22	13	11
– Galveston *Glen Campbell* (Ember)	–	27	18	18
– Time Is Tight *Booker T. and The M.G.s* (Stax)	–	39	30	15
– Tracks Of My Tears *Smokey Robinson and The Miracles* (Tamla Motown)	–	37	30	19
– Higher And Higher *Jackie Wilson* (MCA)	–	–	39	20
– Dick-A-Dum-Dum *Des O'Connor* (Columbia)	–	46	28	14
– Oh Happy Day *The Edwin Hawkins Singers* (Buddah)	–	–	39	13

JUNE 1969

7	14	21	28
1 Dizzy *Tommy Roe* (Stateside)	2	3	6
2 Get Back *The Beatles* (Apple)	5	6	18
3 Man Of The World *Fleetwood Mac* (Immediate)	4	11	–
4 The Ballad Of John And Yoko *The Beatles* (Apple)	1	1	1
5 My Way *Frank Sinatra* (Capitol)	7	7	–
6 The Boxer *Simon and Garfunkel* (CBS)	8	10	–
7 My Sentimental Friend *Herman's Hermits* (Columbia)	18	–	–
8 Behind The Painted Smile *The Isley Brothers* (Tamla Motown)	20	–	–
9 Oh Happy Day *The Edwin Hawkins Singers* (Buddah)	3	2	2
10 Ragamuffin Man *Manfred Mann* (Fontana)	10	15	–
11 Love Me Tonight *Tom Jones* (Decca)	12	19	–
12 Time Is Tight *Booker T. and The M.G.s* (Stax)	6	4	4
13 Tracks Of My Tears *Smokey Robinson and The Miracles* (Tamla Motown)	9	12	10
14 Galveston *Glen Campbell* (Ember)	17	16	–
15 Higher And Higher *Jackie Wilson* (MCA)	11	13	13
16 Aquarius/Let The Sunshine In *Fifth Dimension* (Liberty)	16	–	–
17 I'd Rather Go Blind *Chicken Shack* (Blue Horizon)	19	14	17
18 Dick-A-Dum-Dum *Des O'Connor* (Columbia)	14	–	–
19 Come Back And Shake Me *Clodagh Rodgers* (RCA)	–	–	–
20 Goodbye *Mary Hopkin* (Apple)	–	–	–
25 Big Ship *Cliff Richard* (Columbia)	13	8	11
22 Living In The Past *Jethro Tull* (Island)	15	5	3
– In The Ghetto *Elvis Presley* (RCA)	36	9	5
– Something In The Air *Thunderclap Newman* (Track)	42	17	7
43 Way Of Life *The Family Dogg* (Bell)	34	18	15
35 Proud Mary *Creedence Clearwater Revival* (Liberty)	22	20	9
– Break-A-Way *The Beach Boys* (Capitol)	29	21	8
50 Frozen Orange Juice *Peter Sarstedt* (UA)	24	24	12
26 Gimme Gimme Good Lovin' *Crazy Elephant* (Major Minor)	21	22	14
38 What Is A Man? *The Four Tops* (Tamla Motown)	27	29	16
35 Happy Heart *Andy Williams* (CBS)	25	34	19
– Lights Of Cincinnati *Scott Walker* (Philips)	46	25	20

		5	12	19	26
1	Something In The Air *Thunderclap Newman* (Track)		1	1	3
2	In The Ghetto *Elvis Presley* (RCA)		2	2	4
3	The Ballad Of John And Yoko *The Beatles* (Apple)		3	11	15
4	Living In The Past *Jethro Tull* (Island)		5	12	–
5	Oh Happy Day *The Edwin Hawkins Singers* (Buddah)		11	20	–
6	Time Is Tight *Booker T. and The M.G.s* (Stax)		10	17	19
7	Break-A-Way *The Beach Boys* (Capitol)		6	8	11
8	Way Of Life *The Family Dogg* (Bell)		7	6	10
9	Proud Mary *Creedence Clearwater Revival* (Liberty)		8	10	13
10	Frozen Orange Juice *Peter Sarstedt* (UA)		12	14	–
11	Big Ship *Cliff Richard* (Columbia)		15	–	–
12	Gimme Gimme Good Lovin' *Crazy Elephant* (Major Minor)		14	16	17
13	Dizzy *Tommy Roe* (Stateside)		19	22	–
14	Lights Of Cincinnati *Scott Walker* (Philips)		13	13	14
15	Hello Susie *Amen Corner* (Immediate)		4	5	6
16	Tracks Of My Tears *Smokey Robinson and The Miracles* (Tamla Motown)		–	–	–
17	Higher And Higher *Jackie Wilson* (MCA)		–	–	–
18	I'd Rather Go Blind *Chicken Shack* (Blue Horizon)		–	–	–
19	Baby Make It Soon *The Marmalade* (CBS)		18	9	9
20	My Way *Frank Sinatra* (Reprise)		–	–	–
–	Honky Tonk Women *The Rolling Stones* (Decca)		9	3	1
27	It Mek *Desmond Dekker* (Pyramid)		16	7	7
24	What Is A Man? *The Four Tops* (Tamla Motown)		17	–	–
42	That's The Way God Planned It *Billy Preston* (Apple)		20	15	12
–	Saved By The Bell *Robin Gibb* (Polydor)		25	18	5
32	Make Me An Island *Joe Dolan* (Pye)		29	19	16
–	Goodnight Midnight *Clodagh Rodgers* (RCA)		31	23	8
–	Babarabajagal *Donovan and The Jeff Beck Group* (Pye)		44	25	18
–	Conversations *Cilla Black* (Parlophone)		32	24	20
–	Give Peace A Chance *The Plastic Ono Band* (Apple)		21	4	2

		2	9	16	23	30
1	Honky Tonk Women *The Rolling Stones* (Decca)		1	1	1	2
2	Give Peace A Chance *The Plastic Ono Band* (Apple)		2	4	6	15
3	Saved By The Bell *Robin Gibb* (Polydor)		3	2	2	3
4	In The Ghetto *Elvis Presley* (RCA)		5	11	16	20
5	Something In The Air *Thunderclap Newman* (Track)		12	–	–	–
6	Goodnight Midnight *Clodagh Rodgers* (RCA)		4	6	7	16
7	Make Me An Island *Joe Dolan* (Pye)		7	3	5	5
8	It Mek *Desmond Dekker* (Pyramid)		10	–	–	–
9	Baby Make It Soon *The Marmalade* (CBS)		9	18	–	–
10	Hello Susie *Amen Corner* (Immediate)		18	–	–	–
11	That's The Way God Planned It *Billy Preston* (Apple)		11	16	–	–
12	Babarabajagal *Donovan and The Jeff Beck Group* (Pye)		14	14	–	–
13	Conversations *Cilla Black* (Parlophone)		8	7	9	13
14	Way Of Life *The Family Dogg* (Bell)		20	–	–	–
15	Wet Dream *Max Romeo* (Unity)		–	10	13	18
16	My Cherie Amour *Stevie Wonder* (Tamla Motown)		6	5	4	4
17	Break-A-Way *The Beach Boys* (Capitol)		–	–	–	–
18	When Two Worlds Collide *Jim Reeves* (RCA)		–	17	–	–
19	Bringing On Back The Good Times *The Love Affair* (CBS)		13	9	11	12
20	Time Is Tight *Booker T. and The M.G.s* (Stax)		–	–	–	–
25	I Can Sing A Rainbow/Love Is Blue *The Dells* (Chelsea)		15	15	15	–
29	Peaceful *Georgie Fame* (CBS)		16	–	–	–
21	Early In The Morning *Vanity Fare* (Page One)		17	8	10	10

2		9	16	23	30
34 Curly *The Move* (Regal Zonophone)		19	19	12	14
28 Too Busy Thinking About My Baby *Marvin Gaye* (Tamla Motown)		32	12	8	7
– In The Year 2525 *Zager and Evans* (RCA)		21	13	3	1
37 Viva Bobbie Joe *The Equals* (President)		25	20	14	6
45 Je T'Aime, Moi Non Plus *Jane Birkin and Serge Gainsbourg* (Fontana)		–	32	17	17
– Don't Forget To Remember *The Bee Gees* (Polydor)		–	43	18	9
39 I'm A Better Man *Engelbert Humperdinck* (Decca)		–	28	19	–
– Bad Moon Rising *Creedence Clearwater Revival* (Liberty)		–	49	20	8
– Natural Born Boogie *Humble Pie* (Immediate)		–	–	23	11
– Good Morning Starshine *Oliver* (CBS)		48	31	26	19

SEPTEMBER 1969

6		13	20	27
1 In The Year 2525 *Zager and Evans* (RCA)		1	3	5
2 Bad Moon Rising *Creedence Clearwater Revival* (Liberty)		2	1	1
3 Honky Tonk Women *The Rolling Stones* (Decca)		9	10	18
4 My Cherie Amour *Stevie Wonder* (Tamla Motown)		8	11	16
5 Don't Forget To Remember *The Bee Gees* (Polydor)		3	2	3
6 Too Busy Thinking About My Baby *Marvin Gaye* (Tamla Motown)		5	6	8
7 Viva Bobbie Joe *The Equals* (President)		7	7	9
8 Je T'Aime, Moi Non Plus *Jane Birkin and Serge Gainsbourg* (Fontana)		6	4	2
9 Saved By The Bell *Robin Gibb* (Polydor)		10	12	–
10 Natural Born Boogie *Humble Pie* (Immediate)		4	5	6
11 Make Me An Island *Joe Dolan* (Pye)		12	13	–
12 Early In The Morning *Vanity Fare* (Page One)		14	–	–
13 Curly *The Move* (Regal Zonophone)		13	20	–
14 Good Morning Starshine *Oliver* (CBS)		11	8	7
15 Conversations *Cilla Black* (Parlophone)		–	–	–
16 Give Peace A Chance *The Plastic Ono Band* (Apple)		–	–	–
17 I'm A Better Man *Engelbert Humperdinck* (Decca)		15	18	–
18 Bringing On Back The Good Times *The Love Affair* (CBS)		–	–	–
19 Goodnight Midnight *Clodagh Rodgers* (RCA)		20	–	–
20 Wet Dream *Max Romeo* (Unity)		18	–	–
– Cloud Nine *The Temptations* (Tamla Motown)		16	–	15
– Marrakesh Express *Crosby, Stills and Nash* (Atlantic)		17	–	17
– I'll Never Fall In Love Again *Bobby Gentry* (Capitol)		19	9	4
– Throw Down A Line *Cliff Richard and Hank Marvin* (Columbia)		34	14	14
– A Boy Named Sue *Johnny Cash* (CBS)		41	15	10
– It's Getting Better *Mama Cass* (Stateside)		26	16	11
– Birth *The Peddlers* (CBS)		27	17	–
– Hare Krishna Mantra *Radha Krishna Temple* (Apple)		44	19	19
– Lay Lady Lay *Bob Dylan* (CBS)		30	31	12
– Put Yourself In My Place *The Isley Brothers* (Tamla Motown)		23	28	13
– Nobody's Child *Karen Young* (Major Minor)		35	30	20

Due to print schedules Record Mirror *did not publish a chart for 6 September 1969. However, it would have used the BMRB listing, and this we have done.*

OCTOBER 1969

4		11	18	25
1 Bad Moon Rising *Creedence Clearwater Revival* (Liberty)		3	12	18
2 I'll Never Fall In Love Again *Bobby Gentry* (Capitol)		2	1	2
3 Je T'Aime, Moi Non Plus *Jane Birkin and Serge Gainsbourg* (Major Minor)		1	2	4
4 A Boy Named Sue *Johnny Cash* (CBS)		4	4	10
5 Don't Forget To Remember *The Bee Gees* (Polydor)		7	16	16
6 Good Morning Starshine *Oliver* (CBS)		6	10	12
7 Throw Down A Line *Cliff Richard and Hank Marvin* (Columbia)		8	14	15
8 It's Getting Better *Mama Cass* (Stateside)		9	13	14
9 Lay Lady Lay *Bob Dylan* (CBS)		5	7	9
10 In The Year 2525 *Zager and Evans* (RCA)		18	–	–
11 Natural Born Boogie *Humble Pie* (Immediate)		17	–	–
12 Hare Krishna Mantra *Radha Krishna Temple* (Apple)		12	15	–
13 Viva Bobbie Joe *The Equals* (President)		–	–	–
14 Nobody's Child *Karen Young* (Major Minor)		10	6	7
15 Too Busy Thinking About My Baby *Marvin Gaye* (Tamla Motown)		–	–	–
16 Je T'Aime, Moi Non Plus *Jane Birkin and Serge Gainsbourg* (Fontana)		–	–	–
17 I'm Gonna Make You Mine *Lou Christie* (Buddah)		11	3	3
18 I Second That Emotion *Diana Ross and The Supremes and The Temptations* (Tamla Motown)		–	19	–
19 Love At First Sight *Sounds Nice* (Parlophone)		–	18	19
20 Space Oddity *David Bowie* (Philips)		13	8	6
34 Oh Well *Fleetwood Mac* (Reprise)		14	9	8
25 Put Yourself In My Place *The Isley Brothers* (Tamla Motown)		15	–	–
32 He Ain't Heavy, He's My Brother *The Hollies* (Parlophone)		16	5	5
27 Do What You Gotta Do *The Four Tops* (Tamla Motown)		19	17	11
31 Cloud Nine *The Temptations* (Tamla Motown)		20	–	–
– Sugar Sugar *The Archies* (RCA)		43	11	1
50 Return Of Django/Dollar In The Teeth *The Upsetters* (Island)		37	20	15
44 Love's Been Good To Me *Frank Sinatra* (Capitol)		26	21	13
39 Delta Lady *Joe Cocker* (Regal Zonophone)		39	30	20

NOVEMBER 1969

1		8	15	22	29
1 Sugar Sugar *The Archies* (RCA)		1	1	1	1
2 I'm Gonna Make You Mine *Lou Christie* (Buddah)		3	10	16	–
3 He Ain't Heavy, He's My Brother *The Hollies* (Parlophone)		4	4	11	18
4 Oh Well *Fleetwood Mac* (Reprise)		2	2	3	4
5 Space Oddity *David Bowie* (Philips)		7	16	18	–
6 I'll Never Fall In Love Again *Bobby Gentry* (Capitol)		9	15	–	–
7 Nobody's Child *Karen Young* (Major Minor)		6	9	8	11
8 Return Of Django/Dollar In The Teeth *The Upsetters* (Island)		5	5	5	8
9 Je T'Aime, Moi Non Plus *Jane Birkin and Serge Gainsbourg* (Major Minor)		14	20	–	–
10 A Boy Named Sue *Johnny Cash* (CBS)		12	18	–	–
11 Lay Lady Lay *Bob Dylan* (CBS)		20	–	–	–
12 Delta Lady *Joe Cocker* (Regal Zonophone)		10	11	14	–
13 Love's Been Good To Me *Frank Sinatra* (Reprise)		8	8	12	12
14 Do What You Gotta Do *The Four Tops* (Tamla Motown)		16	–	–	–
15 It's Getting Better *Mama Cass* (Stateside)		–	–	–	–
16 Bad Moon Rising *Creedence Clearwater Revival* (Liberty)		–	–	–	–

1	8	15	22	29
17 Good Morning Starshine *Oliver* (CBS)	–	–	–	–
18 Wonderful World Beautiful People *Jimmy Cliff* (Trojan)	11	7	6	7
19 Don't Forget To Remember *The Bee Gees* (Polydor)	–	–	–	–
20 (Call Me) Number One *The Tremeloes* (CBS)	13	3	2	2
– Something/Come Together *The Beatles* (Apple)	15	6	4	6
22 What Does It Take *Jnr. Walker and The All Stars* (Tamla Motown)	17	13	13	13
38 Cold Turkey *The Plastic Ono Band* (Apple)	18	14	15	16
36 Sweet Dream *Jethro Tull* (Chrysalis)	19	12	7	10
31 The Liquidator *Harry J. and The All Stars* (Trojan)	24	17	17	9
45 Ruby Don't Take Your Love To Town *Kenny Rogers and The First Edition* (Reprise)	21	19	9	5
– Winter World Of Love *Engelbert Humperdinck* (Decca)	–	46	19	15
– Yester-Me, Yester-You, Yesterday *Stevie Wonder* (Tamla Motown)	–	31	10	3
49 Teresa *Joe Dolan* (Pye)	30	28	20	–
– Melting Pot *Blue Mink* (Philips)	–	50	27	14
– Two Little Boys *Rolf Harris* (Columbia)	–	–	32	17
– Onion Song *Mervin Gaye and Tammi Terrell* (Tamla Motown)	–	36	33	19
– Love Is All *Malcolm Roberts* (Major Minor)	–	–	30	20

DECEMBER 1969

6	13	20
1 Sugar Sugar *The Archies* (RCA)	1	3
2 Yester-Me, Yester-You, Yesterday *Stevie Wonder* (Tamla Motown)	4	4
3 Ruby Don't Take Your Love To Town *Kenny Rogers and The First Edition* (Reprise)	2	2
4 (Call Me) Number One *The Tremeloes* (CBS)	6	9
5 Two Little Boys *Rolf Harris* (Columbia)	3	1
6 Oh Well *Fleetwood Mac* (Reprise)	18	–
7 Melting Pot *Blue Mink* (Philips)	5	5
8 Something/Come Together *The Beatles* (Apple)	11	18
9 Sweet Dream *Jethro Tull* (Chrysalis)	16	–
10 Suspicious Minds *Elvis Presley* (RCA)	8	6
11 Wonderful World Beautiful People *Jimmy Cliff* (Trojan)	10	17
12 Winter World Of Love *Engelbert Humperdinck* (Decca)	7	8
13 The Liquidator *Harry J. and The All Stars* (Trojan)	13	11
14 Return of Django/Dollar In The Teeth *The Upsetters* (Island)	–	–
15 Nobody's Child *Karen Young* (Major Minor)	14	–
16 Leavin' (Durham Town) *Roger Whittaker* (Columbia)	19	14
17 Onion Song *Marvin Gaye and Tammi Terrell* (Tamla Motown)	9	13
18 Love's Been Good To Me *Frank Sinatra* (Capitol)	–	–
19 Cold Turkey *The Plastic Ono Band* (Apple)	–	–
20 What Does It Take *Jnr. Walker and The All Stars* (Tamla Motown)	–	–
21 Love Is All *Malcolm Roberts* (Major Minor)	12	15
23 Tracy *The Cuff Links* (MCA)	15	10
27 All I Have To Do Is Dream *Bobby Gentry and Glen Campbell* (Capitol)	17	7
24 Green River *Creedence Clearwater Revival* (Liberty)	20	–
– Without Love *Tom Jones* (Decca)	21	12
30 Good Old Rock 'n' Roll *The Dave Clark Five* (Columbia)	25	16
26 Loneliness *Des O'Connor* (Columbia)	24	19
45 With The Eyes Of A Child *Cliff Richard* (Columbia)	39	20

1969

No big new stars came into 1969's chart reckoning, and the discs which became hits were, by and large, not exceptional.

For some people, the presence at the Number One spot of 'Je T'Aime, Moi Non Plus' from Jane Birkin and Serge Gainsbourg constituted the year's most sensational event. Certainly what appeared on disc as a simulated sound reproduction of the love act was novel and not altogether unpleasant. More interesting, however, was the extraordinary reaction of Philips, the recording company which originally released the record. Philips were presumably aware of the controversy which would surround the record when they recorded it, but when the disc reached the Number Two position they presumably decided that it was too controversial and sold the product to another record company. Record companies have often made hits of records which have failed with other companies, but 'Je T'Aime' would seem to be pop's only case of a hit record changing hands and reaching Number One with the new company, while it was already at a very high position in the charts with the original company.

Another newsworthy record in the charts was 'Give Peace A Chance' which reached Number Two. The song was recorded in a Canadian hotel room, with John Lennon and Yoko Ono being joined by a singing host who received the name of The Plastic Ono Band. Although John and Yoko formed a group of musicians for future recordings, the name of The Plastic Ono Band persisted, and was featured on 'Cold Turkey', one of the most realistic and horrific discs recorded as a single, for it was descriptive of someone coming off heroin.

Much more peaceful was a series of hit records such as 'Sugar Sugar', 'It Mek', 'Ragamuffin Man', and 'Where Do You Go To My Lovely'. The latter was sung by Peter Sarstedt, a brother of Eden Kane, the singer who had achieved several hits in the early 1960s.

Cliff Richard joined forces with Hank Marvin for 'Throw Down A Line', while a group known as Thunderclap Newman, whose line-up included Jimmy McCulough, sang 'Somthing In The Air' – a song which has become one of pop's classics.

For a time 'Swamp' music became popular as an American singer, Creedence Clearwater, assisted by his band known as Creedence Clearwater Revival, had three hits. The first two of these, 'Proud Mary' and 'Bad Moon Rising', were probably the most memorable, while the third, 'Green River', received short shift, and Creedence Clearwater Revival returned to the swamps of obscurity.

The Rolling Stones had a Number One with 'Honky Tonk Women', while Marvin Gaye recorded 'I Heard It Through The Grapevine', one of Tamla Motown's finest singles. Gaye had another hit with 'Too Busy Thinking About My Baby' before joining forces with Tammi Terrell for the 'Onion Song'.

Hits came from Jethro Tull, Joe Cocker, Bob Dylan, and The Beatles bade farewell with 'Get Back' and 'The Ballad Of John And Yoko'. Surprisingly, 'Something', a double A-side with 'Come Together' only reached the Number Four position.

The most unusual hit was 'Babarabajagal' from Donovan and The Jeff Beck Group – a hybrid of artists if ever there was one.

The amount of festivals which were held, and the culture which accompanied them, enlivened what would otherwise have been a rather dull year for pop, and the Top Fifty in particular.

JANUARY 1970

3	10	17	24	31
1 Two Little Boys *Rolf Harris* (Columbia)	1	1	1	2
2 Ruby Don't Take Your Love To Town *Kenny Rogers and The First Edition* (Reprise)	2	4	2	7
3 Sugar Sugar *The Archies* (RCA)	6	6	9	14
4 Suspicious Minds *Elvis Presley* (RCA)	7	2	2	6
5 Melting Pot *Blue Mink* (Philips)	3	7	10	16
6 Yester-Me, Yester-You, Yesterday *Stevie Wonder* (Tamla Motown)	9	14	–	–
7 All I Have To Do Is Dream *Bobby Gentry and Glen Campbell* (Capitol)	4	3	4	5
8 Winter World Of Love *Engelbert Humperdinck* (Decca)	14	16	–	–
9 Tracy *The Cuff Links* (MCA)	4	5	5	11
10 Without Love *Tom Jones* (Decca)	13	11	17	–
11 Onion Song *Marvin Gaye and Tammi Terrell* (Tamla Motown)	11	19	–	–
12 Good Old Rock 'n' Roll *The Dave Clark Five* (Columbia)	8	8	7	13
13 Leavin' (Durham Town) *Roger Whittaker* (Columbia)	12	12	19	18
14 (Call Me) Number One *The Tremeloes* (CBS)	15	–	–	–
15 Love Is All *Malcolm Roberts* (Major Minor)	–	–	–	–
16 The Liquidator *Harry J. and The All Stars* (Trojan)	10	17	15	17
17 But You Love Me Daddy *Jim Reeves* (RCA)	17	15	18	19
18 Loneliness *Des O'Connor* (Columbia)	–	–	–	–
19 Green River *Creedence Clearwater Revival* (Liberty)	–	–	–	–
20 Nobody's Child *Karen Young* (Major Minor)	–	–	–	–
30 Reflections Of My Life *The Marmalade* (Decca)	16	9	3	3
21 Something/Come Together *The Beatles* (Apple)	18	–	–	–
47 Comin' Home *Delaney and Bonnie* (Atlantic)	19	–	16	–
29 If I Thought You'd Ever Change Your Mind *Cilla Black* (Parlophone)	20	–	–	–
– Friends *Arrival* (Decca)	–	18	11	8
– Come And Get It *Badfinger* (Apple)	33	10	8	4
27 Some Day We'll Be Together *Diana Ross and The Supremes* (Tamla Motown)	24	13	14	15
22 With The Eyes Of A Child *Cliff Richard* (Columbia)	22	20	–	–
– Leavin' On A Jet Plane *Peter, Paul and Mary* (Warner Bros.)	–	36	13	9
– Love Grows *Edison Lighthouse* (Bell)	–	–	12	1
– Witches Promise/Teacher *Jethro Tull* (Chrysalis)	–	–	30	10
– I'm A Man *Chicago* (CBS)	–	23	20	12
– I Can't Get Next To You *The Temptations* (Tamla Motown)	–	39	26	20

FEBRUARY 1970

7	14	21	28
1 Love Grows *Edison Lighthouse* (Bell)	1	1	1
2 Two Little Boys *Rolf Harris* (Columbia)	7	10	15
3 Reflections Of My Life *The Marmalade* (Decca)	6	15	–
4 Leavin' On A Jet Plane *Peter, Paul and Mary* (Warner Bros.)	2	3	6
5 Come And Get It *Badfinger* (Apple)	5	13	19
6 Witches Promise/Teacher *Jethro Tull* (Chrysalis)	4	8	12
7 Ruby Don't Take Your Love To Town *Kenny Rogers and The First Edition* (Reprise)	13	18	20
8 I'm A Man *Chicago* (CBS)	9	14	18
9 Friends *Arrival* (Decca)	11	–	–
10 Temma Harbour *Mary Hopkin* (Apple)	8	6	7
11 All I Have To Do Is Dream *Bobby Gentry and Glen Campbell* (Capitol)	15	–	–

7	14	21	28
12 Suspicious Minds *Elvis Presley* (RCA)	17	–	–
13 I Can't Get Next To You *The Temptations* (Tamla Motown)	14	17	17
14 Tracy *The Cuff Links* (MCA)	–	–	–
15 Let's Work Together *Canned Heat* (Liberty)	3	2	3
16 Hitchin' A Ride *Vanity Fare* (Page One)	20	16	–
17 Someday We'll Be Together *Diana Ross and The Supremes* (Tamla Motown)	19	–	–
18 Good Old Rock 'n' Roll *The Dave Clark Five* (Columbia)	–	–	–
19 Sugar Sugar *The Archies* (RCA)	–	–	–
20 The Liquidator *Harry J. and The All Stars* (Trojan)	–	–	–
21 Venus *Shocking Blue* (Penny Farthing)	10	9	8
30 I Want You Back *The Jackson Five* (Tamla Motown)	12	4	4
28 Wedding Bell Blues *Fifth Dimension* (Liberty)	16	–	–
36 Wanderin' Star *Lee Marvin* (Paramount)	18	5	2
– Instant Karma *John Lennon and Yoko Ono with The Plastic Ono Band* (Apple)	–	7	5
49 My Baby Loves Lovin' *White Plains* (Deram)	22	11	9
32 Years May Come, Years May Go *Herman's Hermits* (Columbia)	24	12	11
– United We Stand *Brotherhood Of Man* (Deram)	40	19	10
25 Both Sides Now *Judy Collins* (Elektra)	23	20	14
– Bridge Over Troubled Water *Simon and Garfunkel* (CBS)	–	42	13
41 Raindrops Keep Fallin' On My Head *Sacha Distel* (Warner Bros.)	32	26	16

MARCH 1970

7	14	21	28
1 Wanderin' Star *Lee Marvin* (Paramount)	1	1	2
2 I Want You Back *The Jackson Five* (Tamla Motown)	4	4	12
3 Let's Work Together *Canned Heat* (Liberty)	7	12	14
4 Love Grows *Edison Lighthouse* (Bell)	5	17	19
5 Instant Karma *John Lennon and Yoko Ono with The Plastic Ono Band* (Apple)	6	10	15
6 Leavin' On A Jet Plane *Peter, Paul and Mary* (Warner Bros.)	15	19	–
7 Bridge Over Troubled Water *Simon and Garfunkel* (CBS)	3	2	1
8 Years May Come, Years May Go *Herman's Hermits* (Columbia)	9	7	13
9 My Baby Loves Lovin' *White Plains* (Deram)	14	18	–
10 Temma Harbour *Mary Hopkin* (Apple)	19	–	–
11 United We Stand *Brotherhood Of Man* (Deram)	12	16	17
12 Venus *Shocking Blue* (Penny Farthing)	16	–	–
13 Na Na Hey Hey Kiss Him Goodbye *Steam* (Fontana)	13	9	10
14 Elizabethan Reggae *Boris Gardner* (Duke)	–	–	–
15 Raindrops Keep Fallin' On My Head *Sacha Distel* (Warner Bros.)	10	14	16
16 Something's Burning *Kenny Rogers and The First Edition* (Reprise)	18	13	11
17 Both Sides Now *Judy Collins* (Elektra)	11	–	–
18 Don't Cry Daddy *Elvis Presley* (RCA)	11	8	9
19 That Same Old Feeling *Pickettywitch* (Pye)	8	5	5
20 Two Little Boys *Rolf Harris* (Columbia)	–	20	–
– Let It Be *The Beatles* (Apple)	2	3	4
– Can't Help Falling In Love *Andy Williams* (CBS)	17	6	3
28 Everybody Get Together *The Dave Clark Five* (Columbia)	20	11	8
– Young, Gifted And Black *Bob and Marcia* (Harry J.)	22	15	6
– Knock Knock Who's There *Mary Hopkin* (Apple)	–	–	7
32 Farewell Is A Lonely Sound *Jimmy Ruffin* (Tamla Motown)	29	23	18
48 You're Such A Good Looking Woman *Joe Dolan* (Pye)	28	26	20

APRIL 1970

4		11	18	25
1 Bridge Over Troubled Water *Simon and Garfunkel* (CBS)		1	2	3
2 Knock Knock Who's There *Mary Hopkin* (Apple)		4	4	5
3 Can't Help Falling In Love *Andy Williams* (CBS)		3	3	4
4 Wanderin' Star *Lee Marvin* (Paramount)		5	8	13
5 Young, Gifted And Black *Bob and Marcia* (Harry J.)		8	7	7
6 That Same Old Feeling *Pickettywitch* (Pye)		7	11	19
7 Let It Be *The Beatles* (Apple)		11	16	–
8 Something's Burning *Kenny Rogers and The First Edition* (Reprise)		9	15	18
9 Everybody Get Together *The Dave Clark Five* (Columbia)		15	–	–
10 Don't Cry Daddy *Elvis Presley* (RCA)		14	20	–
11 Na Na Hey Hey Kiss Him Goodbye *Steam* (Fontana)		18	–	–
12 I Want You Back *The Jackson Five* (Tamla Motown)		20	–	–
13 All Kinds Of Everything *Dana* (Rex)		2	1	1
14 Farewell Is A Lonely Sound *Jimmy Ruffin* (Tamla Motown)		13	9	9
15 Spirit In The Sky *Norman Greenbaum* (Reprise)		6	5	2
16 Years May Come, Years May Go *Herman's Hermits* (Columbia)		–	–	–
17 I Can't Help Myself *The Four Tops* (Tamla Motown)		12	10	11
18 You're Such A Good Looking Woman *Joe Dolan* (Pye)		17	17	–
19 Who Do You Love *Juicy Lucy* (Vertigo)		–	14	20
20 Let's Work Together *Canned Heat* (Liberty)		–	–	–
21 Gimme Dat Ding *The Pipkins* (Columbia)		10	6	6
22 When Julie Comes Around *The Cuff Links* (MCA)		16	12	12
39 Never Had A Dream Come True *Stevie Wonder* (Tamla Motown)		19	13	8
37 Good Morning Freedom *Blue Mink* (Philips)		21	18	10
35 Travellin' Band *Creedence Clearwater Revival* (Liberty)		27	19	15
40 House Of The Rising Sun *Frijid Pink* (Deram)		39	21	14
47 Rag Mama Rag *The Band* (Capitol)		33	25	16
– Daughter Of Darkness *Tom Jones* (Decca)		–	33	17

MAY 1970

2		9	16	23	30
1 Spirit In The Sky *Norman Greenbaum* (Reprise)		1	2	2	4
2 All Kinds Of Everything *Dana* (Rex)		3	5	10	–
3 Back Home *The England World Cup Squad* (Pye)		2	1	1	1
4 Bridge Over Troubled Water *Simon and Garfunkel* (CBS)		4	12	14	–
5 Can't Help Falling In Love *Andy Williams* (CBS)		7	11	12	–
6 Never Had A Dream Come True *Stevie Wonder* (Tamla Motown)		9	16	15	–
7 Gimme Dat Ding *The Pipkins* (Columbia)		11	18	–	–
8 Farewell Is A Lonely Sound *Jimmy Ruffin* (Tamla Motown)		16	14	–	–
9 House Of The Rising Sun *Frijid Pink* (Deram)		6	4	6	7
10 When Julie Comes Around *The Cuff Links* (MCA)		12	13	–	–
11 Travellin' Band *Creedence Clearwater Revival* (Liberty)		8	9	11	16
12 Good Morning Freedom *Blue Mink* (Philips)		13	–	–	–
13 Young, Gifted And Black *Bob and Marcia* (Harry J.)		18	–	–	–
14 Knock Knock Who's There *Mary Hopkin* (Apple)		15	–	–	–
15 Daughter Of Darkness *Tom Jones* (Decca)		5	8	5	9
16 Rag Mama Rag *The Band* (Capitol)		19	17	–	–
17 I Can't Help Myself *The Four Tops* (Tamla Motown)		–	–	–	–
18 Who Do You Love *Juicy Lucy* (Vertigo)		–	–	–	–
19 I Can't Tell The Bottom From The Top *The Hollies* (Parlophone)		10	7	9	15
20 You're Such A Good Looking Woman *Joe Dolan* (Pye)		–	–	–	–
27 Brontosaurus *The Move* (Regal Zonophone)		14	10	7	10

2

	9	16	23	30
23 I Don't Believe In If Anymore *Roger Whittaker* (Columbia)	17	15	8	8
35 Question *The Moody Blues* (Threshold)	20	3	4	2
44 Yellow River *Christie* (CBS)	28	6	3	3
26 The Seeker *The Who* (Track)	24	19	–	–
24 I've Got You On My Mind *White Plains* (Deram)	22	20	17	17
– Honey Come Back *Glen Campbell* (Capitol)	38	28	13	5
– Everything Is Beautiful *Ray Stevens* (CBS)	–	40	16	12
29 Do The Funky Chicken *Rufus Thomas* (Stax)	26	25	18	–
28 If I Could *Julie Felix* (RAK)	25	23	19	–
– ABC *The Jackson Five* (Tamla Motown)	–	41	20	11
48 Up The Ladder To The Roof *The Supremes* (Tamla Motown)	39	30	30	6
– Groovin' With Mr Bloe *Mr Bloe* (DJM)	37	36	21	13
– Cottonfields *The Beach Boys* (Capitol)	–	46	32	14
– The Green Manalishi *Fleetwood Mac* (Reprise)	–	–	49	18
50 Don't You Know *Butterscotch* (RCA)	41	31	22	19
– Abraham, Martin And John *Marvin Gaye* (Tamla Motown)	35	33	24	20

JUNE 1970

6	13	20	27
1 Yellow River *Christie* (CBS)	2	2	4
2 Back Home *The England World Cup Squad* (Pye)	3	9	15
3 Question *The Moody Blues* (Threshold)	6	12	17
4 Honey Come Back *Glen Campbell* (Capitol)	5	6	8
5 Daughter Of Darkness *Tom Jones* (Decca)	16	20	–
6 Everything Is Beautiful *Ray Stevens* (CBS)	9	8	11
7 Groovin' With Mr Bloe *Mr Bloe* (DJM)	4	3	2
8 ABC *The Jackson Five* (Tamla Motown)	10	14	–
9 Spirit In The Sky *Norman Greenbaum* (Reprise)	15	–	–
10 Up The Ladder To The Roof *The Supremes* (Tamla Motown)	8	13	12
11 I Don't Believe In If Anymore *Roger Whittaker* (Columbia)	12	19	19
12 Cottonfields *The Beach Boys* (Capitol)	7	5	6
13 In The Summertime *Mungo Jerry* (Dawn)	1	1	1
14 Abraham, Martin And John *Marvin Gaye* (Tamla Motown)	14	11	9
15 Brontosaurus *The Move* (Regal Zonophone)	18	–	–
16 House Of The Rising Sun *Frijid Pink* (Deram)	19	–	–
17 The Green Manalishi *Fleetwood Mac* (Reprise)	13	10	10
18 Don't You Know *Butterscotch* (RCA)	17	–	20
19 I've Got You On My Mind *White Plains* (Deram)	–	–	–
20 Do The Funky Chicken *Rufus Thomas* (Stax)	–	–	–
25 Sally *Gerry Monroe* (Chapter One)	11	7	5
37 Goodbye Sam, Hello Samantha *Cliff Richard* (Columbia)	20	15	7
36 All Right Now *Free* (Island)	27	4	3
34 I Will Survive *Arrival* (Decca)	23	16	16
31 It's All In The Game *The Four Tops* (Tamla Motown)	24	17	13
29 Down The Dustpipe *Status Quo* (Pye)	21	18	14
– Up Around The Bend *Creedence Clearwater Revival* (Liberty)	–	33	18

JULY 1970

4	11	18	25
1 In The Summertime *Mungo Jerry* (Dawn)	1	1	1
2 All Right Now *Free* (Island)	2	2	2
3 Groovin' With Mr Bloe *Mr Bloe* (DJM)	3	8	14
4 Sally *Gerry Monroe* (Chapter One)	7	6	13
5 Cottonfields *The Beach Boys* (Capitol)	6	7	10
6 Goodbye Sam, Hello Samantha *Cliff Richard* (Columbia)	8	9	12
7 Yellow River *Christie* (CBS)	15	17	18

	11	**18**	**25**
8 It's All In The Game *The Four Tops* (Tamla Motown)	5	5	6
9 Up Around The Bend *Creedence Clearwater Revival* (Liberty)	4	3	5
10 The Green Manalishi *Fleetwood Mac* (Reprise)	10	16	17
11 Honey Come Back *Glen Campbell* (Capitol)	14	15	19
12 Down The Dustpipe *Status Quo* (Pye)	12	14	16
13 Abraham, Martin And John *Marvin Gaye* (Tamla Motown)	11	–	–
14 Everything Is Beautiful *Ray Stevens* (CBS)	18	–	–
15 Love Of The Common People *Nicky Thomas* (Trojan)	9	11	9
16 Something *Shirley Bassey* (UA)	13	10	7
17 I Will Survive *Arrival* (Decca)	17	–	–
18 Up The Ladder To The Roof *The Supremes* (Tamla Motown)	–	–	–
19 American Woman *Guess Who* (RCA)	–	–	–
20 Question *The Moody Blues* (Threshold)	–	–	–
22 Lola *The Kinks* (Pye)	16	4	4
28 Lady D'Arbanville *Cat Stevens* (Island)	19	12	11
– The Wonder Of You *Elvis Presley* (RCA)	20	13	3
39 (It's Like A) Sad Old Kinda Movie *Pickettywitch* (Pye)	27	18	–
45 I'll Say Forever My Love *Jimmy Ruffin* (Tamla Motown)	30	19	15
29 Love Like A Man *Ten Years After* (Deram)	24	20	–
48 Neanderthal Man *Hotlegs* (Fontana)	32	21	8
31 Big Yellow Taxi *Joni Mitchell* (Reprise)	25	28	20

AUGUST 1970

1	**8**	**15**	**22**	**29**
1 The Wonder Of You *Elvis Presley* (RCA)	1	1	1	1
2 All Right Now *Free* (Island)	4	5	12	14
3 Lola *The Kinks* (Pye)	2	3	4	5
4 In The Summertime *Mungo Jerry* (Dawn)	6	8	9	16
5 Something *Shirley Bassey* (UA)	5	4	6	8
6 Neanderthal Man *Hotlegs* (Fontana)	3	2	2	3
7 It's All In The Game *The Four Tops* (Tamla Motown)	9	14	–	–
8 Up Around The Bend *Creedence Clearwater Revival* (Liberty)	11	–	–	–
9 I'll Say Forever My Love *Jimmy Ruffin* (Tamla Motown)	7	9	10	13
10 Lady D'Arbanville *Cat Stevens* (Island)	8	12	17	20
11 Love Of The Common People *Nicky Thomas* (Trojan)	13	18	–	–
12 Love Like A Man *Ten Years After* (Deram)	10	10	13	12
13 Goodbye Sam, Hello Samantha *Cliff Richard* (Columbia)	18	20	–	–
14 Cottonfields *The Beach Boys* (Capitol)	19	19	–	–
15 Sally *Gerry Monroe* (Chapter One)	20	–	–	–
16 (It's Like A) Sad Old Kinda Movie *Pickettywitch* (Pye)	–	–	–	–
17 Big Yellow Taxi *Joni Mitchell* (Reprise)	12	13	11	–
18 Signed, Sealed, Delivered, I'm Yours *Stevie Wonder* (Tamla Motown)	15	15	16	18
19 Groovin' With Mr Bloe *Mr Bloe* (DJM)	–	–	–	–
20 Rainbow *The Marmalade* (Decca)	14	7	3	4
22 Song Of Joy *Miguel Rios* (A & M)	16	–	18	–
23 Natural Sinner *Fair Weather* (RCA)	17	6	8	6
29 Tears Of A Clown *Smokey Robinson and The Miracles* (Tamla Motown)	25	11	5	2
30 25 Or 6 To 4 *Chicago* (CBS)	28	16	14	7
37 The Love You Save *The Jackson Five* (Tamla Motown)	24	17	7	10
36 Sweet Inspiration *Johnny Johnson and The Bandwagon* (Bell)	29	23	15	11
– Mama Told Me Not To Come *Three Dog Night* (Stateside)	42	30	19	9
– Love Is Life *Hot Chocolate* (RAK)	–	43	20	17
46 Make It With You *Bread* (Elektra)	37	33	22	15
– Give Me Just A Little More Time *Chairmen Of The Board* (Invictus)	–	–	34	91

SEPTEMBER 1970

5		12	19	26
1 The Wonder Of You *Elvis Presley* (RCA)		2	4	5
2 Tears Of A Clown *Smokey Robinson and The Miracles* (Tamla Motown)		1	2	2
3 Mama Told Me Not To Come *Three Dog Night* (Stateside)		3	5	6
4 Rainbow *The Marmalade* (Decca)		9	11	–
5 Give Me Just A Little More Time *Chairmen Of The Board* (Invictus)		4	3	3
6 Neanderthal Man *Hotlegs* (Fontana)		13	19	–
7 Make It With You *Bread* (Elektra)		5	7	10
8 25 Or 6 To 4 *Chicago* (CBS)		7	12	17
9 Something *Shirley Bassey* (UA)		15	14	–
10 Sweet Inspiration *Johnny Johnson and The Bandwagon* (Bell)		12	16	–
11 Natural Sinner *Fair Weather* (RCA)		17	–	–
12 Lola *The Kinks* (Pye)		18	–	–
13 Wild World *Jimmy Cliff* (Island)		8	9	12
14 The Love You Save *The Jackson Five* (Tamla Motown)		–	–	–
15 Love Is Life *Hot Chocolate* (RAK)		10	6	11
16 I (Who Have Nothing) *Tom Jones* (Decca)		–	–	–
17 It's So Easy *Andy Williams* (CBS)		16	13	–
18 Love Like A Man *Ten Years After* (Deram)		–	–	–
19 I'll Say Forever My Love *Jimmy Ruffin* (Tamla Motown)		–	–	–
20 You Can Get It If You Really Want It *Desmond Dekker* (Trojan)		14	8	4
36 Band Of Gold *Freda Payne* (Invictus)		6	1	1
24 Which Way You Goin' Billy? *The Poppy Family* (Decca)		11	10	7
29 Don't Play That Song *Aretha Franklin* (Atlantic)		19	17	13
30 Montego Bay *Bobby Bloom* (Polydoc)		20	15	8
26 Strange Band *Family* (Reprise)		22	18	14
32 Black Night *Deep Purple* (Harvest)		34	20	9
43 Close To You *The Carpenters* (A & M)		38	31	15
– Ain't No Mountain High Enough *Diana Ross* (Tamla Motown)		32	21	16
– Me And My Life *The Tremeloes* (CBS)		39	30	18
47 Paranoid *Black Sabbath* (Vertigo)		37	28	19
41 Long As I Can See The Light *Creedence Clearwater Revival* (Liberty)		29	26	20

OCTOBER 1970

3		10	17	24	31
1 Band Of Gold *Freda Payne* (Invictus)		1	1	1	3
2 You Can Get It If You Really Want It *Desmond Dekker* (Trojan)		2	3	8	12
3 Montego Bay *Bobby Bloom* (Polydor)		5	7	11	8
4 Tears Of A Clown *Smokey Robinson and The Miracles* (Tamla Motown)		12	16	–	–
5 Black Night *Deep Purple* (Harvest)		3	2	2	5
6 Give Me Just A Little More Time *Chairmen Of The Board* (Invictus)		9	18	–	–
7 Which Way You Goin' Billy? *The Poppy Family* (Decca)		10	9	12	–
8 Paranoid *Black Sabbath* (Vertigo)		4	5	5	6
9 The Wonder Of You *Elvis Presley* (RCA)		11	17	20	–
10 Love Is Life *Hot Chocolate* (RAK)		17	–	–	–
11 Strange Band *Family* (Reprise)		15	12	–	–
12 Mama Told Me Not To Come *Three Dog Night* (Stateside)		18	–	–	–
13 Ain't No Mountain High Enough *Diana Ross* (Tamla Motown)		7	6	7	9

3	**10**	**17**	**24**	**31**
14 Close To You *The Carpenters* (A & M)	6	8	6	11
15 Me And My Life *The Tremeloes* (CBS)	8	4	4	4
16 Make It With You *Bread* (Elektra)	20	–	–	–
17 Wild World *Jimmy Cliff* (Island)	–	–	–	–
18 Don't Play That Song *Aretha Franklin* (Atlantic)	13	–	–	–
19 It's So Easy *Andy Williams* (CBS)	–	–	–	–
20 Black Pearl *Horace Faith* (Trojan)	14	13	15	–
26 Ball Of Confusion *The Temptations* (Tamla Motown)	16	10	9	7
24 Our World *Blue Mink* (Philips)	19	–	17	–
39 Woodstock *Matthews Southern Comfort* (Uni)	24	11	10	1
– Patches *Clarence Carter* (Atlantic)	39	14	3	2
35 The Tip Of My Fingers *Des O'Connor* (Columbia)	33	15	19	17
29 Gasoline Alley Bred *The Hollies* (Parlophone)	23	19	14	16
50 Still Waters *The Four Tops* (Tamla Motown)	27	20	13	10
– War *Edwin Starr* (Tamla Motown)	–	–	16	15
37 Ruby Tuesday *Melanie* (Buddah)	29	21	18	13
49 The Witch *Rattles* (Decca)	41	25	22	14
– It's Wonderful *Jimmy Ruffin* (Tamla Motown)	–	38	27	18
– Indian Reservation *Don Fardon* (Young Blood)	50	44	32	19
– New World In The Morning *Roger Whittaker* (Columbia)	44	28	24	20

NOVEMBER 1970

7	**14**	**21**	**28**
1 Woodstock *Matthews Southern Comfort* (Uni)	1	2	4
2 Patches *Clarence Carter* (Atlantic)	2	4	8
3 Black Night *Deep Purple* (Harvest)	11	–	–
4 Band Of Gold *Freda Payne* (Invictus)	10	17	–
5 War *Edwin Starr* (Tamla Motown)	3	5	6
6 Me And My Life *The Tremeloes* (CBS)	6	12	–
7 Ball Of Confusion *The Temptations* (Tamla Motown)	14	14	–
8 The Witch *Rattles* (Decca)	8	8	15
9 Ruby Tuesday *Melanie* (Buddah)	9	9	14
10 Paranoid *Black Sabbath* (Vertigo)	13	–	–
11 Still Waters *The Four Tops* (Tamla Motown)	15	18	–
12 Indian Reservation *Don Fardon* (Young Blood)	4	3	3
13 Ain't No Mountain High Enough *Diana Ross* (Tamla Motown)	–	–	–
14 Close To You *The Carpenters* (A & M)	20	–	–
15 Voodoo Chile *Jimi Hendrix Experience* (Track)	5	1	2
16 It's Wonderful *Jimmy Ruffin* (Tamla Motown)	12	6	12
17 Gasoline Alley Bred *The Hollies* (Parlophone)	–	–	–
18 San Bernadino *Christie* (CBS)	7	7	11
19 You Can Get It If You Really Want It *Desmond Dekker* (Trojan)	–	–	–
20 The Tip Of My Fingers *Des O'Connor* (Columbia)	–	–	–
24 Julie Do Ya Love Me *White Plains* (Deram)	16	13	10
21 New World In The Morning *Roger Whittaker* (Columbia)	17	–	20
32 Whole Lotta Love *C.C.S.* (RAK)	18	20	13
25 Think About Your Children *Mary Hopkin* (Apple)	19	–	19
31 Ride A White Swan *T. Rex* (Fly)	30	15	7
– I Hear You Knocking *Dave Edmunds* (MAM)	–	16	1
– You've Got Me Dangling On A String *Chairmen Of The Board* (Invictus)	40	19	16
– I've Lost You *Elvis Presley* (RCA)	26	23	9
– Home Lovin' Man *Andy Williams* (CBS)	–	45	17
– It's Only Make Believe *Glen Campbell* (Capitol)	–	38	18
– Cracklin' Rosie *Neil Diamond* (Uni)	29	10	5

DECEMBER 1970

5		12	19	26
1	I Hear You Knocking *Dave Edmunds* (MAM)	1	1	1
2	Voodoo Chile *Jimi Hendrix Experience* (Track)	5	11	19
3	Cracklin' Rosie *Neil Diamond* (Uni)	3	3	6
4	Indian Reservation *Don Fardon* (Young Blood)	9	13	14
5	You've Got Me Dangling On A String *Chairmen Of The Board* (Invictus)	8	10	12
6	When I'm Dead And Gone *McGuiness Flint* (Capitol)	2	2	3
7	Ride A White Swan *T. Rex* (Fly)	6	12	10
8	Julie Do Ya Love Me *White Plains* (Deram)	14	16	16
9	I've Lost You *Elvis Presley* (RCA)	10	14	15
10	It's Wonderful *Jimmy Ruffin* (Tamla Motown)	19	19	–
11	Woodstock *Matthews Southern Comfort* (Uni)	–	–	–
12	My Prayer *Gerry Monroe* (Chapter One)	12	9	9
13	War *Edwin Starr* (Tamla Motown)	20	–	–
14	San Bernadino *Christie* (CBS)	15	–	–
15	I'll Be There *The Jackson Five* (Tamla Motown)	13	5	5
16	Patches *Clarence Carter* (Atlantic)	–	–	–
17	Home Lovin' Man *Andy Williams* (CBS)	7	7	7
18	It's Only Make Believe *Glen Campbell* (Capitol)	4	4	4
19	Whole Lotta Love *C.C.S.* (RAK)	18	–	–
20	Ruby Tuesday *Melanie* (Buddah)	–	–	–
30	Nothing Rhymed *Gilbert O'Sullivan* (MAM)	11	8	8
24	Lady Barbara *Peter Noone and Herman's Hermits* (RAK)	16	17	13
32	Grandad *Clive Dunn* (Columbia)	17	6	2
27	Blame It On The Pony Express *Johnny Johnson and The Bandwagon* (Bell)	22	15	11
35	Brokenhearted *Ken Dodd* (Columbia)	30	18	17
26	It's A Shame *The Motown Spinners* (Tamla Motown)	26	20	–
25	My Way *Frank Sinatra* (Reprise)	24	26	18
–	Apeman *The Kinks* (Pye)	32	32	20

1970

If 1969 lacked a lively Top Fifty, let alone a Top Twenty, then 1970 hardly brought a vast improvement. Admittedly, there were several new names, of which The Jackson Five were the most interesting from a teen sensation point of view. They soon accumulated four Top Ten singles, though their chart positions did not reflect the furore which was created by teen journals and some record papers. They had no Number One or Two discs, and 'ABC' and 'The Love You Save' did not even enter the Top Five.

Marc Bolan, The Carpenters and Hot Chocolate all announced their arrival, though each had only one hit in 1970. For a while Mary Hopkin, a Welsh girl who had been discovered by Paul McCartney and who recorded on The Beatles' Apple label, had promised much, but very little happened for Mary after her third disc in 1970 failed to reach the Top Ten. Her previous records had all entered the Top Ten, and 'Those Were The Days', her first hit in 1968, had been a Number One, but her swan-song 'Think About Your Children' only managed a chart zenith of Number Nineteen.

The regulars from the 1960s found life a trifle sticky. Cliff Richard had one of his worst years since his arrival in 1958 and only managed one hit 'Goodbye Sam, Hello Samantha'. The Hollies had two hits, but Lulu did not appear in the charts at all. Tom Jones appeared in the listings for 1970 with 'Daughter Of Darkness', his only hit of that year. However, Elvis Presley showed resilience with three hits, including a Number One in the form of a powerful ballad with good lyrics called 'The Wonder Of You'. The Stones had no Top Twenty hits during 1970, but Simon and Garfunkel took their 'Bridge Over Troubled Water' into the Top Twenty, where it remained for a total of 13 weeks. Julie Felix, a veteran of Flower Power and folk music, signed with RAK Records, where she was guided by the successful Mickie Most. She recorded several successful songs and one, 'If I Could', gave her the Top Twenty placing for which she had so long strived. Alas, it was her only top disc, though several of her later records bubbled just under the Top Twenty.

Dana, an Irish girl with looks to melt, won the Eurovision Song Contest with 'All Kinds Of Everything', a record which sold two million copies around the world.

Black Sabbath appeared in the Top Five with 'Paranoid', while in completely different vein came Joni Mitchell with 'Big Yellow Taxi'. Hotlegs and their 'Neanderthal Man' entered the charts, an item which is interesting because of the fact that several members of Hotlegs were ex-members of The Mindbenders, Wayne Fontana's backing group in the 1960s. When Hotlegs disbanded, several of the members went on to form 10cc, a successful 1970s band.

Tamla Motown music reigned supreme, even without the aid of The Jackson Five, for many hits came for members of the Motown stable of artists, including Stevie Wonder, The Temptations, The Supremes, Diana Ross, Marvin Gaye, Jimmy Ruffin, The Four Tops, The Motown Spinners and Smokey Robinson.

JANUARY 1971

		2	9	16	23	30
1	I Hear You Knocking *Dave Edmunds* (MAM)		2	2	6	7
2	Grandad *Clive Dunn* (Columbia)		1	1	1	2
3	When I'm Dead And Gone *McGuiness Flint* (Capitol)		3	3	3	17
4	It's Only Make Believe *Glen Campbell* (Capitol)		9	6	12	18
5	I'll Be There *The Jackson Five* (Tamla Motown)		5	5	4	6
6	Cracklin' Rosie *Neil Diamond* (UA)		6	7	14	10
7	Home Lovin' Man *Andy Williams* (CBS)		10	9	15	–
8	Nothing Rhymed *Gilbert O'Sullivan* (MAM)		8	10	17	–
9	My Prayer *Gerry Monroe* (Chapter One)		14	18	–	–
10	Ride A White Swan *T. Rex* (Fly)		4	4	2	4
11	Blame It On The Pony Express *Johnny Johnson and The Bandwagon* (Bell)		7	8	11	11
12	You've Got Me Dangling On A String *Chairmen Of the Board* (Invictus)		11	12	19	–
13	Lady Barbara *Peter Noone and Herman's Hermits* (RAK)		13	14	–	–
14	Indian Reservation *Don Fardon* (Young Blood)		16	–	–	–
15	I've Lost You *Elvis Presley* (RCA)		17	20	–	–
16	Julie Do Ya Love Me *White Plains* (Deram)		19	–	–	–
17	Broken Hearted *Ken Dodd* (Columbia)		15	16	20	–
18	My Way *Frank Sinatra* (Capitol)		–	–	–	–
19	Voodoo Chile *Jimi Hendrix Experience* (Track)		20	–	–	–
20	Apeman *The Kinks* (Pye)		12	11	5	5
31	Blackskin Blue Eyed Boy *The Equals* (President)		18	15	10	9
21	You're Ready Now *Frankie Valli* (Philips)		25	13	18	12
–	You Don't Have To Say You Love Me *Elvis Presley* (RCA)		23	17	9	14
30	Amazing Grace *Judy Collins* (Elektra)		21	19	8	8
–	My Sweet Lord *George Harrison* (Apple)		–	–	7	1
–	The Pushbike Song *The Mixtures* (Polydor)		–	24	13	3
–	No Matter What *Badfinger* (Apple)		35	34	16	13
–	The Resurrection Shuffle *Ashton, Gardner and Dyke* (Capitol)		–	45	26	15
–	She's A Lady *Tom Jones* (MAM)		–	42	21	16
–	Stoned Love *The Supremes* (Tamla Motown)		–	48	24	19
–	Candida *Dawn* (Bell)		–	40	22	20

FEBRUARY 1971

		6	13	20	27
1	My Sweet Lord *George Harrison* (Apple)		1	1	1
2	The Pushbike Song *The Mixtures* (Polydor)		2	2	2
3	Stoned Loved *The Supremes* (Tamla Motown)		3	4	5
4	Grandad *Clive Dunn* (Columbia)		9	9	12
5	No Matter What *Badfinger* (Apple)		6	6	10
6	Amazing Grace *Judy Collins* (Elektra)		5	5	6
7	Ride A White Swan *T. Rex* (Fly)		14	12	–
8	Ape Man *The Kinks* (Pye)		8	11	17
9	The Resurrection Shuffle *Ashton, Gardner and Dyke* (Capitol)		4	3	3
10	I'll Be There *The Jackson Five* (Tamla Motown)		11	–	–
11	You're Ready Now *Frankie Valli* (Philips)		12	15	–
12	Candida *Dawn* (Bell)		10	10	9
13	Your Song *Elton John* (DJM)		7	8	8
14	You Don't Have To Say You Love Me *Elvis Presley* (RCA)		18	18	–
15	Blackskin Blue Eyed Boy *The Equals* (President)		17	–	–
16	When I'm Dead And Gone *McGuiness Flint* (Capitol)		–	–	–
17	She's A Lady *Tom Jones* (MAM)		15	13	16
18	Cracklin' Rosie *Neil Diamond* (UA)		20	–	–
19	I Hear You Knocking *Dave Edmunds* (MAM)		–	–	–

6		13	20	27
20	Blame It On The Pony Express *Johnny Johnson and The Bandwagon* (Bell)	–	–	–
31	It's Impossible *Perry Como* (RCA)	13	7	4
30	Rupert *Jackie Lee* (Pye)	16	16	14
21	It's The Same Old Song *The Weathermen* (B & C)	19	–	–
–	Baby Jump *Mungo Jerry* (Dawn)	–	14	7
39	(Come Round Here) I'm The One You Need *Smokey Robinson and The Miracles* (Tamla Motown)	24	17	13
31	Sunny Honey Girl *Cliff Richard* (Columbia)	22	19	20
23	It's Only Make Believe *Glen Campbell* (Capitol)	25	20	–
–	Sweet Caroline *Neil Diamond* (UA)	–	30	11
–	Forget Me Not *Martha Reeves and The Vandellas* (Tamla Motown)	32	22	15
–	I Think I Love You *The Partridge Family* (Bell)	34	35	18
–	Chestnut Mare *The Byrds* (CBS)	30	38	19
–	Everything's Tuesday *Chairmen Of The Board* (Invictus)	–	26	20

MARCH 1971

6		13	20	27
1	Baby Jump *Mungo Jerry* (Dawn)	1	2	4
2	My Sweet Lord *George Harrison* (Apple)	3	6	7
3	The Pushbike Song *The Mixtures* (Polydor)	6	7	11
4	Another Day *Paul McCartney* (Apple)	2	3	2
5	It's Impossible *Perry Como* (RCA)	5	5	5
6	The Resurrection Shuffle *Ashton, Gardner and Dyke* (Capitol)	11	10	16
7	Amazing Grace *Judy Collins* (Elektra)	9	13	6
8	Stoned Love *The Supremes* (Tamla Motown)	10	17	–
9	Sweet Caroline *Neil Diamond* (UA)	8	9	8
10	Rose Garden *Lynn Anderson* (CBS)	4	4	3
11	Forget Me Not *Martha Reeves and The Vandellas* (Tamla Motown)	15	–	–
12	Tomorrow Night *Atomic Rooster* (B & C)	13	11	14
13	Your Song *Elton John* (DJM)	20	–	–
14	Rupert *Jackie Lee* (Pye)	–	20	–
15	(Come Round Here) I'm The One You Need *Smokey Robinson and The Miracles* (Tamla Motown)	18	–	–
16	No Matter What *Badfinger* (Apple)	19	–	–
17	Hot Love *T. Rex* (Fly)	7	1	1
18	Grandad *Clive Dunn* (Columbia)	16	–	–
19	Everything's Tuesday *Chairmen Of The Board* (Invictus)	12	18	13
20	Candida *Dawn* (Bell)	–	–	–
21	Who Put The Lights Out *Dana* (Rex)	14	16	17
22	Rose Garden *New World* (RAK)	17	15	15
29	Strange Kind Of Woman *Deep Purple* (Purple)	22	8	18
–	Power To The People *John Lennon and The Plastic Ono Band* (Apple)	–	12	12
–	Bridget The Midget *Ray Stevens* (CBS)	34	14	9
–	I Will Drink The Wine *Frank Sinatra* (Capitol)	25	19	–
–	Jack In A Box *Clodagh Rodgers* (RCA)	–	23	10
–	There Goes My Everything *Elvis Presley* (RCA)	–	29	19
39	Walkin' *C.C.S.* (RAK)	32	21	20

APRIL 1971

3		10	17	24
1 Hot Love *T. Rex* (Fly)		1	1	1
2 Bridget The Midget *Ray Stevens* (CBS)		2	2	3
3 Rose Garden *Lynn Anderson* (CBS)		3	3	5
4 Another Day *Paul McCartney* (Apple)		5	11	17
5 Baby Jump *Mungo Jerry* (Dawn)		10	13	–
6 Jack In A Box *Clodagh Rodgers* (RCA)		4	5	10
7 Power To The People *John Lennon and The Plastic Ono Band* (Apple)		8	10	16
8 There Goes My Everything *Elvis Presley* (RCA)		6	7	11
9 It's Impossible *Perry Como* (RCA)		9	12	20
10 Walkin' *C.C.S.* (RAK)		7	9	8
11 Strange Kind Of Woman *Deep Purple* (Purple)		11	17	19
12 If Not For You *Olivia Newton-John* (Pye)		12	8	7
13 Sweet Caroline *Neil Diamond* (UA)		15	–	–
14 My Sweet Lord *George Harrison* (Apple)		14	–	–
15 The Pushbike Song *The Mixtures* (Polydor)		16	19	–
16 I Will Drink The Wine *Frank Sinatra* (Capitol)		–	16	–
17 Rose Garden *New World* (RAK)		19	–	–
18 Tomorrow Night *Atomic Rooster* (B & C)		–	–	–
19 Amazing Grace *Judy Collins* (Elektra)		18	–	–
20 Where Do I Begin (Love Story) *Andy Williams* (CBS)		13	6	4
21 Double Barrel *Dave and Ansil Collins* (Technique)		17	4	2
28 Funny Funny *The Sweet* (RCA)		20	15	14
– Mozart 40 *Waldo de Los Rios* (A & M)		26	14	6
41 Remember Me *Diana Ross* (Tamla Motown)		28	18	13
– Knock Three Times *Dawn* (Bell)		32	20	18
31 Something Old Something New *The Fantastics* (Bell)		21	21	9
– It Don't Come Easy *Ringo Starr* (Apple)		–	29	12
– Rosetta *Fame and Price* (CBS)		49	30	15

MAY 1971

1		8	15	22	29
1 Double Barrel *Dave and Ansil Collins* (Technique)		1	3	5	10
2 Hot Love *T. Rex* (Fly)		6	9	17	–
3 Knock Three Times *Dawn* (Bell)		2	1	1	1
4 Brown Sugar *The Rolling Stones* (RS)		3	2	2	2
5 Mozart 40 *Waldo de Los Rios* (A & M)		5	5	6	12
6 Bridget The Midget *Ray Stevens* (CBS)		10	18	–	–
7 It Don't Come Easy *Ringo Starr* (Apple)		4	4	4	8
8 Where Do I Begin (Love Story) *Andy Williams* (CBS)		8	10	15	–
9 Remember Me *Diana Ross* (Tamla Motown)		7	7	10	13
10 Walkin' *C.C.S.* (RAK)		16	–	–	–
11 If Not For You *Olivia Newton-John* (Pye)		14	–	–	–
12 Rose Garden *Lynn Anderson* (CBS)		17	–	–	–
13 There Goes My Everything *Elvis Presley* (RCA)		–	–	–	–
14 Funny Funny *The Sweet* (RCA)		13	13	–	–
15 Rosetta *Fame and Price* (CBS)		11	19	19	–
16 Something Old Something New *The Fantastics* (Bell)		9	–	–	–
17 Jack In The Box *Clodagh Rodgers* (RCA)		–	–	–	–
18 My Little One *The Marmalade* (Decca)		20	15	–	–
19 Another Day *Paul McCartney* (Apple)		–	–	–	–
20 Indiana Wants Me *R. Dean Taylor* (Tamla Motown)		12	6	3	3
22 Jig A Jig *East Of Eden* (Deram)		15	8	7	7
25 It's A Sin To Tell A Lie *Gerry Monroe* (Chapter One)		18	17	13	15
26 Sugar Sugar *Sakharin* (RCA)		19	12	14	14
32 Un Banc, Un Arbre, Une Rue *Severine* (Philips)		28	11	12	9

1		8	15	22	29
48	Heaven Must Have Sent You *The Elgins* (Tamla Motown)	25	14	8	6
45	Malt And Barley Blues *McGuiness Flint* (Capitol)	23	16	9	5
50	My Brother Jake *Free* (Island)	24	20	11	4
–	Good Old Arsenal *Arsenal 1st Team Squad* (Pye)	44	24	16	–
–	I Am . . . I Said *Neil Diamond* (UA)	33	28	18	11
42	Rain *Bruce Ruffin* (Trojan)	31	27	20	19
–	Rags To Riches *Elvis Presley* (RCA)	–	43	23	16
–	I Did What I Did For Maria *Tony Christie* (MCA)	47	34	24	17
–	I Think Of You *Perry Como* (RCA)	–	38	27	18
–	Oh You Pretty Thing *Peter Noone* (RAK)	–	–	34	20

JUNE 1971

5		12	19	26
1	Knock Three Times *Dawn* (Bell)	1	2	7
2	Indiana Wants Me *R. Dean Taylor* (Tamla Motown)	3	10	15
3	Heaven Must Have Sent You *The Elgins* (Tamla Motown)	5	8	11
4	My Brother Jake *Free* (Island)	6	11	17
5	Brown Sugar *The Rolling Stones* (RS)	10	10	18
6	I Am . . . I Said *Neil Diamond* (UA)	4	9	10
7	Malt And Barley Blues *McGuiness Flint* (Capitol)	11	14	19
8	I Did What I Did For Maria *Tony Christie* (MCA)	2	3	2
9	Rags To Riches *Elvis Presley* (RCA)	13	12	14
10	Jig A Jig *East Of Eden* (Deram)	14	–	–
11	I'm Gonna Run Away From You *Tammi Lynn* (Mojo)	8	5	4
12	Mozart 40 *Waldo de Los Rios* (A & M)	18	20	–
13	Lady Rose *Mungo Jerry* (Dawn)	7	6	5
14	I Think Of You *Perry Como* (RCA)	17	15	20
15	It Don't Come Easy *Ringo Starr* (Apple)	20	–	–
16	The Banner Man *Blue Mink* (Regal Zonophone)	9	4	3
17	Double Barrel *Dave and Ansil Collins* (Technique)	–	–	–
18	It's A Sin To Tell A Lie *Gerry Monroe* (Chapter One)	–	–	–
19	Oh You Pretty Thing *Peter Noone* (RAK)	12	13	12
20	Un Banc, Un Arbre, Une Rue *Severine* (Philips)	–	–	–
22	He's Gonna Step On You Again *John Kongos* (Fly)	15	7	6
36	Chirpy Chirpy Cheep Cheep *Middle Of The Road* (RCA)	16	1	1
23	Sugar Sugar *Sakharin* (RCA)	19	–	–
–	Just My Imagination *The Temptations* (Tamla Motown)	25	17	13
–	Don't Let It Die *Hurricane Smith* (Columbia)	50	18	8
–	Co-Co *The Sweet* (RCA)	33	19	9
40	I Don't Blame You At All *Smokey Robinson and The Miracles* (Tamla Motown)	32	22	16

JULY 1971

3		10	17	24	31
1	Chirpy Chirpy Cheep Cheep *Middle Of The Road* (RCA)	1	1	2	2
2	Don't Let It Die *Hurricane Smith* (Columbia)	3	3	5	9
3	The Banner Man *Blue Mink* (Regal Zonophone)	4	8	9	14
4	He's Gonna Step On You Again *John Kongos* (Fly)	5	9	13	18
5	Co-Co *The Sweet* (RCA)	2	2	3	3
6	I Did What I Did For Maria *Tony Christie* (MCA)	7	18	18	–
7	I'm Gonna Run Away From You *Tammi Lynn* (Mojo)	6	10	14	–
8	Lady Rose *Mungo Jerry* (Dawn)	10	17	–	–
9	Knock Three Times *Dawn* (Bell)	15	–	–	–
10	Just My Imagination *The Temptations* (Tamla Motown)	8	11	10	15
11	I Don't Blame You At All *Smokey Robinson and The Miracles* (Tamla Motown)	12	15	19	–
12	Pied Piper *Bob and Marcia* (Trojan)	11	13	17	20

3	10	17	24	31
13 Oh You Pretty Thing *Peter Noone* (RAK)	–	–	–	–
14 I Am . . . I Said *Neil Diamond* (UA)	19	–	–	–
15 Heaven Must Have Sent You *The Elgins* (Tamla Motown)	20	–	–	–
16 When You Are A King *White Plains* (Deram)	13	14	16	19
17 Monkey Spanner *Dave and Ansil Collins* (Technique)	17	7	7	7
18 Me And You And A Dog Named Boo *Lobo* (Philips)	14	5	4	4
19 Black And White *Greyhound* (Trojan)	9	6	6	6
20 Rags To Riches *Elvis Presley* (RCA)	–	–	–	–
22 River Deep Mountain High *The Supremes and The Four Tops* (Tamla Motown)	16	16	11	13
26 Tom-Tom Turnaround *New World* (RAK)	18	12	8	6
– Get It On *T. Rex* (Fly)	21	4	1	1
– Tonight *The Move* (Harvest)	25	19	12	11
– Leap Up And Down *St. Cecilia* (Polydor)	23	20	–	12
– Never Ending Song Of Love *The New Seekers* (Philips)	49	26	15	5
– Devil's Answer *Atomic Rooster* (B & C)	36	25	20	10
– I'm Still Waiting *Diana Ross* (Tamla Motown)	–	–	–	16
– Won't Get Fooled Again *The Who* (Track)	41	27	22	17

AUGUST 1971

7	14	21	28
1 Get It On *T. Rex* (Fly)	1	3	4
2 Never Ending Song Of Love *The New Seekers* (Philips)	2	2	2
3 Chirpy Chirpy Cheep Cheep *Middle Of The Road* (RCA)	8	8	13
4 Devil's Answer *Atomic Rooster* (B & C)	4	4	7
5 Co-Co *The Sweet* (RCA)	10	14	–
6 Me And You And A Dog Named Boo *Lobo* (Philips)	6	13	19
7 Tom-Tom Turnaround *New World* (RAK)	7	7	11
8 I'm Still Waiting *Diana Ross* (Tamla Motown)	3	1	1
9 Monkey Spanner *Dave and Ansil Collins* (Trojan)	11	18	–
10 Won't Get Fooled Again *The Who* (Track)	9	9	14
11 In My Own Time *Family* (Reprise)	5	5	5
12 Black And White *Greyhound* (Trojan)	15	20	–
13 Heartbreak Hotel *Elvis Presley* (RCA)	14	10	17
14 Tonight *The Move* (Harvest)	16	–	–
15 Leap Up And Down *St. Cecilia* (Polydor)	12	12	16
16 River Deep Mountain High *The Supremes and The Four Tops* (Tamla Motown)	20	–	–
17 Get Down Get With It *Slade* (Polydor)	17	16	18
18 Don't Let It Die *Hurricane Smith* (Columbia)	–	–	–
19 Just My Imagination *The Temptations* (Tamla Motown)	–	–	–
20 La-La Means I Love You *The Delfonics* (Bell)	19	–	–
27 What Are You Doing Sunday *Dawn* (Bell)	13	6	3
21 Soldier Blue *Buffy St. Marie* (RCA)	21	11	8
– Bangla Desh *George Harrison* (Apple)	18	15	10
44 Let Your Yeah Be Yeah *The Pioneers* (Trojan)	25	17	6
39 Hey Girl Don't Bother Me *The Tams* (Probe)	26	19	9
32 Move On Up *Curtis Mayfield* (Buddah)	22	22	12
49 It's Too Late *Carole King* (A & M)	32	24	15
34 We Will *Gilbert O'Sullivan* (MAM)	29	23	20

SEPTEMBER 1971

4		11	18	25
1	I'm Still Waiting *Diana Ross* (Tamla Motown)	1	2	10
2	Never Ending Song Of Love *The New Seekers* (Philips)	4	7	14
3	Hey Girl Don't Bother Me *The Tams* (Probe)	2	1	1
4	In My Own Time *Family* (Reprise)	11	14	20
5	What Are You Doing Sunday *Dawn* (Bell)	3	10	16
6	Let Your Yeah Be Yeah *The Pioneers* (Trojan)	5	13	18
7	Soldier Blue *Buffy St. Marie* (RCA)	7	9	12
8	It's Too Late *Carole King* (A & M)	10	6	15
9	Devil's Answer *Atomic Rooster* (B & C)	–	–	–
10	Get It On *T. Rex* (Fly)	13	–	–
11	Bangla Desh *George Harrison* (Apple)	12	–	–
12	Back-Street Luv *Curved Air* (Warner Bros.)	9	4	11
13	Tom-Tom Turnaround *New World* (RAK)	17	–	–
14	Move On Up *Curtis Mayfield* (Buddah)	16	–	–
15	Won't Get Fooled Again *The Who* (Track)	–	–	–
16	We Will *Gilbert O'Sullivan* (MAM)	18	20	–
17	Did You Ever . . .? *Nancy Sinatra and Lee Hazlewood* (Capitol)	6	3	2
18	Heartbreak Hotel *Elvis Presley* (RCA)	–	–	–
19	Nathan Jones *The Supremes* (Tamla Motown)	8	5	5
20	Leap Up And Down *St. Cecilia* (Polydor)	–	–	–
36	You've Got A Friend *James Taylor* (Warner Bros.)	14	12	9
25	I Believe (In Love) *Hot Chocolate* (RAK)	15	8	8
31	Maggie May *Rod Stewart* (Mercury)	19	11	3
37	Cousin Norman *The Marmalade* (Decca)	20	17	7
24	For All We Know *Shirley Bassey* (UA)	21	15	13
50	Tweedledee, Tweedledum *Middle Of The Road* (RCA)	23	16	4
39	Tap Turns On The Water *C.C.S.* (RAK)	26	18	6
24	When Love Comes Round Again *Ken Dodd* (Columbia)	28	19	–
32	Daddy Don't You Walk So Fast *Daniel Boone* (Penny Farthing)	26	21	17
–	Life Is A Long Song *Jethro Tull* (Chrysalis)	–	25	19

OCTOBER 1971

2		9	16	23	30
1	Hey Girl Don't Bother Me *The Tams* (Probe)	2	3	9	15
2	Maggie May *Rod Stewart* (Mercury)	1	1	1	1
3	Did You Ever . . .? *Nancy Sinatra and Lee Hazlewood* (Capitol)	3	5	8	13
4	Tweedledee, Tweedledum *Middle Of The Road* (RCA)	4	2	3	3
5	Tap Turns On The Water *C.C.S.* (RAK)	6	8	11	14
6	Cousin Norman *The Marmalade* (Decca)	8	7	17	–
7	Nathan Jones *The Supremes* (Tamla Motown)	12	16	–	–
8	You've Got A Friend *James Taylor* (Warner Bros.)	5	4	4	8
9	I Believe (In Love) *Hot Chocolate* (RAK)	10	17	–	–
10	For All We Know *Shirley Bassey* (UA)	7	6	7	6
11	Back-Street Luv *Curved Air* (Warner Bros.)	15	–	–	–
12	Life Is A Long Song *Jethro Tull* (Chrysalis)	11	11	16	–
13	I'm Still Waiting *Diana Ross* (Tamla Motown)	16	–	–	–
14	Never Ending Song Of Love *The New Seekers* (Philips)	20	–	–	–
15	It's Too Late *Carole King* (A & M)	–	–	–	–
16	Soldier Blue *Buffy St. Marie* (RCA)	–	–	–	–
17	Freedom Come, Freedom Go *The Fortunes* (Capitol)	9	10	6	7
18	Daddy Don't You Walk So Fast *Daniel Boone* (Penny Farthing)	19	20	–	–
19	Another Time, Another Place *Engelbert Humperdinck* (MAM)	–	15	13	16

2   **9   16   23   30**

	9	16	23	30
20 Butterfly *Danyel Gerrard* (CBS)	–	13	12	11
21 You Don't Have To Be In The Army To Fight In The War *Mungo Jerry* (Dawn)	13	18	15	–
29 Witch-Queen Of New Orleans *Redbone* (Epic)	14	9	2	2
28 Sultana *Titanic* (CBS)	17	14	10	5
24 Simple Game *The Four Tops* (Tamla Motown)	18	12	5	4
26 Keep On Dancing *The Bay City Rollers* (Bell)	25	19	20	9
33 Spanish Harlem *Aretha Franklin* (Atlantic)	26	21	14	19
– The Night They Drove Old Dixie Down *Joan Baez* (Vanguard)	29	23	18	12
– Tired Of Being Alone *Al Green* (London)	37	28	19	10
46 Look Around *Vince Hill* (Columbia)	33	29	23	17
– Brandy *Scott English* (Horse)	44	33	25	18
– Till *Tom Jones* (MAM)	–	–	22	10

NOVEMBER 1971

6	13	20	27
1 Maggie May *Rod Stewart* (Mercury)	2	4	9
2 Witch-Queen Of New Orleans *Redbone* (Epic)	3	11	16
3 Simple Game *The Four Tops* (Probe)	5	12	20
4 Tired Of Being Alone *Al Green* (London)	6	9	11
5 Till *Tom Jones* (MAM)	4	2	6
6 The Night They Drove Old Dixie Down *Joan Baez* (Vanguard)	9	10	15
7 Sultana *Titanic* (CBS)	10	15	–
8 Coz I Luv You *Slade* (Polydor)	1	1	1
9 For All We Know *Shirley Bassey* (UA)	14	20	–
10 Tweedledee, Tweedledum *Middle Of The Road* (RCA)	15	–	–
11 Freedom Come, Freedom Go *The Fortunes* (Capitol)	19	–	–
12 Look Around *Vince Hill* (Columbia)	13	13	13
13 Brandy *Scott English* (Horse)	12	16	17
14 Spanish Harlem *Aretha Franklin* (Atlantic)	–	–	–
15 You've Got A Friend *James Taylor* (Warner Bros.)	–	–	–
16 Keep On Dancing *The Bay City Rollers* (Bell)	17	–	–
17 I Will Return *Springwater* (Polydor)	8	5	7
18 Butterfly *Danyel Gerrard* (CBS)	–	–	–
19 Johnny Reggae *The Piglets* (Bell)	7	3	5
20 Superstar *The Carpenters* (A & M)	18	19	–
21 The Banks Of The Ohio *Olivia Newton-John* (Pye)	11	6	8
32 Gypsies, Tramps And Thieves *Cher* (MCA)	16	7	4
24 Run Baby Run *The Newbeats* (London)	20	14	12
– Jeepster *T. Rex* (Fly)	37	8	2
– Ernie (The Fastest Milkman In The West) *Benny Hill* (Columbia)	29	17	3
27 Surrender *Diana Ross* (Tamla Motown)	22	18	10
– Tokoloshe Man *John Kongos* (Fly)	–	28	14
– Sing A Song Of Freedom *Cliff Richard* (Columbia)	45	29	18
30 Let's See Action *The Who* (Track)	27	24	19

DECEMBER 1971

4	11	18	25
1 Coz I Luv You *Slade* (Polydor)	3	3	14
2 Ernie (The Fastest Milkman In The West) *Benny Hill* (Columbia)	1	1	1
3 Jeepster *T. Rex* (Fly)	2	2	4
4 Gypsies, Tramps And Thieves *Cher* (MCA)	5	8	10
5 Johnny Reggae *The Piglets* (Bell)	10	14	–
6 Tokoloshe Man *John Kongos* (Fly)	4	6	7

1971

Dave Edmunds had entered the 1970 charts in November with 'I Hear You Knocking', and the record continued to move upwards until it was the first Number One single of 1971. It was Edmunds' only hit for the MAM record label, for his future discs were recorded on Rockfield, his own label which was named after his Welsh recording studios. The wait for another hit for Edmunds was long, for his next Top Twenty entry was not until February 1973, when 'Baby I Love You' entered the charts at Number Thirty-Two.

Clive Dunn, from the *Dad's Army* television series, provided one of 1971's biggest surprises when the chart was only two weeks old with 'Grandad', a song which remained at the Number One position for three weeks.

For Andy Williams, 1971 was a quiet year with only one hit, 'Where Do I Begin (Love Story)'. This was a poor chart performance when compared to Williams' 1970 chart statistics, when he had achieved three hits.

Several major hits came into the charts at the end of January, one of which was 'My Sweet Lord' from the ex-Beatle, George Harrison. Another interesting entry so early in the year was 'Amazing Grace' from Judy Collins. However, The Royal Scots Dragoon Guards Band made another version of this song in 1972, and their version did better in terms of chart positions.

1971 was a good year for Marc Bolan and T. Rex. 'Ride A White Swan', which had entered the charts in 1970, remained in the 1971 charts until late February, and was quickly followed by more success. Bolan's hits were well spaced, for they were issued in March, July and November of 1971.

Elvis Presley achieved five Top Twenty hits, though none of these were very powerful when compared to his 1970 hit 'The Wonder Of You', which had remained in the Top Twenty for 16 weeks. Presley's biggest success of 1971 was achieved by the romantic ballad, 'I Just Can't Help Believing', which remained in the Top Twenty for a total of two months.

Humour of a kind reared its head during the year with

'Bridget The Midget' from Ray Stevens, and with the amazing 'Ernie (The Fastest Milkman In The West)' from Benny Hill. On the other hand there was a brief classical excursion in April called 'Mozart 40' from Waldo de Los Rios.

The Beatles as a group may have disbanded, but in 1971 each member had a chart triumph in his own right. For George Harrison it was 'My Sweet Lord' and 'Bangla Desh', and for John Lennon and his wife Yoko Ono, and The Plastic Ono Band it was a Top Ten triumph with 'Power To The People'. Meanwhile Paul McCartney as a solo artist achieved a hit with 'Another Day', a song which he had co-written with his wife, Linda. Ringo Starr, however, provided the biggest surprise of all with 'It Don't Come Easy', which was a hit on both sides of the Atlantic.

1971 saw the birth of Middle Of The Road with 'Chirpy Chirpy Cheep Cheep', and of The Sweet with 'Funny Funny' and 'Co-Co'. Whereas the latter group continued to achieve hit records, Middle Of The Road ceased to attract the public's attention – a strange phenomenon considering that all of their three 1971 hits reached the Top Five.

Reggae made some impact on the charts owing to the records of such artists as Dave and Ansil Collins, The Pioneers, Greyhound and Bob Andy and Marcia Griffiths.

Dawn, Rod Stewart, The Marmalade, Diana Ross and Tony Christie all had big hits in 1971, but the most significant arrivals in the charts were those of Elton John and Slade.

Slade's lead singer, Noddy Holder, stated 'The fans are fed up with paying to sit on their hands while watching musicians who clearly couldn't care less about the customers. What is wanted is more of a party atmosphere'. Slade certainly created a fun atmosphere, and the fans went back to stomping and leaping around and enjoying themselves. Slade had hit on the formula for success and provided exactly what the fans wanted at the time.

JANUARY 1972

1		8	15	22	29
1	Ernie (The Fastest Milkman In The West) *Benny Hill* (Columbia)	2	3	13	–
2	Jeepster *T. Rex* (Fly)	3	10	18	–
3	Something Tells Me *Cilla Black* (Parlophone)	7	6	12	–
4	I'd Like To Teach The World To Sing *The New Seekers* (Polydor)	1	1	1	1
5	Theme From Shaft *Isaac Hayes* (Stax)	6	14	14	–
6	Softly Whispering I Love You *The Congregation* (Columbia)	4	4	5	14
7	Tokoloshe Man *John Kongos* (Fly)	11	–	–	–
8	No Matter How I Try *Gilbert O'Sullivan* (MAM)	9	12	11	18
9	Soley Soley *Middle Of The Road* (RCA)	5	5	7	11
10	Gypsies, Tramps And Thieves *Cher* (MCA)	19	–	–	–
11	Banks Of The Ohio *Olivia Newton-John* (Pye)	–	–	–	–
12	Morning *Val Doonican* (Philips)	13	15	19	–
13	Sleepy Shores *The Johnny Pearson Orchestra* (Penny Farthing)	8	9	9	12
14	Coz I Luv You *Slade* (Polydor)	16	–	–	–
15	It Must Be Love *Labi Siffre* (Pye)	14	19	–	–
16	I Just Can't Help Believing *Elvis Presley* (RCA)	10	7	6	6
17	Fireball *Deep Purple* (Purple)	15	18	–	–
18	Mother Of Mine *Neil Reid* (Decca)	12	2	2	2
19	Till *Tom Jones* (Decca)	–	–	–	–
20	Is This The Way To Amarillo *Tony Christie* (MCA)	18	–	–	–
21	Kara Kara *New World* (RAK)	17	–	–	–
22	Sing A Song Of Freedom *Cliff Richard* (Columbia)	20	–	–	–
34	Brand New Key *Melanie* (Buddah)	24	8	4	5
–	Horse With No Name *America* (Warner Bros.)	21	11	3	4
36	Morning Has Broken *Cat Stevens* (Island)	30	13	10	9
43	Stay With Me *The Faces* (Warner Bros.)	23	16	8	7
32	Theme From The Onedin Line *The Vienna Philharmonic Orchestra* (Decca)	25	17	15	16
–	Where Did Our Love Go? *Donny Elbert* (London)	–	28	16	8
–	Let's Stay Together *Al Green* (London)	–	29	17	10
–	Moon River *Greyhound* (Trojan)	50	33	24	15
–	Have You Seen Her? *The Chi-Lites* (MCA)	–	40	27	17
27	Theme From The Persuaders *The John Barry Orchestra* (CBS)	27	20	20	13
–	Telegram Sam *T. Rex* (T. Rex)	–	–	–	3
–	All I Ever Need Is You *Sonny and Cher* (MCA)	–	42	30	19
–	Baby I'm A Want You *Bread* (Warner Bros.)	–	38	28	20

FEBRUARY 1972

5		12	19	26
1	Telegram Sam *T. Rex* (T. Rex)	1	2	2
2	I'd Like To Teach The World To Sing *The New Seekers* (Polydor)	4	7	13
3	Mother Of Mine *Neil Reid* (Decca)	3	5	9
4	Horse With No Name *America* (Warner Bros.)	6	11	19
5	Brand New Key *Melanie* (Buddah)	8	14	18
6	Stay With Me *The Faces* (Warner Bros.)	11	–	–
7	Have You Seen Her? *The Chi-Lites* (MCA)	5	3	6
8	Where Did Our Love Go? *Donny Elbert* (London)	12	19	–
9	Let's Stay Together *Al Green* (London)	7	10	12
10	I Just Can't Help Believing *Elvis Presley* (RCA)	13	–	–
11	Son Of My Father *Chicory Tip* (CBS)	2	1	1

5	12	19	26
12 Moon River *Greyhound* (Trojan)	14	14	–
13 Morning Has Broken *Cat Stevens* (Island)	–	–	–
14 Baby I'm A Want You *Bread* (Elektra)	18	15	–
15 Family Affair *Sly and The Family Stone* (Epic)	19	18	–
16 All I Ever Need Is You *Sonny and Cher* (MCA)	10	8	11
17 American Pie *Don MacLean* (UA)	15	6	3
18 Soley Soley *Middle Of The Road* (RCA)	–	–	–
19 Sleepy Shores *The Johnny Pearson Orchestra* (Penny Farthing)	–	–	–
20 Theme From The Persuaders *The John Barry Orchestra* (CBS)	–	–	–
25 Look Wot You Dun *Slade* (Polydor)	9	4	4
23 Storm In A Tea Cup *The Fortunes* (Capitol)	16	9	7
28 Day After Day *Badfinger* (Apple)	17	13	10
26 My World *The Bee Gees* (Polydor)	20	17	16
50 Without You *Nilsson* (RCA)	27	16	5
22 If You Really Love Me *Stevie Wonder* (Tamla Motown)	22	20	20
– Got To Be There *Michael Jackson* (Tamla Motown)	39	22	8
46 Poppa Joe *The Sweet* (RCA)	30	26	14
– Blue Is The Colour *Chelsea F.C.* (Penny Farthing)	–	–	15
– Mother And Child Reunion *Paul Simon* (CBS)	–	28	17

MARCH 1972

4	11	18	25
1 Son Of My Father *Chicory Tip* (CBS)	3	4	12
2 American Pie *Don MacLean* (UA)	2	2	3
3 Without You *Nilsson* (RCA)	1	1	1
4 Look Wot You Dun *Slade* (Polydor)	8	13	18
5 Got To Be There *Michael Jackson* (Tamla Motown)	6	7	8
6 Have You Seen Her? *The Chi-Lites* (MCA)	14	–	–
9 Mother And Child Reunion *Paul Simon* (CBS)	7	5	6
8 Storm In A Tea Cup *The Fortunes* (Capitol)	11	14	–
9 Blue Is The Colour *Chelsea F.C.* (Penny Farthing)	5	8	11
10 Day After Day *Badfinger* (Apple)	13	16	–
11 Poppa Joe *The Sweet* (RCA)	12	12	7
12 Beg, Steal Or Borrow *The New Seekers* (Polydor)	4	3	2
13 Mother Of Mine *Neil Reid* (Decca)	15	10	15
14 Telegram Sam *T. Rex* (T. Rex)	18	–	–
15 I'd Like To Teach The World To Sing *The New Seekers* (Polydor)	–	–	20
16 My World *The Bee Gees* (Polydor)	20	–	–
17 Say You Don't Mind *Colin Blunstone* (CBS)	17	15	–
18 All I Ever Need Is You *Sonny and Cher* (MCA)	–	–	–
19 I Can't Help Myself *Donny Elbert* (Avco)	16	11	13
20 Let's Stay Together *Al Green* (London)	–	–	–
23 Alone Again (Naturally) *Gilbert O'Sullivan* (MAM)	9	6	14
22 Meet Me On The Corner *Lindisfarne* (Charisma)	10	9	5
21 Give Ireland Back To The Irish *Wings* (Apple)	19	17	16
50 Floy Joy *The Supremes* (Tamla Motown)	27	18	10
33 It's One Of Those Nights *The Partridge Family* (Bell)	25	19	15
– Desiderata *Les Crane* (Warner Bros.)	23	20	9
44 Hold Your Head Up *Argent* (Epic)	30	21	7
47 Too Beautiful To Last *Engelbert Humperdinck* (Decca)	37	26	19

APRIL 1972

1	8	15	22	29
1 Without You *Nilsson* (RCA)	1	2	2	3
2 Beg, Steal Or Borrow *The New Seekers* (Polydor)	2	3	6	12
3 Alone Again (Naturally) *Gilbert O'Sullivan* (MAM)	4	8	10	–
4 American Pie *Don MacLean* (UA)	7	16	–	–
5 Hold Your Head Up *Argent* (Epic)	5	6	8	16
6 Meet Me On The Corner *Lindisfarne* (Charisma)	6	13	–	–
7 Desiderata *Les Crane* (Warner Bros.)	9	9	12	19
8 Mother And Child Reunion *Paul Simon* (CBS)	14	–	–	–
9 Floy Joy *The Supremes* (Tamla Motown)	10	14	16	–
10 Got To Be There *Michael Jackson* (Tamla Motown)	–	–	–	–
11 It's One Of Those Nights *The Partridge Family* (Bell)	12	15	–	–
12 Blue Is The Colour *Chelsea F.C.* (Penny Farthing)	19	–	–	–
13 I Can't Help Myself *Donny Elbert* (Avco)	–	–	–	–
14 Too Beautiful To Last *Engelbert Humperdinck* (Decca)	17	20	–	–
15 Sweet Talking Guy *The Chiffons* (London)	8	5	4	4
16 Son Of My Father *Chicory Tip* (CBS)	–	–	–	–
17 Heart Of Gold *Neil Young* (Warner Bros.)	11	10	11	17
18 Back Off Boogaloo *Ringo Starr* (Apple)	15	4	3	2
19 The Young New Mexican Puppeteer *Tom Jones* (Decca)	13	7	7	6
20 What Is Life *Olivia Newton-John* (Pye)	16	18	17	–
31 Amazing Grace *Royal Scots Dragoon Guards Band* (RCA)	3	1	1	1
26 Until It's Time For You To Go *Elvis Presley* (RCA)	18	19	5	10
23 Crying, Laughing, Loving, Lying *Labi Siffre* (Pye)	20	11	13	15
41 Debora *Tyrannosaurus Rex* (Magni Fly)	27	12	15	7
29 Run Run Run *Jo Jo Gunne* (Asylum)	21	17	9	8
– Come What May *Vicky Leandros* (Philips)	39	26	14	5
42 Radancer *The Marmalade* (Decca)	30	21	16	9
50 Stir It Up *Johnny Nash* (CBS)	43	24	19	13
– Could It Be Forever *David Cassidy* (Bell)	35	34	20	11
– A Thing Called Love *Johnny Cash and The Evangel Temple Choir* (CBS)	–	37	28	14
– Tumbling Dice *The Rolling Stones* (RS)	–	–	–	18
33 I Am What I Am *Greyhound* (Trojan)	37	25	27	20

MAY 1972

6	13	20	27
1 Amazing Grace *Royal Scots Dragoon Guards Band* (RCA)	1	2	3
2 Back Off Boogaloo *Ringo Starr* (Apple)	11	12	–
3 Come What May *Vicky Leandros* (Philips)	2	4	4
4 Could It Be Forever *David Cassidy* (Bell)	3	3	2
5 Sweet Talking Guy *The Chiffons* (London)	10	11	–
6 Run Run Run *Jo Jo Gunne* (Asylum)	8	10	17
7 A Thing Called Love *Johnny Cash* (CBS)	4	6	7
8 Debora *Tyrannosaurus Rex* (Magni Fly)	12	16	–
9 Radancer *The Marmalade* (Decca)	6	9	1
10 Without You *Nilsson* (RCA)	15	–	–
11 The Young New Mexican Puppeteer *Tom Jones* (Decca)	13	–	–
12 Rocket Man *Elton John* (DJM)	7	5	5
13 Until It's Time For You To Go *Elvis Presley* (RCA)	16	–	–
14 Tumbling Dice *The Rolling Stones* (RS)	5	7	9
15 Stir It Up *Johnny Nash* (CBS)	14	18	–
16 Take A Look Around *The Temptations* (Tamla Motown)	17	13	18
17 Hold Your Head Up *Argent* (Epic)	–	–	–
18 Crying, Laughing, Loving, Lying *Labi Siffre* (Pye)	–	–	–
19 Runnin' Away *Sly and The Family Stone* (Epic)	–	17	–
20 Saturday Night At The Movies/At The Club *The Drifters* (Bell)	19	8	8

6

	13	20	27
– Metal Guru *T. Rex* (T. Rex)	9	1	1
27 Oh Babe What Would You Say *Hurricane Smith* (Columbia)	18	15	6
42 Leeds United *Leeds United F.C.* (Chapter One)	20	14	10
– Lady Eleanor *Lindisfarne* (Charisma)	29	19	12
24 Amazing Grace *Judy Collins* (Elektra)	23	20	–
– Vincent *Don MacLean* (UA)	36	29	11
32 A Whiter Shade Of Pale *Procol Harum* (Chrysalis)	26	22	14
28 Me And Julio Down By The School Yard *Paul Simon* (CBS)	24	23	15
– Sister Jane *New World* (RAK)	31	27	16
34 Isn't Life Strange *The Moody Blues* (Threshold)	39	24	19
– California Man *The Move* (Harvest)	46	34	20

JUNE 1972

3

	10	17	24
1 Metal Guru *T. Rex* (T. Rex)	1	1	4
2 Rocket Man *Elton John* (DJM)	5	11	19
3 At The Club/Saturday Night At The Movies *The Drifters* (Bell)	6	4	5
4 Oh Babe What Would You Say *Hurricane Smith* (Columbia)	4	8	12
5 Vincent *Don MacLean* (UA)	2	1	1
6 Lady Eleanor *Lindisfarne* (Charisma)	3	6	10
7 Could It Be Forever *David Cassidy* (Bell)	7	14	–
8 Amazing Grace *Royal Scots Dragoon Guards Band* (RCA)	11	18	–
9 A Thing Called Love *Johnny Cash* (CBS)	19	–	–
10 Come What May *Vicky Leandros* (Philips)	17	–	–
11 California Man *The Move* (Harvest)	8	7	7
12 Leeds United *Leeds United F.C.* (Chapter One)	16	–	–
13 Isn't Life Strange *The Moody Blues* (Threshold)	15	15	–
14 Tumbling Dice *The Rolling Stones* (RS)	–	–	–
15 A Whiter Shade Of Pale *Procol Harum* (Chrysalis)	13	20	–
16 Sister Jane *New World* (RAK)	9	9	11
17 Take A Look Around *The Temptations* (Bell)	–	–	–
18 Doobedood'ndoobe *Diana Ross* (Tamla Motown)	18	12	–
19 Me And Julio Down By The School Yard *Paul Simon* (CBS)	20	–	–
20 Mary Had A Little Lamb *Wings* (Apple)	12	10	9
22 Rockin' Robin *Michael Jackson* (Tamla Motown)	10	5	3
25 Take Me Bak 'Ome *Slade* (Polydor)	14	3	2
31 Song Sung Blue *Neil Diamond* (UA)	23	16	15
32 Supersonic Rocket Ship *The Kinks* (RCA)	24	17	16
35 Little Bit Of Love *Free* (Island)	28	19	20
– Rock And Roll Part 2 *Gary Glitter* (Bell)	37	21	6
– Little Willie *The Sweet* (RCA)	47	23	8
– Puppy Love *Donny Osmond* (MGM)	–	36	13
37 Oh Girl *The Chi-Lites* (MCA)	25	25	14
34 The First Time Ever I Saw Your Face *Roberta Flack* (Atlantic)	26	22	17
– Ooh-Wakka-Doo-Wakka-Day *Gilbert O'Sullivan* (MAM)	–	40	18
23 What's Your Name *Chicory Tip* (RCA)	21	13	–

JULY 1972

1

	8	15	22	29
1 Take Me Bak 'Ome *Slade* (Polydor)	3	3	8	16
2 Vincent *Don MacLean* (UA)	5	8	19	–
3 Puppy Love *Donny Osmond* (MGM)	1	1	1	1
4 Little Willie *The Sweet* (RCA)	4	6	6	11
5 Rock And Roll Part 2 *Gary Glitter* (Bell)	2	2	2	3
6 Rockin' Robin *Michael Jackson* (Tamla Motown)	7	10	15	–
7 California Man *The Move* (Harvest)	10	14	–	–
8 An American Trilogy *Elvis Presley* (RCA)	9	9	10	18

1		8	15	22	29
9	Mary Had A Little Lamb *Wings* (Apple)	11	15	–	–
10	At The Club/Saturday Night At The Movies *The Drifters* (Bell)	–	–	–	–
11	Circles *The New Seekers* (Polydor)	6	5	4	6
12	Ooh-Wakka-Doo-Wakka-Day *Gilbert O'Sullivan* (MAM)	8	11	11	–
13	Little Bit Of Love *Free* (Island)	15	18	–	–
14	Song Sung Blue *Neil Diamond* (UA)	17	–	–	–
15	Metal Guru *T. Rex* (T. Rex)	–	–	–	–
16	The First Time Ever I Saw Your Face *Roberta Flack* (Atlantic)	14	17	–	–
17	Sister Jane *New World* (RAK)	18	–	–	–
18	Oh Girl *The Chi-Lites* (MCA)	18	–	–	–
19	Supersonic Rocket Ship *The Kinks* (RCA)	–	–	–	–
20	Oh Babe What Would You Say *Hurricane Smith* (Columbia)	–	–	–	–
25	I Can See Clearly Now *Johnny Nash* (CBS)	12	7	5	7
28	Sylvia's Mother *Dr Hook and The Medicine Show* (CBS)	13	4	3	2
22	Join Together *The Who* (Track)	16	12	9	13
21	Walking In The Rain With The One You Love *Love Unlimited* (UA)	19	16	16	14
24	Nut Rocker *B. Bumble and The Stingers* (Stateside)	20	19	–	–
–	Breaking Up Is Hard To Do *The Partridge Family* (Bell)	30	13	7	4
41	Starman *David Bowie* (RCA)	29	20	18	10
–	Seaside Shuffle *Terry Dactyl and The Dinosaurs* (UK)	–	29	12	5
32	Betcha By Golly Wow *The Stylistics* (Avco)	25	25	13	15
43	Mad About You *Bruce Ruffin* (Rhino)	35	23	14	9
–	School's Out *Alice Cooper* (Warner Bros.)	–	44	17	6
49	Silver Machine *Hawkwind* (UA)	40	37	20	12
–	Automatically Sunshine *The Supremes* (Tamla Motown)	–	35	25	17
–	Popcorn *Hot Butter* (Pye)	–	–	41	19
–	My Guy *Mary Wells* (Tamla Motown)	48	38	26	20

AUGUST 1972

5		12	19	26
1	Puppy Love *Donny Osmond* (MGM)	4	4	10
2	School's Out *Alice Cooper* (Warner Bros.)	1	1	1
3	Sylvia's Mother *Dr Hook and The Medicine Show* (CBS)	5	8	16
4	Seaside Shuffle *Terry Dactyl and The Dinosaurs* (UK)	2	2	5
5	Breaking Up Is Hard To Do *The Partridge Family* (Bell)	3	6	8
6	Rock And Roll Part 2 *Gary Glitter* (Bell)	9	12	18
7	Silver Machine *Hawkwind* (UA)	7	3	3
8	I Can See Clearly Now *Johnny Nash* (CBS)	8	16	15
9	Circles *The New Seekers* (Polydor)	10	–	19
10	Automatically Sunshine *The Supremes* (Tamla Motown)	12	17	–
11	Popcorn *Hot Butter* (Pye)	6	5	6
12	Starman *David Bowie* (RCA)	11	18	–
13	Mad About You *Bruce Ruffin* (Rhino)	13	19	–
14	My Guy *Mary Wells* (Tamla Motown)	15	–	–
15	Join Together *The Who* (Track)	18	–	–
16	Betcha By Golly Wow *The Stylistics* (Avco)	14	–	–
17	Little Willy *The Sweet* (RCA)	20	–	–
18	Take Me Bak 'Ome *Slade* (Polydor)	–	–	–
19	Ooh-Wakka-Doo-Wakka-Day *Gilbert O'Sullivan* (MAM)	–	–	–
20	10538 Overture *The Electric Light Orchestra* (Harvest)	17	14	9
24	It's Four In The Morning *Faron Young* (Fontana)	16	10	12
26	Run To Me *The Bee Gees* (Polydor)	19	9	11
–	You Wear It Well *Rod Stewart* (Mercury)	23	7	2
–	All The Young Dudes *Mott The Hoople* (CBS)	22	11	4
–	Layla *Derek and The Dominoes* (Polydor)	25	13	7

5

	12	**19**	**26**
27 The Locomotion *Little Eva* (London)	21	15	13
23 Working On A Building Of Love *Chairmen Of The Board* (Invictus)			
– Standing In The Road *Blackfoot Sue* (DJM)	24	20	–
28 I Get The Sweetest Feeling *Jackie Wilson* (MCA)	23	24	17
– Sugar Me *Lynsey de Paul* (MAM)	–	47	20

SEPTEMBER 1972

2

	9	**16**	**23**	**30**
1 You Wear It Well *Rod Stewart* (Mercury)	2	2	4	11
2 Mama Weer All Crazee Now *Slade* (Polydor)	1	1	1	3
3 School's Out *Alice Cooper* (Warner Bros.)	11	16	–	–
4 Silver Machine *Hawkwind* (UA)	7	13	19	–
5 All The Young Dudes *Mott The Hoople* (CBS)	3	7	14	–
6 It's Four In The Morning *Faron Young* (Fontana)	5	3	6	7
7 Layla *Derek and The Dominoes* (Polydor)	9	11	–	–
8 Popcorn *Hot Butter* (Pye)	14	17	–	–
9 Standing In The Road *Blackfoot Sue* (DJM)	4	6	11	19
10 Seaside Shuffle *Terry Dactyl and The Dinosaurs* (UK)	15	–	–	–
11 The Locomotion *Little Eva* (London)	12	15	–	–
12 Sugar Me *Lynsey de Paul* (MAM)	6	5	5	15
13 Run To Me *The Bee Gees* (Polydor)	13	–	–	–
14 I Get The Sweetest Feeling *Jackie Wilson* (MCA)	10	9	13	13
15 10538 Overture *The Electric Light Orchestra* (Harvest)	17	–	–	–
16 Breaking Up Is Hard To Do *The Partridge Family* (Bell)	20	–	–	–
17 Puppy Love *Donny Osmond* (MGM)	19	–	–	–
18 Virginia Plain *Roxy Music* (Island)	8	4	7	10
19 I Can See Clearly Now *Johnny Nash* (CBS)	–	–	–	–
20 Ain't No Sunshine *Michael Jackson* (Tamla Motown)	16	8	8	8
25 Lean On Me *Bill Withers* (A & M)	18	18	–	–
– How Can I Be Sure *David Cassidy* (Bell)	–	10	3	1
– Living In Harmony *Cliff Richard* (Columbia)	21	12	12	12
– Children Of The Revolution *T. Rex* (T. Rex)	–	14	2	2
– Too Busy Thinking About My Baby *Mardi Gras* (Bell)	24	19	–	–
– Come On Over To My Place *The Drifters* (Bell)	27	20	10	9
– Too Young *Donny Osmond* (MGM)	–	22	9	5
– Wig-Wam Bam *The Sweet* (RCA)	48	25	15	6
38 Walk In The Night *Jnr. Walker and The All Stars* (Tamla Motown)	25	21	16	10
39 Big Six *Judge Dread* (Big Shot)	29	23	17	17
46 Suzanne Beware Of The Devil *Dandy Livingstone* (Horse)	33	28	18	16
– Mouldy Old Dough *Lieutenant Pigeon* (Decca)	–	38	20	4
– I Didn't Know I Loved You (Till I Saw You Rock 'n' Roll) *Gary Glitter* (Bell)	–	–	27	14
– You're A Lady *Peter Skellern* (Decca)	–	–	43	18

OCTOBER 1972

7

	14	**21**	**28**
1 How Can I Be Sure *David Cassidy* (Bell)	2	4	12
2 Children Of The Revolution *T. Rex* (T. Rex)	5	10	17
3 Mouldy Old Dough *Lieutenant Pigeon* (Decca)	1	1	1
4 Wig-Wam Bam *The Sweet* (RCA)	6	8	10
5 Too Young *Donny Osmond* (MGM)	7	14	–
6 You're A Lady *Peter Skellern* (Decca)	3	3	7
7 Mama Weer All Crazee Now *Slade* (Polydor)	16	–	–
8 I Didn't Know I Loved You (Till I Saw You Rock 'n' Roll) *Gary Glitter* (Bell)	4	5	6

	7	14	21	28
9 It's Four In The Morning *Faron Young* (Fontana)		13	—	—
10 Come On Over To My Place *The Drifters* (Bell)		15	17	—
11 Burning Love *Elvis Presley* (RCA)		8	7	8
12 Big Six *Judge Dread* (Big Shot)		11	11	15
13 Ain't No Sunshine *Michael Jackson* (Tamla Motown)		—	—	—
14 Suzanne Beware Of The Devil *Dandy Livingstone* (Horse)		14	16	—
15 Virginia Plain *Roxy Music* (Island)		—	—	—
16 Living In Harmony *Cliff Richard* (Columbia)		—	—	—
17 Donna *10cc* (UK)		10	2	2
18 In A Broken Dream *Python Lee Jackson* (Young Blood)		9	6	3
19 Walk In The Night *Jnr. Walker and The All Stars* (Tamla Motown)		20	—	—
20 John I'm Only Dancing *David Bowie* (RCA)		12	13	13
34 Elected *Alice Cooper* (Warner Bros.)		17	9	4
22 Backstabbers *The O'Jays* (Philadelphia)		18	20	14
26 There Are More Questions Than Answers *Johnny Nash* (CBS)		19	12	9
– Clair *Gilbert O'Sullivan* (MAM)		—	15	5
– Goodbye To Love *The Carpenters* (A & M)		22	18	11
– Burlesque *Family* (Reprise)		23	19	19
– Guitar Man *Bread* (Elektra)		21	22	16
– Hallelujah Freedom *Jnr. Campbell* (Deram)		39	24	18
– Loop Di Love *Shag* (UK)		46	26	20

NOVEMBER 1972

	4	11	18	25
1 Mouldy Old Dough *Lieutenant Pigeon* (Decca)		2	5	12
2 Clair *Gilbert O'Sullivan* (MAM)		1	1	3
3 Donna *10cc* (UK)		3	3	16
4 In A Broken Dream *Python Lee Jackson* (Young Blood)		7	12	—
5 Elected *Alice Cooper* (Warner Bros.)		4	11	17
6 Leader Of The Pack *The Shangri-Las* (Kama Sutra)		8	3	6
7 Loop Di Love *Shag* (UK)		5	4	7
8 You're A Lady *Peter Skellern* (Decca)		16	—	—
9 Burning Love *Elvis Presley* (RCA)		14	—	—
10 There Are More Questions Than Answers *Johnny Nash* (CBS)		12	18	—
11 Goodbye To Love *The Carpenters* (A & M)		9	15	15
12 I Didn't Know I Loved You (Till I Saw You Rock 'n' Roll) *Gary Glitter* (Bell)		17	—	—
13 Hallelujah Freedom *Jnr. Campbell* (Deram)		10	17	18
14 Burlesque *Family* (Reprise)		13	16	—
15 Big Six *Judge Dread* (Big Shot)		18	—	—
16 John I'm Only Dancing *David Bowie* (RCA)		—	—	—
17 Wig-Wam Bam *The Sweet* (RCA)		—	—	—
18 How Can I Be Sure *David Cassidy* (Bell)		—	—	—
19 Let's Dance *Chris Montez* (London)		15	9	11
20 Guitar Man *Bread* (Elektra)		—	—	—
23 My Ding-A-Ling *Chuck Berry* (Chess)		6	2	1
24 Here I Go Again *Archie Bell and The Drells* (Atlantic)		11	14	14
31 I'm Stone In Love With You *The Stylistics* (Avco)		19	10	9
42 Crocodile Rock *Elton John* (DJM)		20	8	5
– Why *Donny Osmond* (MGM)		21	6	4
– Crazy Horses *The Osmonds* (MGM)		27	7	2
– New Orleans *Harley Quinne* (Bell)		23	19	—
– Hi-Ho Silver Lining *Jeff Beck* (RAK)		22	20	19
– Gudbuy T'Jane *Slade* (Polydor)		—	—	8
– Angel/What Made Milwaukee Famous *Rod Stewart* (Mercury)		—	23	10
– Looking Through The Windows *The Jackson Five* (Tamla Motown)		40	21	13
34 Lay Down *The Strawbs* (A & M)		31	26	20

DECEMBER 1972

2	9	16	23/30
1 My Ding-A-Ling *Chuck Berry* (Chess)	1	1	2
2 Crazy Horses *The Osmonds* (MGM)	2	3	5
3 Why *Donny Osmond* (MGM)	6	6	9
4 Gudbuy T'Jane *Slade* (Polydor)	3	2	6
5 Crocodile Rock *Elton John* (DJM)	5	7	7
6 Angel/What Made Milwaukee Famous *Rod Stewart* (Mercury)	4	9	12
7 Clair *Gilbert O'Sullivan* (MAM)	14	–	–
8 Leader Of The Pack *The Shangri-Las* (Kama Sutra)	20	–	–
9 Looking Through The Windows *The Jackson Five* (Tamla Motown)	10	12	20
10 I'm Stone In Love With You *The Stylistics* (Avco)	15	–	–
11 Let's Dance *Chris Montez* (London)	–	–	–
12 Stay With Me *Blue Mink* (Regal Zonophone)	13	11	15
13 Lay Down *The Strawbs* (A & M)	12	14	–
14 Mouldy Old Dough *Lieutenant Pigeon* (Decca)	–	–	–
15 Loop Di Love *Shag* (UK)	19	–	–
16 Ben *Michael Jackson* (Tamla Motown)	7	8	8
17 Hi-Ho Silver Lining *Jeff Beck* (RAK)	17	17	–
18 Rock Me Baby *David Cassidy* (Bell)	11	13	17
19 Oh Carol *Neil Sedaka* (RCA)	–	–	–
20 Donna *10cc* (UK)	–	–	–
– Solid Gold Easy Action *T. Rex* (EMI)	8	4	3
27 Long Haired Lover From Liverpool *Little Jimmy Osmond* (MGM)	9	5	1
21 Shotgun Wedding *Roy C.* (UK)	16	10	11
28 Help Me Make It Through The Night *Gladys Knight and The Pips* (Tamla Motown)	18	19	14
33 Nights In White Satin *The Moody Blues* (Deram)	21	15	10
– Happy Christmas (War Is Over) *John Lennon and Yoko Ono, The Plastic Ono Band and The Harlem Community Choir* (Apple)	23	16	4
23 Keeper Of The Castle *The Four Tops* (Tamla Motown)	25	18	–
36 Little Drummer Boy *Royal Scots Dragoon Guards Band* (RCA)	28	20	13
– The Jean Genie *David Bowie* (RCA)	33	31	16
– Big Seven *Judge Dread* (Big Shot)	50	32	18
48 Getting A Drag *Lynsey de Paul* (MAM)	30	28	19

1972

'Morning Has Broken' from Cat Stevens rang through the early 1972 air; a hymn, though some people were probably not aware of the song's derivation. Another religious melody numbed the British public in April as 'Amazing Grace' from The Royal Scots Dragoon Guards Band tugged at the nation's heartstrings. The bagpipe hit also revived interest in the Judy Collins version of the song from 1971, for her version of the song enjoyed further Top Twenty success.

Two television themes also enjoyed chart success; the 'Theme From The Persuaders' from The John Barry Orchestra, and the 'Theme From The Onedin Line' by The Vienna Philharmonic Orchestra.

Some newcomers of 1971 did fairly well, for Slade had four hits, while The Sweet had three. However, Elton John appeared in the Top Twenty twice only with 'Rocket Man' and 'Crocodile Rock', the former being his most successful chart single. It is surprising that, despite all his album and American successes, John has never reached the Number One position in the British singles charts.

All other groups in 1972 appeared to live in the shadow of Marc Bolan and T. Rex, who had five hits in that year, including 'Debora', a disc which had been recorded in Bolan's Tyrannosaurus Rex days.

These hit makers, however, met fierce resistance from a new batch of stars of 1972. Whereas the year's most passionate, tear-jerking record was undoubtedly 'Mother Of Mine' from the schoolboy Neil Reid, a totally different kind of passion came into being, for 1972 saw the emergence of Donny Osmond with 'Puppy Love', his first British hit. It was also the beginning of a phenomenon which was given the label of Osmondmania. Donny and his brothers achieved a hit in November 1972 entitled 'Crazy Horses' and Donny on his own with 'Why' fought himself and his brothers with 'Crazy Horses' for the top chart placing.

The Osmonds and Donny were joined in their roles as heart-throbs by David Cassidy. Cassidy's chart run had begun in April 1972, two months before that of Donny and, strictly speaking, he had even preceded The Osmonds, for in February 1971 he had enjoyed success with The Partridge Family with 'I Think I Love You'.

Paul Gadd, alias Paul Raven, alias Gary Glitter came to the fore in 1972 as a major chart force. However, his 'Rock And Roll Part 2' took four months to make any chart impact.

The year saw the arrival of some classic songs, two of which came from Don MacLean with 'American Pie' and 'Vincent'. Together these records gave MacLean 20 weeks of chart occupancy. Another classic was Nilsson's 'Without You', surprisingly his only British hit. June 1972 saw 'The First Time Ever I Saw Your Face' become a world-wide hit sung by Roberta Flack. The song was written by the British folk writer Ewan McColl.

Apart from teen heroes, one other major chart artist, David Bowie, began his successive chart entries. He had achieved a hit, 'Space Oddity', in 1969 but with a change of image in the 1970s, Bowie had three hits in 1972. For Bowie, 1973 was to be even more successful.

JANUARY 1973

6	**13**	**20**	**27**
1 Long Haired Lover From Liverpool *Little Jimmy Osmond* (MGM)	1	1	2
2 Solid Gold Easy Action *T. Rex* (EMI)	3	7	17
3 Crazy Horses *The Osmonds* (MGM)	4	8	18
4 The Jean Genie *David Bowie* (RCA)	2	3	3
5 Gudbuy T'Jane *Slade* (Polydor)	9	14	–
6 Happy Christmas (War Is Over) *John Lennon and Yoko Ono, The Plastic Ono Band and The Harlem Community Choir* (Apple)	15	–	–
7 My Ding-A-Ling *Chuck Berry* (Chess)	14	–	–
8 Shotgun Wedding *Roy C.* (UK)	11	12	–
9 Nights In White Satin *The Moody Blues* (Deram)	13	13	–
10 Hi Hi Hi/C. Moon *Wings* (Apple)	5	5	7
11 Big Seven *Judge Dread* (Big Shot)	8	10	12
12 Ben *Michael Jackson* (Tamla Motown)	12	19	–
13 Always On My Mind *Elvis Presley* (RCA)	10	9	11
14 Help Me Make It Through The Night *Gladys Knight and The Pips* (Tamla Motown)	18	11	–
15 Ball Park Incident *Wizzard* (Harvest)	6	6	6
16 Why *Donny Osmond* (MGM)	17	–	–
17 Crocodile Rock *Elton John* (DJM)	20	–	–
18 Getting A Drag *Lynsey de Paul* (MAM)	–	–	–
19 Little Drummer Boy *The Royal Scots Dragoon Guards Band* (RCA)	–	–	–
20 You're So Vain *Carly Simon* (Elektra)	7	4	4
– Blockbuster *The Sweet* (RCA)	16	2	1
22 Desperate Dan *Lieutenant Pigeon* (Decca)	19	17	20
– Wishing Well *Free* (Island)	26	15	8
28 Can't Keep It In *Cat Stevens* (Island)	21	16	13
– Papa Was A Rolling Stone *The Temptations* (Tamla Motown)	37	18	14
27 Come Softly To Me *The New Seekers* (Polydor)	24	20	30
– Do You Wanna Touch Me *Gary Glitter* (Bell)	–	34	5
– If You Don't Know Me By Now *Harold Melvin and The Blue notes* (CBS)	30	23	9
– Daniel *Elton John* (DJM)	–	38	10
– Paper Plane *Status Quo* (Vertigo)	40	24	15
– Me And Mrs Jones *Billy Paul* (Epic)	42	25	16
– Part Of The Union *The Strawbs* (A & M)	–	–	19

FEBRUARY 1973

3	**10**	**17**	**24**
1 Blockbuster *The Sweet* (RCA)	1	1	1
2 Do You Wanna Touch Me *Gary Glitter* (Bell)	2	3	3
3 You're So Vain *Carly Simon* (Elektra)	4	8	12
4 Long Haired Lover From Liverpool *Little Jimmy Osmond* (MGM)	6	9	17
5 The Jean Genie *David Bowie* (RCA)	13	–	–
6 Daniel *Elton John* (DJM)	5	4	7
7 Part Of The Union *The Strawbs* (A & M)	3	2	2
8 Wishing Well *Free* (Island)	7	13	–
9 If You Don't Know Me By Now *Harold Melvin and The Bluenotes* (CBS)	11	15	–
10 Ball Park Incident *Wizzard* (Harvest)	19	–	–
11 Paper Plane *Status Quo* (Vertigo)	8	10	13
12 Me And Mrs Jones *Billy Paul* (Epic)	12	16	–
13 Hi Hi Hi/C. Moon *Wings* (Apple)	20	–	–

3	10	17	24
14 Always On My Mind *Elvis Presley* (RCA)	–	–	–
15 Can't Keep It In *Cat Stevens* (Island)	14	–	–
16 Big Seven *Judge Dread* (Big Shot)	–	–	–
17 Roll Over Beethoven *The Electric Light Orchestra* (Harvest)	10	6	8
18 Papa Was A Rolling Stone *The Temptations* (Tamla Motown)	15	–	–
19 Crazy Horses *The Osmonds* (MGM)	–	–	–
20 Help Me Make It Through The Night *Gladys Knight and The Pips* (Tamla Motown)	–	–	–
21 Sylvia *Focus* (Polydor)	9	5	4
23 Whisky In The Jar *Thin Lizzy* (Decca)	16	7	6
24 Superstition *Stevie Wonder* (Tamla Motown)	17	11	11
27 Take Me Home Country Roads *Olivia Newton-John* (Pye)	18	18	15
32 Baby I Love You *Dave Edmunds* (Rockfield)	28	12	10
49 Lookin' Through The Eyes Of Love *The Partridge Family* (Bell)	22	14	9
– Cindy Incidentally *The Faces* (Warner Bros.)	–	17	5
– Hello Hurray *Alice Cooper* (Warner Bros.)	44	19	14
34 Take Me Girl I'm Ready *Jnr. Walker and The All Stars* (Tamla Motown)	25	20	16
39 Reelin' And Rockin' *Chuck Berry* (Chess)	29	23	18
– Doctor My Eyes *The Jackson Five* (Tamla Motown)	–	27	19
33 Hocus Pocus *Focus* (Polydor)	30	22	20

MARCH 1973

3	10	17	24	31
1 Cum On Feel The Noize *Slade* (Polydor)	1	1	1	2
2 Part Of The Union *The Strawbs* (A & M)	4	12	20	–
3 Blockbuster *The Sweet* (RCA)	5	14	–	–
4 Sylvia *Focus* (Polydor)	12	9	–	–
5 Cindy Incidentally *The Faces* (Warner Bros.)	2	5	9	18
6 Do You Wanna Touch Me *Gary Glitter* (Bell)	13	–	–	–
7 Whisky In The Jar *Thin Lizzy* (Decca)	10	15	–	–
8 Baby I Love You *Dave Edmunds* (Rockfield)	11	10	–	20
9 Lookin' Through The Eyes Of Love *The Partridge Family* (Bell)	15	16	–	–
10 Feel The Need In Me *The Detroit Emeralds* (Janus)	6	4	5	6
11 Daniel *Elton John* (DJM)	–	–	–	–
12 Doctor My Eyes *The Jackson Five* (Tamla Motown)	9	11	15	–
13 Hello Hurray *Alice Cooper* (Warner Bros.)	7	6	8	15
14 Supersition *Stevie Wonder* (Tamla Motown)	18	–	–	–
15 Roll Over Beethoven *The Electric Light Orchestra* (Harvest)	–	–	–	–
16 Gonna Make You An Offer You Can't Refuse *Jimmy Helms* (Cube)	17	8	10	14
17 Take Me Home Country Roads *Olivia Newton-John* (Pye)	–	–	–	–
18 Long Haired Lover From Liverpool *Little Jimmy Osmond* (MGM)	20	–	–	–
19 Killing Me Softly With His Song *Roberta Flack* (Atlantic)	8	7	6	9
20 Reelin' And Rockin' *Chuck Berry* (Chess)	–	–	–	–
– 20th Century Boy *T. Rex* (EMI)	3	3	3	5
– The Twelfth Of Never *Donny Osmond* (MGM)	14	2	2	1
22 Pinball Wizard/See Me Feel Me *The New Seekers* (Polydor)	16	17	17	19
29 Nice One Cyril *Cockerel Chorus* (Young Blood)	19	18	14	16
– Power To All Our Friends *Cliff Richard* (Columbia)	–	13	4	4
36 Heart Of Stone *Kenny* (RAK)	25	19	12	11
42 Never Never Never *Shirley Bassey* (UA)	31	20	11	10
– Get Down *Gilbert O'Sullivan* (MAM)	–	30	7	3
32 Why Can't We Live Together *Timmy Thomas* (Mojo)	28	23	13	12
– Tie A Yellow Ribbon *Dawn* (Bell)	38	32	16	7

3		**10**	**17**	**24**	**31**
28	That's When The Music Takes Me *Neil Sedaka* (RCA)	24	24	18	–
46	Love Train *The O'Jays* (CBS)	40	28	19	13
–	I'm A Clown/Some Kind Of A Summer *David Cassidy* (Bell)	–	–	35	8
–	Pyjamarama *Roxy Music* (Island)	45	31	23	17

APRIL 1973

7		**14**	**21**	**28**
1	Get Down *Gilbert O'Sullivan* (MAM)	1	3	3
2	The Twelfth Of Never *Donny Osmond* (MGM)	4	6	8
3	Tie A Yellow Ribbon *Dawn* (Bell)	2	1	1
4	Power To All Our Friends *Cliff Richard* (Columbia)	7	7	14
5	I'm A Clown/Some Kind Of A Summer *David Cassidy* (Bell)	3	5	4
6	Tweedle Dee *Little Jimmy Osmond* (MGM)	6	4	5
7	Cum On Feel The Noize *Slade* (Polydor)	13	19	–
8	Never Never Never *Shirley Bassey* (UA)	8	9	11
9	Love Train *The O'Jays* (CBS)	9	12	13
10	Killing Me Softly With His Song *Roberta Flack* (Atlantic)	19	20	–
11	Feel The Need In Me *The Detroit Emeralds* (Janus)	18	–	–
12	Heart Of Stone *Kenny* (RAK)	12	16	–
13	Pyjamarama *Roxy Music* (Island)	10	10	10
14	Why Can't We Live Together *Timmy Thomas* (Mojo)	15	–	–
15	20th Century Boy *T. Rex* (EMI)	17	–	–
16	Nice One Cyril *Cockerel Chorus* (Young Blood)	–	–	–
17	Hello Hello I'm Back Again *Gary Glitter* (Bell)	5	2	2
18	Crazy *Mud* (RAK)	14	14	12
19	Hello Hurray *Alice Cooper* (Warner Bros.)	–	–	–
20	Amanda *Stuart Gillies* (Philips)	20	13	15
21	All Because Of You *Geordie* (EMI)	11	11	6
–	Drive-in Saturday *David Bowie* (RCA)	16	8	7
43	My Love *Wings* (Apple)	25	15	9
22	Duelling Banjos *Eric Weissberg and Steve Mandel* (Warner Bros.)	21	17	19
28	God Gave Rock 'n' Roll To You *Argent* (Epic)	29	18	–
–	See My Baby Jive *Wizzard* (Harvest)	–	27	16
–	Giving It All Away *Roger Daltrey* (Track)	31	24	17
–	Brother Louie *Hot Chocolate* (RAK)	33	21	18
–	Big Eight *Judge Dread* (Big Shot)	–	29	20

MAY 1973

5		**12**	**19**	**26**
1	Tie A Yellow Ribbon *Dawn* (Bell)	1	3	4
2	Hello Hello I'm Back Again *Gary Glitter* (Bell)	3	4	8
3	Drive-in Saturday *David Bowie* (RCA)	8	6	16
4	Hell Raiser *The Sweet* (RCA)	2	2	2
5	Tweedle Dee *Little Jimmy Osmond* (MGM)	16	20	–
6	See My Baby Jive *Wizzard* (Harvest)	4	1	1
7	All Because Of You *Geordie* (EMI)	11	12	–
8	Get Down *Gilbert O'Sullivan* (MAM)	12	–	–
9	Brother Louie *Hot Chocolate* (RAK)	7	8	9
10	I'm A Clown/Some Kind Of A Summer *David Cassidy* (Bell)	15	19	–
11	Giving It All Away *Roger Daltrey* (Track)	5	7	10
12	My Love *Wings* (Apple)	9	11	14
13	No More Mr Nice Guy *Alice Cooper* (Warner Bros.)	10	10	15
14	Pyjamarama *Roxy Music* (Island)	–	–	–
15	Crazy *Mud* (RAK)	–	–	–
16	Big Eight *Judge Dread* (Big Shot)	14	16	19

5

	12	19	26
17 Amanda *Stuart Gillies* (Philips)	–	–	–
18 The Twelfth Of Never *Donny Osmond* (MGM)	–	–	–
19 Good Grief Christina *Chicory Tip* (CBS)	–	17	–
20 And I Love You So *Perry Como* (RCA)	6	5	3
25 Wonderful Dream *Ann-Marie David* (Epic)	13	13	13
29 The Right Thing To Do *Carly Simon* (Elektra)	17	–	–
21 Never Never Never *Shirley Bassey* (UA)	18	–	–
42 Also Sprach Zarathustra (2001) *Deodato* (Creed Taylor)	19	9	7
30 Could It Be I'm Falling In Love *The Detroit Spinners* (Alanttic)	20	18	12
34 One And One Is One *Medicine Head* (Polydor)	24	14	6
45 Brokendown Angel *Nazareth* (Mooncrest)	27	15	11
– Can The Can *Suzi Quatro* (RAK)	–	34	5
– Walk On The Wild Side *Lou Reed* (RCA)	32	24	17
– You Are The Sunshine Of My Life *Stevie Wonder* (Tamla Motown)	–	35	18
27 Mean Girl *Status Quo* (Pye)	22	21	20

JUNE 1973

2

	9	16	23	30
1 See My Baby Jive *Wizzard* (Harvest)	1	3	6	15
2 Can The Can *Suzi Quatro* (RAK)	2	1	3	7
3 And I Love You So *Perry Como* (RCA)	4	7	11	14
4 One And One Is One *Medicine Head* (Polydor)	3	4	9	12
5 Hell Raiser *The Sweet* (RCA)	8	–	–	–
6 Tie A Yellow Ribbon *Dawn* (Bell)	9	14	13	16
7 You Are The Sunshine Of My Life *Stevie Wonder* (Tamla Motown)	7	9	17	–
8 Also Sprach Zarathustra (2001) *Deodato* (Creed Taylor)	14	–	–	–
9 Brokendown Angel *Nazareth* (Mooncrest)	12	17	–	–
10 Walk On The Wild Side *Lou Reed* (RCA)	13	13	–	–
11 Could It Be I'm Falling In Love *The Detroit Spinners* (Atlantic)	16	–	–	–
12 You Want It You Got It *The Detroit Emeralds* (Westbound)	15	19	–	–
13 Rubber Bullets *10cc* (UK)	5	2	1	2
14 Walking In The Rain *The Partridge Family* (Bell)	10	10	12	13
15 Hello Hello I'm Back Again *Gary Glitter* (Bell)	20	–	–	–
16 Giving It All Away *Roger Daltrey* (Track)	–	–	–	–
17 Albatross *Fleetwood Mac* (CBS)	6	5	2	3
18 Brother Louie *Hot Chocolate* (RAK)	–	–	–	–
19 Wonderful Dream *Ann-Marie David* (Epic)	–	–	–	–
20 Stuck In The Middle With You *Stealers Wheel* (A & M)	11	8	8	10
38 Give Me Love (Give Me Peace On Earth) *George Harrison* (Apple)	17	11	10	8
22 Armed And Extremely Dangerous *First Choice* (Bell)	18	16	16	–
26 Welcome Home *Peters and Lee* (Philips)	19	18	5	4
– The Groover *T. Rex* (EMI)	–	6	4	5
39 Snoopy Versus The Red Baron *The Hot Shots* (Mooncrest)	25	12	7	6
– Live And Let Die *Wings* (Apple)	37	15	14	9
35 Sweet Illusion *Jnr. Campbell* (Deram)	21	20	15	19
33 Frankenstein *The Edgar Winter Group* (Epic)	22	25	18	–
– Born To Be With You *Dave Edmunds* (Rockfield)	48	28	19	11
– Can You Do It *Geordie* (EMI)	–	31	20	18
– Skweeze Me Pleeze Me *Slade* (Polydor)	–	–	–	1
– Take Me To The Mardi Gras *Paul Simon* (CBS)	–	36	24	17
– Hallelujah Day *The Jackson Five* (Tamla Motown)	41	27	25	20

JULY 1973

7		14	21	28
1	Skweeze Me Pleeze Me *Slade* (Polydor)	1	4	6
2	Welcome Home *Peters and Lee* (Philips)	2	1	2
3	Rubber Bullets *10cc* (UK)	6	13	19
4	Life On Mars *David Bowie* (RCA)	3	3	3
5	Albatross *Fleetwood Mac* (CBS)	8	14	–
6	Snoopy Versus The Red Baron *The Hot Shots* (Mooncrest)	4	10	13
7	Born To Be With You *Dave Edmunds* (Rockfield)	5	8	10
8	The Groover *T. Rex* (EMI)	19	–	–
9	Take Me To The Mardi Gras *Paul Simon* (CBS)	7	9	11
10	Give Me Love (Give Me Peace On Earth) *George Harrison* (Apple)	10	–	–
11	Live And Let Die *Wings* (Apple)	11	16	20
12	Stuck In The Middle With You *Stealers Wheel* (A & M)	–	–	–
13	Can You Do It *Geordie* (EMI)	15	–	–
14	Honaloochie Boogie *Mott The Hoople* (CBS)	12	19	–
15	Rock-A-Doodle-Doo *Linda Lewis* (Raft)	17	17	–
16	Tie A Yellow Ribbon *Dawn* (Bell)	20	–	–
17	And I Love You So *Perry Como* (RCA)	16	20	–
18	Sweet Illusion *Jnr. Campbell* (Deram)	–	–	–
19	Can The Can *Suzi Quatro* (RAK)	–	–	–
20	Hallelujah Day *The Jackson Five* (Tamla Motown)	–	–	–
36	Saturday Night's Alright For Fighting *Elton John* (DJM)	9	7	7
23	Randy *Blue Mink* (EMI)	13	11	9
27	Step By Step *Joe Simon* (Mojo)	14	18	17
–	Going Home *The Osmonds* (MGM)	18	6	5
–	I'm The Leader Of The Gang (I Am) *Gary Glitter* (Bell)	–	2	1
43	Alright Alright Alright *Mungo Jerry* (Dawn)	23	5	4
32	Gaye *Clifford T. Ward* (Charisma)	24	12	8
30	Pillow Talk *Sylvia* (London)	22	15	14
47	Yesterday Once More *The Carpenters* (A & M)	34	26	12
–	Touch Me In The Morning *Diana Ross* (Tamla Motown)	50	27	15
–	Spanish Eyes *Al Martino* (Capitol)	42	31	16
–	Bad Bad Boy *Nazareth* (Mooncrest)	–	34	18

AUGUST 1973

4		11	18	25
1	I'm The Leader Of The Gang (I Am) *Gary Glitter* (Bell)	1	1	3
2	Welcome Home *Peters and Lee* (Philips)	2	4	8
3	Alright Alright Alright *Mungo Jerry* (Dawn)	3	6	10
4	Going Home *The Osmonds* (MGM)	6	10	–
5	Life On Mars *David Bowie* (RCA)	7	13	19
6	48 Crash *Suzi Quatro* (RAK)	4	3	7
7	Yesterday Once More *The Carpenters* (A & M)	5	2	2
8	Spanish Eyes *Al Martino* (Capitol)	8	5	6
9	Touch Me In The Morning *Diana Ross* (Tamla Motown)	11	14	14
10	Randy *Blue Mink* (EMI)	14	–	–
11	Bad Bad Boy *Nazareth* (Mooncrest)	10	12	17
12	Gaye *Clifford T. Ward* (Charisma)	13	20	–
13	Ying Tong Song *The Goons* (Decca)	9	9	15
14	Saturday Night's Alright For Fighting *Elton John* (DJM)	20	–	–
15	Skweeze Me Pleeze Me *Slade* (Polydor)	–	–	–
16	Pillow Talk *Sylvia* (London)	17	–	–
17	Hypnosis *Mud* (RAK)	16	–	–
18	You Can Do Magic *Limmie and The Family Cookin'* (Avco)	12	7	5
19	Born To Be With You *Dave Edmunds* (Rockfield)	–	–	–
20	Snoopy Versus The Red Baron *The Hot Shots* (Mooncrest)	–	–	–

SEPTEMBER 1973

OCTOBER 1973

6		**13**	**20**	**27**
1 Eye Level *The Simon Park Orchestra* (Columbia)		1	1	2
2 The Ballroom Blitz *The Sweet* (RCA)		3	7	12
3 Monster Mash *Bobby Pickett and The Crypt Kickers* (London)		5	5	13
4 My Friend Stan *Slade* (Polydor)		2	3	3
5 Nutbush City Limits *Ike and Tina Turner* (UA)		4	4	9
6 Angel Fingers *Wizzard* (Harvest)		11	15	–
7 For The Good Times *Perry Como* (RCA)		7	9	7
8 The Laughing Gnome *David Bowie* (Deram)		6	6	8
9 Joybringer *Manfred Mann Earthband* (Vertigo)		10	13	–
10 Rock On *David Essex* (CBS)		17	–	–
11 Caroline *Status Quo* (Vertigo)		9	8	5
12 Oh No Not My Baby *Rod Stewart* (Mercury)		13	–	–
13 All The Way From Memphis *Mott The Hoople* (CBS)		16	–	–
14 Angie *The Rolling Stones* (RS)		–	–	–
15 Spanish Eyes *Al Martino* (Capitol)		15	19	–
16 Goodbye Yellow Brick Road *Elton John* (DJM)		12	10	6
17 I've Been Hurt *Guy Darrell* (Santa Ponsa)		18	–	–
18 Ooh Baby *Gilbert O'Sullivan* (MAM)		19	–	–
19 Dancing On A Saturday Night *Barry Blue* (Bell)		–	–	–
20 Say, Has Anybody Seen My Sweet Gypsy Rose *Dawn* (Bell)		–	–	–
– Daydreamer/Puppy Song *David Cassidy* (Bell)		8	2	1
23 A Hard Rain's Gonna Fall *Bryan Ferry* (Island)		14	11	10
24 Ghetto Child *The Detroit Spinners* (Atlantic)		20	12	11
44 Showdown *The Electric Light Orchestra* (Harvest)		29	14	16
– Sorrow *David Bowie* (RCA)		–	16	4
25 That Lady *The Isley Brothers* (Epic)		22	17	14
34 Knockin' On Heaven's Door *Bob Dylan* (CBS)		26	18	17
– 5.15 *The Who* (Track)		40	20	–
37 Let There Be Peace On Earth (Let It Begin With Me) *Michael Ward* (Philips)		24	24	15
35 Deck Of Cards *Max Bygraves* (Pye)		38	26	18
– Top Of The World *The Carpenters* (A & M)		–	36	19
– This Flight Tonight *Nazareth* (Mooncrest)		45	23	20

NOVEMBER 1973

3		**10**	**17**	**24**
1 Daydreamer/Puppy Song *David Cassidy* (Bell)		1	3	11
2 Eye Level *The Simon Park Orchestra* (Columbia)		6	15	20
3 Sorrow *David Bowie* (RCA)		3	4	5
4 Let Me In *The Osmonds* (MGM)		2	2	2
5 Caroline *Status Quo* (Vertigo)		7	20	–
6 Goodbye Yellow Brick Road *Elton John* (DJM)		10	19	–
7 Ghetto Child *The Detroit Spinners* (Atlantic)		8	10	–
8 My Friend Stan *Slade* (Polydor)		16	–	–
9 Top Of The World *The Carpenters* (A & M)		5	7	9
10 For The Good Times *Perry Como* (RCA)		9	12	16
11 The Laughing Gnome *David Bowie* (Deram)		–	–	–
12 Showdown *The Electric Light Orchestra* (Harvest)		12	18	–
13 A Hard Rain's Gonna Fall *Bryan Ferry* (Island)		18	–	–
14 Knockin' On Heaven's Door *Bob Dylan* (CBS)		15	–	–
15 This Flight Tonight *Nazareth* (Mooncrest)		11	11	15
16 Nutbush City Limits *Ike and Tina Turner* (UA)		–	–	–
17 Deck Of Cards *Max Bygraves* (Pye)		14	13	19
18 Let There Be Peace On Earth (Let It Begin With Me) *Michael Ward* (Philips)		19	–	–
19 Won't Somebody Dance With Me *Lynsey de Paul* (MAM)		17	14	18

3

	10	17	24
20 Dyna-Mite *Mud* (RAK)	4	5	4
24 Photograph *Ringo Starr* (Apple)	13	8	10
31 Do You Wanna Dance *Barry Blue* (Bell)	20	9	7
– I Love You Love Me Love *Gary Glitter* (Bell)	–	1	1
– When I Fall In Love *Donny Osmond* (MGM)	23	6	6
28 Daytona Demon *Suzi Quatro* (RAK)	22	16	14
– Why Oh Why Oh Why *Gilbert O'Sullivan* (MAM)	48	17	12
– Paper Roses *Marie Osmond* (MGM)	–	24	3
50 My Coo-Ca-Choo *Alvin Stardust* (Magnet)	36	27	8
– Lamplight *David Essex* (CBS)	38	23	13
33 Helen Wheels *Wings* (Apple)	28	26	17

DECEMBER 1973

1

	8	15	22/29
1 I Love You Love Me Love *Gary Glitter* (Bell)	1	2	2
2 My Coo-Ca-Choo *Alvin Stardust* (Magnet)	4	3	5
3 Paper Roses *Marie Osmond* (MGM)	2	5	6
4 When I Fall In Love *Donny Osmond* (MGM)	12	12	15
5 Dyna-Mite *Mud* (RAK)	6	11	–
6 Why Oh Why Oh Why *Gilbert O'Sullivan* (MAM)	9	10	13
7 You Won't Find Another Fool Like Me *The New Seekers* (Polydor)	3	4	3
8 Lamplight *David Essex* (CBS)	7	7	8
9 Do You Wanna Dance *Barry Blue* (Bell)	10	19	–
10 Let Me In *The Osmonds* (MGM)	5	16	19
11 Photograph *Ringo Starr* (Apple)	14	–	–
12 Helen Wheels *Wings* (Apple)	15	15	–
13 Daydreamer/Puppy Song *David Cassidy* (Bell)	–	–	–
14 Top Of The World *The Carpenters* (A & M)	17	20	–
15 Sorrow *David Bowie* (RCA)	20	–	–
16 Street Life *Roxy Music* (Island)	11	9	10
17 Roll Away The Stone *Mott The Hoople* (CBS)	8	8	9
18 Daytona Demon *Suzi Quatro* (RAK)	18	–	–
19 Won't Somebody Dance With Me *Lynsey de Paul* (MAM)	–	–	–
20 Truck On (Tyke) *T. Rex* (EMI)	13	14	12
23 Amoureuse *Kiki Dee* (Rocket)	16	13	18
– I Wish It Could Be Christmas Every Day *Wizzard* (Harvest)	19	6	4
– Merry Xmas Everybody *Slade* (Polydor)	–	1	1
28 Love On A Mountain Top *Robert Knight* (Monument)	22	17	16
25 Keep On Truckin' *Eddie Kendricks* (Tamla Motown)	24	18	–
– The Show Must Go On *Leo Sayer* (Chrysalis)	–	24	7
42 Forever *Roy Wood* (Harvest)	32	31	11
– Gaudete *Steeleye Span* (Chrysalis)	48	27	14
– Dance With The Devil *Cozy Powell* (RAK)	46	38	17
– Pool Hall Richard/I Wish It Would Rain *The Faces* (Warner Bros.)	38	26	20

1973

Did 1973 begin with disaster? It could be said that it did, for Little Jimmy Osmond opened the New Year's charts at Number One with 'Long Haired Lover From Liverpool'. 1973 saw Little Jimmy have a follow-up hit with 'Tweedle Dee', while his big brother Donny achieved two Number Ones and a Number Four. His top chart positions were held by 'The Twelfth Of Never', which had been made popular by Johnny Mathis in the 1950s, and 'Young Love', which had given Hit Parade success to both Tab Hunter and Sonny James in 1957. Donny's other hit was 'When I Fall In Love', which had been a huge hit for Nat 'King' Cole in April 1957.

The Osmonds had two Top Five discs with 'Going Home' and 'Let Me In' and Marie Osmond, their younger sister, arrived on the scene with 'Paper Roses', a record which almost reached the Number One position.

David Cassidy had a good year with two hits in his own right and another two with The Partridge Family. At last David Essex found deserved fame and became a chart force with 'Rock On' which reached Number Three, and his follow-up, 'Lamplight', which entered the Top Ten.

Other teen heroes with chart success in 1973 included The Sweet, Slade, a slightly reticent Marc Bolan, Gary Glitter and Mud. Glitter's successes in the charts were very impressive statistically, for two of his discs reached Number Two in the charts, while another two, 'I'm The Leader Of The Gang' and 'I Love You Love Me Love' both reached Number One.

Mud achieved their first hit with 'Crazy' and were just one group signed to the RAK record label, a company owned by Mickie Most. The RAK label achieved 14 chart entries out of 18 releases and another successful label, Bell, achieved 16 hits out of 57 releases, i.e. a ratio of 1 : 3. This is very impressive when compared to the Decca record company's ratio of 1 : 31, or 20 hits out of 620 releases.

RAK's successes were achieved by Mud, Hot Chocolate, Cozy Powell, and Suzi Quatro, a girl singer discovered in Detroit by Mickie Most.

The record industry created a demand for teen stars, but most of these failed although minor hits were obtained by Andy and David Williams, The Dougal Brothers and The Handley Family.

Philadelphia groups came to the fore and successful discs were recorded by Billy Paul, The Stylistics, The Detroit Emeralds, The Detroit Spinners, Harold Melvin and The Bluenotes, The O'Jays, while artists on the Tamla Motown label also achieved a few hits.

A number of exciting new groups such as Mott The Hoople, Roxy Music, Wings and a re-born Status Quo all established themselves in the charts. Following on the heels of their late 1972 hit, 'Donna', 10cc continued to build upon their chart reputation. Perhaps the most memorable of all recording successes of 1973 were those of David Bowie, as his discs, act, personality and his 'cult' following made him a very important figure indeed.

5	12	19	26
1 Merry Xmas Everybody *Slade* (Polydor)	1	3	12
2 You Won't Find Another Fool Like Me *The New Seekers* (Polydor)	2	1	5
3 I Love You Love Me Love *Gary Glitter* (Bell)	7	13	13
4 I Wish It Could Be Christmas Every Day *Wizzard* (Harvest)	4	16	–
5 My Coo-Ca-Choo *Alvin Stardust* (Magnet)	5	5	6
6 Paper Roses *Marie Osmond* (MGM)	14	8	14
7 The Show Must Go On *Leo Sayer* (Chrysalis)	3	2	3
8 Lamplight *David Essex* (CBS)	10	15	15
9 Roll Away The Stone *Mott The Hoople* (CBS)	13	17	18
10 Street Life *Roxy Music* (Island)	15	19	–
11 Forever *Roy Wood* (Harvest)	12	9	8
12 Why Oh Why Oh Why *Gilbert O'Sullivan* (MAM)	17	18	–
13 Love On A Mountain Top *Robert Knight* (Monument)	11	12	10
14 Dance With The Devil *Cozy Powell* (RAK)	6	4	4
15 Truck On (Tyke) *T. Rex* (EMI)	18	–	–
16 Pool Hall Richard/I Wish It Would Rain *The Faces* (Warner Bros.)	8	11	11
17 Gaudete *Steeleye Span* (Chrysalis)	16	–	–
18 When I Fall In Love *Donny Osmond* (MGM)	20	–	–
19 Amoureuse *Kiki Dee* (Rocket)	–	–	–
20 Vaya Con Dios *Millican and Nesbitt* (Pye)	–	–	–
26 Radar Love *Golden Earring* (Track)	9	7	7
22 Vado Via *Drupi* (A & M)	19	–	17
– Teenage Rampage *The Sweet* (RCA)	–	6	2
– Tiger Feet *Mud* (RAK)	–	10	1
36 Solitaire *Andy Williams* (CBS)	22	14	9
43 All Of My Life *Diana Ross* (Tamla Motown)	38	20	16
– Rockin' Roll Baby *The Stylistics* (Avco)	–	29	19
– How Come *Ronnie Lane* (GM)	49	25	20

2	9	16	23
1 Tiger Feet *Mud* (RAK)	1	1	2
2 Teenage Rampage *The Sweet* (RCA)	2	4	11
3 You Won't Find Another Fool Like Me *The New Seekers* (Polydor)	8	20	–
4 The Show Must Go On *Leo Sayer* (Chrysalis)	7	10	–
5 Dance With The Devil *Cozy Powell* (RAK)	3	6	17
6 Solitaire *Andy Williams* (CBS)	4	5	7
7 Radar Love *Golden Earring* (Track)	11	17	–
8 My Coo-Ca-Choo *Alvin Stardust* (Magnet)	16	–	–
9 Forever *Roy Wood* (Harvest)	10	18	–
10 Love On A Mountain Top *Robert Knight* (Monument)	13	14	–
11 How Come *Ronnie Lane* (GM)	12	11	–
12 Rockin' Roll Baby *The Stylistics* (Avco)	6	8	12
13 The Man Who Sold The World *Lulu* (Polydor)	5	3	5
14 All Of My Life *Diana Ross* (Tamla Motown)	9	9	9
15 Pool Hall Richard/I Wish It Would Rain *The Faces* (Warner Bros.)	–	–	–
16 I Love You Love Me Love *Gary Glitter* (Bell)	–	–	–
17 Paper Roses *Marie Osmond* (MGM)	–	–	–
18 Teenage Lament '74 *Alice Cooper* (Warner Bros.)	15	12	–
19 Lamplight *David Essex* (CBS)	–	–	–
20 Living For The City *Stevie Wonder* (Tamla Motown)	17	15	19
– Devil Gate Drive *Suzi Quatro* (RAK)	14	2	1

2		9	16	23
– Teenage Dream *Marc Bolan* (EMI)		18	13	16
26 Wombling Song *The Wombles* (CBS)		19	7	4
34 Love's Theme *Love Unlimited Orchestra* (Pye)		20	19	10
– Ma He's Making Eyes At Me *Lena Zavaroni* (Philips)		30	16	13
– Jealous Mind *Alvin Stardust* (Magnet)		–	22	3
– Rebel Rebel *David Bowie* (RCA)		–	–	6
– The Air That I Breathe *The Hollies* (Polydor)		33	26	8
32 Never Never Gonna Give Ya Up *Barry White* (Pye)		23	21	14
– You're Sixteen *Ringo Starr* (Apple)		–	–	15
– Remember (Sha-La-La-La) *The Bay City Rollers* (Bell)		47	38	18
– The Most Beautiful Girl *Charlie Rich* (CBS)		–	46	20

MARCH 1974

2	9	16	23	30
1 Devil Gate Drive *Suzi Quatro* (RAK)	2	6	14	–
2 Jealous Mind *Alvin Stardust* (Magnet)	1	2	5	17
3 The Air That I Breathe *The Hollies* (Polydor)	3	3	2	4
4 Wombling Song *The Wombles* (CBS)	7	10	13	–
5 Rebel Rebel *David Bowie* (RCA)	5	13	16	–
6 Tiger Feet *Mud* (RAK)	16	–	–	–
7 You're Sixteen *Ringo Starr* (Apple)	4	5	4	7
8 Remember (Sha-La-La-La) *The Bay City Rollers* (Bell)	6	7	8	16
9 The Man Who Sold The World *Lulu* (Polydor)	17	–	–	–
10 Ma He's Making Eyes At Me *Lena Zavaroni* (Philips)	13	14	17	–
11 The Most Beautiful Girl *Charlie Rich* (Epic)	9	4	3	2
12 Love's Theme *Love Unlimited Orchestra* (Pye)	15	18	–	–
13 Solitaire *Andy Williams* (CBS)	20	–	–	–
14 Never Never Gonna Give Ya Up *Barry White* (Pye)	14	16	–	–
15 Billy, Don't Be A Hero *Paper Lace* (Bus Stop)	8	1	1	1
16 It's You *Freddie Starr* (Tiffany)	12	9	9	13
17 Jet *Wings* (Apple)	10	8	7	10
18 Rockin' Roll Baby *The Stylistics* (Avco)	–	–	–	–
19 Happiness Is Me And You *Gilbert O'Sullivan* (MAM)	19	20	–	–
20 Burn Baby Burn *Hudson Ford* (A & M)	18	15	19	–
28 Candle In The Wind *Elton John* (DJM)	11	12	11	14
– I Get A Little Sentimental Over You *The New Seekers* (Polydor)	24	11	6	5
50 School Love *Barry Blue* (Bell)	25	17	12	11
48 Jambalaya *The Carpenters* (A & M)	40	19	18	12
– Emma *Hot Chocolate* (RAK)	–	36	10	6
– Seven Seas Of Rhye *Queen* (EMI)	45	30	15	15
– Seasons In The Sun *Terry Jacks* (Bell)	–	–	20	3
– Remember Me This Way *Gary Glitter* (Bell)	–	–	–	8
– Angel Face *The Glitter Band* (Bell)	–	–	26	9
– Long Live Love *Olivia Newton-John* (Pye)	–	28	21	18
– You Are Everything *Diana Ross and Marvin Gaye* (Tamla Motown)	–	–	25	19
– Everlasting Love *Robert Knight* (Monument)	35	24	22	20

APRIL 1974

6	13	20	27
1 Seasons In The Sun *Terry Jacks* (Bell)	1	1	1
2 Billy, Don't Be A Hero *Paper Lace* (Bus Stop)	2	10	15
3 Emma *Hot Chocolate* (RAK)	6	6	14
4 Remember Me This Way *Gary Glitter* (Bell)	3	7	12
5 Angel Face *The Glitter Band* (Bell)	5	4	5
6 Everyday *Slade* (Polydor)	4	3	7

6	13	20	27
7 I Get A Little Sentimental Over You *The New Seekers* (Polydor)	12	20	–
8 The Most Beautiful Girl *Charlie Rich* (Epic)	9	16	–
9 You Are Everything *Diana Ross and Marvin Gaye* (Tamla Motown)	7	5	6
10 The Air That I Breathe *The Hollies* (Polydor)	–	–	–
11 Seven Seas Of Rhye *Queen* (EMI)	10	14	17
12 You're Sixteen *Ringo Starr* (Apple)	–	–	–
13 School Love *Barry Blue* (Bell)	16	–	–
14 Jambalaya *The Carpenters* (A & M)	13	–	–
15 Jet *Wings* (Apple)	–	–	–
16 Long Live Love *Olivia Newton-John* (Pye)	11	19	–
17 Candle In The Wind *Elton John* (DJM)	19	–	–
18 It's You *Freddie Starr* (Tiffany)	–	–	–
19 Everlasting Love *Robert Knight* (Monument)	–	–	–
20 Rock Around The Clock *Bill Haley and The Comets* (MCA)	17	12	13
– The Cat Crept In *Mud* (RAK)	8	2	3
23 Doctor's Orders *Sunny* (CBS)	14	9	8
25 I'm Gonna Knock On Your Door *Jimmy Osmond* (MGM)	15	13	11
21 Golden Age Of Rock 'n' Roll *Mott The Hoople* (CBS)	18	18	10
36 Remember You're A Womble *The Wombles* (CBS)	20	8	4
28 Homely Girl *The Chi-Lites* (Brunswick)	22	11	9
38 A Walkin' Miracle *Limmie and The Family Cookin'* (Avco)	23	15	12
– Waterloo *Abba* (Epic)	–	17	2
43 Long Legged Woman Dressed In Black *Mungo Jerry* (Dawn)	36	25	18
– Don't Stay Away Too Long *Peters and Lee* (Philips)	–	38	19
– He's Misstra Know It All *Stevie Wonder* (Tamla Motown)	40	31	20

MAY 1974

4	11	18	25
1 Waterloo *Abba* (Epic)	1	2	6
2 The Cat Crept In *Mud* (RAK)	12	17	–
3 Seasons In The Sun *Terry Jacks* (Bell)	9	20	–
4 Remember You're A Womble *The Wombles* (CBS)	3	5	13
5 Homely Girl *The Chi-Lites* (Brunswick)	7	8	15
6 A Walkin' Miracle *Limmie and The Family Cookin'* (Avco)	8	8	12
7 Doctor's Orders *Sunny* (CBS)	17	–	–
8 You Are Everything *Diana Ross and Marvin Gaye* (Tamla Motown)	15	–	–
9 Rock And Roll Winter *Wizzard* (Warner Bros.)	6	6	11
10 Angel Face *The Glitter Band* (Bell)	19	–	–
11 Don't Stay Away Too Long *Peters and Lee* (Philips)	4	3	4
12 Shang-A-Lang *The Bay City Rollers* (Bell)	5	4	2
13 Everyday *Slade* (Polydor)	–	–	–
14 Long Legged Woman Dressed In Black *Mungo Jerry* (Dawn)	13	19	20
15 I'm Gonna Knock On Your Door *Jimmy Osmond* (MGM)	–	–	–
16 Year Of Decision *The Three Degrees* (Philadelphia)	20	13	19
17 He's Misstra Know It All *Stevie Wonder* (Tamla Motown)	10	11	17
18 Emma *Hot Chocolate* (RAK)	–	–	–
19 Rock Around The Clock *Bill Haley and The Comets* (MCA)	–	–	–
20 Remember Me This Way *Gary Glitter* (Bell)	–	–	–
– Sugar Baby Love *The Rubettes* (Polydor)	2	1	1
– Red Dress *Alvin Stardust* (Magnet)	11	10	7
– The Night Chicago Died *Paper Lace* (Bus Stop)	14	7	5
– I Can't Stop *The Osmonds* (MGM)	16	15	12
– Spiders And Snakes *Jim Stafford* (MGM)	18	14	14
48 This Town Ain't Big Enough For Both Of Us *Sparks* (Island)	27	9	–
21 Behind Closed Doors *Charlie Rich* (Epic)	23	16	–
38 Break The Rules *Status Quo* (Vertigo)	26	18	8

4		11	18	25
– There's A Ghost In My House *R. Dean Taylor* (Tamla Motown)		34	24	9
– If I Didn't Care *David Cassidy* (Bell)		29	21	10
46 Go *Gigliola Cinquetti* (CBS)		37	22	16
43 I See A Star *Mouth and McNeal* (Decca)		42	29	18

JUNE 1974

1	8	15	22	29
1 Sugar Baby Love *The Rubettes* (Polydor)	1	6	12	–
2 This Town Ain't Big Enough For Both Of Us *Sparks* (Island)	2	4	9	–
3 The Night Chicago Died *Paper Lace* (Bus Stop)	6	12	–	–
4 There's A Ghost In My House *R. Dean Taylor* (Tamla Motown)	5	3	4	5
5 Don't Stay Away Too Long *Peters and Lee* (Philips)	11	20	–	–
6 Hey Rock And Roll *Showaddywaddy* (Bell)	3	2	3	4
7 Shang-A-Lang *The Bay City Rollers* (Bell)	14	–	–	–
8 Go *Gigliola Cinquetti* (CBS)	12	11	–	–
9 If I Didn't Care *David Cassidy* (Bell)	9	15	–	–
10 Red Dress *Alvin Stardust* (Magnet)	19	–	–	–
11 Break The Rules *Status Quo* (Vertigo)	10	–	–	–
12 I See A Star *Mouth and McNeal* (Decca)	8	10	15	–
13 The Streak *Ray Stevens* (Janus)	4	1	2	3
14 I Can't Stop *The Osmonds* (MCA)	17	–	–	–
15 Waterloo *Abba* (Epic)	–	–	–	–
16 The In Crowd *Bryan Ferry* (Island)	13	14	19	–
17 Judy Teen *Cockney Rebel* (EMI)	7	7	5	12
18 Spiders And Snakes *Jim Stafford* (MGM)	–	–	–	–
19 Remember You're A Womble *The Wombles* (CBS)	20	–	–	–
20 (You Keep Me) Hanging On *Cliff Richard* (EMI)	15	13	–	–
22 A Touch Too Much *The Arrows* (RAK)	16	9	8	9
24 Jarrow Song *Alan Price* (Warner Bros.)	17	8	6	10
– Always Yours *Gary Glitter* (Bell)	–	5	1	2
30 Don't Let The Sun Go Down On Me *Elton John* (DJM)	24	16	17	16
28 Summer Breeze *The Isley Brothers* (Epic)	21	17	16	17
36 Liverpool Lou *The Scaffold* (Warner Bros.)	22	18	7	11
31 The Man In Black *Cozy Powell* (RAK)	26	19	20	18
– I'd Love You To Want Me *Lobo* (UK)	37	24	10	7
– She *Charles Aznavour* (Barclay)	–	–	11	1
– One Man Band *Leo Sayer* (Chrysalis)	–	25	13	6
– Kissin' In The Back Row *The Drifters* (Bell)	–	39	14	8
44 Guilty *The Pearls* (Bell)	29	22	18	13
– Going Down The Road *Roy Wood* (Harvest)	–	37	21	14
– Can't Get Enough *Bad Company* (Island)	37	21	23	15
– Wall Street Shuffle *10cc* (UK)	–	34	28	19
– Easy, Easy *The Scotland World Cup Squad* (Polydor)	–	–	30	20

JULY 1974

6	13	20	27
1 She *Charles Aznavour* (Barclay)	1	1	2
2 Kissin' In The Back Row *The Drifters* (Bell)	2	2	4
3 Always Yours *Gary Glitter* (Bell)	9	10	–
4 Bangin' Man *Slade* (Polydor)	3	5	8
5 Hey Rock And Roll *Showaddywaddy* (Bell)	11	16	–
6 I'd Love You To Want Me *Lobo* (UK)	5	7	10
7 The Streak *Ray Stevens* (Janus)	16	–	–
8 One Man Band *Leo Sayer* (Chrysalis)	6	18	–
9 Young Girl *Gary Puckett and The Union Gap* (CBS)	8	6	6

	13	20	27
10 Guilty *The Pearls* (Bell)	15	–	–
11 Wall Street Shuffle *10cc* (UK)	10	12	13
12 Banana Rock *The Wombles* (CBS)	12	9	12
13 A Touch Too Much *The Arrows* (RAK)	–	–	–
14 Liverpool Lou *The Scaffold* (Warner Bros.)	–	–	–
15 Rock Your Baby *George McCrae* (Jayboy)	4	3	1
16 Going Down The Road *Roy Wood* (Harvest)	13	–	–
17 There's A Ghost In My House *R. Dean Taylor* (Tamla Motown)	–	–	–
18 Don't Let The Sun Go Down On Me *Elton John* (DJM)	19	–	–
19 Judy Teen *Cockney Rebel* (EMI)	–	–	–
20 Jarrow Song *Alan Price* (Warner Bros.)	–	–	–
27 Band On The Run *Wings* (Apple)	7	4	5
24 Too Big *Suzi Quatro* (RAK)	14	19	–
21 Beach Baby *The First Class* (UK)	17	13	18
– The Six Teens *The Sweet* (RCA)	18	11	9
26 If You Go Away *Terry Jacks* (Bell)	20	8	11
– Born With A Smile On My Face *Stephanie De Sykes and Rain* (Bradley's)	–	14	3
25 Laughter In The Rain *Neil Sedaka* (Polydor)	22	15	16
– When Will I See You Again *The Three Degrees* (Philadelphia)	33	17	7
47 She's A Winner *The Intruders* (Philadelphia)	29	20	19
– You Make Me Feel Brand New *The Stylistics* (Avco)	44	30	14
– Tonight *The Rubettes* (Polydor)	40	21	15
– Amateur Hour *Sparks* (Island)	–	42	17
50 My Girl Bill *Jim Stafford* (MGM)	31	23	20

AUGUST 1974

3	10	17	24	31
1 Rock Your Baby *George McCrae* (Jayboy)	1	2	6	16
2 Born With A Smile On My Face *Stephanie De Sykes and Rain* (Bradley's)	3	5	14	–
3 Band On The Run *Wings* (Apple)	8	12	–	–
4 When Will I See You Again *The Three Degrees* (Philadelphia)	2	1	1	2
5 She *Charles Aznavour* (Barclay)	17	–	–	–
6 Kissin' In The Back Row Of The Movies *The Drifters* (Bell)	9	–	–	–
7 Young Girl *Gary Puckett and The Union Gap* (CBS)	14	–	–	–
8 You Make Me Feel Brand New *The Stylistics* (Avco)	4	3	2	3
9 Amateur Hour *Sparks* (Island)	7	11	16	–
10 If You Go Away *Terry Jacks* (Bell)	–	–	–	–
11 The Six Teens *The Sweet* (RCA)	19	–	–	–
12 Tonight *The Rubettes* (Polydor)	12	13	18	–
13 Rocket *Mud* (RAK)	6	7	8	15
14 She's A Winner *The Intruders* (Philadelphia)	18	18	–	–
15 Rock The Boat *The Hues Corporation* (RCA)	10	6	7	11
16 Banana Rock *The Wombles* (CBS)	–	–	–	–
17 Summerlove Sensation *The Bay City Rollers* (Bell)	5	4	3	5
18 Laughter In The Rain *Neil Sedaka* (Polydor)	–	–	–	–
19 Beach Baby *The First Class* (UK)	–	–	–	–
20 Bangin' Man *Slade* (Polydor)	–	–	–	–
25 What Becomes Of The Broken Hearted *Jimmy Ruffin* (Tamla Motown)	11	8	4	6
22 It's Only Rock 'n' Roll *The Rolling Stones* (RS)	13	10	11	20
31 I Shot The Sheriff *Eric Clapton* (RSO)	15	9	9	13
21 Please Please Me *David Cassidy* (Bell)	16	16	–	–
26 My Girl Bill *Jim Stafford* (MGM)	20	–	–	–
33 I'm Leaving It All Up To You *Donny and Marie Osmond* (MGM)	21	14	5	4

3	10	17	24	31
42 Just For You *The Glitter Band* (Bell)	22	15	10	17
43 Hello Summertime *Bobby Goldsboro* (UA)	27	17	17	14
36 Honey Honey *Sweet Dreams* (Bradley's)	29	19	13	10
30 Your Baby Ain't Your Baby Anymore *Paul Da Vinci* (Penny Farthing)	23	20	–	–
– Mr Soft *Cockney Rebel* (EMI)	39	23	12	8
– Y Viva Espana *Sylvia* (Sonet)	46	28	15	7
– Love Me For A Reason *The Osmonds* (MGM)	–	–	19	1
– Na Na Na *Cozy Powell* (RAK)	48	29	20	12
– Kung Fu Fighting *Carl Douglas* (Pye)	–	42	29	9
– Annie's Song *John Denver* (RCA)	–	37	26	18
– Rock 'n' Roll Lady *Showaddywaddy* (Bell)	–	32	22	19

SEPTEMBER 1974

7	14	21	28
1 Love Me For A Reason *The Osmonds* (MGM)	1	2	4
2 I'm Leaving It All Up To You *Donny and Marie Osmond* (MGM)	3	5	11
3 When Will I See You Again *The Three Degrees* (Philadelphia)	7	15	–
4 Kung Fu Fighting *Carl Douglas* (Pye)	2	1	1
5 Y Viva Espana *Sylvia* (Sonet)	4	6	5
6 You Make Me Feel Brand New *The Stylistics* (Avco)	13	17	–
7 Annie's Song *John Denver* (RCA)	5	3	2
8 What Becomes Of The Broken Hearted *Jimmy Ruffin* (Tamla Motown)	8	12	18
9 Mr Soft *Cockney Rebel* (EMI)	11	20	–
10 Honey Honey *Sweet Dreams* (Bradley's)	12	13	–
11 Hang On In There Baby *Johnny Bristol* (MGM)	6	4	3
12 Summerlove Sensation *The Bay City Rollers* (Bell)	19	–	–
13 Na Na Na *Cozy Powell* (RAK)	10	10	14
14 Hello Summertime *Bobby Goldsboro* (UA)	20	18	–
15 Rock 'n' Roll Lady *Showaddywaddy* (Bell)	18	16	–
16 Queen Of Clubs *K. C. and The Sunshine Band* (Jayboy)	15	9	7
17 Rainbow *Peters and Lee* (Philips)	–	19	–
18 Just For You *The Glitter Band* (Bell)	–	–	–
19 You You You *Alvin Stardust* (Magnet)	9	7	6
20 Can't Get Enough Of Your Love Babe *Barry White* (Pye)	17	8	8
24 Baby Love *Diana Ross and The Supremes* (Tamla Motown)	14	14	12
22 The Black-Eyed Boys *Paper Lace* (Bus Stop)	16	11	13
29 Rock Me Gently *Andy Kim* (Capitol)	24	22	9
– Long Tall Glasses *Leo Sayer* (Chrysalis)	48	23	10
– Sad Sweet Dreamer *Sweet Sensation* (Pye)	44	34	15
– Gee Baby *Peter Shelley* (Magnet)	42	33	16
27 Smoke Gets In Your Eyes *Bryan Ferry* (Island)	22	21	17
28 Another Saturday Night *Cat Stevens* (Island)	23	24	19
– Knock On Wood *David Bowie* (RCA)	–	–	20

OCTOBER 1974

5	12	19	26
1 Kung Fu Fighting *Carl Douglas* (Pye)	4	14	–
2 Annie's Song *John Denver* (RCA)	1	5	12
3 Hang On In There Baby *Johnny Bristol* (MGM)	7	15	–
4 Long Tall Glasses *Leo Sayer* (Chrysalis)	6	6	14
5 Sad Sweet Dreamer *Sweet Sensation* (Pye)	3	1	3
6 Gee Baby *Peter Shelley* (Magnet)	5	4	5
7 You You You *Alvin Stardust* (Magnet)	8	–	–
8 Rock Me Gently *Andy Kim* (Capitol)	2	8	8
9 Can't Get Enough Of Your Love Babe *Barry White* (Pye)	9	–	–

		12	**19**	**26**
10	Queen Of Clubs *K. C. and The Sunshine Band* (Jayboy)	12	–	–
11	Y Viva Espana *Sylvia* (Sonet)	18	–	–
12	The Black-Eyed Boys *Paper Lace* (Bus Stop)	–	–	–
13	Everything I Own *Ken Boothe* (Trojan)	11	2	1
14	Love Me For A Reason *The Osmonds* (MGM)	–	–	–
15	The Bitch Is Back *Elton John* (DJM)	16	–	–
16	I'm Leaving It All Up To You *Donny and Marie Osmond* (MGM)	–	–	–
17	Knock On Wood *David Bowie* (RCA)	10	16	–
18	Reggae Tune *Andy Fairweather Low* (A & M)	13	10	13
19	Smoke Gets In Your Eyes *Bryan Ferry* (Island)	–	–	–
20	Machine Gun *The Commodores* (Tamla Motown)	20	20	–
31	I Get A Kick Out Of You *Gary Shearston* (Charisma)	14	9	7
27	Farewell/Bring It On Home To Me *Rod Stewart* (Mercury)	15	7	11
29	You're Having My Baby *Paul Anka* (UA)	17	12	8
21	I Got The Music In Me *The Kiki Dee Band* (Rocket)	19	–	–
–	Far Far Away *Slade* (Polydor)	–	3	2
–	All Of Me Loves All Of You *The Bay City Rollers* (Bell)	31	11	4
39	I Can't Leave You Alone *George McCrae* (Jayboy)	22	13	9
–	All I Want Is You *Roxy Music* (Island)	49	17	16
28	You Little Trust Maker *The Tymes* (RCA)	23	18	20
–	Gonna Make You A Star *David Essex* (CBS)	42	19	10
–	Down On The Beach Tonight *The Drifters* (Bell)	46	25	15
44	Happy Anniversary *Slim Whitman* (UA)	33	28	17
–	Hey There Lonely Girl *Eddie Holman* (ABC)	–	31	18
–	Let's Get Together Again *The Glitter Band* (Bell)	–	48	19

NOVEMBER 1974

		9	**16**	**23**	**30**
1	Everything I Own *Ken Boothe* (Trojan)	1	3	5	16
2	Far Far Away *Slade* (Polydor)	5	6	–	–
3	Gonna Make You A Star *David Essex* (CBS)	2	1	1	1
4	All Of Me Loves All Of You *The Bay City Rollers* (Bell)	4	7	10	–
5	Killer Queen *Queen* (EMI)	3	2	2	5
6	Sad Sweet Dreamer *Sweet Sensation* (Pye)	18	–	–	–
7	You're Having My Baby *Paul Anka* (UA)	9	12	–	–
8	Down On The Beach Tonight *The Drifters* (Bell)	7	8	11	–
9	I Can't Leave You Alone *George McCrae* (Jayboy)	11	16	–	–
10	Let's Get Together Again *The Glitter Band* (Bell)	8	11	12	–
11	Hey There Lonely Girl *Eddie Holman* (ABC)	6	4	4	8
12	I Get A Kick Out Of You *Gary Shearston* (Charisma)	13	–	–	–
13	Gee Baby *Peter Shelley* (Magnet)	–	–	–	–
14	Let's Put It All Together *The Stylistics* (Avco)	10	9	9	4
15	All I Want Is You *Roxy Music* (Island)	12	14	19	–
16	Never Turn Your Back On Mother Earth *Sparks* (Island)	15	13	18	–
17	Minuetto Allegretto *The Wombles* (CBS)	16	19	–	–
18	Farewell/Bring It On Home To Me *Rod Stewart* (Mercury)	–	–	–	–
19	You Little Trust Maker *The Tymes* (RCA)	–	–	–	–
20	Reggae Tune *Andy Fairweather Low* (A & M)	–	–	–	–
21	Happy Anniversary *Slim Whitman* (UA)	14	–	–	–
26	Pepper Box *The Peppers* (Spark)	17	10	6	9
23	Da Doo Ron Ron *The Crystals* (Warner Spector)	19	15	17	19
38	You're The First, The Last, My Everything *Barry White* (20th Century)	20	5	3	2
40	Magic *Pilot* (EMI)	30	17	15	11
–	The Wild One *Suzi Quatro* (RAK)	37	18	14	7
48	No Honestly *Lynsey de Paul* (Jet)	22	20	7	13
–	Juke Box Jive *The Rubettes* (Polydor)	–	23	8	4
39	Too Good To Be Forgotten *The Chi-Lites* (Brunswick)	27	21	13	10
–	Oh Yes You're Beautiful *Gary Glitter* (Bell)	–	–	16	3

2	9	16	23	30
– You Ain't Seen Nothing Yet *Bachman Turner Overdrive* (Mercury)	–	34	20	6
– Tell Him *Hello* (Bell)	43	32	23	12
– My Boy *Elvis Presley* (RCA)	–	40	28	15
45 Costafine Town *Splinter* (Dark Horse)	28	22	22	17
– Lucy In The Sky With Diamonds *Elton John* (DJM)	–	–	34	18
– Ire Feelings (Skanga) *Rupie Edwards* (Cactus)	–	–	38	20

DECEMBER 1974

7	14	21/28
1 You're The First, The Last, My Everything *Barry White* (20th Century)	1	4
2 Gonna Make You A Star *David Essex* (CBS)	5	–
3 Juke Box Jive *The Rubettes* (Polydor)	8	3
4 Oh Yes You're Beautiful *Gary Glitter* (Bell)	2	9
5 You Ain't Seen Nothing Yet *Bachman Turner Overdrive* (Mercury)	3	2
6 Tell Him *Hello* (Bell)	7	10
7 Hey There Lonely Girl *Eddie Holman* (ABC)	–	–
8 My Boy *Elvis Presley* (RCA)	6	7
9 Killer Queen *Queen* (EMI)	–	–
10 Ire Feelings (Skanga) *Rupie Edwards* (Cactus)	9	14
11 Magic *Pilot* (EMI)	12	–
12 Pepper Box *The Peppers* (Spark)	–	–
13 Too Good To Be Forgotten *The Chi-Lites* (Brunswick)	13	–
14 Get Dancing *Discotex and The Sex-o-lettes* (Chelsea)	11	8
15 Lucy In The Sky With Diamonds *Elton John* (DJM)	10	11
16 The Wild One *Suzi Quatro* (RAK)	15	–
17 No Honestly *Lynsey de Paul* (Jet)	–	–
18 Costafine Town *Splinter* (Dark Horse)	17	–
19 Lonely This Christmas *Mud* (RAK)	4	1
20 How Long *Ace* (Anchor)	–	–
39 Streets Of London *Ralph McTell* (Reprise)	14	6
23 Junior's Farm *Wings* (Apple)	16	–
21 Where Did All The Good Times Go *Donny Osmond* (MGM)	18	–
24 Tell Me Why *Alvin Stardust* (Magnet)	19	16
34 Down Down *Status Quo* (Vertigo)	20	15
47 Wombling Merry Christmas *The Wombles* (CBS)	21	5
28 You Can Make Me Dance, Sing Or Anything *Rod Stewart and The Faces* (Warner Bros.)	23	12
41 Father Christmas Do Not Touch Me/The Inbetweenies *The Goodies* (Bradley's)	28	13
25 Sound Your Funky Horn *K. C. and The Sunshine Band* (Jayboy)	32	17
– Christmas Song *Gilbert O'Sullivan* (MAM)	44	18
– I Can Help *Billy Swann* (Monument)	27	19
22 Sha La La *Al Green* (London)	22	20

1974

Mud headed the top disc listing for 1974 with 'Tiger Feet', and by the year's end they were celebrating the fact that 'Lonely This Christmas' had sold more than half a million copies.

Also catching the public's imagination were David Essex, Showaddywaddy, The Three Degrees, Ringo Starr, Paper Lace and George McCrae. It was an outstanding year for Alvin Stardust, too, a singer who had been in the charts of 1963 with 'Cindy's Birthday' under the name of Shane Fenton. Stardust had made his first chart foray in the latter part of 1973 with 'My Coo-Ca-Choo' and this success continued into 1974 with 'Jealous Mind', 'You You You' and 'Red Dress'.

1974 also saw the emergence of The Wombles, whose music was carefully supervised by the ingenious Mike Batt. In mass popularity terms even the Wimbledon Common team's glory was stolen by the re-emergence of The Bay City Rollers, Scotland's major chart force.

The Bay City Rollers had entered the charts in 1971 with 'Keep On Dancing' and nothing had been seen of them since. However, their fortunes changed in 1974 and they spent endless weeks in the charts with hits such as 'All Of Me Loves All Of You', 'Remember' and 'Summerlove Sensation'. However, once their records slipped in the chart placings, they disappeared quickly which is why no Bay City Roller disc appears in the Top Thirty table of discs which have the longest individual disc residencies.

Several hits reflected certain occurences in the media. Abba achieved great success with their Eurovision-winning song 'Waterloo', and television helped Stephanie De Sykes with 'Born With A Smile On My Face'. The popularity of Kung Fu, as a result of the television programme of the same name, saw Carl Douglas in the Top Ten with 'Kung Fu Fighting'.

In the black music market, Britain's first soul group, Sweet Sensation, also entered the charts in 1974, while in 'soft' soul terms, the talking-singing Barry White had arrived. Reggae had a brief spell of chart fortune, and predictions of a mass outbreak of reggae in the charts were heard, but this was not to be, although two people in particular, Ken Boothe and John Holt, both had big hits.

Age proved to be no barrier for Charles Aznavour and Charlie Rich, as they both had hits with 'She' and 'The Most Beautiful Girl' respectively.

Humour was largely to be had from Ray Stevens with 'The Streak', and new names included Queen and Sparks. The reward for a record company's faith and patience came after six months of waiting for 'Y Viva Espana' to enter the charts, but when it did the disc threatened to stay forever.

When compared to the previous year, 1974 showed some startling changes for the worse for such artists as Jimmy, Marie and Donny Osmond, David Cassidy and The Sweet. However, of these names, only Marie and Jimmy Osmond failed to make a comeback in the charts during the following year.

JANUARY 1975

4		11	18	25
1 Lonely This Christmas *Mud* (RAK)		1	8	17
2 Wombling Merry Christmas *The Wombles* (CBS)		5	20	–
3 Juke Box Jive *The Rubettes* (Polydor)		10	18	–
4 Streets Of London *Ralph McTell* (Reprise)		2	2	4
5 My Boy *Elvis Presley* (RCA)		13	14	16
6 You Ain't Seen Nothing Yet *Bachman Turner Overdrive* (Mercury)		12	16	–
7 The Inbetweenies/Father Christmas Do Not Touch Me *The Goodies* (Bradley's)		11	13	19
8 You're The First, The Last, My Everything *Barry White* (20th Century)		–	–	–
9 Oh Yes You're Beautiful *Gary Glitter* (Bell)		–	–	–
10 Down Down *Status Quo* (Vertigo)		3	1	5
11 Get Dancing *Discotex and The Sex-o-lettes* (Chelsea)		8	9	15
12 Christmas Song *Gilbert O'Sullivan* (MAM)		–	–	–
13 Hey Mister Christmas *Showaddywaddy* (Bell)		–	–	–
14 Lucy In The Sky With Diamonds *Elton John* (DJM)		17	19	–
15 Tell Him *Hello* (Bell)		–	–	–
16 You Can Make Me Dance, Sing Or Anything *Rod Stewart and The Faces* (Warner Bros.)		14	–	–
17 I Can Help *Billy Swann* (Monument)		9	6	12
18 Ire Feelings (Skanga) *Rupie Edwards* (Cactus)		–	–	–
19 Tell Me Why *Alvin Stardust* (Magnet)		–	–	–
20 Gonna Make You A Star *David Essex* (CBS)		–	–	–
21 The Bump *Kenny* (RAK)		4	3	3
23 Never Can Say Goodbye *Gloria Gaynor* (MGM)		6	4	2
27 Ms Grace *The Tymes* (RCA)		7	5	1
28 Are You Ready To Rock *Wizzard* (Warner Bros.)		15	10	8
26 Stardust *David Essex* (CBS)		16	7	10
29 Help Me Make It Through The Night *John Holt* (Trojan)		18	12	6
32 Crying Over You *Ken Boothe* (Trojan)		19	11	11
22 Under My Thumb *Wayne Gibson* (Pye)		20	17	–
40 The Morning Side Of The Mountain *Donny and Marie Osmond* (MGM)		26	15	7
– January *Pilot* (EMI)		–	27	9
– Promised Land *Elvis Presley* (RCA)		–	22	13
– Goodbye My Love *The Glitter Band* (Bell)		–	47	14
– Something For The Girl With Everything *Sparks* (Island)		–	44	18
– Purely By Coincidence *Sweet Sensation* (Pye)		–	49	20

FEBRUARY 1975

1		8	15	22
1 January *Pilot* (EMI)		1	1	2
2 Ms Grace *The Tymes* (RCA)		4	–	–
3 The Bump *Kenny* (RAK)		7	6	–
4 Never Can Say Goodbye *Gloria Gaynor* (MGM)		5	–	–
5 Morning Side Of The Mountain *Donny and Marie Osmond* (MGM)		6	8	–
6 Down Down *Status Quo* (Vertigo)		–	–	–
7 Help Me Make It Through The Night *John Holt* (Trojan)		9	16	–
8 Goodbye My Love *The Glitter Band* (Bell)		2	4	6
9 Promised Land *Elvis Presley* (RCA)		10	13	20
10 Sugar Candy Kisses *Mac and Katie Kissoon* (Polydor)		3	3	4
11 Are You Ready To Rock *Wizzard* (Warner Bros.)		20	–	–
12 Boogie On Reggae Woman *Stevie Wonder* (Tamla Motown)		15	19	–
13 Streets Of London *Ralph McTell* (Reprise)		19	–	–

1	8	15	22
14 Purely By Coincidence *Sweet Sensation* (Pye)	11	18	–
15 Please Mr Postman *The Carpenters* (A & M)	8	2	3
16 Stardust *David Essex* (CBS)	–	–	–
17 Crying Over You *Ken Boothe* (Trojan)	–	–	–
18 Angie Baby *Helen Reddy* (Capitol)	13	5	8
19 I Can Help *Billy Swann* (Monument)	–	–	–
20 Now I'm Here *Queen* (EMI)	12	11	16
21 Black Superman (Muhammed Ali) *Johnny Wakelin and The Kinshasa Band* (Pye)	14	7	10
25 Footsee *Wigan's Chosen Few* (Pye)	16	10	9
22 Something For The Girl With Everything *Sparks* (Island)	17	–	–
24 Star On A TV Show *The Stylistics* (Avco)	18	12	14
– Make Me Smile (Come Up And See Me) *Steve Harley and Cockney Rebel* (EMI)	33	9	1
30 Your Kiss Is Sweet *Syreeta* (Tamla Motown)	25	14	13
– Shame Shame Shame *Shirley and Company* (All Platinum)	38	15	7
40 Good Love Can Never Die *Alvin Stardust* (Magnet)	22	17	11
28 It May Be Winter Outside *Love Unlimited* (20th Century)	24	20	15
– The Secrets That You Keep *Mud* (RAK)	–	26	5
39 My Eyes Adored You *Frankie Valli* (Private Stock)	31	21	12
32 I'm Stone In Love With You *Johnny Mathis* (CBS)	28	24	17
37 Please Tell Him That I Said Hello *Dana* (GTO)	29	25	18
– Only You Can *Fox* (GTO)	–	50	19

MARCH 1975

1	8	15	22	29
1 Make Me Smile (Come Up And See Me) *Steve Harley and Cockney Rebel* (EMI)	2	3	13	–
2 If *Telly Savalas* (MCA)	1	1	2	4
3 Please Mr Postman *The Carpenters* (A & M)	6	14	–	–
4 The Secrets That You Keep *Mud* (RAK)	3	5	7	–
5 Only You Can *Fox* (GTO)	4	4	3	7
6 Shame Shame Shame *Shirley and Company* (All Platinum)	7	12	–	–
7 My Eyes Adored You *Frankie Valli* (Private Stock)	5	6	12	–
8 Sugar Candy Kisses *Mac and Katie Kissoon* (Polydor)	–	–	–	–
9 January *Pilot* (EMI)	–	–	–	–
10 Footsee *Wigan's Chosen Few* (Pye)	10	–	–	–
11 It May Be Winter Outside *Love Unlimited* (20th Century)	14	–	–	–
12 Your Kiss Is Sweet *Syreeta* (Tamla Motown)	17	–	–	–
13 Good Love Can Never Die *Alvin Stardust* (Magnet)	16	–	–	–
14 Angie Baby *Helen Reddy* (Capitol)	20	–	–	–
15 Black Superman (Muhammed Ali) *Johnny Wakelin and The Kinshasa Band* (Pye)	–	–	–	–
16 Goodbye My Love *The Glitter Band* (Bell)	–	–	–	–
17 Please Tell Him That I Said Hello *Dana* (GTO)	12	8	16	18
18 Star On A TV Show *The Stylistics* (Avco)	–	–	–	–
19 I'm Stone In Love With You *Johnny Mathis* (CBS)	11	10	18	20
20 Now I'm Here *Queen* (EMI)	–	–	–	–
– Bye Bye Baby *The Bay City Rollers* (Bell)	8	2	1	1
22 Pick Up The Pieces *The Average White Band* (Atlantic)	9	7	6	12
24 Dreamer *Supertramp* (A & M)	13	15	15	17
21 How Does It Feel *Slade* (Polydor)	15	16	–	–
29 Young Americans *David Bowie* (RCA)	18	–	19	–
30 Sweet Music *Showaddywaddy* (Bell)	19	18	14	16
44 There's A Whole Lot Of Loving *Guys and Dolls* (Magnet)	26	9	4	2
26 Mandy *Barry Manilow* (Arista)	21	11	11	13
– What Am I Gonna Do With You *Barry White* (20th Century)	30	13	5	5
– Girls *Moments and Whatnauts* (All Platinum)	35	17	9	3
– Fancy Pants *Kenny* (RAK)	36	19	8	6

1	**8**	**15**	**22**	**29**
– I Can Do It *The Rubettes* (State)	31	20	10	9
– Play Me Like You Play Your Guitar *Duane Eddy and The Rebelettes* (GTO)	47	29	17	11
– Philadelphia Freedom *The Elton John Band* (DJM)	29	24	20	15
– The Funky Gibbon/Sick Man Blues *The Goodies* (Bradley's)	–	37	23	8
– Fox On The Run *The Sweet* (RCA)	–	42	21	10
– Swing Your Daddy *Jim Gilstrap* (Chelsea)	–	44	26	14
– Reach Out I'll Be There *Gloria Gaynor* (MGM)	45	31	22	19

APRIL 1975

5	**12**	**19**	**26**
1 Bye Bye Baby *The Bay City Rollers* (Bell)	1	1	1
2 There's A Whole Lot Of Loving *Guys and Dolls* (Magnet)	3	6	19
3 Girls *Moments and Whatnauts* (All Platinum)	6	7	–
4 Fancy Pants *Kenny* (RAK)	5	8	–
5 Fox On The Run *The Sweet* (RCA)	2	2	3
6 What Am I Gonna Do With You *Barry White* (20th Century)	15	19	–
7 I Can Do It *The Rubettes* (State)	9	12	–
8 Swing Your Daddy *Jim Gilstrap* (Chelsea)	7	4	5
9 Play Me Like You Play Your Guitar *Duane Eddy and The Rebelettes* (GTO)	10	11	–
10 The Funky Gibbon/Sick Man Blues *The Goodies* (Bradley's)	4	5	8
11 Love Me Love My Dog *Peter Shelley* (Magnet)	8	3	4
12 Let Me Be The One *The Shadows* (EMI)	13	15	–
13 Philadelphia Freedom *The Elton John Band* (DJM)	12	17	20
14 Reach Out I'll Be There *Gloria Gaynor* (MGM)	14	20	–
15 Only You Can *Fox* (GTO)	–	–	–
16 The Ugly Duckling *Mike Reid* (Pye)	11	10	15
17 If *Telly Savalas* (MCA)	18	–	–
18 Pick Up The Pieces *The Average White Band* (Atlantic)	–	–	–
19 Sweet Music *Showaddywaddy* (Bell)	–	–	–
20 Mandy *Barry Manilow* (Arista)	–	–	–
21 Skiing In The Snow *Wigan's Ovation* (Spark)	16	13	12
23 Lady Marmalade *Labelle* (Epic)	17	–	17
31 Honey *Bobby Goldsboro* (UA)	19	9	2
39 A Little Love And Understanding *Gilbert Becaud* (Decca)	20	–	13
49 Life Is A Minestrone *10cc* (Mercury)	23	14	9
– The Tears I Cried *The Glitter Band* (Bell)	29	16	14
– Ding-A-Dong *Teach-In* (Polydor)	26	18	18
– Oh Boy *Mud* (RAK)	–	–	6
– Loving You *Minnie Riperton* (Epic)	49	23	7
45 Hurt So Good *Susan Cadogan* (Magnet)	34	25	10
– Take Good Care Of Yourself *The Three Degrees* (Philadelphia)	40	22	11
36 Hold On To Love *Peter Skellern* (Decca)	21	24	16

MAY 1975

3	**10**	**17**	**24**	**31**
1 Oh Boy *Mud* (RAK)	1	2	3	15
2 Loving You *Minnie Riperton* (Epic)	2	3	4	13
3 Honey *Bobby Goldsboro* (UA)	5	8	–	–
4 Hurt So Good *Susan Cadogan* (Magnet)	4	4	8	17
5 Bye Bye Baby *The Bay City Rollers* (Bell)	8	19	–	–
6 Love Me Love My Dog *Peter Shelley* (Magnet)	16	–	–	–
7 Life Is A Minestrone *10cc* (Mercury)	15	20	–	–
8 The Tears I Cried *The Glitter Band* (Bell)	11	18	–	–
9 Take Good Care Of Yourself *The Three Degrees* (Philadelphia)	9	15	–	–

3

	10	17	24	31
10 Fox On The Run *The Sweet* (RCA)	–	–	–	–
11 Swing Your Daddy *Jim Gilstrap* (Chelsea)	18	–	–	–
12 A Little Love And Understanding *Gilbert Becaud* (Decca)	10	13	–	–
13 Ding-A-Dong *Teach-In* (Polydor)	19	–	–	–
14 Hold On To Love *Peter Skellern* (Decca)	20	–	–	–
15 The Funky Gibbon/Sick Man Blues *The Goodies* (Bradley's)	–	–	–	–
16 The Night *Frankie Valli and The Four Seasons* (Mowest)	7	9	15	19
17 Let Me Try Again *Tammy Jones* (Epic)	6	5	7	9
18 Only Yesterday *The Carpenters* (A & M)	14	7	10	14
19 Skiing In The Snow *Wigan's Ovation* (Spark)	–	–	–	–
20 We'll Find Our Day *Stephanie De Sykes* (Bradley's)	17	17	–	–
23 Stand By Your Man *Tammy Wynette* (Epic)	3	1	1	1
21 I Wanna Dance Wit Choo *Discotex and The Sex-o-lettes* (Chelsea)	12	6	11	8
25 Love Like You And Me *Gary Glitter* (Bell)	13	10	20	–
32 The Way We Were *Gladys Knight and The Pips* (Buddah)	22	11	5	4
– Sing Baby Sing *The Stylistics* (Avco)	36	12	6	3
– Thanks For The Memory *Slade* (Polydor)	–	14	12	7
46 Don't Do It Baby *Mac and Katie Kissoon* (State)	27	16	9	12
– Whispering Grass *Windsor Davies and Don Estelle* (EMI)	–	28	2	2
– Three Steps To Heaven *Showaddywaddy* (Bell)	–	50	13	5
– Send In The Clowns *Judy Collins* (Elektra)	–	39	14	6
– Roll Over Lay Down *Status Quo* (Vertigo)	–	37	16	10
– Autobahn *Kraftwerk* (Vertigo)	38	22	17	16
43 Once Bitten Twice Shy *Ian Hunter* (CBS)	28	25	18	20
– The Israelites *Desmond Dekker* (Cactus)	40	21	19	11
– The Proud One *The Osmonds* (MGM)	–	–	34	18

JUNE 1975

	14	21	28
1 Whispering Grass *Windsor Davies and Don Estelle* (EMI)	1	1	2
2 Stand By Your Man *Tammy Wynette* (Epic)	5	7	16
3 Three Steps To Heaven *Showaddywaddy* (Bell)	2	3	3
4 Sing Baby Sing *The Stylistics* (Avco)	4	8	14
5 Try To Remember/The Way We Were *Gladys Knight and The Pips* (Buddah)	7	9	19
6 Send In The Clowns *Judy Collins* (Elektra)	8	11	–
7 The Proud One *The Osmonds* (MGM)	6	5	7
8 I'm Not In Love *10cc* (Mercury)	3	2	1
9 Roll Over Lay Down *Status Quo* (Vertigo)	13	18	–
10 The Israelites *Desmond Dekker* (Cactus)	14	19	–
11 Autobahn *Kraftwerk* (Vertigo)	12	16	–
12 Thanks For The Memory *Slade* (Polydor)	17	–	–
13 I Wanna Dance Wit Choo *Discotex and The Sex-o-lettes* (Chelsea)	–	–	–
14 Once Bitten Twice Shy *Ian Hunter* (CBS)	18	20	–
15 Imagine Me, Imagine You *Fox* (GTO)	19	–	–
16 Let Me Try Again *Tammy Jones* (Epic)	–	–	–
17 Don't Do It Baby *Mac and Katie Kissoon* (State)	–	–	–
18 Listen To What The Man Said *Wings* (Apple)	10	6	9
19 Swing Low Sweet Chariot *Eric Clapton* (RSO)	–	–	–
20 Disco Queen *Hot Chocolate* (RAK)	11	12	17
22 The Hustle *Van McCoy* (Avco)	9	4	4
30 Oh What A Shame *Roy Wood* (Jet)	15	13	15
23 Disco Stomp *Hamilton Bohannon* (Brunswick)	16	10	8
21 I'll Do For You Anything You Want Me To *Barry White* (20th Century)	20	–	–
– Tears On My Pillow *Johnny Nash* (CBS)	29	14	5

7	14	21	28
42 Baby I Love You, OK *Kenny* (RAK)	24	15	12
40 Mr Raffles (Man It Was Mean) *Steve Harley and Cockney Rebel* (EMI)	23	17	13
– Doing Alright With The Boys *Gary Glitter* (Bell)	–	22	6
– Misty *Ray Stevens* (Janus)	–	35	10
– Moonshine Sally *Mud* (RAK)	–	26	11
– My White Bicycle *Nazareth* (Mooncrest)	36	24	18
– I Don't Love You But I Think I Like You *Gilbert O'Sullivan* (MAM)	41	25	20

JULY 1975

5	12	19	26
1 I'm Not In Love *10cc* (Mercury)	4	8	14
2 Tears On My Pillow *Johnny Nash* (CBS)	1	2	3
3 The Hustle *Van McCoy* (Avco)	3	4	7
4 Whispering Grass *Windsor Davies and Don Estelle* (EMI)	9	15	–
5 Misty *Ray Stevens* (Janus)	2	3	4
6 Disco Stomp *Hamilton Bohannon* (Brunswick)	8	9	15
7 Three Steps To Heaven *Showaddywaddy* (Bell)	12	–	–
8 Doing Alright With The Boys *Gary Glitter* (Bell)	6	18	–
9 Have You Seen Her/Oh Girl *The Chi-Lites* (Brunswick)	5	6	6
10 Moonshine Sally *Mud* (RAK)	11	13	–
11 The Proud One *The Osmonds* (MGM)	–	–	–
12 Listen To What The Man Said *Wings* (Apple)	–	–	–
13 Baby I Love You, OK *Kenny* (RAK)	16	–	–
14 I Don't Love You But I Think I Like You *Gilbert O'Sullivan* (MAM)	17	–	–
15 Eighteen With A Bullet *Pete Wingfield* (Island)	10	7	8
16 Mr Raffles (Man It Was Mean) *Steve Harley and Cockney Rebel* (EMI)	–	–	
17 My White Bicycle *Nazareth* (Mooncrest)	14	17	
18 Make The World Go Away *Donny and Marie Osmond* (MGM)	18	–	–
19 Foe-Dee-O-Dee *The Rubettes* (State)	15	–	19
20 Oh What A Shame *Roy Wood* (Jet)	–	–	–
– Give A Little Love *The Bay City Rollers* (Bell)	7	1	1
37 Barbados *Typically Tropical* (Gull)	13	5	2
32 Je T'Aime *Judge Dread* (Cactus)	19	10	9
30 D.I.V.O.R.C.E. *Tammy Wynette* (Epic)	20	16	12
47 Rolling Stone *David Essex* (CBS)	26	11	5
28 Jive Talkin' *The Bee Gees* (RSO)	23	12	11
33 Sealed With A Kiss *Brian Hyland* (ABC)	24	14	10
23 Black Pudding Bertha *The Goodies* (Bradley's)	22	19	–
21 Mama Never Told Me *Sister Sledge* (Atlantic)	27	20	–
– It's In His Kiss *Linda Lewis* (Arista)	41	28	13
– If You Think You Know How To Love Me *Smokey* (RAK)	–	40	16
– Action *The Sweet* (RCA)	47	27	17
36 I Write The Songs *David Cassidy* (RCA)	30	23	18
– New York City *T. Rex* (EMI)	39	30	20

AUGUST 1975

2	9	16	23	30
1 Give A Little Love *The Bay City Rollers* (Bell)	2	4	11	–
2 Barbados *Typically Tropical* (Gull)	1	2	4	8
3 Tears On My Pillow *Johnny Nash* (CBS)	10	14	–	–
4 Misty *Ray Stevens* (Janus)	20	–	–	–
5 Jive Talkin' *The Bee Gees* (RSO)	5	6	9	17
6 If You Think You Know How To Love Me *Smokey* (RAK)	4	3	5	10

204

	9	16	23	30
7 Sealed With A Kiss *Brian Hyland* (ABC)	7	12	16	–
8 It's In His Kiss *Linda Lewis* (Arista)	6	9	13	–
9 The Hustle *Van McCoy* (Avco)	–	–	–	–
10 Je T'Aime *Judge Dread* (Cactus)	9	16	–	–
11 Rolling Stone *David Essex* (CBS)	17	–	–	–
12 I Can't Give You Anything (But My Love) *The Stylistics* (Avco)	3	1	1	1
13 Have You Seen Her/Oh Girl *The Chi-Lites* (Brunswick)	–	–	–	–
14 Eighteen With A Bullet *Pete Wingfield* (Island)	–	–	–	–
15 Action *The Sweet* (RCA)	19	–	–	–
16 Delilah *The Sensational Alex Harvey Band* (Vertigo)	8	7	17	15
17 I Write The Songs/For Love *David Cassidy* (RCA)	11	18	–	–
18 D.I.V.O.R.C.E. *Tammy Wynette* (Epic)	–	–	–	–
19 New York City *T. Rex* (EMI)	15	17	–	–
20 Highwire *Linda Carr and The Love Squad* (Chelsea)	–	15	–	–
22 Sherry *Adrian Baker* (Magnet)	12	10	12	16
28 It's Been So Long *George McCrae* (Jayboy)	13	8	6	4
29 The Last Farewell *Roger Whittaker* (EMI)	14	5	3	3
21 Blanket On The Ground *Billie Jo Spears* (UA)	16	11	7	6
23 Dolly My Love *The Moments* (All Platinum)	18	13	10	11
33 El Bimbo *Bimbo Jet* (EMI)	26	19	14	12
50 Best Thing That Ever Happened *Gladys Knight and The Pips* (Buddah)	30	20	15	7
– Sailing *Rod Stewart* (Warner Bros.)	–	24	2	2
48 That's The Way I Like It *K. C. and The Sunshine Band* (Jayboy)	38	23	8	5
45 Summer Of '42 *The Biddu Orchestra* (Epic)	35	26	18	14
41 Fame *David Bowie* (RCA)	33	30	19	–
– Super Womble *The Wombles* (CBS)	36	28	20	–
– Summertime City *Mike Batt* (Epic)	–	49	36	9
– Funky Moped/Magic Roundabout *Jasper Carrott* (DJM)	–	50	45	13
– Love In The Sun *The Glitter Band* (Bell)	44	40	29	18
– Julie-Ann *Kenny* (RAK)	–	47	35	19
– A Child's Prayer *Hot Chocolate* (RAK)	50	43	28	20

SEPTEMBER 1975

6		13	20	27
1 Sailing *Rod Stewart* (Warner Bros.)		1	1	1
2 Can't Give You Anything (But My Love) *The Stylistics* (Avco)		3	12	–
3 The Last Farewell *Roger Whittaker* (EMI)		2	3	6
4 That's The Way (I Like It) *K. C. and The Sunshine Band* (Jayboy)		5	10	19
5 It's Been So Long *George McCrae* (Jayboy)		11	15	–
6 Summertime City *Mike Batt* (Epic)		6	4	13
7 Blanket On The Ground *Billie Jo Spears* (UA)		14	–	–
8 A Child's Prayer *Hot Chocolate* (RAK)		7	8	9
9 Best Thing That Ever Happened *Gladys Knight and The Pips* (Buddah)		9	17	–
10 Funky Moped/Magic Roundabout *Jasper Carrott* (DJM)		8	5	5
11 Moonlighting *Leo Sayer* (Chrysalis)		4	2	3
12 Julie-Ann *Kenny* (RAK)		10	11	15
13 El Bimbo *Bimbo Jet* (EMI)		–	–	–
14 Dolly My Love *Moments* (All Platinum)		–	–	–
15 Summer Of '42 *The Biddu Orchestra* (Epic)		17	–	–
16 Love In The Sun *The Glitter Band* (Bell)		15	20	–
17 Fame *David Bowie* (RCA)		–	–	–
18 Barbados *Typically Tropical* (Gull)		–	–	–
19 If You Think You Know How To Love Me *Smokey* (RAK)		–	–	–
20 Super Womble *The Wombles* (CBS)		–	–	–

1975

Disco sounds continued to make their assault on the charts in 1975, a trend which had begun in 1974. It could be said that records were made popular by the discos and then entered the charts – a statement which could certainly be verified by a glance at the charts of 1975 with hits from K. C. and The Sunshine Band, Hamilton Bohannon, Jasper Carrott, Pete Wingfield, Chris Spedding, Wigan's Ovation, Jackie Wilson, The Sharonettes, Gloria Gaynor, B.T. Express and Silver Convention. The Chi-Lites' hit of January 1972 'Have You Seen Her?' became a hit all over again in July 1975, and there were many other disco records from the All Platinum record label. Other disco records which entered the charts came from The Tymes, Eddie Holman, Wayne Gibson, and Discotex and The Sex-o-lettes.

Girl artists came to the fore, and at one time about 18 girls made the Top Fifty – an unprecedented figure when taking into consideration the fact that in most other years it is hard to find even 10 girl artists entering the charts during a 12-month period.

1975 will be remembered as the year in which Johnny Mathis entered the charts again with 'I'm Stone In Love With You', his first hit single for 17 years, although an album of Mathis' had entered the Top Ten album charts in 1960.

For Dana, the Irish Eurovision song winner of 1970, 1975 showed compassion. In 1970 and 1971 she had achieved hits with 'All Kinds Of Everything' and 'Who Put The Lights Out', but fruitless years had followed until the welcome arrival of 'Please Tell Him That I Said Hello', a disc which made the 1975 charts in the last week of January at Number Thirty-Eight.

As far as the Top Twenty was concerned in 1975, The Glitter Band, The Rubettes, Status Quo, The Bay City Rollers, The Carpenters, Mac and Katie Kissoon, Pilot, Alvin Stardust and Kenny, a new teen group, all enjoyed success. Particularly pleasing was the appearance in the charts of The Average White Band with 'Pick Up The Pieces', a funky sound from a British group.

1975 promised much for some bands, but in fact yielded very little. Pilot seemed likely to become the next teen chart force, but this was not to be, while the Canadian exponents of the thudding bass, Bachman Turner Overdrive, did not live up to the potential they had shown in 1974. Another teen prospect, Arrows, floundered and even Suzi Quatro lost much of her chart appeal of the previous two years. Slade had Hit Parade successes with 'How Does It Feel' and 'Thanks For The Memory', but they were in America for most of the year, which could explain why their chart impact in Britain was not greater.

A new label, GTO, under the ex-Bell Records, hit-making prowess of Dick Leahy, not only made Dana a chart force with which to be reckoned again, but also signed Fox, an exciting new band who had two hits with 'Only You Can' and 'Imagine Me Imagine You'.

Rod Stewart, after months of legal disputes, returned to the charts with 'Sailing', and after years of non-action came two golden oldies, 'Sealed With A Kiss' from Brian Hyland and 'Honey' from Bobby Goldsboro.

Humour came from The Goodies, Mike Reid and Jasper Carrott, for those who examined words and vocal gesture rather than beat.

Frankie Valli of The Four Seasons patiently waited months for 'My Eyes Adored You' to enter the charts, and when it eventually did it gave the Private Stock record label its first major chart triumph. Telly Savalas of *Kojak* fame talked his way into the charts with 'If', while Barry White again talked and growled his way into the Top Ten.

Peter Shelley did well singing and producing records, but 1975 tended to lack any definite character and domination except by possibly The Bay City Rollers, who put the emphasis on teenage tartan clothes, half-mast trousers and Scottish scarves. It was estimated that The Rollers attracted merchandising of £2,000,000 in Britain in 1975 alone, while at least the same amount was projected for them in America, assuming that the much-planned Roller onslaught was successful. And if it wasn't, well, there was always next month's sensation.

SIMPLY POP

All the facts and personal details you could wish for on David, Elton, Donny, Slade, the Rollers and many, many more, along with some terrific pictures of them all, on stage and off. SIMPLY POP is a great new large format paperback (it measures $9\frac{1}{2}'' \times 7\frac{1}{2}''$!) and is just one of the titles in the Queen Anne Press Pop Library. As well as stories about your favourite stars, it is full of things to do—games and crosswords; facts and features to read and enjoy, *and* the first-ever 'O' level/CSE exam paper in pop! You can even find out how to become a pop journalist.

Get your copy of this great new pop book and see if *you* can pass the exam paper at the back. Enough games, facts and quizzes to keep you going right through the year. Be top in Pop: SIMPLY POP!

Available from your bookseller or newsagent, 95p

In case of difficulty, please send a cheque/P.O. made out to Queen Anne Press Limited, for £1.05 including postage and packing, to:
Queen Anne Press Limited, 12 Vandy Street, London EC2A 2EN
Please allow up to four weeks for delivery.

ROLLERS IN AMERICA

The Queen Anne Press Pop Library is proud to present this exclusive souvenir of the ROLLERS' trip to America in the autumn of 1975. If you hurry you could well be lucky enough to obtain a copy of this beautifully produced full colour souvenir album of pictures of the group. Here they are preparing for the trip, travelling to the States, the tour itself, and there are holiday pictures, too, of their stop-off in Bermuda on the way home.

If you are a ROLLERS fan you can't afford to miss this beautiful full colour collection of pictures with amusing captions and an introduction to each section by Bess Coleman, their public relations officer. All the photographs are by Allan Ballard, who went with them everywhere on the tour.

Available at your newsagents for only 65p. Magazine format.

In case of difficulty, please send a cheque/P.O. made out to Queen Anne Press Limited, for 80p including postage and packing, to:
Queen Anne Press Limited, 12 Vandy Street, London EC2A 2EN
Please allow up to four weeks for delivery.